The Blue Guides

Please write in with your comments, suggestions and corrections for the next edition of the Blue Guide. Writers of the most helpful letters will be awarded a free Blue Guide of their choice.

City Guide
Barcelona

Annie Bennett

A&C Black • London
WW Norton • New York

BLUE GUIDE • CITY GUIDE • BLUE GUIDE

Second edition May 2002

Published by A & C Black Publishers Ltd
37 Soho Square, London W1D 3QZ

www.acblack.com

© Annie Bennett, 2002
First edition © Michael Jacobs, 1992
Illustrations © Peter Spells
Maps by Eugene Fleury © A & C Black (Publishers) Limited. Metro map on inside back cover
kindly supplied by the Barcelona transport authority and the Spanish National Tourist Office.

ISBN O–7136–5213–6

All rights reserved. No part of this publication may be reproduced or used in any form or by
any means—photographic, electronic or mechanical, including photocopying, recording,
taping of information and retrieval systems—without permission of the publishers.

The rights of Annie Bennett to be identified as the author of this work have been asserted by
her in accordance with the Copyright Designs and Patents Act, 1988.

'Blue Guides' is a registered trademark.
A CIP catalogue record of this book is available from the British Library.

Published in the United States of America by
W W Norton & Company, Incorporated
500 Fifth Avenue, New York, NY 10110

Published simultaneously in Canada by
Penguin Books Canada Limited
10 Alcorn Avenue, Toronto
Ontario M4V 3BE

ISBN 0–393–32133–9 USA

The author and the publishers have done their best to ensure the accuracy of all the
information in Blue Guide Barcelona; however, they can accept no responsibility for any
loss, injury or inconvenience sustained by any traveller as a result of information or
advice contained in the Guide.

For permission to reproduce the extract from *Homage to Catalonia* by George Orwell, p 88,
the publishers would like to thank A.M. Heath & Co. Ltd and Harcourt Trade Division;
and for permission to reproduce the extract from *Forbidden Territory* by Juan Goytisolo,
p 146, the publishers are grateful to Quartet Books Ltd and Farrar, Straus & Giroux Inc.

Cover photograph: details of Gaudí's colourful polychrome work at Parc Güell,
© Phil Robinson.

Annie Bennett is a writer and translator specialising in Spanish tourism and culture. After
graduating in Modern Languages, she lived in Spain for ten years, and now divides her time
between London and Spain.

A & C Black uses paper produced with elemental chlorine-free pulp, harvested from managed sustainable forests.

Printed and bound in Great Britain by Butler & Tanner Ltd, Frome and London.

Contents

Background information

The Guide

Walks

Days out

Maps and plans

Introduction

Barcelona has cleverly managed to reinforce its character while revamping itself for the 21st century. With its astounding architecture, first-rate cultural venues, sensational cuisine, buzzing street life and chic shops, it is undoubtedly one of the most dynamic and stylish cities in Europe.

La Rambla, Barcelona's famous boulevard, rates among the most entertaining urban landscapes in the world. But stroll down to the end of it and you become part of a totally different scene, where the lazy pleasures of the Mediterranean take over from the bustle of the city. Along the waterside, a promenade leads to a marina packed with yachts and flanked by fish restaurants, and around the corner a strip of golden sand stretches for miles.

The waterfront has already created its own distinctive character, taking its place alongside Barcelona's more established districts. A decade after Barcelona reinvented itself so spectacularly for the 1992 Olympic Games, the city's energetic programme of urban renewal is still very much underway. The city is expanding along the northern seaboard, creating a new residential, business and leisure district called Diagonal-Mar. A cornerstone of this development is the site of the Universal Forum of Cultures, a major international event which will take place in 2004.

The city is also rediscovering its rich heritage of industrial architecture, restoring late-19C buildings to their former glory and putting them to 21C uses. Designers and dot.com businesses are rapidly snapping up the dilapidated warehouses and factories in the Poblenou area, creating a new technological hotbed called 22@BCN, which is already being dubbed the Silicon Valley of Catalunya.

The Fàbrica Casaramona, a vast Modernista textile mill at the base of Montjuïc hill, has been redesigned to house the contemporary art collection of the Fundació La Caixa, an exciting addition to an already vibrant cultural scene.

The MACBA contemporary art museum has brought a new energy to the previously seedy Raval quarter. A drastic programme of urban improvements—including the demolition of entire streets—has contributed to its renaissance, with new galleries, bars and shops opening every week.

Barcelona is a very popular destination all year round, and you need to book well in advance to get into most of the city-centre hotels. When planning what you want to do, bear in mind that only major museums and shops stay open all day. Most places close for at least two hours, but that gives you plenty of time to enjoy a good lunch. Catalan food is quite different from what you may have tried in other parts of Spain, and it is well worth seeking out bars and restaurants that serve authentic local cuisine, whether traditional or modern. *Cava*, the Catalan version of champagne, is regarded as an everyday drink, and certainly not just for special occasions. While in Barcelona, try adopting the local habit of having a flute of *cava* in a bar at around noon, which is perhaps the most civilised of Catalan customs.

Acknowledgements

I would like to thank Gemma Davies, Judy Tither and Sue Harper for their help in producing this book. Maria Lluisa Albacar and her team at Turisme de Barcelona provided essential assistance, as did the staff at the Spanish Tourist Office in London, particularly Pituca Caton, Inma Felip and Claire Turner.

Highlights

If you only have two or three days, you can still see a good range of the major sights. Start by walking down the **Rambla**, then branch off into the **Plaça Reial** and the **Barri Gòtic**, or old town. Visit the **Cathedral** and the nearby Museu d'Història de la Ciutat, a fantastic museum which will provide you with the basics about Barcelona's history and development. Also close by is the very popular Museu Picasso and the Església de Santa Maria, which many local citizens regard as their most important church. The winding lanes of the old town are packed with atmospheric bars and restaurants, as well as traditional shops and funky boutiques.

Start your **Gaudí explorations** by visiting La Pedrera, his most extravagant residential creation. Inside, the Espai Gaudí provides an excellent insight into the great architect's work, with displays detailing all his buildings. The highpoint for most visitors, however, is a visit to the swirling rooftop, with panoramic views across the city. If you are visiting in summer, don't miss coming here at night when the terrace is open as a bar. After looking at a few of the many other Modernista gems in the vicinity, head for the Sagrada Família, Gaudí's final and most ambitious project, then spend some time in the hypnotic Park Güell.

Walk along the waterfront to the **Port Vell**, the old harbour that is now a sparkling marina, and visit the Museu d'Història de Catalunya before a sumptuous seafood lunch at one of the outdoor restaurants. If the weather is good and you have time, stroll along the boardwalk to the Port Olímpic for a drink at the Hotel Arts or in one of the many bars in the marina.

Take the **cable car** from the seafront across the bay to **Montjuïc hill**. The thrilling ride gives you a breathtaking view of the city and port. Explore the Olympic complex and visit the Fundació Joan Miró and the Museu Nacional d'Art de Catalunya. On your way downhill, the Mies van der Rohe Pavilion, the CaixaForum arts centre and the Poble Espanyol—which contains reproductions of architectural styles from all over Spain—are just a few of the options on offer. Have a look at Walk 8 for more details. In the evening, don't miss the spectacular water displays at the nearby Font Màgica.

Football fans should head for the Nou Camp and visit the entertaining museum devoted to **F.C. Barcelona**. Not too far away is the Monestir de Pedralbes, which houses the **Thyssen Collection**. For more wonderful views, head up Tibidabo hill and zoom up the Collserola tower.

PRACTICAL INFORMATION

 Planning your trip

When to go

Barcelona has a mild Mediterranean climate, with average temperatures of 10°C (50°F) in January, its coldest month, and 25°C (78°F) during July and August. As it is by the sea, Barcelona never experiences the excessive heat of Madrid or Seville, but the humidity can be oppressive at the very height of summer. June and September are good months to choose, when you can expect warm weather and the city is in full swing.

Passports and formalities

UK visitors need a passport but other EU nationals can simply use their national identity cards. For stays of longer than 90 days, all EU citizens need to apply for a residence permit. US, Canadian and Australian citizens need passports to enter Spain. Visas are only required for stays of more than ninety days.

For further information or to apply for a visa, contact a Spanish consulate or embassy.

UK

Spanish Embassy, 39 Chesham Place, London SW1X 8SB, ☎ 020 7235 5555;
Spanish Consulates: 20 Draycott Place, London SW3 2RZ, ☎ 020 7589 8989,
and Suite 1A, Brook House, 70 Spring Gardens, Manchester M22 2BQ,
☎ 0161 236 1262.

USA

Spanish Embassy, 2375 Pennsylvania Ave, NW, Washington DC 20037,
☎ 202 452 0100.
Spanish Consulates: 150 E 58th St, New York, NY 10155, ☎ 212 355 4080,
and 5055 Wilshire Boulevard, Suite 960, Los Angeles, CA 90036,
☎ 323 938 0158.

Canada

Spanish Embassy, 74 Stanley Avenue, Ottawa, Ontario K1M 1P4,
☎ 613 747 2252.
Spanish Consulate, Simcoe Place, 200 Front St, Ste. 2401, Toronto, Ontario
M5V 3K2, ☎ 416 977 1661.

Australia

Spanish Embassy, 15 Arkana Street, Yarrakumla, P.O. Box 9076/Deakin, ACT 2600, Canberrra, ☎ 02 6273 3555.
Spanish Consulate, 24th Floor, St Martin Tower, 3131 Market Street, Sydney NSW 200, ☎ 02 9261 2433.

National Tourist Boards

The Spanish National Tourist Office provides an extensive range of maps and leaflets on accommodation, culture, transport, sport and festivals. Contact details:

UK
22–23 Manchester Square, London W1U 3PX, ☎ 020 7486 8077, www.tourspain.co.uk, www.uk.tourspain.es, email: londres@tourspain.es

Netherlands
Laan Van Meerdervoor 8A, 2517 AJ Den Haag, ☎ 31 70 346 5900, www.spaansverkeersbureau.nl, email: lahaya@tourspain.es

USA
666 5th Ave, New York, NY 10103, ☎ 212 265 8822, www.okspain.org, email: oetny@tourspain.es
8383 Wilshire Boulevard, Suite 960, Beverly Hills, CA 90211, ☎ 323 658 7188, email: losangeles@tourspain.es
Water Tower Place, Suite 915, East 845 North Michigan Ave, Chicago, Ill 60611, ☎ 312 642 1992, email: chicago@tourspain.es
1221 Brickell Ave, Miami, Fl. 33131, ☎ 305 358 1992, email: miami@tourspain.es

Canada
2 Bloor St West, 3th Floor, Toronto, Ontario M4W 3E2, ☎ 416-961 3131, www.tourspain.toronto.on.ca, email: toronto@tourspain.es

Tour operators

Most major city break operators feature Barcelona in their brochures. Prices are usually slightly higher than booking independently, but often include transfers and sometimes a pass for public transport and discounted museum entrances. Reputable operators include the following:
Cresta, ☎ 0870 161 0900, www.crestaholidays.co.uk
Kirker, ☎ 020 7231 3333, www.kirker.ping.co.uk
Magic of Spain, ☎ 0990 462442, www.magictravel.co.uk
Mundicolor, ☎ 020 7828 6021, www.mundicolor.co.uk
Travelscene, ☎ 0870 777 4445, www.travelscene.co.uk

Cultural tours with guest lecturers are operated by:
Ace Study Tours, ☎ 01223 835055, www.study-tours.org
Martin Randall Travel, ☎ 020 8742 3355, email: info@martinrandall.co.uk
Prospect Music & Art Tours, ☎ 020 8995 2151, email: sales@prospect-tours.com

Opera packages can be booked through:
JMB Travel, ☎ 01905 830099, www.jmb-travel.co.uk
Travel for the Arts, ☎ 020 7483 4466, travelforthearts.co.uk
Dance Holidays ☎ 01206 577000, www.danceholidays.com organises salsa and tango weekends.

Maps

Tourist offices provide a free map that marks the major sights but does not have a street index. *Falkplan* and *Michelin* are good city maps. *Edicions de la Tramuntana* produces a map in book form, which is easier to consult as you are walking around. *Geoplaneta* and *Editorial Pamias* publish heftier map books, which cover a larger area and also contain useful listings.

Health and insurance

No vaccinations are required. EU citizens may obtain free emergency medical cover by means of the E111 reciprocal arrangement scheme. In the UK, E111 forms are contained in the *Health Advice for Travellers* leaflet, which is available at post offices, or you can obtain one by calling ☎ 0800 555 777. The scheme only covers limited treatment with the Spanish national healthcare system (*Seguridad Social*). Take photocopies of your form as well as the original.

You are strongly recommended to take out private travel insurance for more comprehensive medical care and also to cover lost or stolen property, cash and valuables as well as personal health care. See also Emergencies on p 54.

Currency

The Euro € was introduced at the beginning of 2002, replacing the *Peseta*. One euro is worth 166 pesetas—just over 60 UK pence or just under one US dollar. One UK pound equals about 1.50 Euros. One US dollar equals about 1.10 euros. One Australian dollar equals about 60 cents.

There are seven denominations of notes: €500, €200, €100, €50, €20, €10 and €5. There are also eight coins: €2, €1, and 50, 20, 10, five, two and one cents.

See also the section on banks, bureaux de change and credit cards on p 51.

Travellers with disabilities

The city is making a huge effort to improve conditions for people with disabilities, but there is a long way to go. As a rule of thumb, anything built or modified since 1992 is accessible to people with physical disabilities and in wheelchairs. This applies to hotels, museums, shops and entertainment and sports venues. The whole Vila Olímpica area, for example, is wheelchair-friendly, with easy access to the beaches, promenades and marina. Barceloneta and Nova Icària beaches have assistants available during summer weekends for people who need help. Call ☎ 93 435 1370 or ask at Red Cross (Cruz Roja) first-aid centres for more information. The Centre Municipal de Vela (Port Olímpic 100, ☎ 93 221 1499) offers sailing courses for people with disabilities.

Places that are totally accessible with above-average facilities include the MACBA Contemporary Art Museum, the Liceu opera house, the Auditori concert hall and the Icària Yelmo multiplex cinema, which shows films in the original version with subtitles. See the relevant sections below for contact details.

For information on public transport, contact *SIPTRE*, a helpline for people with mobility problems that publishes a guide to transport services and answers specific transport queries (☎ 93 486 0752). See also the **Getting around** section below. The general city helpline (☎ 010 from Barcelona, ☎ 93 402 7000 from elsewhere) is a good starting point for all sorts of mobility and accessibility queries. Ask for an English-speaking operator. The **Institut Municipal de Persones Amb Disminució** (C/Llacuna 161, 3a, ☎ 93 291 8410) is dedicated to improving facilities in Barcelona, and publishes a very useful map, the *Plano de la Barcelona Accesible*, which shows accessibility at tourist sights, public transport, etc.

In the UK, information can be obtained from the *Spanish Tourist Office* and also from the *Royal Association for Disability and Rehabilitation* (RADAR) at

12 City Forum, 250 City Road, London EC1V 8AF (☎ 020 7250 3222, www.radar.org.uk) and Holiday Care Services, 2nd floor, Imperial Buildings, Victoria Road, Horley, Surrey R6 7PZ (☎ 01293 774535).

Getting there

By air

From the UK
Flights from the UK take just under two hours.
Iberia, Venture House, 27–29 Glasshouse Street, London W1R 6JU, ☎ 0990 341341, www.iberia.com
British Airways, 156 Regent Street, London W1R 6LB, ☎ 0345 222111, www.british-airways.com
Both Iberia and British Airways fly several times a day from London Heathrow and Gatwick, Manchester and Birmingham.
British Midland bmi, Donington Hall, Castle Donington, Derby, East Midlands, DE74 2SB, ☎ 0870 6070 555, www.flybmi.com, flies from Heathrow.
Go, ☎ 0845 6054321, www.go-fly.com, flies from Stansted and Bristol.
Easyjet, ☎ 0870 600 0000, www.easyjet.com, flies from Luton and Liverpool.
   Reliable **agents** for cheap flights include:
Spanish Travel Services, 138 Eversholt Street, London NW1 1BL, ☎ 020 7387 5337, www.apatraveluk.com/sts
Avro, Wren Court, 17 London Road, Bromley, Kent BR1 1DE, ☎ 0870 036 0111, www.avro-flights.co.uk

From the USA
Iberia, ☎ 1 800 772 4642, www.iberia.com, flies direct from New York. Other major airlines require a change in London or Madrid.

By train
Using *Eurostar* (Eurostar House, Waterloo Station, London SW1 8SE, ☎ 0870 160 6600, www.eurostar.co.uk) from London to Paris, the journey takes a total of around 18 hours. For information, contact *Rail Europe*, ☎ 08705 848 848, www.raileurope.co.uk, or visit the *Rail Europe Travel Shop*, 179 Piccadilly, London W1V 0BA.

By coach
Eurolines (UK) Ltd, 4 Cardiff Road, Luton LU1 1PP, ☎ 08705 143219, www.eurolines.co.uk, runs a regular bus service from London to Barcelona. Buses leave from Victoria Coach Station and the journey time is about 25 hours.

By car
You need two days to drive to Barcelona from the UK. You can put your car on a cross-channel ferry or the Eurotunnel shuttle to northern France, followed by a 15-hour drive. You can also take a ferry to northern Spain, which reduces the

driving time by half. *P&O Stena Line* (Channel House, Channel View Road, Dover, Kent CT17 9TJ, ☎ 0870 600 0600, www.posl.com) sails from Portsmouth to Bilbao (35-hour voyage). *Brittany Ferries* (Millbay, Plymouth, Devon PL1 3EW, ☎ 08705 561600, www.brittanyferries.co.uk) sails from Plymouth to Santander (24-hour voyage). See **Driving** below for documents required to drive in Spain.

On arrival

By air

El Prat International Airport is 12km (7.5 miles) south of the city centre and has three terminals. International flights use terminals A and B, domestic flights use B, and C handles the Barcelona-Madrid shuttle (Pont Aeri/Puente Aereo). Facilities include cash dispensers, banks, currency exchange, tourist information, left luggage, postal services, cafés and restaurants and a wide range of shops.

Transport to the city The **Aerobus** service runs to Plaça de Catalunya every 15 minutes from 06.00–24.00 Mon–Fri, and 06.30–24.00 Sat, Sun & public holidays. Buses have luggage space, low boarding decks, electronic ramps and wide aisles. Journey time is 25–40 minutes, depending on traffic. The fare is about €3, payable on the bus. See p 14 for more public transport information.

Trains to the centre leave the airport every 30 minutes from approximately 06.00–22.30 and stop at Sants (the main rail station) and Plaça de Catalunya (20 minutes). The fare is slightly cheaper than the bus. The station is a good five minutes' walk from the terminals, although partly on moving walkways.

A metro line is being constructed and is scheduled to open in 2004.

A **taxi** to the centre costs around €18 including supplements (see also p 17).

By train

Most trains arrive at Sants station in the west of the city, which has all the facilities of an airport, including tourist information. Lines 3 and 5 of the metro provide links to the centre. A taxi to Plaça de Catalunya costs around €6, including supplements.

By coach

Most coaches arrive at Barcelona-Nord station to the northeast near Ciutadella Park and adjacent to Arc de Triomf metro station. A taxi to the centre should cost about €4.

Tourist information

The main tourist office run by the city council, Turisme de Barcelona, is underneath Plaça de Catalunya, on the Corte Inglés side (☎ 906 301282 from Spain, ☎ 93 304 3421 from abroad, www.barcelonaturisme.com). Open 09.00–21.00 daily, there is also a hotel reservation service and a book and gift shop. There are branches in the town hall in the Plaça de Sant Jaume (open 10.00–20.00

Mon–Sat, 10.00–14.00 Sun & public holidays), and in Sants train station (open 08.00–20.00 daily June–Sept; 08.00–20.00 Mon–Fri, 08.00–14.00 Sat, Sun & public holidays Oct–May). In summer, there are also information kiosks at key points around the city, including the Sagrada Familia, and multilingual staff—easily recognisable in red jackets—patrol the streets.

General information on the city is available by calling the municipal helpline on ☎ 010 from within Barcelona, or ☎ 93 402 7000 from anywhere else. English-speaking operators are available on request. The city council's website is also very useful, with most information in English, www.bcn.es.

The tourist office of the Catalan regional government is based in the Palau Robert, Passeig de Gràcia 107 (☎ 93 238 4000, www.gencat.es/probert). Open 10.00–19.00 Mon–Sat, 10.00–14.30 Sun. Information on all Catalunya, as well as a book and gift shop. They also run the tourist information desks at the airport (open 09.30–20.00 Mon–Sat, 09.30–15.00 Sun).

There is a further information centre in the Palau de la Virreina at La Rambla 99 (☎ 93 301 7775), run by the culture department of the city council. This is a very useful office for concerts, exhibitions and other cultural events. Tickets for some events are also available here. The adjoining bookshop is well-stocked with books on Barcelona.

Getting around

It goes without saying that by far the best way of getting to know Barcelona is on foot, and this is perfectly possible in the Ciutat Vella or Old Town, where the distances are manageable. Once you enter the Eixample, however, walking can become tiring, not least because of the monotony of the regular grid plan.

Public transport in Barcelona is both cheap and—as with most aspects of this city's life—exceptionally efficient. Tickets are all flat-fare and there is a wealth of money-saving multi-trip tickets, which are explained below. *TMB*, the public transport company, has information centres at Universitat, Diagonal, Sagrada Familia and Sants metro stations, and also at the FGC local train stations at Plaça de Catalunya, Plaça de Espanya and Provença. Call ☎ 93 412 0000 or the municipal helpline ☎ 010 for information. Comprehensive information in English is available on the website, www.tmb.net. For information on facilities for disabled travellers, call ☎ 93 486 0752. As well as at *TMB* information centres, **metro maps** are available at the ticket booths at all stations and **bus maps** are available from tourist offices.

Tickets A single ticket for the bus or metro costs about €1 Euro. While very reasonable compared to other cities, it is much cheaper to buy one of the multi-trip tickets. The basic travelcard, or *targeta*, is the T-10, which costs about €6 and allows ten rides on the metro, bus, FGC trains and Renfe local trains (*rodalies*) within Zone (*Corona*) 1, which covers just about everywhere you are likely to want to go in the city. Cards must be punched in a machine at the front of buses, or put through the turnstile for the metro and trains. The card may be shared by two or more people, provided it is punched the appropriate number of times per journey. Changes as part of a journey are allowed within one hour, but you must put your ticket back in the stamping machine (it will not be stamped twice).

The **T-Dia** is a one-day travelcard covering unlimited travel and costs around €5. The **T-50/30** allows 50 journeys within a period of 30 days. The **T-Mes** allows unlimited travel for a month.

The **Abonament 3 Dies** or **5 Dies** is a three or five day transport pass, allowing unlimited travel.

All the above are available at metro and FGC stations. Travelcards are also sold at some newsstands and lottery shops. You can also get them from ServiCaixa machines (payable by credit card), which are found in major branches of La Caixa bank, usually next to the cash machine.

The **Barcelona Card** allows unlimited travel for 24, 48 or 72 hours, as well as discounts on museum entrances, city sights, entertainment and in some shops and restaurants. It costs approximately €18, €22 and €24 respectively and is available from municipal tourist offices.

By metro

The metro is the fastest and most practical transport system within the centre of the city. There are five lines and stations near most places of tourist interest. Be aware that it closes at 23.00 during the week. Trains run 05.00–23.00 Mon–Thur; 05.00–02.00 Fri, Sat & the eves of public holidays; 06.00–24.00 Sun; 06.00–23.00 public holidays that fall on weekdays, and 06.00–02.00 public holidays followed by another public holiday.

Most of the metro system is currently not easy for people with physical disabilities or in wheelchairs. Line 2 is the exception, with lifts and ramps at all stations, and there are lifts at some stations on Line 1.

At some smaller stations, different street entrances lead straight down to a particular platform, so be sure to look at signs to check you are going in the right direction. At Liceu station on the Rambla, for example, the two entrances on the right as you walk down towards the sea take you to the southbound platform (next station Drassanes), while the two entrances on the left take you to the northbound platform (next station Catalunya).

By bus

Routes and the direction the bus is going are marked on all stops, making them very easy to use. Buses start at 05.00 or 06.00 and run until 22.30–24.00, depending on the route, and usually come along every 10–15 minutes. Services are reduced on Sundays and public holidays. You can buy a single flatfare ticket from the driver (change given) or punch your travelcard in the machine at the front of the bus. Always get on at the front and off in the middle. Buses are single decker with low boarding platforms and an increasing number have electronic ramps for wheelchair users. To use these, attract the attention of the driver when the bus pulls into the stop for him to activate the mechanism. When you are ready to get off, push the blue button near the exit door. These buses also have a designated space for wheelchair users. The bus map provided by the tourist office indicates which routes offer this facility.

Useful routes include the **14**, which goes from uptown through the Plaça de Catalunya and La Rambla, then along the waterfront to the Port Olimpic; the **17**, which goes from Barceloneta up the Via Laietana past the Cathedral, then through the shopping district of Passeig de Gràcia and Diagonal to the Blue Tram terminus; the **50**, which you can take across town from the Sagrada Familia to Montjuïc, and the **24**, which goes from Plaça de Catalunya up Passeig de Gràcia to the Park Güell.

Night buses run from 22.30 to approximately 05.00. Most routes cross Plaça de Catalunya and all are equipped for wheelchairs.

By FGC train

A third transport system is the commuter train network known as the *Ferrocarrils de la Generalitat de Catalunya*, which have their terminals in Plaça d'Espanya and Plaça de Catalunya, and are often indistinguishable from the metro trains. They serve not only such nearby districts as Gràcia and Sarrià, but also faraway places such as Terrassa and Montserrat. Within greater Barcelona, TMB travelcards and multi-trip tickets are valid for travel.

By car

Driving around the centre is not advisable given the all-day traffic jams, numerous one-way systems, impatient locals and parking problems. Although not a legal requirement, an International Driving Licence may help if you have to deal with the police. If driving your own car, you should have an International Motor Insurance Certificate (Green Card) and a Bail Bond. It is obligatory to carry spare bulbs, a warning triangle and have beam benders.

Parking on the street is permissible in pay-and-display *Zones Blaves* (Blue Zones), with blue markings on the road. Ticket machines detail restrictions, usually a maximum two-hour period during peak times. Red markings mean no parking, and yellow usually means loading and unloading only. Parking is severely restricted in downtown areas, particularly in the Barri Gòtic and anywhere with narrow streets. If you are unlucky enough to have your car towed away (and this is all too likely if you are parked illegally), call the municipal car pound (*dipòsit municipal*) on ☎ 93 428 4595. Car parks, called *parkings*, are signposted by a white P on a blue background and are a much safer option. Central ones include Moll de la Fusta on the waterfront, under Plaça de Catalunya, Passeig de Gràcia and Avinguda de la Catedral.

To hire a car, you must be over 21 and have held a licence for at least a year. A credit card is usually required as a guarantee. As well as in the city centre, all major companies have offices at the airport (*Avis*, ☎ 902 135531; *Hertz*, ☎ 902 402405; *Europcar*, ☎ 902 105030).

The Spanish motoring organisation, the *Real Automóvil Club de España* (*RACE*) C/José Abascal 10, ☎ 900 112222) and its Catalan counterpart, the *Reial Automòbil Club de Catalunya* (*RACC*) (Avinguda Diagonal 687, ☎ 902 307307) have reciprocal arrangements for breakdown cover with the British *AA* and *RAC*.

Diato (C/Almogávers 142, ☎ 93 309 6131/608 697280) provides a 24-hour repair service. *Vidrauto* (C/Mallorca 342, ☎ 93 458 3644) replaces broken windscreens.

By bicycle/moped

The downtown area is quite flat and there are even some cycle lanes. (Call the municipal helpline on ☎ 010 or check the website www.bcn.es for details.) A bike is a good option for exploring the seafront as you can ride along the promenades. Bikes can be hired from **Un Cotxe Menys** (C/Esparteria 3, ☎ 93 268 2195) in the Born district, which also organises cycling tours of the old town and waterfront, and from **Scenic** (C/Marina 22, ☎ 93 221 1666), which runs fun trips on various quirky means of transport.

Mopeds are a good way to get around too, and can be hired from **Vanguard** (C/Londres 31, ☎ 93 439 3880). You must be over 18 and have held a licence for at least a year.

By taxi

Taxis are black with a yellow stripe on the side. A green light on the roof and *Libre/Lliure* (Free) sign against the windscreen indicate when a cab is free. Although plentiful and inexpensive, drivers do not always have a thorough knowledge of the city. It helps if you know the area where you are going as well as the address.

The flagfall fare is about €2, and rises per kilometre or period of time if stuck in traffic. The basic fare tariff applies from 06.00–22.00 Mon–Fri, with slightly higher rates from 22.00–06.00 and on Sat, Sun & public holidays. There are supplements for each piece of luggage measuring 55 x 35 x 35cm, and trips to and from the airport. Details of these and other supplements are shown on an information panel on the side window of taxis, and it is worth checking that you are not being overcharged.

A receipt is *un recibo/un rebut*. If you want to make a complaint, make sure you get a properly-completed receipt with the registration, licence number, fare and the date, and call the municipal helpline on ☎ 010. It is usual (but not obligatory) to tip about 10 per cent.

Cabs can usually be flagged down in the street without too many problems and there are ranks all around the city as well as at transport hubs (look for a rectangular street sign showing a white T on a blue background). The most difficult times to find a taxi are on Friday and Saturday nights, but it is easy to telephone for one. You can arrange to be picked up at a given crossroads or other specific place, as well as at an address. The cab company asks for your name and you are given a number to quote to the driver. The main taxi companies are: **Barnataxi**, ☎ 93 355 7755; **Taxi Radiomòbil**, ☎ 93 358 11 11 and **Radio Taxi**, ☎ 93 225 0000. All these have cabs adapted for people in wheelchairs, or call specialists **Taxi Adaptado** on ☎ 93 357 7755.

Other means of transport

Bus Turístic

Take the stress out of sightseeing by hopping on and off the Bus Turístic, an open-top doubledecker with two routes around the city, passing all the major points of interest. The buses run every ten minutes in summer. Service is slightly less frequent at other times of year, depending on visitor numbers. Tickets are available from tourist offices or on the bus, which has designated stops at key points around the city. It costs approximately €15 for one day and €19 for two days, and includes a book of vouchers that give discounts at all the museums and attractions along the route, as well as on the other means of transport detailed below and at fast-food cafés and shops. The vouchers are valid till the end of the year when the bus ticket is purchased, so you can use them throughout your stay. Just riding around on the bus is a great way to get to grips with the layout of the city, and there are terrific views from Tibidabo and Montjuïc.

Montjuïc funicular
The funicular runs from near Paral·lel metro station up Montjuïc hill, stopping near the Fundació Miró. It operates every day in summer from 10.00–21.30. In winter, times change to 10.00–19.30, sometimes restricted to Sat, Sun & public holidays in quieter months.

Montjuïc cable car
The cable car runs from the funicular terminus on Montjuïc up the hill to the castle. In summer, it operates every day from 10.00–21.30. In winter, this changes to 10.00–19.30, usually daily, but sometimes restricted as above.

Blue tram
The **Tramvia Blau** is a traditional wooden tram that began operating in 1901. It runs from Plaça J.F. Kennedy up to Plaça Dr Andreu on Tibidabo hill, 10.00–21.30 daily in summer and 10.00–19.30 in winter. As above, the winter timetable is sometimes restricted to weekends.

Tibidabo funicular
This funicular takes you up to the Tibidabo funfair from Plaça Dr Andreu. Times vary throughout the year in line with when the funfair is open.

Port cable car
The **Transbordador Aeri cable cars** run from the Torre de Sant Sebstià on the Barceloneta quayside to the Miramar station on Montjuïc, with a stop at the Torre de Jaume I by the World Trade Center on the Moll (Quay) Barcelona. They run 10.30–20.00 in summer, slightly less often during the rest of the year.

Golondrines boats
These pleasure boats run trips around the harbour and down to the Port Olímpic. Harbour trips leave every hour on weekdays, more frequently at weekends and in summer. Port Olímpic trips are less frequent, between three and six a day, depending on demand. All boats leave from Plaça Portal de la Pau at the bottom of the Rambla, metro Drassanes.

Globus balloon
Hot-air balloon trips over Barcelona run daily in summer from 10.30–23.00, less frequently in winter, according to demand. The balloons leave from a site on the corner of Passeig de Circumval·lació and Carrer de Wellington, near Ciutadella Park, and stop in the Port Olímpic. Further information on departures from tourist offices or guides on the Bus Turístic.

Where to stay

As Barcelona is both a major business and leisure destination, its hotels operate at near maximum capacity all year round and it is advisable to book as far in advance as possible. The numerous trade fairs and special events taking place in the city mean that there is often a shortage of space, despite the many new hotels that have opened in the last decade.

If your first choices are full, try places lower down the scale, which are more likely to have rooms as they are not usually used by business visitors. Just after noon is the best time to call, when hotels know what they have available.

The star system is often misleading and rates vary greatly. Hotels are graded according to size and facilities, with no regard for architecture, decoration or service. Rates are always quoted by room rather than by person. Tax (IVA) is levied at 7 per cent, and is not usually included in quoted rates. Check whether or not breakfast is included. In four and five star places, breakfast is sometimes extortionately priced (around €18), compared to around €5 in a bar. If you only want juice, coffee and toast, it is probably better to go out, and the quality is often higher. Even in five star hotels, breakfast coffee is sometimes ghastly and juice is not freshly squeezed.

The Spanish Tourist Office provides a comprehensive hotel list, though only basic details are given. The tourist offices in Barcelona, including at the airport (p 13) offer a helpful hotel reservation service.

There are numerous websites for booking hotels, which include:

www.hotel-barcelona.com
www.bestbarcelonahotels.com
www.1stbarcelonahotels.com
www.spainonline.com

www.lastminute.com
www.expedia.com
www.hoteldiscounts.com

All hotels listed here are centrally located, most near Plaça de Catalunya, the Rambla or the seafront. Despite Barcelona's reputation as a design capital, the vast majority of hotels are decorated in anonymous international style. Some that do have a more individual décor include the Arts, Claris, Colón, Rivoli Ramblas, Park, Oriente, Mesón Castilla, Nouvel and Espanya.

Noise is often a problem, particularly below four-star standard. Ask for *una habitación tranquila*. Quieter rooms are however usually *interior*, meaning that they give onto a stairwell or inner courtyard and are often dark. If you need natural light, ask for *una habitación exterior*, but bear in mind that these usually give onto the street. Air-conditioning is an advantage in July and August, and heating is essential from November to April. If you are travelling by car, check that the hotel has parking facilities. You may have to pay extra for this, but it saves a lot of hassle and is much safer.

The rates given below are for a double room (*habitación doble*). A single room (*individual*) is usually about 30 per cent cheaper. Most hotels also offer double rooms for single use (*doble para uso individual*) for about 20 per cent less than the normal rate. As single rooms are often tiny and dark, it is worth investigating this option. Paying for a double in a one star hotel may well be a better deal than a single in a three star. All places listed here have private bathrooms. This also applies to the *hostales* listed—but specify *con baño individual* when booking, in case not all rooms have ensuite bathrooms.

Hostales are small, no-frills establishments, often family-run. It is a very broad category, with some looking just like a simple hotel, while others are effectively a converted large flat in an apartment block. They are rated from one to three stars and there are often half a dozen or so in the same building. If you can put up with basic facilities, the money saved is considerable. Here I have concentrated on places that to all intents and purposes are the same as hotels. The newly-refurbished **Urquinaona**, for example, is an excellent option, with all the facilities you would expect in a three-star hotel at half the price.

The following rates are given as a guideline only:

Five star €180–500
Four star €150–300
Three star €90–180
Two star €60–100
One star €45–75

Dial the international prefix + 34 before the numbers given.

Five star hotels

Arts, C/de la Marina 19-21. ☎ 93 221 1000, fax 93 221 1070, www.harts.es. Overlooking the beach on the seafront in the Port Olímpic, this 45-floor stylish hotel is decorated in distinctive contemporary style. A favourite with celebrities. Good bars and restaurants. Outdoor pool. Fitness centre. 455 rooms, suites and apartments with spectacular views. Wheelchair access and adapted rooms.

Claris, C/Pau Claris 150. ☎ 93 487 6262, fax 93 215 7970, www.derbyhotels.es. 19C mansion converted into swish hotel decorated with antiques and designer furniture. Near Gaudí buildings and shops on Passeig de Gràcia. Rooftop pool. 120 rooms and suites (some duplex). Wheelchair access.

Ritz, Gran Vía de les Corts Catalanes 668. ☎ 93 318 5200, fax 93 318 0148, www.ritzbcn.com. Opened in 1919, the hotel has been revamped to embrace all the traditional splendour of Ritz establishments. 125 rooms and suites. Non-smoking floor. Wheelchair access.

Four star hotels

Barcino, C/Jaume I, 6. ☎ 93 302 2012, fax 93 301 4242, www.hotelbarcino.com. Smart hotel in Gothic Quarter, near Rambla, Cathedral and shops. 53 rooms and suites.

Colón, Avda de la Catedral 7. ☎ 93 301 1404, fax 93 317 2915, www.hotelcolon.es. Opposite the cathedral, in the heart of the Gothic Quarter. Built in 1951, lots of old-fashioned charm and very comfortable. 147 rooms. Wheelchair access and adapted rooms.

Condes de Barcelona, Passeig de Gràcia 73–75. ☎ 93 467 4780, fax 93 467 4785, www.hotelcondesdebarcelona.com. Stylish hotel situated in two historic buildings, one dating from late-19C with lots of Modernista details. Good service. Rooftop pool and bar with views of La Pedrera. 183 rooms.

Duques de Bergara, C/Bergara 11. ☎ 93 301 5151, fax 93 317 3442, www.hoteles-catalonia.es. Characterful Modernista building near Plaça de

Catalunya. Friendly service. 146 rooms and suites. Outdoor pool. Wheelchair access and adapted rooms.

Gótico, C/Jaume I, 14. ☎ 93 315 2211, fax 93 315 2213, www.hotelgotico.com. Central location in heart of Gothic Quarter. Refurbished in 1999. Friendly staff. 81 rooms, some with balcony.

Majèstic, Passeig de Gràcia 68. ☎ 93 487 3939, fax 93 487 9790, www.hotelmajestic.es. Well-established and fully refurbished in 1997. Handy location. Lively bars and renowned restaurant. 303 rooms. Garage. Rooftop pool.

Millennium, Ronda de Sant Pau 14. ☎ 93 441 4177, fax 93 324 8150, www.hotel-millennium.com. 19C building converted into stylish hotel in 2001. On edge of Raval district, near the seafront and Montjuïc. Call or check website for details of discount rates. 46 rooms and suites. Fitness centre and sauna.

Regente, Rambla de Catalunya 76. ☎ 93 487 5989, fax 93 487 3227, www.hoteles-centro-ciudad.es. Historic Modernista building in handy location. Comfortable, good service. Top floor rooms have terraces with great views. 79 rooms. Rooftop pool. Wheelchair access and adapted rooms.

Rivoli Ramblas, La Rambla 128. ☎ 93 302 6643, fax 93 317 5053, www.rivolihotels.com. Art Deco building, revamped in spectacular style. Roof terrace with bar. 90 rooms and suites. Garage.

Three star hotels

Allegro, Avda. Portal de l'Angel 15–17. ☎ 93 318 4141, fax 93 301 2631, www.hoteles-catalonia.es. Smart hotel on pedestrianised shopping street near Plaça de Catalunya. Late-19C mansion converted in 1998. 74 rooms, some with balconies. Wheelchair access and adapted rooms.

Flor Parks, La Rambla 70. ☎ 93 342 9760, fax 93 342 9788, email hotel-flor-parks@ctv.es. Contemporary design, with rooms overlooking Rambla or a tree-filled courtyard at the back.

Gran Via, Gran Via de les Corts Catalanes 642. ☎ 93 318 1900, fax 93 318 9997. Converted mansion with lots of old-world charm near Passeig de Gràcia. Roof terrace. 53 rooms.

Metropol, C/Ample 31. ☎ 93 310 5100, fax 93 319 1276, www.hesperia-metropol.com. Near the seafront, Rambla and Gothic Quarter in quiet street. 71 rooms. Wheelchair access and adapted rooms.

Montblanc, Via Laietana 61. ☎ 93 343 5555, fax 93 343 5558, www.hoteles-centro-ciudad.es. Convenient location for sights, shops and seafront, opened in 2000. 79 rooms.

Nouvel, C/de Santa Ana 18–20. ☎ 93 301 8274, fax 93 301 8370, www.hotelnouvel.com. Refurbished Modernista building with wrought-iron balconies and carved stone façade. Just off the Rambla near Plaça de Catalunya. 54 rooms. Wheelchair access.

Oriente, La Rambla 45. ☎ 93 302 2558, fax 93 412 3819, www.husa.es. Dating back to 1842, the Oriente used to be very grand. It is still a characterful place to stay, though no longer so luxurious. See p 92. Great location. 142 rooms.

Park, Avda Marquès de Argentera 11. ☎ 93 319 6000, fax 93 319 4519, www.parkhotelbarcelona.com. With its distinctive 1950s' architecture (see p 156), this is one of the most stylish hotels in Barcelona. Restored and refurbished in 1990. Location handy for waterfront, Ciutadella park and lively Born district. 91 rooms. Full wheelchair access and adapted rooms.

Sant Agustí, Plaça Sant Agustí 3. ☎ 93 318 1658, fax 93 317 2928, www.hotelsa.com. Contemporary and traditional design are combined successfully at the friendly Sant Agustí, just off the Rambla. Some rooms have balconies overlooking the square. Good breakfasts. 77 rooms. Wheelchair access and adapted rooms.

Two star hotels

Cuatro Naciones, La Rambla 40. ☎ 93 317 3624, fax 93 302 6985. At the bottom end of the Rambla, this hotel dates back to the mid-19C. Recently refurbished, the top floor rooms have large terraces. 34 rooms.

Espanya, C/Sant Pau 9. ☎ 93 318 1758, fax 93 317 1134, email hotelespanya@tresnet.com. Rooms are nothing out of the ordinary but the dining rooms were designed by the top Modernista architect Domènech i Montaner and decorated by Ramon Casas. See p 145. 69 rooms.

Mesón Castilla, C/Valldoncella 5. ☎ 93 318 2182, fax 93 412 4020, email hmesoncastilla@teleline.es. The two-star rating undervalues this charming hotel with good facilities and lots of character. Near Plaça de Catalunya and MACBA museum. Garage. 56 rooms.

Hostales and one star hotels

Call, C/de l'Arc de San Ramon del Call 4. ☎ 93 302 1123, fax 93 301 3486. Situated on a tiny street in former Jewish quarter. Rooms are basic but have bathrooms and phone. Great for exploring the Gothic Quarter but not suitable if you need a taxi to the door. Lift.

Dalí, C/Boquería 12. ☎ 93 318 5580, fax 93 318 5580. 18C building just off the Rambla. Popular with younger crowd. 57 rooms with bathrooms.

Del Mar, Pla del Palau 19. ☎ 93 319 3302/3047, fax 902 118227, www.gargallo-hotels.com. Friendly, comfortable place near the seafront. 68 rooms with bathrooms. Lift.

Eden, C/Balmes 55. ☎ 93 452 6620, fax 93 452 6621, www.barcelona-on-line.es/hostaleden. Funky hostal in Eixample, handy for galleries and shops. Enterprising young owners. Some rooms are just okay, others bright and spacious, and some even have jacuzzis or fridges. On 1st and 2nd floor of apartment block. No lift.

Grau, C/Ramelleres 27, ☎ 93 301 8135, www.intercom.es/grau. Characterful hostal with friendly, helpful staff in Raval district. Near MACBA museum, Rambla and Plaça de Catalunya. Note that not all rooms have ensuite bathrooms and there is no lift.

Jardí, Plaça Sant Josep Oriol 1. ☎ 93 301 5900, fax 93 318 3664. Justifiably popular hotel on pretty pedestrianised square in the Gothic Quarter. Rooms vary in size but all have bathrooms. Try to get one with a view.

Orleans, Avda Marquès de l'Argentera 13. ☎ 93 319 7382, fax 93 319 7382. Surprisingly luxurious rooms on 1st floor of apartment block near seafront and Ciutadella park. All new furniture, fittings and bathrooms. 17 rooms with TV, phone and heating. No lift.

Peninsula, C/Sant Pau 34. ☎ 93 302 3138, fax 93 412 3699. Formerly a convent, the Peninsula has basic rooms set around an airy courtyard filled with plants and contemporary art. Breakfast served in attractive café. 80 rooms with bathrooms, air-conditioning and phone. Lift.

Ramos, C/Hospital 36. ☎ 93 302 0723, fax 93 302 0430. Good budget choice in convenient location off Rambla. Rooms, on 1st and 2nd floors, are set around a courtyard and all have bathrooms, TV, phone, heating and air-conditioning. No lift.

Roma Reial, Plaça Reial 11. ☎ 93 302 0366, fax 93 301 1839. Great (if noisy) location on lively, atmospheric Plaça Reial, just off Rambla. 52 rooms with bathrooms, phone and heating. Best ones have balconies giving onto the square.

Urquinaona, Ronda de Sant Pere 24. ☎ 93 268 1336, fax 93 295 4137, www.barcelonahotel.com/urquinaona. Refurbished *hostal* with above average facilities, near Plaça de Catalunya. Rooms have TV, phone, fridge and air-conditioning.

Windsor, Rambla de Catalunya 84. ☎ 93 215 1198. Characterful place on smart, lively street. Good location for Modernista architecture and shopping. 15 rooms with private bathrooms.

Youth hostels

Information is available from the *Xarxa d'Albergs de Joventut*, ☎ 93 483 8363, fax 93 483 8350.

Alberg Gothic Point, C/Vitagans 5. ☎ 93 268 7808, email badia@intercom.es. Central location, near Jaume I metro station, so handy for most sights and waterfront. Good facilities with accommodation in single or double rooms. Lockers available and there is also a free internet service.

Alberg Mare de Déu de Montserrat, Passeig Mare de Déu del Coll 41–51. ☎ 93 210 5151, fax 93 210 0798. The hostel is 4km from the centre, on the 28 bus route from Plaça de Catalunya.

Alberg Kabul, Plaça Reial 17. ☎ 93 318 5190, fax 93 301 4034, www.kabul-hostel.com. Privately-run hostel in good location.

Alberg Juvenil Palau, C/Palau 6. ☎ 93 412 5080. Small, private hostel in the heart of the Gothic Quarter.

Alberg Pere Tarrès, C/Numància 149. ☎ 93 410 2309, fax 93 419 6268, www.peretarres.org. Ten minutes' walk from Sants train station. More than 90 beds, but strict rules.

Campsites

The Generalitat de Catalunya tourist office (p 13) publishes a useful booklet on campsites.

Cala Gogó, Carretera de la Platja, El Prat de Llobregat. ☎ 93 379 4600, fax 93 379 4711. Large campsite with good facilities, 7km south of centre near airport and Prat beach. Bus 65 from Plaça de Espanya.

Masnou, N11 road, turning at km 633, El Masnou. ☎/fax 93 555 1503. 10km north of the centre near beach. Open year round. Take the local train (*rodalies*) to Masnou from Plaça de Catalunya.

Food and drink

The Catalan love of food is exemplified in the character of Pepe Carvalho, the protagonist of a popular series of detective novels by the leading Catalan writer, Vázquez Montalbán. Carvalho is a passionate cook and gourmet whose obsession with what he eats is unaffected by crises in both his professional and personal life, his obsession being such that Montalbán was able to bring out a book dedicated solely to *The Recipes of Pepe Carvalho* (Barcelona, 1989). It is with a heavy heart that this fat and balding hedonist is forced on one occasion to leave his home town of Barcelona and go off on an assignment to Madrid, a place which, in his own words, 'has given no more than a stew, an omelette and a dish of tripe to the gastronomic culture of our country'. Most Madrilenians would rightly take offence at Carvalho's assessment of their gastronomy, though few of them would retaliate with an attack on Catalan food, which in certain Spanish circles is regarded as the Catalans' main saving grace.

The virtues of Catalan food were outlined as far back as the 14C, in an encyclopaedic manual of learning written by a Franciscan monk, Francesc Eiximenis, from the Catalan town of Girona. Eiximenis, who came from a wealthy mercantile family, was a man of broad international outlook who had travelled widely throughout Europe, including Paris, Cologne, Oxford and Rome. Such a background lent an added authority to the section of his manual that was entitled 'Why the Catalans eat more finely and in a better way than other nations' (*Com catalans menjen plus graciosament ab millor manere que altres nacions*). Among the reasons that he gave were that the Catalans avoid excess and superfluity, that they accompany their food with wines rather than beers or sweet brews, that their diet is a regular and balanced one that takes into account both the nutritional and dietary elements of the food, and that in their table manners and cutting of meat they show a respect for hygiene not generally found elsewhere. Further reflections on Catalan food are to be found in another 14C treatise, the *Llibre de Sent Soví*, but the first Catalan cookery book was not to appear until the end of the following century.

This work, the *Llibre de Coch*, was written by Robert de Nola, a cook who claimed to have worked in the service of Ferdinand I of Aragon. Translated shortly afterwards into Castilian, the book was perhaps the most influential of its kind in 16C Spain. Certain of its recipes might not be entirely to present-day tastes, such as the one for roast cat (*menjar de gat rostit*), which involves roasting the animal in oil, garlic and herbs and serving it in slices with more garlic. Catalan refinement and hygienic concerns were in this case reflected in the delicate detail of removing the cat's brain beforehand, as it was considered prejudicial to human sanity.

Many of the principles of modern Catalan cookery were outlined in the book, but the basic repertory of so-called traditional Catalan dishes does not seem to have been established until the late 19C, at a time of growing Catalan nationalism. The two leading cookery writers of this period were Ignasi Domènech Puigcercós—the author of some 30 books on the subject—and Ferran Agulló, a lawyer and journalist who was born in Girona in 1863. Agulló's most important work was the *Llibre de la cuina catalana* (The Book of Catalan Food), the introduction to which begins with the words: 'Catalunya, just as it has its own language, constitution, customs, history and political ideals, has its own cuisine. There are regions, nations, peoples, who have their own gastronomic specialities, but not a cuisine. Catalunya has this, and it has something more: it has an extraordinary capacity to assimilate the specialities of other cusines such as that of France or Italy; it appropriates these specialities and modifies them in accordance with its own tastes and traditions.'

To this ability to assimilate should be added the exceptional natural resources of Catalunya, a region that can be divided into three main gastronomic areas: one reliant on the exceptional variety of seafood from the Mediterranean, another on the cattle farming and rich vegetable produce of the densely agricultural hinterland and a third on the abundance of game in the mountains. Within each of these areas there exists a wealth of local variations in the cuisine, particularly in the agricultural parts of the interior. The dishes that Barcelona itself has contributed to this rich gastronomic culture have been much debated, but what is certain is that it has acted as a melting-pot to the many strands of the regional cuisine, bringing together the culinary traditions of the maritime, agricultural and mountainous areas of Catalunya, as well as those of the many peoples who have settled in the city from other parts of Spain and Europe.

From the Romantic period onwards, tourists have tended to denigrate the food of Spain generally, and there is certainly an irony in the fact that this very tourism, particularly in the coastal resorts, has been a major contributory factor to the decline of traditional Catalan cuisine. Vázquez Montalbán, in a polemical book on Catalan food written in 1979, expressed his worry that the food of his region was becoming so blandly international in character that soon all that would be left of Catalunya's gastronomic traditions would be a piece of soggy toast rubbed with oil and tomato and spread with a layer of ham as thin and tasteless as clingfilm.

Fortunately, the decline in the local gastronomy has recently been halted, thanks to a combination of resurgent regional pride and the beneficial influence of *nouvelle cuisine*, the principles of which were ideally suited to Catalan food, which has traditionally been characterised by a meticulous care in its preparation, an insistence on freshness of produce, a preference for quality over quantity and a love of unusual combinations. Nonetheless, the ubiquitous *pa amb tomaquet* or bread rubbed with oil and tomato—which is not only a dish in its own right when served with ham, but is also an accompaniment to most other dishes—has become as integral to the gastronomic image of Catalunya as pasta has to that of Italy, or dumplings to that of the Czech Republic.

The four sauces

Agulló, and most other cookery writers from the 19C onwards, have defined the true essence of Catalan food as lying in the four sauces known as the *sofregit*, the *picada*, the *samfaina* and the *allioli*. In contrast to other parts of Spain, both fish and meat in Catalunya are rarely presented simply in a fried, boiled, baked, grilled or roasted state, but with an accompanying sauce. The two most important ones are the *sofregit* (which means literally 'a fry-up') and the *picada* (literally 'chopped-up').

Sofregit is prepared—preferably in a terracotta casserole or *cassola de fang*—by slowly frying an onion in oil or lard, and then adding a chopped and peeled tomato. Garlic and parsley are usually added to the resulting mixture, which should have the consistency of jam.

The *picada* is a more complex sauce and varies slightly according to the dishes it accompanies. The one essential element is the mortar in which all the ingredients are pounded together. The most usual ingredients are garlic, saffron, pine nuts, almonds, biscuits, fried or toasted breadcrumbs, and fish, chicken or other livers (which can be put in either raw or cooked). Dry or sweet wine, or even anisette, is frequently used to make the mixture more liquid, and honey, sugar and grated chocolate are often added as sweeteners. Mixing sweet and sour ingredients together is very popular in Catalan cuisine.

Samfaina is the Catalan equivalent of the French ratatouille and is made with onions, tomatoes, red or green peppers and, occasionally, pumpkin.

Allioli, which is common to several Mediterranean regions, including Provence, Greece, North Africa and southern Italy, is a paste made by pounding garlic in a mortar and slowly amalgamating olive oil. Other ingredients, such as cheese, can be added to create a thicker mixture. The most common addition is egg yolk, which produces a garlic mayonnaise. The exact origins of *allioli* are not known, though a comparable sauce is mentioned in the *Llibre de Sent-Soví*.

Typical meals

A typical Catalan meal is likely to begin with a salad, a vegetable dish or a soup. One of the most common salads is the *escalivada*, which in its most basic form comprises skinned and roasted peppers and aubergines cut into strips and dressed with oil, salt and vinegar. This should not be confused with an *esqueixada* (with which it is sometimes served), which is a salad of shredded salt cod.

Vegetable dishes include cabbage (*col*) with *allioli*, spinach with currants and pinenuts (*espinac amb pases i pinyons*). Numerous stews are made with beans (*mongetes*), broad beans (*faves*) or chickpeas (*cigrons*), usually also involving pieces of the ubiquitous Catalan pork sausage known as the *botifarra*. Two of the finest soup dishes are made with *rap* (monkfish) and *bolets* (ceps), both of which feature a *picada* of saffron, garlic and toasted almonds.

The main fish or meat dishes, though usually prepared or served with a sauce, are rarely accompanied by vegetables other than potatoes. A popular **fish** dish which is claimed to be of Barcelona origin is dried salt cod (*bacallà*) with *samfaina*. Other traditional ways of preparing this *bacallà* are *a la llauna* (with paprika, garlic, parsley and white wine) and with honey (*mel*).

Almost certainly originating from the fish restaurants of the Barcelona district of Barceloneta is the *sarsuela*, a name borrowed from a Spanish form of operetta but applied in culinary usage to the Catalan equivalent of the Provençal *bouillabaisse*. The mixture of seafood used usually includes mussels, monkfish, langoustines and squid, and is cooked in a *sofregit* to which saffron, garlic and parsley are added. Owing to its relatively recent origin, this is a dish that has horrified traditionalists, including the leading Catalan writer Josep Pla, who not only complained of its 'horrible name' of theatrical origin, but also opined that it comprised a ratio of one good fish to every six fishes of the 'vilest quality'.

Pla was unimpressed by all mixtures of seafood, and reserved his strongest criticism for the *parrillada*, a culinary fashion of even more recent origin than the *sarsuela*. Described by Pla as a dry version of the latter, this mixture of grilled or deep-fried seafood can indeed have a desiccated, archaeological character when served in some of the cheaper restaurants of Barceloneta. A better bet is the *suquet*, a seafood stew originating in the Costa Brava, and prepared in both a *sofregit* and *picada*.

Meat, game and poultry The variety of meat, game and poultry dishes is very great in Catalunya, poultry in particular being more commonly and interestingly served than it is in other parts of Spain. As with the fish recipes, most of these dishes gain their distinction from the use of the *sofrito*, *picada*, *samfaina* and *allioli* sauces. Traditional dishes include duck cooked with pears (*ànec amb peras*) and rabbit with chestnuts and ceps (*conill amb castanyas i bolets*). *Gall dindi farcit a la Catalana* is a Christmas dish of turkey stuffed with ham, sausages, plums, apricots, currants, pine nuts, chestnuts, wine and cinnamon.

Meat, game and poultry are sometimes prepared together with seafood. An excellent—if rare and very expensive—example is lobster with chicken (*llagosta amb pollastre*). A Barcelona invention of the 1950s was the *mar i muntanya* (literally 'sea and mountain'), which, as its name suggests, brings together a veritable excess of ingredients, including snails, cuttlefish, trotters, sausages, rabbit, mussels, chicken, tomatoes, onions, almonds, pine nuts, chocolate and hazelnuts. In the debased form in which this dish is usually served today, this rich mixture has been pared down to a chicken and prawn ragout.

The most famous of all Catalan dishes, and a meal in itself, is the *escudella i carn d'olla*, which is a variant of the Castilian *cocido* and the Andalusian *puchero*. This is a stew made with potatoes, cabbage, chickpeas, chicken and a variety of meats, including the *botifarra* sausage. The broth is served as a first course, usually today with noodles, but traditionally with pasta cut into alphabet shapes, an addition that inspired Miguel de Unamuno to write that the Catalans were 'such lovers of culture that they even eat the letters of the alphabet'. The vegetables and meats are piled up separately on a large plate.

Rice and pasta dishes are very common in Catalunya, the former being an import from the neighbouring region of Valencia. The Catalan equivalent of *paella* is the *arròs a la Catalana*, but a more traditional rice dish is the *arroseixat*, in which saffron-flavoured rice is prepared with potatoes, onions and fish. The delicious *arròs negre* or 'black rice' is rice cooked in cuttlefish ink.

Pasta dishes, though of distant Italian origin, have become one of the great Catalan specialities, in particular cannelloni, which are known in Catalan as *canalons*. An unappetising version of cannelloni is usually found in the cheaper restaurants, but this is traditionally a festive dish, prepared with the remains of roast or stewed meats. The pasta is usually filled with a sauce made of onions, pork, veal, chicken livers and chicken breasts, and covered with a bechamel flavoured with nutmeg. The other main pasta dishes are macaroni (*maccarons*) and noodles (*fideus*). Macaroni is usually served with a thick sauce made of tomatoes, bechamel and pieces of ham, sausage or bacon. The classic Catalan way of preparing noodles is *a la cazuela*, a dish unlike any Italian one, comprising noodles incorporated into a stew of pork ribs, *botifarra* sausages, tomatoes and wine.

Desserts The sweet tooth of the Catalans is evident more in their use of sugar, honey and chocolate in savoury dishes than it is in the range of their desserts. The usual restaurant stand-by is the *crema catalana*, a cream custard with a caramelised crust as in the French *crème brulée*. As in other parts of Spain, many of the more elaborate desserts and pastries are only to be found around Easter and Christmas.

Wine

Catalunya is one of the most important wine-producing regions in Spain, with ten officially recognised production areas (*Denominación de Orígen*, or *D.O.*). The Catalan government is currently trying to set up the *D.O. Catalunya*, which will bring the different areas under one umbrella with the idea of improving production methods and quality.

The **Penedès** district extends to the south of Barcelona and produces the most famous of Catalunya's wines. The region is traditionally known for its whites, but producers are now making some good reds too, using mainly French grape varieties. Renowned producers include Torres and Jean Leon.

Although geographically within Penedès, the champagne-like sparkling wines known as **cavas** have their own *D.O.* Production is based in and around the town of Sant Sadurni d'Anoia (see p 228). The quality of *cavas* has improved tremendously in recent years. The best known in Spain and internationally are Freixenet and Codorníu, but while in Barcelona it is worth seeking out other producers, such as Caus, Agustí Torello and Juvé Camps.

South of the Penedès district lies the wine-growing district of **Tarragona** and further south still is the **Priorato**. Both these districts specialise in full-bodied reds and are also renowned for their sweet dessert wines.

The **Alella** region is just north of Barcelona and is also traditionally renowned for its whites. After years in the doldrums—and losing quite a few vineyards to the expanding city—production is now concentrated in the interior and has taken on a new dynamism. The increasing use of foreign grape varieties means that the whites have a quite different character, and the area is also producing rosés and reds. Leading wineries include Parxet, which produces the well-known Marqués de Alella, and Roura, which produces a good rosé.

The inland **Costers del Segre** region in Lleida province is also gaining interest, largely due to one winery: Raimat. Established in 1918 by the director of Codorníu, Raimat produces some excellent Cabernet Sauvignons.

Cold drinks

When ordering soft drinks (*refrescos*), it is usual to specify a brand name. Fresh fruit juices are not as common as you might expect—usually orange is the only one that does not come out of a carton or bottle. Ask for *zumo natural* or *zumo recién exprimido*. Although widely available at breakfast time, people do not usually drink juice with meals. Tap water (*agua del grifo*) is safe to drink but does not taste great in Barcelona. Mineral water (*agua mineral*) is inexpensive.

Alcoholic mixed drinks (*copas*) are served in long glasses with plenty of ice (*hielo*) in much larger measures than other European countries. Always specify a brand when ordering spirits (particularly whisky), otherwise you will be given the cheapest, which is often low quality and can give you a terrible headache even if you only have one drink. **Beer** (*cerveza*) is available in cafés as well as bars, and is usually draught.

Hot drinks

Coffee is invariably made in an espresso machine. *Café solo* is a straight espresso.

Café con leche is an espresso shot with about twice the quantity of hot milk. *Café cortado* is espresso with a dash of hot milk. *Café americano* is an expresso topped up with hot water. Cappuccino is becoming increasingly popular.

Tea is widely available, but not always great quality. To get milk, wait until the tea is served then ask for *un poco de leche fría*. Herb teas (*infusiones*) are also popular, particularly camomile (*manzanilla*) and peppermint (*poleo*).

Food and drink glossary
Listed in Catalan then Spanish

Common preparation terms:
a la planxa/a la plancha, cooked on the griddle
a la romana/a la romana, fried in batter
al romesco/al romesco, almond, garlic and tomato sauce
al forn/al horno, baked
rostit/asado, roast or baked
a la brasa/a la brasa, chargrilled

a la graella/a la parrilla, grilled
a la llauna/a la llauna, baked in a tin
bullit/cocido, boiled
fregit/frito, fried
al vapor/al vapor, steamed
poc fet/poco hecho, rare
a punt/en su punto, medium rare
ben fet/muy hecho, well done

Restaurant terms
carta/carta, menu
compte/cuenta, bill (check)
got/vaso, glass
pa/pan, bread

pebre/pimienta, pepper
sal/sal, salt
tovalló/servilleta, napkin

Some common ingredients
allioli/allioli, garlic and olive oil dressing, sometimes an egg mayonnaise
arròs/arroz, rice
cargols/caracoles, snails

fideus/fideos, noodles
formatge/queso, cheese
oli/aceite, oil

Vegetables (*verdures/verduras*)
albergínies/berenjenas, aubergines
all/ajo, garlic
amanida/ensalada, salad
àpi/apio, celery
bledes/acelgas, Swiss chard
bolet/seta, wild mushroom
calçot/cebolleta, large spring onion
carbassó/calabacín, courgette (zucchini)
carxofe/alcachofa, artichoke
ceba/cebolla, onion
cigrons/garbanzos, chickpeas
endivies/endibias, chicory
espàrrecs/espárragos, asparagus
espinacs/espinacas, spinach
faves/habas, broad beans

enciam/lechuga, lettuce
llenties/lentejas, lentils
mongetes/alubias, dried beans
mongetes blancs/judias blancas, butter beans
mongetes tendres/judias verdes, green beans
pastanagues/znahorias, carrots
patates/patatas, potatoes
pebrots/pimientos, peppers
pèsols/guisantes, peas
porro/puerro, leek
remolatxa/remolacha, beetroot
tòfona/trufa, truffle
tomàquet/tomate, tomato
xampinyons/champiñones, mushrooms

Eggs (*ous/huevos*)

remenats/revueltos, scrambled

ruita/tortilla, omelette

Fish and seafood (*peix i marisc/pescados y mariscos*)

anguila/anguila, eel
anxova/anchoa, anchovy
bacallà/bacalao, salt cod
besu/besugo, sea bream
calamars/calamares, squid
calamarsó/chipirón, baby squid
cloïsses/almejas, clams
cranc de mar/cangrejo, crab
cranc de riu/cangrejo de río, freshwater crayfish
cigales or escamarlà/cigalas, Dublin Bay prawns, langoustines
daurada/dorada, gilthead sea bream
emperador/emperador, swordfish
eriçó/erizo, sea urchin
gamba/gamba, prawn
llagosta/langosta, spiny or rock lobster
llagosti/langostino, large prawn
llamantol/bogavante, (large-clawed) lobster

llenguado/lenguado, sole
llobarro/lubina, sea bass
lluç/merluza, hake
moll/salmonete, red mullet
musclo/mejillón, mussel
nero/mero, grouper
ostra/ostra, oyster
percebes/percebes, goose barnacles
pop/pulpo, octopus
rajada/raya, skate
rap/rape, monkfish
rèmol/rodaballo, turbot
salmó/salmón, salon
sardina/sardina, sardine
seitons/boquerones, fresh anchovies
sípia/sepia, cuttlefish
tonyina/bonito or *atún*, tuna
truita/trucha, trout
vieira/vieria, scallop

Poultry and meat (*aviram i carn/aves y carnes*)

ànec/pato, duck
anyell or *xai/cordero*, lamb
bou/buey or *ternera*, beef
botifarra/butifarra, pork sausage
cabrit/cabrito, kid goat
caça/caza, game
cevell/sesos, brains
cèrvol/ciervo, venison
conill/conejo, rabbit
costella/chuleta, cutlet
faisa/faisán, pheasant
fetge/hígado, liver
gall dindi/pavo, turkey
ganso/oca, goose

guatlle/codorniz, quail
llebre/liebre, hare
llom/lomo, pork loin
mandonguilles/albóndigas, meatballs
perdiu/perdiz, partridge
pernil/jamón, ham
pollastre/pollo, chicken
porc/cerdo, pork
ronyons/riñones, kidneys
salsitxa/salchicha, sausage
senglar/jabalí, wild boar
tripa/callos, tripe
vedella/ternera lechal, veal

Nuts (*nous/frutos secos*)

ametller/almendra, almond
avellana/avellana, hazelnut

castanya/castaña, chestnut
pinyó/piñon, pinenut

Fruit (*fruïta*/*fruit*)

albercoc/*albaricoque*, apricot
ananàs/*piña*, pineapple
cirera/*cereza*, cherry
codony/*membrillo*, quince
figa/*higo*, fig
gerd/*frambuesa*, raspberry
llimona/*limón*, lemon
maduixa/*fresa*, strawberry
meló/*melón*, melon

pera/*pera*, pear
pinya/*piña*, pineapple
plàtan/*plátano*, banana
poma/*manzana*, apple
préssec/*melocotón*, peach
raïm/*uva*, grape
síndria/*sandía*, watermelon
taronja/*naranja*, orange

Desserts (*postres*/*postres*)

crem cremat/*crema catalana*, vanilla
   custard with caramelised crust
flam/*flan*, crème caramel
gelat/*helado*, ice cream
mató/*requesón*, fresh cheese
pastis/*pastel*, cake

rebosteria/*repostería*, cakes and pastries
nata/*nata*, cream
mel/*miel*, honey
xarop/*almíbar*, syrup

Drinks (*begudes*/*bebidas*)

cervesa/*cerveza*, beer
vi blanc/*vino blanco*, white wine
vi negre/*vino tinto*, red wine
vi rosat/*vino rosado*, rosé wine
refresc/*refresco*, soft drink
suc/*zumo*, juice
llet/*leche*, milk
batut/*batido*, milkshake

aigua/*agua mineral*, mineral water
   sense gas/*sin gas*, still
   amb gas/*con gas*, sparkling
cafè/*café*, coffee
   sol/*solo*, black
   amb llet/*con leche*, with milk
   tallat/*cortado*, with a dash of milk
te/*té*, tea
xocolata/*chocolate*, chocolate

Restaurants, bars and cafés

Not only does Catalunya have its own distinctive cuisine, but also eating and drinking habits that are very different from those of the rest of the peninsula. The Catalans tend to eat slightly earlier than people in the rest of Spain, with lunch starting at around 13.30 and dinner at 21.00. The Spanish love of tapas or bar snacks, often as a substitute for a meal, is not characteristic of Catalunya. Nevertheless, given the large numbers of Andalusians and people from other regions of Spain in Barcelona, anyone who wishes to follow the Spanish tradition of going out on a tapas crawl will have no difficulty finding suitable bars.

The city's prosperity since the 19C has ensured that this is one of the great restaurant centres of Spain, with the whole range of international and regional Spanish cuisine represented. The earliest of the grand Barcelona restaurants were establishments of wholly French leanings, and carried such pretentious names as 'Le Grand Restaurant de France', 'Chez Martin' or 'La Maison Dorée'.

Only in comparatively recent times have the more important restaurants discovered the virtues of Catalunya's own cuisine, and overcome their bias towards French food. Even so, a French-style elegance characterises the decoration of even some of the more moderately priced of Barcelona's restaurants, and you will rarely find here the homely wooden beam interiors so typical of Castile. Smart fashionable surroundings tend to be regarded here as having the same importance as the actual food, and in recent years Barcelona's restaurants have been struck by the city's all-consuming obsession with *disseny* (design).

Many restaurants offer a fixed-price menu at lunchtime, which is usually a real bargain, particularly in more upmarket places. While dinner at a smart restaurant might set you back at least €40, the set lunch will probably cost less than €15. So even if you are on a tight budget, you can still eat at elegant places in Barcelona.

It is rarely necessary to book more than one day ahead, except at top of the range restaurants. Many restaurants close on Sunday and some on Monday too. A considerable number of places close for at least half of August. Nearly everywhere takes the major credit cards, but it is usual to pay cash in budget places. Cheques are rarely used. It is usual to tip about 10 per cent.

A set-price lunch at a no-frills restaurant should cost under €12. Dinner at a mid-range place costs around €20. A meal at one of the top traditional restaurants will probably come to €35–40 with wine, and you should expect to pay at least €60 for the best of new Catalan cuisine. To give an idea of prices, the restaurants listed here are categorised as follows, based on a three-course meal with wine and coffee:

(€) up to €25
(€€) up to €50
(€€€) more than €50

Gourmet

El Raco d'en Freixa (€€€), C/Sant Elíes 22 (☎ 93 2097559, freixa@chi.es). Walks 7 & 10. Ramón Freixa is one of the most talented chefs in Spain and his restaurant is consistently rated among the best in the country. Innovative Catalan cuisine with excellent service in unstuffy atmosphere.

Gaig (€€€), Passeig Maragall 402 (☎ 93 4291017). Walk 11. Carles Gaig puts a modern spin on classic Catalan dishes, such as wild pheasant lasagna with prunes, spinach and macadamia nuts. Taster menu. Best *humidor* in town and excellent wine cellar.

Jean Luc Figueras (€€€), C/Santa Teresa 10 (☎ 93 4152877). Walk 7. Innovative cuisine in intimate restaurant with only ten tables. Specialities include fillet steak with black truffles and foie gras. Taster menu. Excellent desserts.

La Dama (€€€), Avinguda Diagonal 423 (☎ 93 2020686). Walk 7. Chef Josep Bullich creates lavish dishes in the setting of a sumptuous Modernista building.

Neichel (€€€), C/Beltrán i Rózpide 16 bis (☎ 93 203 8408, neichel@virtualsd.es). Walk 9. Exquisite seasonal Catalan cuisine with a lot of French touches. Taster menu.

Ot (€€€), C/Torres 25 (☎ 93 2847752). Walks 7 & 10. This elegant yet informal restaurant in the Gràcia area serves only a set menu, comprising eight dishes. It is run by a young enthusiastic team with lots of good ideas and only just nudges into the upper price category.

Roig Robi (€€), C/Séneca 20 (☎ 93 2189222, roigrobi@abonados.cplus.es).
Walk 7. Market cuisine at reasonable prices by Mercé Navarro and her
daughter Inma Crossas. Taster menu. Typical dishes include fishcakes made
with hake, prawns and cuttlefish. Courtyard tables.

Traditional Catalan

Ca l'Isidre (€€€), C/les Flors 12 (☎ 93 4411139, www.isidre.mhp.es). Walk 4.
One of the city's most established restaurants and a favourite of King Juan
Carlos. The Gironés family specialises in updating traditional recipes, making
good use of seasonal ingredients. Excellent wine list.

Can Culleretes (€), C/Quintana 5 (☎ 93 3173022). Walks 1 & 2. Founded in
1786, this very popular restaurant serves traditional Catalan dishes at reasonable prices in a series of old-fashioned dining rooms.

Can Lluís (€), C/Cera 49 (☎ 93 4411187). Walk 4. Run by the same family for
three generations, this award-winning restaurant has always been popular
with artists and writers. Traditional décor. The set-price lunch is a real bargain.

Casa Leopoldo (€€), C/San Rafael 24 (☎ 93 4413014). Walk 4. Founded in
1929, this very popular restaurant in the Raval area is renowned for its classic
cuisine, served in large portions.

Gargantúa y Pantagruel (€€), C/Aragó 214 (☎ 93 253 2020). Walk 7. Family-
run, specialising in the cuisine of Lleida province. Interesting selection of
Catalan wines.

Senyor Parellada (€€), C/Argenteria 37 (☎ 93 3105094). Walks 2 & 3.
Housed in an 18C building with open-brick walls in a buzzy downtown loca-
tion, Senyor Parellada is fashionable but not faddy or fussy, serving authentic
Catalan cuisine with a creative twist.

Set Portes (€€), Passeig de Isabel II 14 (☎ 93 3193033, www.7portes.com).
Walks 5 & 6. Founded in 1836, this huge, traditional restaurant specialises in
rice dishes. Chef Josep Lladonosa has written several books on Catalan cuisine.
Although undeniably touristy, it is very popular with locals too.

Modern Catalan

Abac (€€), C/Rec 78–89 (☎ 93 3196600). Walks 3 & 5. Renowned chef
Ramón Pellicer's latest restaurant is one of the best choices in the trendy Born
area. Try the sea bass with aubergine caviar. Separate room to enjoy a cigar
with coffee.

Acontraluz (€€), C/Milanesat 19 (☎ 93 2030658). Walk 10. Stylish inside, but
even better in warm weather when you can eat in the garden surrounded by
jasmine. Seasonal cuisine with excellent vegetable, pasta and rice dishes.

Ateneu Gastronòmic (€), Plaça Sant Miquel 2 bis (☎ 93 302 1198,
www.ateneu.com). Walk 2. The imaginative menu offers some unusual
combinations—but at very reasonable prices. Good place to surprise your taste
buds with dishes inspired by the countries bordering the Mediterranean. Great
wine list too.

Can Travi Nou (€€), C/Jorge Manrique (☎ 93 4280301). Walk 11. Situated in
a mansion in the uptown Horta district, this is a delightful choice for lunch or
dinner, particularly in summer when you can eat outside.

Casa Calvet (€€), C/Casp 48 (☎ 93 4134012). Walk 7. The combination of the setting—a Gaudí building decorated with tiling and stained glass—and chef Miguel Alija's Mediterranean cuisine make this a very popular choice.

Collegi d'Arquitectes (€), Plaça Nova 5 (☎ 93 3015000). Walk 2. Housed in the basement of the architecture school, this is a surprising and original restaurant with daily-changing menu of creative cuisine. Only open Mon–Fri, 08.00–17.00. Also good for breakfast.

La Balsa (€€), C/Infanta Isabel 4 (☎ 93 2115048). Walk 12. Magnificent location on hill overlooking the city. La Balsa has won architectural awards and is renowned as much for its glamorous clientele as its Mediterranean cuisine. Ask for a table on the terrace.

La Llotja (€), Museu Marítim, Avinguda Drassanes (☎ 93 302 6402). Walks 1 & 5. Surprisingly smart restaurant in the vast former trading hall of the royal shipyards, now the Maritime Museum. Good value set lunch, but the à la carte cuisine in the evening is more imaginative.

La Taverna del Teatre (€), C/Casp 21 (☎ 93 3187575). Walk 7. Great value, large, busy brasserie. Good choice for lunch if you are shopping near Plaza de Catalunya.

La Venta (€), Plaça Doctor Andreu (☎ 93 2126455). Walk 12. On Tibidabo hill at the terminus of the Blue Tram, La Venta is a pretty restaurant with a large glassed-in terrace decorated with tiles. Interesting seasonal menu and laidback atmosphere.

L'Hostal de Rita (€), C/Aragó 279 (☎ 93 4872376 but no booking). Walk 7. The elegant colonial bistro décor makes this feel like a smart restaurant, which for once is not matched by the prices. Excellent value fixed-price and à la carte menus make this and the other restaurants in the group (*Les Quinze Nits*, *La Fonda*) very popular choices. Worth queueing for.

L'Olive (€), C/Balmes 47 (☎ 93 4521990). Walk 7. Always busy owing to great Catalan cooking at good prices.

Salero (€), C/Rec 60 (☎ 93 3198022). Walk 3. Fashionable and funky, Salero serves imaginative food at reasonable prices to an arty crowd. Open late.

Silenus (€), C/Angels 8 (☎ 93 3922680). Walk 4. Great place for lunch or dinner after visiting the MACBA museum and galleries of the up-and-coming Raval area. Varied menu with lots of salads. Also good for a coffee and a snack.

Tragaluz (€€), Pasaje de la Concepció 5 (☎ 93 4870196). Fashionable, romantic and stylish with lots of vegetarian and light dishes. Light floods in through glass ceiling.

Seafood

Agua (€), Passeig Marítim 30, Marina Village (☎ 93 2251272). Walk 5. Good seafood and rice dishes in a fresh, informal atmosphere with tables right on the beach. Open late at weekends.

Can Majó (€€), C/Almirall Aixada 23 (☎ 93 2215455). Walk 5. Famed for its rice dishes and quality of its fish, Can Majó has been going for more than 30 years. Outdoor tables by the beach.

El Suquet de L'Almirall (€€), Passeig de Joan de Borbó 65 (☎ 93 2216223). Walk 5. Overlooking the Port Vell marina with outdoor tables, this is one of the best of the seafood restaurants on this strip. Family-run with friendly service, it serves traditional and more creative fish dishes and has a terrific wine list.

Els Pescadors (€€), Plaça Prim 1 (☎ 93 2252018). Walk 5. This used to be a neighbourhood place but is quite smart now with top quality seafood. Specialities include baked fish. In summer, request a table on the terrace in the square.

Passadis d'en Pep (€€€), Plaça Palau 2 (☎ 93 3101021). Chic yet relaxed restaurant run by the legendary Pep Manubens. No menu as such, as dishes of exquisite seafood and other delicacies are brought to your table, usually accompanied by *cava*, then you choose a main course from the daily suggestions. Hidden away down a corridor next to La Caixa bank, this is a unique experience and worth seeking out.

Regional Spanish

Asturian

El Furacu (€), C/Girona 52 (☎ 93 2651783). Walk 7. Unpretentious, small, busy restaurant serving traditional Asturian dishes such as *fabada* bean stew and hake in cider sauce. Good desserts and wonderful selection of Asturian cheeses. Also good for tapas at the bar.

Basque

Beltxenea (€€€), C/Mallorca 275 (☎ 93 2153024). Walk 7. In the elegant setting of a Modernista building, chef Mikel Ezcurra creates exquisite Basque cuisine with Catalan influences. Very smart with a lovely garden for eating outside in summer and first-class wine cellar.

Gorria (€€), C/Diputación 421 (☎ 93 451164). Walk 7. Top-quality seasonal ingredients are used to prepare superb Basque cuisine.

Jaizquibel (€€), C/Sicilia 180 (☎ 93 245 8569). Walks 6 & 7. Great selection of shellfish, fish and meat. Start with the mixed appetisers, which consists of seven dishes. Also good for a tapas lunch or dinner at the bar, with lots of wines to try by the glass.

Castilian

El Asador de Aranda (€€), Avinguda Tibidabo 31 (☎ 93 4170133). Walk 12. Housed in a Modernista building, this attractive restaurant serves authentic Castilian cuisine, specialising in roast meats.

El Yantar de la Ribera (€€), C/Roger de Flor 114 (☎ 93 2656309). Walk 7. Excellent lamb and suckling pig, roasted in separate woodburning ovens. Lots of specialities from the rich cuisine of the province of Burgos, accompanied by Ribera del Duero wines. Great range of cigars.

Galician

Botafumeiro (€€€), C/Gran de Gràcia 81 (☎ 93 2184230, www.botafumeiro.es). Walk 10. Top-quality seafood and meat dishes. Excellent but also pricey and touristy. You can also eat at the bar, where prices are more reasonable.

Casa Darío (€€), C/Consell de Cent 256 (☎ 93 4533135). Walk 7. Galician specialities include tuna pie, baked turbot and top-quality seafood. Prices are reasonable for the quality.

Mesón Morriña (€€), C/Parlament 46 (☎ 93 4419336). Walk 4. Very popular family-run place that uses top-quality ingredients and also has terrific wines.

International

Conducta Ejemplar (€), C/Consell de Cent 403 (☎ 93 2655112). Walk 7.
Brazilian restaurant specialising in chargrilled steaks. Great range of salads.

Il Bellini (€€), C/Muntaner 101 (☎ 93 4543125). Walk 7. Upmarket, authentic
Italian cuisine prepared by chef Danielle Corradini. Good range of Italian wines.

Kaitensushi (€), C/Villaorroel 220 (☎ 93 4190527). Walk 7. Japanese restaurant with fixed-price buffet. Customers can choose what they want from the
dishes on the conveyor belt.

La Muscleria (€), C/Mallorca 290 (☎ 93 4589844). Walk 7. Boisterous
Belgian restaurant specialising in mussels and French fries.

La Rosa del Desierto (€), Plaça Narcís Oller 7 (☎ 93 2374590). Walk 7. Well-
established Moroccan restaurant, specialising in couscous.

La Verónica (€), C/Avinyó 21 (☎ 93 4121122). Walk 2. Situated between the
boutiques and bars in the newly-trendy Carrer Avinyó, this is a fun place
serving great pizzas and desserts.

Lahore (€), C/Torrent de l'Olla 159 (☎ 93 2189511). Walk 10. Pakistani and
Indian cuisine at reasonable prices.

Le Quattro Stagioni (€€), C/Doctor Roux 37 (☎ 93 2052279). Walk 10. Pretty
uptown restaurant with a garden, serving first-class traditional Italian cuisine
at reasonable prices. Different menu according to the season. In summer,
request an outdoor table.

Margarita Blue (€), C/Josep Anselm Clavé 6 (☎ 93 3177176). Walks 1 & 2.
Funky restaurant and bar with TexMex food. Good value fixed-price lunch.
Open late, and very popular. Live performances.

Mesopotamia (€), C/Verdi 65 (☎ 93 2371563). Walk 10. Excellent traditional
Mesopotamian cuisine, including chicken flavoured with rose water and
croquettes with minced meat, almonds and raisins.

Pekín (€), C/Rosselló 202 (☎ 93 2150177). Walk 7. Chinese restaurant that
has won awards for its avant-garde design. The menu combines Mandarin and
Cantonese specialities, with plenty of choice for vegetarians.

Punjab (€), C/Joaquim Costa 1 (☎ 93 4433899). Walk 4. Very popular—and
very cheap—no-frills restaurant with a menu of Pakistani specialities.

Riera (€), C/Joaquim Costa 30 (☎ 93 4433293). Walk 4. Bangladeshi dishes at
bargain prices. Lots of vegetarian options.

Río Azul (€), C/Balmes 92 (☎ 93 2159333). Walk 7. First-class Cantonese
cuisine in an elegant setting. Good selection of vegetarian dishes.

Sushi & News (€), C/Santa Mònica 2 (☎ 93 3185857). Walks 1 & 4. Just off
the Ramblas, this is a lively, fashionable Japanese restaurant where you can eat
sushi and sashimi at the bar or have a sit-down meal.

Thai Gardens (€€), C/Diputación 273 (☎ 93 4879898). Walk 7. Sumptuous
restaurant with broad range of exquisite Thai dishes. The taster menu comprises 12 dishes and is good value. Ask for one of the traditional Thai tables.

Vegetarian

Juicy Jones (€), C/Cardenal Casañas 7 (☎ 93 3024330). Walks 1 & 2. Funky
juice bar with tables in the back. Good selection of mostly vegan dishes on a
daily-changing menu

La Batequilla (€), C/Girona 88 (☎ 93 2658660). Walk 7. Pretty place with a
very reasonable set-price lunch.

La Flauta Mágica (€), C/Banys Vells 18 (☎ 93 2684694). Walk 2. Upmarket restaurant serving creative cuisine. Organic meat dishes also served. Booking advisable.
L'Hortet (€), C/Pintor Fortuny 32 (☎ 93 3176189). Walk 4. Good-value daily set menu, in the Raval area. Cosy atmosphere but no alcohol.
L'Illa de Gràcia (€), C/Sant Doménec 19 (☎ 93 2380229). Walk 10. Not as holier-than-thou as some vegetarian places with no restrictions on smoking and drinking. Good value, particularly at lunchtime.
Oolong (€), C/Gignàs 25 (☎ 93 3151259). Walk 2. Mostly vegetarian menu with imaginative dishes drawing from many cuisines. Open till 02.00. Good live and recorded music.

Tapas bars

Tapas may not be a great tradition in Barcelona, but there are plenty of bars nevertheless. Basque bars are proliferating in Barcelona (and all around Spain). These places follow the model of the bars in San Sebastián, which specialise in *pintxos*—thick slices of bread with an enormous variety of toppings. These are displayed on platters on the counter. Customers just help themselves, keeping the cocktail sticks spearing the *pintxos* as a tally.
   Most of the bars listed here are in the Barri Gòtic, with the greatest concentration in and around C/Mercé.
Bar Celta, C/Mercè 16 (☎ 93 3150006). Try the Galician specialities such as octopus and Padrón peppers, washed down with Ribeiro wine served in the traditional white china bowls.
Bodega Sepúlveda, C/Sepúlveda 173 (☎ 93 4547094). In business for more than fifty years, this is one of the most renowned tapas bars in town, with specialities from all over Spain. Great range of cheeses and charcuterie. A good place to try *habas a la catalana*—broad beans braised with herbs, sausage and garlic.
Cal Pep, Plaça de les Olles 8 (☎ 93 3107961, www.calpep.net). Terrific daily specials (mostly seafood) are cooked by Pep Manubens and his team. At lunchtime, get there at 13.00 just as it opens for any chance of getting a seat at the bar.
Can Ramonet, C/Maquinista 17 (☎ 93 319 3064). Claimed to be the oldest bar in Barcelona, dating back to 1763. Now rather swish, barrels serve as tables for the good-quality (though not cheap) tapas and wines. There is a restaurant too, but it has become over-touristy with prices to match.
El Portalón, C/Banys Nous 20 (☎ 93 3021187). Wonderful old bodega that has been in business since the 1860s. Wines from the barrel, marble tables, peeling paint, gloomy lighting and all manner of paraphernalia make this one of the most atmospheric bars in town.
El Tropezón, C/Regomir 26 (☎ 93 3101864). Always packed bar, owing to superior tapas. Specialities include *patatas bravas* and *bombas picantes* (spicy round croquettes).
El Vaso de Oro, C/Balboa 2 (☎ 93 3193098). People have been flocking to this tiny bar for more than 40 years for the excellent draught beer. Tapas include spicy tuna and Russian salad.
El Xampanyet, C/Montcada 22 (☎ 93 3297003). Touristy but still attractive *bodega* with tiled walls and marble tables. The speciality is *cava* sparkling wine—ask for a *brut* otherwise you might get the sickly *semiseco*. Try the anchovies with house dressing and the *mojama* (cured tuna) from Huelva.

Euskal Etxea, Placeta de Montcada 1 (☎ 93 310 2185). Very popular Basque bar near Picasso museum. Good service, buzzy atmosphere and great selection of freshly-made *pintxos*.

La Cova Fumada, C/Baluard 56 (☎ 93 2214061). Opposite the market in Barceloneta, this family-run bar has marble tables and ancient wooden fridges. Try the Catalan sausages, sardines and squid. Open workmen's hours: 09.00–15.00, 17.30–20.30.

La Jarra, C/Mercè 9 (☎ 93 3151759). The speciality here is cured ham from the Canaries, served with chunks of potato.

La Palma, C/Palma de Sant Just 7 (☎ 93 3150656). Traditional old *bodega* where wines are served straight from the barrel. Basic tapas include cheese and charcuterie.

La Plata, C/Mercè 28 (☎ 93 3151009). Popular local haunt decorated with tiles that has been run by the same family for more than 50 years. Order anchovies or sardines with a tomato, olive and onion salad.

La Vinya del Senyor, Plaça Santa Maria 5 (☎ 93 3103379). This tiny bar with lots of outdoor tables by Santa Maria church has perhaps the best selection of wines in Barcelona. At least 20 are available by the glass, accompanied by Modern Catalan specialities.

La Socarrena, C/Mercè 21 (☎ 93 2680505). The tapas in this rustic bar mainly feature specialities from Asturias and other parts of northern Spain. Try the Cabrales blue cheese from the Picos de Europa, cider-flavoured *chorizo* sausage and *cecina* cured beef from León.

Quimet y Quimet, C/Poeta Cabanyes 25 (☎ 93 4423142). Traditional tapas bar that has been run by the Quimet family for nearly a century. Great variety of good quality dishes. One of the best and most authentic tapas bars in Barcelona. The many specialities include *bicicletas*—diced potatoes stuffed with minced beef.

Taberna Basca Irati, C/Cardenal Cassanyes 17 (☎ 93 3923084). Always busy Basque bar, which means the *pintxos* are always fresh too, which is not the case everywhere. There are lots of tables at the end of the long counter, if you need to sit down.

Santa Maria, C/Comerç 17 (☎ 93 3151227). Chic but informal bar with plenty of tables and an imaginative menu of gourmet tapas.

Txacolín, C/Marquès de Argentera 19 (☎ 93 2681781). Busy Basque bar with overwhelming range of *pintxos* on the bar. Try the slightly fizzy Txacolí white wine.

Va de Vi, C/Banys Vells 16 (☎ 93 3192900). Open 12.00–01.00. Hidden away in a listed building down an alley near the Picasso Museum, this is a haven for wine lovers with an enormous range from Spain and the rest of the world. Gourmet tapas. Parts of the arched space have original Visigothic and Romanesque features.

Cafés

Barcelona is packed with cafés where you can have a coffee or a beer at any time of day. Many of the places listed below cross over into the bar and restaurant categories, as they usually also serve food—whether tapas, sandwiches, full meals or cakes. Some stay open late, until at least midnight, so are also useful for a drink after dinner.

An institution peculiar to Catalunya are the milk-bars known as *granjas*,

where you can eat pastries, cakes and *bunyuelos* (a type of doughnut), traditionally accompanied by thick hot chocolate or coffee. There are several on C/Petrixol
in the Barri Gòtic.

Bauma, C/Roger de Llúria 124 (☎ 93 459 0566). Just off Diagonal, this much-
loved café has been a favourite of literary and theatrical people for more than
half a century. Tables on the covered terrace are the most coveted.

Bracafé, C/Casp 4 (☎ 93 3023082). Near Plaça de Catalunya, Bracafé serves
wonderful coffee and is good for breakfast or a break from shopping.

Café de L'Hivernacle, Parc de la Ciutadella, Passeig Picasso (☎ 93 3102291).
Part of this former hothouse in Ciutadella park is now a delightful café.
Classical and jazz concerts are held regularly in summer.

El Café del Sol, Plaça del Sol 16 (☎ 93 4155663). One of the most popular
meeting places in the Gràcia neighbourhood, with tables in the square. Open
until 02.30.

Els Quatre Gats, C/Montió 3 bis (☎ 93 3024140). Founded in 1897 in a
Modernista building. See p 128 for full history. Set lunch menu.

La Confitería, C/Sant Pau 128 (☎ 93 443 0458). Open 10.00–02.00, this café
with original Modernista décor attracts a theatrical crowd.

Laie Librería Café, C/Pau Claris 85 (☎ 93 3027310). This large café above one
of Barcelona's best bookshops is a terrific place to collapse after touring the
Eixample district. Covered terrace at the back. Cakes, sandwiches and meals
available. Open until 02.00.

Mama Café, C/Doctor Dou 10 (☎ 93 3012940). Open 13.00–01.00, this is a
laid-back place for a coffee, lunch or dinner, with lots of organic food and
plenty of options for vegetarians. Cool rather than hippyish, and near the
MACBA museum.

Mesón del Café, C/Llibreteria 16 (☎ 93 3150754). This tiny, family-run café in
the Barri Gòtic serves wonderful coffee and has been going for nearly a century.

Mudanzas, C/Vidriera 15 (☎ 93 3191137). Open from 10.00 until at least
02.30, this is a popular hangout for the arty residents of the Born area. Music
is gentle and very much in the background until late in the evening, when the
volume is turned up and the mood changes.

Muebles Navarro, C/Riera Alta 4–6 (☎ 907 189096). Open 17.00 until at
least 01.00, this funky American-run café in the Raval area was formerly a
furniture shop. Live music, exhibitions, a great mix of people and delicious
cheesecake.

Taxidermista, Plaça Reial 8 (☎ 93 412 4536). Fashionable bistro designed by
Beth Galí under the arches of the Plaça Reial. Open 10.00–02.30, this is also a
good choice for lunch or an informal dinner.

Tèxtil Café, C/Montcada 12 (☎ 93 2682598). At the entrance to the Textile
Museum, this is a good spot for breakfast, lunch or dinner as well as coffee and
drinks. Tables in the medieval courtyard are much in demand on summer
nights.

Xocoa, C/Petrixol 11 (☎ 93 3011197). Modern *granja* serving excellent hot
chocolate, cakes and sandwiches.

Zurich, C/Pelai 39 (☎ 93 3179153). Touristy but very entertaining café
(see p 175) with lots of pavement tables and a stream of streetlife to observe.
Useful meeting place.

Late-night bars and clubs

The bars and nightlife of Barcelona have become as integral to the romantic tourist image of the city as have the buildings of Gaudí. Jean Genet was one of the many writers enamoured of the nightlife of the notorious Barri Xinès (see p 146), as was Juan Goytisolo, who as a young man from a cultured middle-class background was struck down by *l'amour de boue* (literally, the love of mud). The main place of pilgrimage today for those seeking out the squalid, old-fashioned bar is the *Bar Marsella*, where it is possible to drink absinthe.

Those interested in the Barcelona of today will have to visit instead the so-called 'designer bars', a type of bar that originated in Barcelona and is more prevalent here than in any other Spanish city. These are for the most part bars *de copas*, places that cater for the Spanish love of following an evening meal with a *copa* or strong drink. Popular choices are whisky, gin, vodka or rum with coke, tonic or lemon. Always specify a brand when ordering spirits, or you might be given a low-quality drink. Beer or soft fizzy drinks are also popular, but coffee and wine are not usually available. Despite the generally loud music and discotheque element of many of these places, these bars attract a wide clientèle, and are by no means restricted to the young, smart and beautiful.

There are dozens of bars in the Barri Gòtic, particularly in and around the Plaça Reial. The Born and Raval areas are also rich in nightlife. In summer, head for the Port Olímpic marina, which is packed with bars, restaurants and clubs. Things start warming up sometime after midnight, and the action continues until dawn.

The phenomenon of the **designer bar** originated in Barcelona in the late 1970s. One of the first signature bars was *Zig-Zag*, which was designed by Alicia Núñez and and Guillermo Bonet in 1980. This same team was responsible five years later for the creation of the legendary *Otto Zutz*. This, and contemporary bars such as *Si Si Si* and *Universal*, were characterised by the sparsity of their design, the latter having the character of some futuristic prison. A new phase in bar design was initiated in 1986 by Eduardo Samso's *Nick Havanna*, which went in for extravagant, varied and humorous effects. This trend was pursued to an even greater degree in the near contemporary *Velvet* and *Network*, which were inspired respectively by the films *Blue Velvet* and *Blade Runner*. Both bars were the work of Alfredo Arribas who, together with the designer Mariscal, went on to create *Torres de Avila*.

The absurdity of the whole phenomenon of the designer-bar was admirably expressed in Eduardo Mendoza's witty and satirical novel, *No News of Gurb* (1990), which is set in a Barcelona of the near future, and deals with an extra-terrestial's search for the elusive and similarly extra-terrestial Gurb. The search takes the protagonist through all of the city's fashionable bars, and details are given of whether or not a place has received, or was a finalist for, the prestigious award for design presented by the *Foment de les Arts Decoratives* (FAD). Eventually, after a succession of designer bars which has included a bar in Poble Nou which has won the 'FAD award for the renovation of urban spaces', the protagonist throws up in the Plaça Urquinaona, and then in the Plaça de Catalunya, and again on the pedestrian crossing at the corner of Muntaner and Aragó, and finally in the taxi which takes him home after his nocturnal ordeal through a designer hell.

Abaixadors Deu, C/Abaixadors 10 (☎ 93 2681019). Open 18.00 until at least 03.00. A multifunctional space that offers cinema, theatre and performances as well as eating, drinking and dancing.

Al Limón Negro, C/Escudellers Blancs 8 (☎ 93 3189770). Open 18.00–03.00. Very popular place amid a clutch of bars in nightlife hub off the Rambla. All sorts of people come here for drinks and light suppers, as well as for the live music, performances and exhibitions.

Antilla BCN, C/Aragó 141–143 (☎ 93 4512151). Open 23.00 until at least 03.00. See live salsa bands at Barcelona's most popular Latin club—and be prepared to join in the frenetic dancing.

Atlàntic, C/Lluís Muntadas 2 (☎ 93 4187161). Open 22.00 until at least 03.00. High up on Tibidabo hill, this chic bar in a Modernista house attracts a glamorous crowd. Fabulous views from the terrace.

Bar Ra, Plaça de la Gardunya (☎ 93 3014163). Open 09.00–02.00. Lively spot in the square behind La Boqueria market, with outdoor tables. Although primarily a bar, breakfast, lunch and dinner are available.

Benidorm, C/Joaquim Costa 39 (☎ 93 3178052). Open 18.00–02.00. Kitsch décor and visiting DJs make this small club a popular choice for drinking and dancing.

Boadas, C/Tallers 1 (☎ 93 318 9592). Open 12.00–02.00. Art Deco cocktail bar on the corner of the Rambla. Founded in 1933 by Miguel Boadas, who grew up in Cuba with his Catalan parents and now run by his daughter, it is a popular haunt of people returning from the Teatre Liceu, and is renowned in particular for its daquiris and dry martinis. Picasso, Hemingway and Miró were all regulars in their time.

Dry Martini, C/Aribau 166 (☎ 93 2175072. Open 18.30–02.30. Classic cocktail bar that has been a staple of the Barcelona scene since the beginning of the 1980s.

Gimlet, C/Santaló 46 (☎ 93 201 5306) & C/Rec 24 (☎ 93 3101027). Open from 18.30 and 20.00 respectively until 02.30, 03.00 at weekends. Well-established, stylish and understated cocktail bars. The Santaló one is a welcome refuge after shopping around Diagonal.

Harlem Jazz Club, C/Comtessa de Sobradiel 8 (☎ 93 3100755). Open 20.00 until at least 04.00. Tucked away down an alley in the Barri Gòtic, the Harlem holds a range of jazz gigs, featuring bands from all over the world.

La Paloma, C/Tigre 27 (☎ 93 3016897). Open 18.00–21.30 & 23.30 until at least 03.30 Thu–Sat, 18.00–21.30 Sun. Opened in 1902, this is an old-fashioned dance hall par excellence, where you can try out your pasodoble or tango. After midnight, it changes character completely, when the beat switches to a throbbing techno.

London, C/Nou de la Rambla 34 (☎ 93 3185261). Open 19.00 until at least 04.30. Modernista bar that has drawn bohemians since 1910. Live music and cabaret (see p 94).

Luz de Gas, C/Muntaner 246 (☎ 93 2097711). Open 23.00 until at least 04.00. This former music-hall, still bedecked with red velvet and gilt, hosts jazz, pop and salsa concerts, with dancing afterwards.

Luz de Luna, C/Comerç 21 (☎ 93 3107542). Open 22.00 until at least 04.00. Lively salsa club with spectacular dancing.

Marsella, C/Sant Pau 65 (☎ 93 4427263). Open 22.00 until at least 02.30.

This characterful vestige of the old Barri Xinès, open since 1820, still has a loyal clientèle and is a big hit with foreigners who come here to drink absinthe (see p 147).

Mirablau, Plaça del Dr Andreu, Tibidabo (☎ 93 4185879). Open 11.00–04.30. Floor-to-ceiling windows provide a stunning view across Barcelona to the Mediterranean at this chic bar. Have dinner at *La Venta* opposite and come here for drinks before or afterwards. The neighbouring *Merbeyé* and *Mirabé* bars are also recommended.

Moog, C/Arc del Teatre 3 (☎ 93 3185966). Open 23.00 until at least 05.00. Former cabaret theatre is now a very popular club with prestigious guest DJs. Two dance-floors and chill-out room.

Nick Havanna, C/Rosselló 208 (☎ 93 2156591). Open 23.00 until at least 04.00. One of the leading designer bars of the 1980s, and still going strong. See p 200.

Otto Zutz, C/Lincoln 15 (☎ 93 2380722). Open 23.00–06.00. No longer the hippest club in town, but still worth a visit. Worth going for a late dinner (not available every night, so call to check), then staying for a drink or two.

Salsitas, C/Nou de la Rambla 22 (☎ 93 3180840). Open 20.00 until at least 02.30. Very busy place that works as a restaurant until around midnight then turns into a club.

Torres de Avila, Poble Espanyol (☎ 93 4249309). Open 23.00–06.00 Fri & Sat. Spectacular space designed by Mariscal and Alfredo Arribas. See p 200.

Universal, C/Marià Cubi 182–184 (☎ 93 2013596). Open 23.00 until at least 03.30. One of the original designer bars, the *Universal* still draws the crowds to its downstairs dancefloor and upstairs café.

Zig-Zag, C/Plató 13 (☎ 93 2016207). Open 22.00 until at least 03.30. One of the original designer bars, it still attracts a fashionable crowd and gets very crowded at weekends. No dancefloor.

 # Shopping

Shopping hours are usually 09.00–14.00, and 17.00–20.00 Monday–Saturday, although smaller shops may close on Saturday afternoons. Some shops in the centre stay open all day. Some small convenience shops stay open until at least 22.00 every day. Most shops have sales lasting from the second week of January to the end of February, and from late June to the end of July.

Barcelona has a wealth of interesting shops, from the most stylish boutiques to musty old bookshops. There are several shopping areas, spread over a vast area, so some planning is advisable. From *El Corte Inglés* department store on Plaça de Catalunya, you could head down the pedestrianised Avinguda del Portal de l'Angel and explore the side streets, which combine traditional and modern shops. Carrer de la Portaferrissa is packed with shops for younger customers. The Barri Gòtic has some surprisingly funky boutiques, particularly along Carrer d'Avinyó, and the area around the *MACBA* contemporary art museum is a growing hotbed of young designers. For international big names, go to Passeig de Gràcia, Diagonal, Rambla de Catalunya and cross-streets.

The tiny streets of the Born area are packed with workshops and studios, which are often open to the public and a good hunting ground for unusual gifts. Many museums have good shops too, particularly the *Museu Tèxtil*, *MACBA*, *La Pedrera*, *Museu Picasso* and *Fundació Miró*.

As well as the main store on Plaça de Catalunya, *El Corte Inglés* has two smaller branches on Avinguda Diagonal, at the crossroads with Plaça Maria Cristina and Plaça Francesc Macià. There is also a branch specialising in books, music and electronic equipment on Av. Portal de l'Angel.

Shopping centres include *L'Illa* (Avenida Diagonal 557), *Pedralbes Center* (Diagonal 609), *Centre Glòries* (Glorieta de les Glòries Catalanes), *El Triangle* (Plaça Catalunya), *Bulevard Rosa* (Passeig de Gracia.53) and *Diagonal Mar* (end of Diagonal on waterfront).

Antiques

The Barri Gòtic is great for browsing round antique shops, particularly Carrer de la Palla, Carrer Banys Nous and nearby streets.

L'Arca de l'Avia (C/dels Banys Nous 20) specialises in antique lace, silk and linen.

Bulevar dels Antiquaris (Passeig de Gràcia 55) is a modern mall containing around 70 antique shops with different specialities.

Mercantic (C/Rius i Taulet 120, Sant Cugat) is a gallery of around 50 antique dealers north of the centre on Collserola hill (take the FGC train). Best on Sunday, when the shops spill out onto the pavement and stay open until 15.00.

Otranto (Passeig de Sant Joan 142) specialises in architectural salvage.

See also Markets.

Books

Altaïr (Gran Via 616) is an excellent specialist travel bookshop.

BCN Books (corner of C/Roger de Lluria and C/Provença) stocks dictionaries, cards and English books.

Come In (C/Provença 203) and *English Bookshop* (C/Entença 63) only sell English books and educational material.

Crisol (C/Consell de Cent 341 & Rambla de Catalunya 81) stocks a good range of English books, as well as magazines and music.

Happy Books (C/Provença 286) also has a café and specialises in discount coffee-table books.

Laie (C/Pau Claris 85) has an English section and a great café upstairs.

Pròleg (C/Dagueria 13) is a feminist bookshop and information centre with a programme of cultural activities.

Museum shops are good for books on Barcelona, particularly *Museu d'Història de la Ciutat*, *Fundació Miró*, *Museu d'Història de Catalunya* and *Centre de Cultura Contemporània de Barcelona* (*CCCB*). The *Palau de la Virreina* cultural centre (La Rambla 99) has an excellent selection of art, design and photography books, as does the bookshop at the *Maeght gallery* (C/Montcada 25).

Ceramics, crafts and traditional goods

Art Escudellers (C/Escudellers 23–25) displays traditional and contemporary ceramics on the ground floor, while the basement contains an excellent selection of Catalan food and wines.

Casa Oliveres (C/Dagueria 11) is a lace specialist.

Cerería Subirà (Baixada de la Libreteria 7) is a candle specialist, founded in 1761 and is the oldest shop in Barcelona.

Figueras (Ronda de Sant Pere 14) is the place to find mantilla shawls.

Kastoria (Av. Catedral 6-8), *Mils* (Passeig de Gràcia 11) and *Pla de l'Os* (C/Boqueria 8) all stock a good range of Lladró and Majorica porcelain.

La Caixa de Fang (C/Freneria 1) stocks traditional ceramics from all over Spain.

Ramon Santaeularia (Rambla de Catalunya 40) is the place to find all kinds of buttons.

Children's gifts

Casa Palau (C/Pelai 34) specialises in train sets.

Dos Bis (C/Bisbe Irurita 2 bis) has unusual handmade toys.

Drap (C/del Pi 14) specialises in dolls' houses.

El Ingenio (C/Rauric 6) is a wonderful old shop, founded in 1838, where they make papier maché figures and theatrical props.

El Rei de la Màgia (C/Princesa 11) is a treasure trove for magicians.

Els Tres Tombs (Travessera de Gràcia 96) has a great stock of educational toys and books.

Jacadi (Rambla de Catalunya 79) sells exquisite clothes for babies and children.

La Lloca Dido (C/del Pi 8) sells good-quality ragdolls, puppets and wooden toys.

Les Golfes (C/Diputació 256), on the other side of the same street, specialises in dolls.

Menkes (Gran Via 646) stocks flamenco dresses.

Puzzlemanía (C/Diputació 225) stocks jigsaws.

Ventilador (C/Diputació 212) is a kite specialist.

Xalar (Baixada de la Llibreteria 4) stocks reproductions of old toys.

Cigars

Gimeno (Rambla de les Flors 100 & Passeig de Gràcia 101) was founded in 1920 and stocks a wide range of cigars, as well as pipes and smoking accoutrements in general.

L'Estanc de Laietana (Vía Laietana 4) dates back to 1927 and stores its cigars in its own cellar.

Clothes

Leading Catalan designers include:

Antoni Miró (C/Consell de Cent 349 & *Groc* at Rambla de Catalunya 100), who designs understated yet unusual clothes for men and women.

Josep Font (Passeig de Gràcia 106) who is renowned for his quirky designs.

David Valls (C/València 235) who specialises in avant-garde knitwear.

Armand Basi (Passeig de Gràcia 49), a label that produces stylish day and clubwear.

Antoni Pernas (C/Consell de Cent 314) designs elegant, high-quality clothes.

Adolfo Domínguez (Passeig de Gràcia 32 & 89, Diagonal 490, Av. Pau Casals 5 & branches) is also well-known.

Other designers to look out for include *Purificación García* (Av. Pau Casals 4) and *Lydia Delgado* (C/Minerva 21).

International names are clustered along and around Diagonal, with *Armani* at 490 & 620, *Gucci* at 415, *DKNY* at 618 and *Yves Saint Laurent* at 624. *Jean Pierre Bau* at 469 stocks Sybilla, Marni, Gaultier, Dries van Noten and other leading labels.

Nearby are *Chanel* at Passeig de Gràcia 70, *Christian Dior* at Av. Pau Casals 7 and *Hermès* at Av. Pau Casals 13. *Las Terrenas* (C/Tenor Viñas 3) stocks Amaya Arzuaga, Antik Batik, Plein Sud and Lacroix.

On C/Avinyó in the Barri Gòtic, check out *Tribu* at 12, *Loft* at 22, *So Da* at 24 and *Zsu Zsa* at 50.

Zara is an excellent low-price chain for men, women and children with branches all around town, including Av. Portal de l'Angel 24, Diagonal 280, C/Pelai 58 and C/València 245.

Mango (Passeig de Gràcia 65 & branches) caters for a slightly younger market, with the latest styles at budget prices.

There are several shops specialising in **larger sizes for women**, including *Marina Rinaldi* (Passeig de Gràcia 23), *Elena Miró* (Travessera de Gràcia 2), *La Botiga* (C/Parlament 35), *Podium Plus* (C/Canadas 28) and *Súper Línea* (C/Valencia 254).

Designer discount shops include:
Contribuciones (C/Riera de Sant Miquel 30), which has top labels at half price, though stock is often from the previous season.
Preu Bo (C/Comtal 22, C/Balmes 308 and C/Craywinckel 5) offers good discounts on mainly Spanish designers.
Stock House (C/Balmes 67) carries previous-season labels.

The Raval area is the best hunting-ground for **second hand shops**. Look out for *I.Shop* and *Argot* (C/Hospital 82 & 107), *Holala* (C/Carmen 72) and *Recicla, Recicla* (Riera Baixa 13).

Designer products

BD Ediciones (C/Mallorca 291) has won numerous awards and is unmissable for anyone interested in Barcelona's design heritage (see p 179).
Imagine (C/Enric Granados 67) specialises in furniture and household objects by top Catalan designers.
Insòlit (Diagonal 353) and *D Barcelona* (Diagonal 367) are both good hunting grounds for unusual gifts.
Les Muses del Palau (C/Sant Pere Mes Alt 1) has lots of Gaudí and Dalí merchandise.
Ras (C/Doctor Deu 10) stages exhibitions and stocks work by avant-garde designers and architects.
Vinçon (Passeig de Gràcia 96) is Barcelona's principal temple to modern design, with a vast range of household goods, furniture and accessories, all presented in witty, original guises (see p 182).
Zeta (C/Avinyó 22) has a good range of funky lamps.

Food and wine

Cacao Sampaka (C/Consell de Cent 292) sells top-quality chocolate with some highly unusual fillings, including olives, curry and blue cheese, all in beautiful minimalist packaging.

Caelum (C/de la Palla 8) in the Barri Gòtic sells cheeses, biscuits, teas, wine and other things made at convents and monasteries around Spain.

Can Gispert (C/Sombrerers 23) has been roasting almonds and other locally-grown nuts since the mid-19C, and uses the same oven today. Also good for olive oil and other gourmet products.

Colmado Quílez (Rambla de Catalunya 63) is renowned for its superb range of groceries.

El Magnífico (C/Argenteria 64), run by the Sans family, is the best place to buy coffee.

La Boqueria (La Rambla 91) is Barcelona's best-known and most spectacular food market (see p 90), and the best place to get an idea of the high quality and magnificent range of local produce.

Queviures Murria (C/Roger de Llúria 85) is housed in a Modernista building and carries a wide selection of Catalan and Spanish foods and wines.

Planells-Donat (C/Cucurulla & Av. Portal de l'Angel 7, 25 & 27) is the most traditional place to buy *turrón* nougat.

El Celler de Gèlida (C/Vallespir 65, near Sants station) has helpful staff who provide expert advice on their comprehensive stock of Catalan and other wines.

Mas Saloni (C/Enric Granados 68) specialises in Catalan wines and *cavas*.

Vila Viniteca (C/Agullers 7-9) in the Born neighbourhood is a friendly, family-run wine shop with an excellent range to choose from.

Xampany (C/València 200) sells only *cava*.

Jewellery and watches

Bagués (Passeig de Gràcia 41), housed in the Casa Amatller, stocks Modernista jewellery by Masriera i Carreras.

Escofet Balart (Plaça Francesc Macià) stocks work by several leading designers.

Joaquín Berao (C/Rosselló 275) is one of Spain's top contemporary jewellery designers.

Maurer (Rambla de Catalunya 52) stocks a wide range of well-known brands of watches.

Roca (Passeig de Gràcia 18) has been in business since 1988, with a beautiful shop designed by Josep Lluís Sert (see p 176).

Tous (Passeig de Gràcia 75) stocks both contemporary and traditional jewellery.

Markets

Els Encants (Plaça de les Glòries, corner of C/Dos de Maig). Monday, Wednesday, Friday and Saturday from 09.00 onwards. Although open till dusk, many stall-holders pack up at around 15.00. Off the tourist beat, this is a real flea market selling all manner of junk. Good for earthenware, textiles, old posters, hats and vintage clothes.

There are several specialist markets on Sunday mornings, including second-hand books at the *Mercat de Sant Antoni* (at the junction of Ronda de Sant Pau and Ronda de Sant Antoni), coins and stamps in the Plaça Reial and a string of antique stalls on the quayside at Plaça Portal de la Pau at the bottom of the Rambla. Antique stalls are set up every Thursday in the Plaça Nova in front of the cathedral. See also Food and Wine above.

Music

Casa Beethoven (La Rambla 97) stocks sheet music.
Castelló (C/Tallers 3) stocks all kinds of music, with a separate classical music section at no. 7 of the same street.
Jazz Collectors (Passatge Forasté 4 bis) has a huge stock of all jazz genres.
Planet Music (C/Mallorca 214) sells all sorts of music in an avant-garde store.
Ricoma & Fills (Gran Vía de les Corts Catalanes 571, C/Balmes 426 and C/Entença 192–194) specialises in flamenco and classical guitars.
Virgin Megastore is at Passeig de Gràcia 16, near Plaça de Catalunya.
There are several **record shops**, including second-hand dealers, along C/Tallers.

Photographic equipment and services

There is no shortage of express developing outlets around the centre, including *Fotosistema Prisma* (C/Jaume I, 18) and *Fotoprix* (C/Ferran 33, C/Pelai 6 & many branches).
Arpi (La Rambla 38) specialises in camera equipment and has expert staff.
Laboratori Fotogràfic 5/6 (C/Muntaner 393) provides professional developing services.

Shoes and accessories

Top Spanish and Catalan designers include *Camper* (Triangle shopping centre on Plaça de Catalunya, C/València 249 and branches around town), *Cristina Castañer* (C/Mestre Nicolau 23), *Muxart* (C/Rosselló 230 & Rambla de Catalunya 47) and *Farrutx* (C/Rosell 218).
Casas (Av. Portal de l'Angel 40, Rambla Canaletes 125 & C/Portaferrissa 25), *Tascón* (Rambla de Catalunya 42, Passeig de Gràcia 64 & branches in shopping centres and at the airport) and *Vogue* (Passeig de Gràcia 30, Av. Portal de l'Angel 12 & branches) all stock fashionable, good-quality shoes.
Lurueña (Diagonal 580) specialises in classic, elegant shoes.
Sara Navarro (Diagonal 598) is one of Spain's most creative footwear designers.
Solé (C/Ample 7) specialises in handmade shoes from all over Spain, and also in large sizes.
La Manual Alpargatera (C/Avinyó 7) is famous for its custom-made espadrilles and counts the Pope, Jack Nicholson and Michael Douglas among its customers.

Most of these shoe shops also sell bags, but specialist shops include *Mandarina Duck* (C/Rosselló 218), *Mi-Sa-Ko* (C/Calvet 38) or *Gala* (Vía Augusta 31).
Seek out *Sombreria Obach* (C/Call 2) for berets and other hats.
Mil (C/Fontanella 20) is another millinery specialist.
Rius de Forns (C/Calvet 60) makes one-off hat designs.
Paraguas (La Rambla 104) specialises in umbrellas and fans.
Guantes Ramblas (La Rambla 132) further down the street specialises in gloves.

Sport and outdoor activities

Corre Corre (C/Calvet 36-38) is the place for trainers.
Cuylás Sports (Via Augusta 37) is good for skiwear.
La Botiga del Barça (F.C. Barcelona stadium & Maremagnum centre) will please the many fans of Barcelona football club (see p 210).

La Tenda (C/Pau Claris 118-120) stocks everything you need for camping, hiking and mountaineering.

Nus Esports de Muntanya (Plaça Diamant 9) specialises in adventure sports such as whitewater rafting.

Only Golf (C/Villaroel 253) should meet your needs for equipment or clothing.

Pro-Bike (C/París 128) or *Tomás Domingo* (C/Rocafort 173) can sort out most mountain bike problems.

Stamp collecting

Monge (C/Boters 2) specialises in stamps issued in Barcelona.

X & F Calicó (Plaça de l'Angel 1–3) was founded in 1784 and is one of the most renowned stamp dealers in Spain.

Stationery

Casa de la Estilográfica (C/Fontanella 17) stocks an excellent range of fountain pens and other writing materials.

Konema (C/Consell de Cent 296) stocks beautiful stationery and all sorts of gifts.

Papirum (Baixada de la Llibreteria 2) has been specialising in hand-decorated paper for more than two hundred years.

Raima (C/Comtal 27) stocks a wide range of notebooks, diaries, paper, pens etc.

 # Entertainment

The *Guía del Ocio* (www.guiadelociobcn.com) listings magazine comes out every Thursday and covers cinema, theatre, concerts, exhibitions, restaurants and nightlife. The daily papers also contain entertainment information and on Fridays publish entertainment supplements. Look out for *Barcelona Metropolitan*, a free monthly English magazine available in hotels and some bars and boutiques. The website www.barcelona.lanetro.com is a good source for checking what is happening before you travel.

As well as from the respective box offices, concert, opera and theatre tickets are usually available from *Tel-Entrada* (☎ 902 101212, or ☎ 0034 93 3262945 from the UK, www.telentrada.com) or *ServiCaixa* (☎ 902 332211 or ☎ 0034 93 4170060 from the UK, www.serviticket.com). Tickets can also be purchased from the ServiCaixa machines at branches of La Caixa bank.

Bullfighting

Plaza de Toros Monumental, Gran Via de les Corts Catalanes 743 (☎ 93 2455804). Metro Monumental. Bus 6, 7, 56, 62. Bullfights are not as popular in Barcelona as in most other parts of Spain, but fights are held every Sunday from Easter to October.

Ticket prices range from €10–80 and are available from the bullring or from the ticket office at C/Muntaner 24 (☎ 93 453 3821). Neither accepts credit cards. See also Museums.

Cinema

Film is very popular in Barcelona with cinemas all over town showing the latest blockbusters and independent films. Foreign films are usually dubbed into Spanish or Catalan, but there are several cinemas that show films in the original version (V.O.). These include the *Icària Yelmo Cineplex* (C/Salvador Espriu 61) in the Port Olímpic, *La Filmoteca* (Avinguda de Sarrià 31–33), *Verdi* (C/Verdi 32), *Boliche* (Diagonal 508), *Renoir-Les Corts* (C/Eugeni d'Ors 12), *Méliès Cinemes* (C/Villaroel 102), *Maldà* (C/Pi 5), *Alexis* (Rambla de Catalunya 90) and *Casablanca* (Passeig de Gràcia 115). Admission is cheaper than in most European cities, usually around €6, with discounts on the *día del espectador*, usually Monday or Wednesday.

Classical music and opera

As well as the publications mentioned above, look out for the monthly leaflet called *Informatiu Musical*, available from tourist offices and the Palau de la Virreina information centre (La Rambla 99), which lists concerts at small, lesser-known venues as well as the main places listed here. See the beginning of this section for ticket information.

L'Auditori, C/Lepant 150 (☎ 93 2479300, www.auditori.com). Box office open 10.00–21.00 daily. Designated space for wheelchair users in halls (mention your requirements when booking). Orchestral, chamber and other concerts are held on an almost daily basis in the main auditorium and smaller hall. A special bus service runs to Plaça de Catalunya after concerts. See p 171.

Palau de la Música Catalana, C/Sant Francesc de Paula 2 (☎ 93 2957200, www.palaumusica.org). Box office open Mon–Sat 10.00–21.00 and one hour before performances on Sundays. Packed programme of orchestral, choral and chamber music. See p 130.

Gran Teatre del Liceu, La Rambla 51–59 (☎ 93 4859913, www.liceubarcelona.com). Box office hours vary according to season, usually summer Mon–Fri 08.00–15.00, 10.00–13.00, winter 15.00–19.00. First-class programme of opera and dance. See p 91.

Auditori Winterthur, L'ILLA shopping centre, Diagonal 547 (☎ 93 2901090). Classical and contemporary music in new concert hall with excellent acoustics.

Dance

The main venue for contemporary dance is *L'Espai*, Travessera de Gràcia 63 (☎ 93 4143133), which runs a varied programme from Sept–June, including experimental music. Ballet is performed at the *Gran Teatre del Liceu* (see above) and the *Teatre Nacional* (see Theatre below). Several arts venues also regularly include dance in their programmes of cultural activities, including the CCCB (see Museums).

Flamenco has no place in Catalan culture, but there are plenty of venues run by Andalusian residents. Some of these are tourist traps, but interesting places to try include *Los Juanele* (C/Aldana 4, no phone), *Los Tarantos* (Plaça Reial 17, ☎ 93 3183067) and *La Macarena* (C/Nou de Sant Francesc 5, ☎ 93 3175436).

Jazz and rock music

Concerts by major pop artists are often held at sports stadia, notably the *Palau de Sant Jordi* and the *Estadi Olímpic*, both on Montjuïc. Classical music venues including *L'Auditori*, *Palau de la Música Catalana* and the **Gran Teatre del Liceu** are occasionally used too. Smaller venues include *Razzmatazz* (C/Pamplona 88/C/Almogàvers 122), which has three spaces, *Bikini* (C/Déu i Mata 105) and *La Boite* (Diagonal 477).

Jazz venues include *Harlem Jazz Club* (C/Contessa de Sobradiel 8), *La Cova del Drac* (C/Vallmajor 33), *Jazz Si Club* (C/Requesens 2) and *Jamboree* (Plaça Reial 17). *Luz de Gas* (C/Muntaner 246) is a fun venue with all sorts of live music. Salsa bands play at *Antilla BCN* (C/Aragó 141–143). The **Festival Internacional de Jazz** runs from October to December. **Sonar** is a festival of experimental music, held annually in June at the CCCB (see Museums). Concerts are also held at other major arts venues, including the *Fundació Joan Miró* and *CaixaForum*. Check the *Guía del Ocio* for details.

Theatre

There is a lively mainstream and fringe theatre scene in Barcelona. Performances are increasingly given in Catalan rather than Spanish, but the language is usually stated in listings. Many theatres close in July and August, but the **Festival del Grec** from late June to early August has a rich theatre programme. See information on obtaining tickets at the beginning of this section.

TNC-Teatre Nacional de Catalunya, Plaça de les Arts 1 (☎ 93 3065700). Works by major international playwrights, usually in Catalan. See p 171.

Teatre Poliorama, La Rambla 115 (☎ 93 3188181). Specialises in works by leading Catalan companies.

Teatre Romea, C/Hospital 51 (☎ 93 3177189). Open since the mid-19C and formerly run by the Catalan government, the Romea programmes classical and contemporary plays in Spanish and Catalan.

Ciutat del Teatre is a new theatrical centre at the base of Montjuïc (Plaça Margarida Xirgu), which includes the Mercat de les Flors (☎ 93 4261875) and the Teatre Lliure, which has moved into the Palau de l'Agricultura building. There are plans to further extend the complex into adjoining buildings.

Fringe theatres include the *Espai Joan Brossa* (C/Allada Vermell 11, ☎ 93 3101364), *Artenbrut* (C/Perill 9, ☎ 93 4579705), *Malic* (C/Fusina 3, ☎ 93 3107035), *Sala Beckett* (C/alegre de Dalt 55, ☎ 93 2845312), *Teatreneu* (C/Terol 26.-28, ☎ 93 2847733), *Nou Tantarantana* (C/de les Flors 22, ☎ 93 4417022) and *La Caldera* (C/Torrent d'en Vidalet 43, ☎ 93 4156851).

 # Sports

Golf clubs

Can Dragó (C/Rosselló i Pòrcel 7, ☎ 93 2760480) has three greens and very cheap daily rates. *Club de Golf Sant Cugat* (C/Villa s/n, Sant Cugat del Vallès, ☎ 93 6743908) is one of the most established clubs in Barcelona and considerably more expensive for non-members, particularly at weekends. Visitors can hire clubs.

Gyms

Dir (☎ 901 304030) is a chain of fitness centres with several branches in Barcelona, including C/Casp 34, C/Castillejos 388, Avinguda del Doctor Marañon 17 and C/Gran de Gràcia 3. Day and short-term membership available. Excellent gym facilities and a range of exercise classes. ***Poliesportiu Municipal Aiguajoc*** (C/Comte Borrell 21–33, ☎ 93 4430355) is a large public sports centre (near Poble Sec metro station) with a gym, squash courts, exercise classes and pool with wave machine.

Swimming pools

Piscines Municipals Bernat Picornell (Av. De l'Estadi 30-40, ☎ 93 4234041, ww.bcn.es/picornell) complex on Montjuïc has fantastic indoor and outdoor pools (open June–end Sep Mon–Sun 09.00–20.00; Oct–end May Mon–Sat 09.00–21.00, Sun & public holidays 09.00–14.30). Inexpensive for non-members with discount for senior citizens. Towel hire available. Also has a gym and a programme of exercise classes. See p 201.

Club Natació Atlètic Barceloneta (Plaça del Mar, ☎ 93 2210010) is a municipal swimming and sports complex situated right on the beach at Barceloneta. Reasonable rates for non-members, and super indoor and outdoor pools (open Mon–Sat 10.00–22.30, Sun & public holidays 10.00–16.30). You can also hire canoes to use in the sea.

Tennis

There are municipal courts on Montjuïc, Tennis Municipal Pompeia (Av. Marquès de Comillas 29–41, ☎ 93 4239747). Non-members can play at reasonable rates at the Complex Esportiu Bon Pastor (C/Arbeca 1, ☎ 93 3120702), which also has pools and gym facilities but is outside the centre.

Football

F.C. Barcelona plays at the Camp Nou stadium (Av. Arístides Maillol s/n, ☎ 93 4963600 for general enquiries, ☎ 93 4963702 for ticket information, www.fcbarcelona.com). Tickets are available two days before matches from the stadium. Online ticket sales planned but not available at time of writing. Check website for information. See p 210.

Espanyol, Barcelona's other team, plays at the Estadi Olímpic on Montjuïc (Av. De l'Estadi s/n, ☎ 93 4248800). Tickets available from the stadium in advance and from 10.00 on match days.

General information

Banking services

The normal banking hours are Monday-Friday 08.30–14.00, though main branches may open till 16/17.00. Most banks are also open on Saturday mornings 08.30–12.00/13.00, though not in July and August. The banks at the airport and Sants railway station are open throughout the day up to 23.00 and 22.00 respectively, including Sundays and public holidays. There are bureaux de change (*canvi/cambio*) all over the city, where the rate may be slightly lower than the banks, but they do not usually charge commission. You can also change money at El Corte Inglés and at most hotels. The Caixa Catalunya has a branch in the tourist office at Plaça de Catalunya where you can change money from Mon–Sat 09.00–21.00, Sun 09.00–14.00. Make sure you are given enough low-denomination notes. The easiest and cheapest way to get cash is to use your normal debit card at any ATM (cashpoint machine, *caixer/cajero*). Just check that the symbols (Visa, Delta, Cirrus etc.) on your card match those on the machine, and there should be no problem. You can choose to have the instructions in English, so the process is pretty much the same as using your card at home. Your bank may charge a fee or a percentage for this service, and there is a limit to how much you can withdraw per day.

Credit cards are widely accepted in shops and restaurants, and can also be used to draw cash from ATMs.

If your cards are lost or stolen, call the following emergency numbers:

Mastercard	☎ 900 971231 or 93 3152512
American Express	☎ 902 375637 or 91 5720303
Visa	☎ 900 974445 or 93 3152512
Diners Club	☎ 91 5474000

Instant **international money transfers** can be arranged by Western Union (☎ 900 633633) or MoneyGram (☎ 900 201010), which operate through most banks. You can also transfer money through American Express, which has branches in Barcelona at C/Rosselló 61 (☎ 93 2170070) and La Rambla 74 (☎ 93 3011116).

Children

There is plenty to keep children of all ages amused along the waterfront from the bottom of La Rambla to the Port Vell marina. As well as the cable cars to Montjuïc, the *golondrines* pleasure boats and the Globus hot-air balloon (p 18), you can take them to the Aquarium (p 152) or the IMAX cinema. Also in ths area are the child-friendly wax museum, the Museu de Cera (p 95), the Museu Marítim (p 150) and the Museu d'Història de Catalunya (p 156). Of course, most kids will love the zoo (p 167) and the Tibidabo funfair (see p 223), and older ones will like the Torre de Collserola (p 223). Happy Parc (C/Pau Claris 97, ☎ 93 3178660, and C/Comtes de Bell-lloc 74–78, ☎ 93 4900835) is an indoor play area with inflatables, slides and lots of other fun things where you can leave the kids with trained supervisors for an hour or two.

If you have a car, you could go to Planet Bowling, which is just outside Barcelona (Autopista A-16, Gavà exit, ☎ 93 6383650). Open every day from 13.00 till past midnight. As well as 26 lanes, there are pool tables, a playground and an amusement arcade.

The Port Aventura theme park (☎ 977 779090) is 100km from Barcelona, but has its own train station so is easily accessible. Rides include the Dragon Khan rollercoaster. Open daily 10.00–20.00, July–mid-Sept extended to 10.00–24.00.

Children are welcome at most restaurants and there are plenty of branches of the major fastfood chains if you are desperate. Barcelona is however full of informal café/restaurants which are ideal for children. A good place to take younger children, particularly at weekends, is the big and boisterous *Central Catalana del Pollastre* (C/Ramon Turró 13), which serves spit-roast chicken and chips.

Consulates
Australia: Gran Via Carles III 98, ☎ 93 3309496
Canada: Passeig de Gràcia 77, ☎ 93 2150704
Netherlands: Avinguda Diagonal 601, ☎ 93 4106210
New Zealand: Travessera de Gràcia 64, ☎ 93 2090399
Republic of Ireland: Gran Via Carles III 94, ☎ 93 4915021
UK: Avinguda Diagonal 477, ☎ 93 4199044
USA: Passeig de la Reina Elisenda 23–25, ☎ 93 2802227

Crime and personal security
Pickpocketing and mugging are rife in downtown Barcelona, and the thieves have an ever more ingenious repertoire of scams. The city is one of the most dangerous in Europe with respect to personal security, and tourists are the prime target. Keep important things on your person rather than in a bag, but not in back pockets, and do not carry more money than you need. The worst areas are the Rambla, Barri Gòtic and Raval, Montjuïc and other park areas, the metro and the beach in summer. Avoid quiet streets at night and never leave anything in a car. Keep your bag visible and if possible attached to you in bars and restaurants (never hang it on the back of your chair).

The city council is however making an enormous effort to improve the situation. There is a designated multilingual service, **Turisme Atenció**, at La Rambla 43 (☎ 93 3019060), where you can report a crime—a process known as a *denuncia*—which is necessary for insurance purposes. You can also get legal advice and help with contacting members of your family. Open Mon–Thur & Sun 07.00–24.00, Fri & Sat 07.00–02.00. You can also report a crime at the **police station** (*comisaria*) at C/Nou de la Rambla 80. The general police phone number is 091. See also Emergencies below.

Cultural organisations
British Council, C/Amigó 83 (☎ 93 2419977). Major centre for the teaching of English, but also has a library with newspapers (open to anyone, but you have to join to take books out), and offers a programme of cultural events and films.
Institute for North American Studies, Via Augusta 123 (☎ 93 2002467). English courses, cultural events and extensive library, but you have to be a member (low annual fee).
Arxiu Històric de la Ciutat, C/Santa Llúcia 1 (☎ 93 3181195). Books on all aspects of Barcelona, newspaper library and archive of city records. Housed in historic Gothic building (see p 111). One-day access possible just with passport, but after that you need to provide two photographs and pay a small fee to obtain a pass.

Customs and etiquette
When introduced to people, it is usual to kiss lightly on both cheeks. Try to remember to greet everyone (waiters, taxi drivers, shop assistants etc) with a cheery *bon dia* (good morning) or *bona tarda* (good afternoon or evening). If invited to someone's house for a meal, it is customary to take a small gift—chocolates, wine or flowers are all fine. Remember that Barcelona is primarily a major city rather than a tourist resort, and people tend to dress smartly. Keep beachwear for the beach.

Drugs
Cannabis is legal in Spain in small amounts for personal use. Although it is not unusual to see people openly smoking joints in parks and some bars, this is illegal and not advisable, particularly for foreigners. All other drugs are illegal.

Electric current
220V AC 50Hz. Round two-pin continental plugs.

Emergencies
All emergency services ☎ 012.
Police ☎ 091.
Ambulance ☎ 061.
In a medical emergency, treatment will be provided free at state-run hospitals if you have an E111 form (see Health and insurance p 11). Go to the Accident & Emergency (*Urgències*) department at one of the following:
Hospital Clínic at C/Villaroel 170 (☎ 93 2275400) in the Eixample, which has an adjacent first-aid centre at C/València 184.
Centre d'Urgències Perecamps at Avinguda Drassanes 13–15 (☎ 93 4410600) at the bottom of La Rambla.
Hospital del Mar at Passeig Marítim 25–29 (☎ 93 2483000) by the beach between Barceloneta and the Port Olímpic. See also Pharmacies below.

If you **lose your passport**, report it to the police (see Crime and personal security above) and contact the relevant consulate (see p 53). If you are a British citizen and plan to return to the UK the same day, the British Consulate will provide you with an emergency passport to enable you to travel. It normally takes five working days to issue a new full passport, but this can sometimes be done faster in emergencies. See Banking services above for information on how to cancel credit cards and how to get cash transferred quickly.

Newspapers
British and American newspapers are readily available on newsstands throughout the city centre, but particularly along the Rambla. Most British papers are printed in Spain, so are on sale early in the morning. They are expensive, however, costing from €2 upwards. Look out for *Broadsheet* and *Barcelona Metropolitan*, both free monthly magazines aimed at English-speaking residents, that are available in some hotels, boutiques and bars.

Pensioners
Discounts are often available in museums. Most senior citizen discounts on public transport only apply to residents with the appropriate pass. Transport aimed primarily at tourists usually does offer a discount, however. Unlike some European cities, most bars and cafés in Barcelona are full of older people, so you need never worry about feeling out of place.

Pharmacies
Spanish pharmacists are highly qualified and knowledgeable and therefore a good first port of call for medical problems. There is a rota system for late-night and weekend opening (*farmàcie de guàrdia*), which is shown in pharmacy windows and listed in newspapers. You can also call ☎ 010 and request this

information. Medication is reasonably priced compared with other European cities. Several pharmacies open 24 hours every day, including **Farmàcia Clapés** at La Rambla 98 and **Farmàcia Alvarez** at Passeig de Gràcia 26.

Photography
Always check whether it is permitted to take photographs in churches and museums, and if you are allowed to use a flash. See Shopping for information on developing and photographic services.

Public holidays
There are 16 public holidays a year, when most shops and all banks are closed, as well as some bars and restaurants. Museums usually open Sunday hours. Be careful when planning your trip, particularly if shopping is important to you. There are often bargain minibreaks to be had around the 6 and 8 December holidays, for example, which are advertised as Christmas shopping trips, even though the shops are closed on those days. If a holiday falls on a Tuesday or Thursday, many people take the preceding Monday or following Friday off to create a long weekend, known as a *puente* (bridge).

1 January	New Year's Day
6 January	Epiphany
(movable)	Good Friday and Easter Monday
1 May	Labour Day
(movable)	Whit Monday
24 June	St John's Day; fireworks and bonfires are lit the night before throughout the city
15 August	Assumption
11 September	*Diada*, Catalan National Day; Catalan flags are hung from many of the houses
24 September	the *Mercè* holiday, a local city holiday preceding a week of festivities
12 October	Columbus Day, the Feast of the Spanish-speaking nations
1 November	All Saints' Day
6 December	Constitution Day
8 December	Immaculate Conception
25 December	Christmas Day
26 December	Boxing Day

The **festival of St George** (Sant Jordi), on 23 April, when it is customary to exchange a book and a rose as a sign of love and friendship, is not a public holiday, and all shops and museums are open that day.

Religion
Catholicism is the national religion of Spain. Mass is held in English at the Parròquia Maria Reina (Avinguda de Espluges 103, ☎ 93 2034115) at 10.00 Sun. A **Protestant** service is held at 11.00 Sun at Saint George's Church (C/Horaci 38, ☎ 93 4178867). Prayers are held at the **synagogue** (C/Avenir 24, ☎ 93 2006148) at Mon–Thur 07.30, Fri 08.00 & 21.00, Sat 09.00 & 20.30, and Sun 08.30. At the **Centre Islàmic** (Avinguda Meridiana 326, ☎ 93 3514901), worship takes place every day from 17.00–20.00, plus Fri 14.45.

Telephones, postal and internet services

Most payphones accept coins, phonecards (*targeta/tarjeta telefónica*) and credit cards. Phonecards are available from news-stands, tobacconists and post offices. You can also make calls from the phone centres (*locutorios*), located in Sants train station, Nord bus station and in El Corte Inglés department stores. Privately-run phone centres include *Europhil* (C/Corders 13) and *Cambios Sol* (La Rambla 88).

From Barcelona

UK dial 00, then 44 followed by the local code (without the initial 0) and the number. To make a reverse charge call to the UK, dial 900 9900 44, which connects you with the international operator in the UK.

USA and Canada 1
Australia 61
New Zealand 64

To call **Barcelona from the UK**, dial 00 34, then the nine-digit number, which will begin with the 93 Barcelona code.

Local calls: you need to dial the 93 code even when calling within Barcelona, which means you dial a total of nine digits for any local number.

Operator: ☎ 1009 (Spain); ☎ 1008 (Europe); ☎ 1009 (rest of the world).

Directory enquiries: ☎ 1003 (Spain); ☎ 025 (international).

The main **post office** (Correu Central) is on the corner of Via Laietana and Plaça d'Antoni López, and is open Mon–Sat 08.30–21.30, Sun 09.00–14.00. The address for the Poste Restante service is Lista de Correos, 08070 Barcelona, Espanya. A passport is required for identification when picking up mail.

Other central post offices include:
Ronda Universitat 23, open Mon–Fri 08.30–20.30, Sat 09.30–13.00.
Plaça Urquinaona 6 and Plaça Bonsuccés, both open Mon–Fri 08.30–14.30, Sat 09.30–13.00, all of which are near Plaça de Catalunya.
C/Aragó 282 in the Eixample, open Mon–Fri 08.30–20.30, Sat 09.30–13.00.
C/Valencia 231 also in the Eixample, open Mon–Fri 08.30–14.30, Sat 09.30–13.00.
Plaça Sant Miquel in the Barri Gòtic, a post office in the town hall, open Mon–Fri 08.30–14.30, Sat 09.30–13.00.
El Corte Inglés at Diagonal 617 has a post office which is open the same hours as the store, Mon–Sat 10.00–21.00.

Stamps (*timbres/sellos*) are also available at all tobacconists (*estancs/estancos*), recognisable by their maroon sign with the word *tabacs/tabacos* in yellow lettering. All branches of El Corte Inglés also have an *estanc*. **Post boxes** (*bústia/buzón*) are yellow, most with only one collection at 17.00.

There are **internet cafés** all over Barcelona, including *easyEverything* at La Rambla 31 and Ronda Universitat 35 (near Plaça de Catalunya), which are open 24 hours every day. Also centrally located are *bcnet* at C/Barra de Ferro 3 (near Museu Picasso), *Travelbar* at C/Boqueria 27 (Barri Gòtic), *inetcorner* at Plaça Ramon Berenguer 2 (near Cathedral) and C/Sardenya 306 (near Sagrada Familia), *ciberopcion* at Gran Via de les Corts Catalanes 602 and *Cybermundo* at C/Bergara 3 (both near Plaça de Catalunya).

Time

Barcelona is one hour ahead of Greenwich Mean Time and British Summer Time. It is six hours ahead of New York. In summer, it is light until 21.30, but dusk falls around 17.30 in winter.

Toilets

There is a dearth of public toilets, but fortunately no shortage of bars to nip into. It is not obligatory to also order a drink when you want to use the facilities, but it is courteous. It is also worth bearing in mind that you can nearly always access the toilets in museums without going into the museum itself.

Women travellers

Barcelona is a great city for visiting alone, given the wealth of cultural and shopping possibilities. There are also plenty of cafés and informal restaurants, where a woman eating alone will not attract attention. If you feel self-conscious sitting at a table, choose one of the many places with stools at the bar, where you will certainly not be the only person on your own.

Women should expect to get comments from passing men on the street. Although this practice goes by the charming name of *piropos* (compliments), the comments are often sexually explicit. Just ignore them and keep walking. This behaviour is all bravado, and there is little danger of getting into serious difficulties, provided you use your common sense.

 # Languages

The Spanish and Catalan languages have equal status in Barcelona, but though everyone who speaks Catalan is fluent also in Spanish, the opposite is not true. Owing to the large immigrant population from other parts of Spain, and the fact that many of the city's older inhabitants were brought up at a time when the Catalan language was officially prohibited, the city's fluent Catalan speakers account for little more than 50 per cent of the population. All street names and signs are however now solely in Catalan, as are most information panels in museums, exhibition catalogues, restaurant menus and so on.

In some cases you are more likely to find a Catalan text translated into English than into Spanish, and there are certain Catalan nationalists who have even argued that Catalan authors who do not write in Catalan, such as Juan Goytisolo and Eduardo Mendoza, have no right to receive sponsorship from the Catalan Government. Not even the most fervent of these nationalists will take offence if a foreigner addresses them in Spanish, but on the other hand if you belong to that tiny minority of visitors to Catalunya who have bothered to learn some Catalan, you will find yourself welcomed into the Catalan community in a way which few others will experience. Anyone who is planning an extended stay in Barcelona would be well advised to try to learn Catalan as well as Spanish.

The Catalan language is spoken not only throughout Catalunya, but also (with variations) in the Valencian provinces of Valencia, Castelló and Alacant (Alicante), the Balearic Islands, a narrow strip of eastern Aragon, the Republic of Andorra and the town of Alguer (Alghero) in Sardinia. Altogether it has more speakers than have Albanian, Danish, Finnish, Gaelic, Lithuanian or Norwegian. It is a member of the Romance family of languages, and anyone with a basic command of Spanish will have few problems at least in understanding the gist of a Catalan text. An additional knowledge of French or Italian will also greatly help, as many Catalan words or phrases are closer to these two languages than they are to Spanish—for instance *si us plau* (please) or *menjar* (eat).

The main difficulties come with the pronunciation, which is complex compared to Spanish, and affected by more accents (thus, whereas in Spanish the sole accents are the acute and the tilde, in Catalan the accents are the acute, grave, umlaut and the cedilla). Among the more idiosyncratic features of the pronunciation are that the *h* is always silent, *j* is pronounced like the French *j* or *g* (and not as an *h* as in Spanish); *ny* is the equivalent of the Spanish tilde, ~, even at the end of a word; *ll* without a dot has a strong consonantal *y* sound as in the English *lli*; *ig* at the end of a syllable is like the English *tch*; *gu* is pronounced *gw* and *x* sounds like the English *sh*. For example, to use names that you will come across again and again on a trip to Barcelona, Joan Maragall (the great Catalan poet) = *Jhone Maraga-ye*, Puig i Cadafalch (the Modernista architect) = *Putch ee Kadafalk*, and Güell (Gaudí's patron) = *Gwe-ye*.

Useful words and phrases
Listed in Catalan then Spanish

Hello *hola, holá*
Goodbye *adéu, adiós*
Good morning (until lunchtime)
  bon dia, buenos días
Good afternoon/evening *bona tarda, buenas tardes*
Good night *bona nit, buenas noches*

Yes *sí, sí*
No *no, no*
Okay *d'acord, vale*
Please *si us plau, por favor*
Thank you *gràcies, gracias*

Today *avui, hoy*
Tomorrow *demà, mañana*
Yesterday *ahir, ayer*
Now *ara, ahora*
Later *més tard, más tarde*

cold *fred, frío*
hot *calenta, caliente*
open *obert, abierto*
cheap *barat, barato*
expensive *car, caro*

left *esquerra, izquierda*
right *dreta, derecha*
straight on *recte, recto*
near *a prop, cerca*
far *lluny, lejos*

railway station *estació de tren, estación de trenes*
bus station *estació d'autobusos, estación de autobuses*
airport *aeroport, aeropuerto*
ticket *bitllet, billete*

toilets *serveis, servicios*
tourist office *oficina de turisme, oficina de turismo*
police station *comissaria de policia, comisaría de policía*
hospital *hospital, hospital*
doctor *doctor, médico*
dentist *dentista, dentista*
chemist *farmàcia, farmacia*
aspirin *aspirina, aspirina*

What is your name? *Com es diu, Com et dius?, ¿Cómo se llama usted, Cómo te llamas?*
My name is... *Em dic, me llamo*
I would like... *Voldria, querría*
Do you speak English? *Parla anglès?, ¿Habla inglés?*
I don't understand *No ho entenc, no entiendo*
Where is...? *On és?, ¿Dónde está?*
What time is it? *Quina hora és?, ¿Qué hora es?*
At what time? *A quina hora?, ¿A qué hora?*
How much is it? *Quant és?, ¿Cuánto es?*

Monday *dilluns, lunes*
Tuesday *dimarts, martes*
Wednesday *dimecres, miércoles*
Thursday *dijous, jueves*
Friday *divendres, viernes*
Saturday *dissabte, sábado*
Sunday *diumenge, domingo*

January *gener, enero*
February *febrer, febrero*
March *març, marzo*
April *abril, abril*
May *maig, mayo*
June *juny, junio*
July *juliol, julio*
August *agost, agosto*
September *setembre, septiembre*
October *octubre, octubre*
November *novembre, noviembre*
December *desembre, diciembre*

spring *primavera, primavera*
summer *estiu, verano*
autumn *tardor, otoño*
winter *hivern, invierno*

1 *un, uno*
2 *dos, dos*
3 *tres, tres*
4 *quatre, cuatro*
5 *cinc, cinco*
6 *sis, seis*
7 *set, siete*
8 *vuit, ocho*
9 *nou, nueve*
10 *deu, diez*
11 *onze, once*
12 *dotze, doce*
13 *tretze, trece*
14 *catorze, catorce*
15 *quinze, quince*
16 *setze, dieciseis*
17 *disset, diecisiete*
18 *divuit, dieciocho*
19 *dinou, diecinueve*
20 *vint, veinte*
30 *trenta, treinta*
40 *quaranta, cuarenta*
50 *cinquanta, cincuenta*
60 *seixanta, sesenta*
70 *setanta, sesenta*
80 *vuitanta, ochenta*
90 *noranta, noventa*
100 *cent, cien*

Museums and galleries

More detailed information on most of the museums listed below is given in the walks. Although major venues stay open all day, many smaller places close at lunchtime, usually from 14.00–17.00, and some only open in the morning. Many are however open until 20.00, so you can pack a lot into a couple of days with a little advance planning. Many museums are closed on Sunday afternoon and all day Monday. Sunday opening times usually apply on public holidays. Opening hours tend to change by half an hour or so between summer and winter. The times listed here were correct at the time of writing, but museums sometimes vary their hours.

Entrance charges and special tickets Entrance fees are cheap compared with most other European cities—rarely more than €5—and there are several discount schemes. Senior citizens of any nationality qualify for a discount at many museums. The **Articket**, available from tourist offices and participating museums, costs approximately €16 and includes entrance to the Museu Nacional d'Art de Catalunya, Museu d'Art Modern, Fundació Joan Miró, Fundació Antoni Tàpies, Museu d'Art Contemporani de Barcelona (MACBA), Centre de Cultura Contemporània de Barcelona (CCCB) and La Pedrera. If you visit all these museums, the saving is around 40 per cent on individual entrance prices. The Articket is valid for three months. The **Ruta del Modernisme** (available from Centre del Modernisme, Casa Amatller, Passeig de Gràcia 41) costs approximately €5 and comprises an informative book (available in English) and vouchers giving free entrance or discounts at the museums and buildings along the route, which include the Palau Güell, Palau de la Música Catalana, La Pedrera and the Sagrada Família. Discounts are also available with the **Barcelona Card** and with **Bus Turístic** vouchers, details of which are given in the Getting Around section.

For up to date information on exhibitions, buy the weekly listings magazine *Guía del Ocio*, or visit their website, www.guiadelocio.com. Also useful is the quarterly *Museums of Barcelona* booklet, which is available from museum shops.

Museums, Foundations and Cultural Centres

Casa-Museu Gaudí, Park Güell, Carretera del Carmel (☎ 93 219 3811). Open every day, Nov–Feb 10.00–18.00; Mar, Apr & Oct 10.00–19.00; May–Sept 10.00–20.00. Fee. Metro Lesseps. Bus 24, 25. Walk 11. The house where Gaudí lived from 1906 until 1926. Exhibits include examples of his work, and artworks by Picasso and others.

Centre d'Art Santa Mònica, Rambla Santa Mònica 7 (☎ 93 316 2810, http://cultura.gencat.es). Open Mon–Sat 11.00–14.00, 17.00–20.00, Sun & public holidays 11.00–15.00. Free. Metro Drassanes. Bus 14, 38, 59, 91. Wheelchair access. Walk 2. Art venue that stages major international exhibitions as well as showcasing cutting-edge Catalan artists.

Centre de Cultura Contemporània de Barcelona (**CCCB**), C/Montealegre 5 (☎ 93 306 4100, www.cccb.org). Late Sept–mid June Tue, Thu, Fri 11.00–14.00, 16.00–20.00, Wed & Sat 11.00–20.00, Sun & public holidays 11.00–19.00. Mid-June–late Sept Tue–Sat 11.00–20.00, Sun & public holidays 11.00–15.00. Fee. Metro Catalunya & Universitat. Bus 14, 16, 17, 38 or any to Plaça de Catalunya or Plaça de Universitat. Book and gift shop. Café/restaurant. Wheelchair access. Guided tours. Walk 4. Major temporary exhibitions and lively programme of cultural events.

Col·lecció Thyssen-Bornemisza, Reial Monestir de Santa Maria de Pedralbes, Baixada del Monestir 9 (☎ 93 280 1434, www.museothyssen.org). Open Tue–Sun 10.00–14.00. Fee. Free first Sunday each month. Metro Maria Cristina. FGC train station Reina Elisenda. Bus 22, 63, 64, 75, 114. Bookshop. Wheelchair access. Walk 9. Part of the collection of Baron Thyssen-Bornemisza, housed in Monastery of Pedralbes. The collection includes work by

Fra Angelico, Veronese, Titian, Zurbarán and Canaletto. See also Museu Monastir de Pedralbes below.

Fundació Antoni Tàpies, C/Aragó 255 (☎ 93 487 0315, email: museu@ftapies.com). Open Tue–Sun 10.00–20.00. Fee. Metro Passeig de Gràcia. Bus 7, 16, 17, 22, 24, 28. Bookshop. Library. Wheelchair access. Walk 7. Works from all periods of the artist's life, including paintings, drawing and sculptures. Temporary exhibitions.

Fundació Francisco Godia, C/València 284 (☎ 93 272 3180, www.fundacionfgodia.org). Open Mon, Wed–Sun 10.00–20.00. Fee. Metro Passeig de Gràcia. Bus 7, 16, 17, 22, 24, 28. Shop. Wheelchair access. Walk 7. Important collection of paintings, sculpture and ceramics from the 12C to 21C. Temporary exhibitions.

Fundació Joan Miró, Parc de Montjuïc (☎ 93 443 9470, www.bcn.fjmiro.es). Open Oct–June Tue, Wed, Fri & Sat 10.00–19.00, Thu 10.00–21.30, Sun & public holidays 10.00–14.30; July–Sept Tue, Wed, Fri & Sat 10.00–20.00, Thu 10.00–21.30, Sun & public holidays 10.00–14.30. Fee. Metro Espanya. Bus 50. Montjuïc funicular. Book and gift shop. Café/restaurant. Wheelchair access. Guided tours. Walk 8. The permanent exhibition of Joan Miró's work spans his whole working life, from 1914 to 1978, and includes drawings, paintings and sculpture. Temporary exhibitions focus on different stages or aspects of his work, as well as shows by other artists. The foundation also organises regular cultural events.

Galeria Olímpica, Estadi Olímpic de Montjuïc, Passeig Olímpic (☎ 906 301 775, www.fundaciobarcelonaolimpica.es). Open Oct–Mar Mon–Sat 10.00–13.00, 16.00–18.00, public holidays 10.00–14.00; April & May Mon–Sat 10.00–14.00, 16.00–18.00, public holidays 10.00–14.00; June Tue–Sat 10.00–14.00, 16.00–20.00, Sun & public holidays 10.00–14.00; July–Sept Mon–Sat 10.00–14.00, 16.00–20.00, Sun & public holidays 10.00–14.00. Fee. Metro Espanya. Bus 50. Shop. Walk 8. Exhibits illustrate the history of the Olympic Games, with a detailed section on the 1992 Barcelona event.

La Pedrera, C/Provença 261–265, corner Passeig de Gràcia (☎ 93 484 5530, www.caixacat.es/cccc). Open Mon–Sun 10.00–20.00. Rooftop also open July–Sept daily 21.00–24.00. Fee. Metro Passeig de Gràcia and Diagonal. Bus 7, 16, 17, 22, 24, 28. Book and gift shop. Café. Wheelchair access. Guided tours. Walk 7. Gaudí's Casa Milà, better known as La Pedrera, contains an exhibition area charting Gaudí's career in the attic space. Visitors also see a flat in the building, furnished in the style of the turn of the 20C, as well as an exhibition of the changes taking place in Barcelona at that time. Temporary exhibitions.

Museu Barbier-Mueller d'Arte Precolombí, C/Montcada 12–14 (☎ 93 310 4516, www.bcn.es/icub). Open Tue–Sat 10.00–18.00, Sun & public holidays 10.00–15.00. Fee. Free first Saturday of the month. Metro Jaume I. Bus 14, 17, 19 & any to Via Laietana. Guided tours. Bookshop. Café. Wheelchair access. Walk 3. Pre-Columbian art, donated by the Barbier-Mueller Museum in Geneva. Sculpture, textiles, ritual objects and ceramics from Central and South America.

Museu-Casa Verdaguer, Vil·la Joana, Vallvidrera (☎ 93 315 1111, www.museuhistoria.bcn.es). Open Oct–May Sat & Sun 11.00–15.00; Jun–Sep Sat 11.00–14.00, 15.00–18.00, Sun 11.00–15.00. Free. FGC train station Baixador de Vallvidrera. Walk 12. 19C farmhouse on Collserola hill, which was the last home of writer Jacint Verdaguer, who died in 1902. Exhibits include examples of his work and personal belongings.

Museu d'Arqueologia de Catalunya, Passeig Santa Madrona 39–41, Parc de Montjuïc (☎ 93 423 2149, www.mac.es). Open Tue–Sat 09.30–19.00, Sun & public holidays 10.00–14.30. Fee. Metro Espanya. Bus 55. Bookshop. Wheelchair access. Walk 8. Housed in a pavilion from the 1929 Exhibition, the museum contains displays from the Palaeolithic to Visigothic periods, including the Dama de Ibiza, a bust richly studded with jewellery.

Museu d'Art Contemporani de Barcelona (MACBA), Plaça dels Angels (☎ 93 412 0810. www.macba.es). Open Mon, Wed–Fri 11.00–19.30/20.00, Sat 10.00–20.00, Sun & public holidays 10.00–15.00. Fee. Metro Catalunya & Universitat. Bus any to Plaça de Catalunya or Plaça Universitat. Bookshop. Café. Wheelchair access. Walk 4. Art from mid-20C onwards, including works by Solano, Broto, Merz, Tàpies, Calder, Brossa and Perejaume. Temporary exhibitions.

Museu d'Art Modern, Parc de la Ciutadella (☎ 93 319 5728, www.mnac.es). Open Tue–Sat 10.00–19.00, Sun & public holidays 10.00–14.30. Fee. Free first Thursday each month. Metro Arc de Triomf. Bus 14, 39, 40, 41, 42, 51, 141. Shop. Wheelchair access. Guided tours. Walk 6. The paintings, sculpture and furniture on display date from the beginning of the 19C to the 1930s, with the emphasis on artists working during the Modernista period. There are plans to transfer the collections to the Museu Nacional d'Art de Catalunya.

Museu de Carrosses Fúnebres, C/Sancho d'Avila 2 (☎ 93 484 1720, www.funerariabarcelona.com). Open Mon–Fri 10.00–13.00, 16.00–18.00. Free. Metro Marina. Bus 6, 10, 40, 42. Collection of hearse carriages from the end of the 19C to mid-20C.

Museu de Cera, Passatge Banca 7, Rambla de Santa Mònica (☎ 93 317 2649). Open Oct–June Mon–Fri 10.00–13.30, 16.00–19.30, Sat, Sun and public holidays 11.00–14.00, 16.30–20.30; July–Sept every day 10.00–22.00. Fee. Metro Drassanes. Bus 14, 36, 38, 57, 59, 64, 91. Shop. Café. Wheelchair access. Walk 1. Waxworks of more than 350 famous figures, including Salvador Dalí, many displayed in period settings.

Museu de Ceràmica, Palau Reial, Avinguda Diagonal 686 (☎ 93 280 1621, www.museuceramica.bcn.es). Open Tue–Sat 10.00–18.00, Sun & public holidays 10.00–15.00. Fee. Free first Sunday each month. Metro Palau Reial. Bus 7, 33, 63, 68, 69, 74, 75, 78. Shop. Wheelchair access. Walk 9. Spanish ceramics from 11C to present day. Exhibits from major centres of ceramic production, such as Manises, Paterna and Teruel. Also pieces by artists including Picasso and Miró.

Museu de Geologia, Parc de la Ciutadella (☎ 93 319 6895, www.museugeologia.bcn.es). Open Tue, Wed, Fri, Sat & Sun 10.00–14.00, Thu 10.00–18.30. Fee (includes entrance to adjacent Zoology Museum). Free first Sunday each month. Metro Arc de Triomf or Jaume I. Bus 14, 39, 41, 51. The displays of minerals, fossils and rocks chart the geological landscape of Catalunya. Temporary exhibitions.

Museu de la Catedral, Pla de la Seu (☎ 93 310 2580). Open Mon–Sun 10.00–13.00, 16.00–18.30. Fee. Metro Jaume I. Bus 17, 19, 40, 45. Shop. Walk 2. Paintings from the 14C–18C, including Bermejo and Huguet.

Museu de la Música, Avinguda Diagonal 373 (☎ 93 416 1157,

www.museumusica.bcn.es). Open Tue–Sun 10.00–14.00, also Wed afternoons
17.00–20.00, except during July–Sept). Fee. Free first Sunday of each month.
Metro Diagonal. Bus 6, 15, 33, 34. Walk 7. Musical instruments from Spain
and other parts of the world, with a particularly good collection of guitars.
Currently housed in Modernista building by Puig i Cadafalch, but there are
plans to transfer the museum to the Auditori concert hall.

Museu de la Xocolata, Carrer de Comerç 36 (☎ 93 268 7878). Open Mon,
Wed–Sat 10.00–19.00, Sun & public holidays 10.00–15.00. Fee. Metro Jaume 1,
Arc de Triomf. Bus 14, 39, 51. Shop. Café. Wheelchair access. Walk 3. Learn about
the history of chocolate in this entertaining new museum. Tasting sessions.

Museu de l'Eròtica, La Rambla 96 (☎ 93 318 9865,
www.eroticamuseum.com). Open Oct–May Mon–Sun 10.00–22.00; June–Sept
Mon–Sun 10.00–24.00. Fee. Metro Liceu. Bus 14, 38, 59. 91. Wheelchair
access. Walk 2. Exhibits illustrate the development of erotic art and culture
over the centuries.

Museu de les Arts Decoratives, Palau Reial, Avinguda Diagonal 686
(☎ 93 280 5054, www.museuartsdecoratives.bcn.es). Open Tue–Sat
10.00–18.00, Sun & public holidays 10.00–15.00. Fee. Metro Palau Reial. Bus
7, 33, 67, 68, 74, 75. Shop. Wheelchair access. Walk 9. Displays from the 13C
to contemporary industrial design. Exhibits include fans, jewellery boxes and
chests, as well as furniture and household objects by leading designers including Mariscal and Oscar Tusquets. Temporary exhibitions.

Museu de Zoologia, Parc de la Ciutadella (☎ 93 319 6912,
www.museuzoologia.bcn.es). Open Tue, Wed, Fri, Sat & Sun 10.00–14.00, Thu
10.00–18.30. Fee (includes entrance to adjacent Geology Museum). Free first
Sunday each month. Metro Arc de Triomf or Jaume 1. Bus 14, 39, 41, 51.
Walk 6. The permanent displays deal with the classification of animals and
other living beings, with emphasis on the species found in Catalunya.
Temporary exhibitions.

Museu del Calçat, Plaça de Sant Felip Neri 5 (☎ 93 301 4533). Open
Tue–Sun 11.00–14.00. Fee. Metro Jaume I or Liceu. Bus 14, 17, 19, 38, 40,
45, 59, 91. Wheelchair access. Walk 2. Examples of shoes and the tools and
machinery used over the last two thousand years. Also display of shoes that
belonged to famous figures.

Museu del Clavegueram, Passeig de Sant Joan 98 (☎ 93 209 1526). Open
Tue–Fri 10.00–13.00, 16.00–18.00, Sat & Sun 10.00–14.00. Fee. Metro
Verdaguer. Bus 6, 15, 19, 33, 34, 50, 51, 55. Wheelchair access. Walk 7. The
museum charts the development of the drainage and sewerage systems from
Roman times to the present day. At weekends, visitors can also tour the sewers
below.

Museu del Futbol Club Barcelona, Estadio del F.C. Barcelona, Avinguda
Arístides Maillol, Entrance 7 or 9 (☎ 93 496 3600, www.fcbarcelona.es). Open
Mon–Sat 10.00–18.30, Sun & public holidays 10.00–14.00. Fee. Metro
Collblanc, Maria Cristina or Palau Reial. Bus 54, 75 or any along Diagonal to
Plaça de Pius XII. Shop. Café. Wheelchair access. Walk 9. Situated in the sta-
dium, photographs, trophies, posters and kit are used to illustrate the club's
history. Visitors can also go out onto the stands. Temporary exhibitions.

Museu del Perfum, Passeig de Gràcia 39 (☎ 93 216 0146,
www.perfum-museum.com). Open Mon–Fri 10.30–13.30, 16.30–20.00, Sat

10.30–13.30. Free. Metro Passeig de Gràcia. Bus 7, 16, 17, 22, 24, 28. Walk 7. Perfume bottles from Ancient Egypt to the present day, including Greek, Roman, Arabic and Oriental exhibits.

Museu del Temple Expiatori de la Sagrada Família, C/Mallorca 401 (☎ 93 207 3031, www.sagradafamilia.org). Open Nov–Feb Mon–Sun 09.00–18.00; March, Sept & Oct Mon–Sun 09.00–19.00; Apr–Aug Mon–Sun 09.00–20.00. Fee. Metro Sagrada Família. Bus 10, 19, 33, 34, 43, 44, 50, 51. Shop. Wheelchair access. Walk 7. The construction of the cathedral is illustrated by means of drawings, models, plans and photographs. One section deals with the life of Gaudí. Visitors also have access to the interior of the cathedral and can take a lift up one of the towers.

Museu dels Autòmats del Tibidabo, Parc d'Atraccions del Tibidabo (☎ 93 211 7942). Open daily 12.00–20.00. Fee. Admission included with fun-fair ticket. FGC train station Avinguda Tibidabo, then Tramvia Blau tram and funicular. Walk 12. Housed in a theatre from the early 20C, the displays include clockwork toys from fairgrounds and theatres.

Museu Diocesà de Barcelona (Pia Almoina), Avinguda de la Catedral 4 (☎ 93 315 2213, www.arquebisbatbcn.es). Open Tue–Sat 10.00–14.00, 17.00–20.00, Sun 11.00–14.00. Fee. Metro Jaume I or Urquinaona. Bus 17, 19, 40, 45. Shop. Wheelchair access. Walk 2. Artworks from parish churches in the Barcelona diocese, from 12C onwards, with Romanesque, Gothic, Renaissance and Baroque exhibits. Temporary exhibitions.

Museu d'Història de Catalunya, Palau de Mar, Plaça Pau Vila 3 (☎ 93 225 4700, http://cultura.gencat.es/museus/mhc). Open Tue, Thur–Sat 10.00–19.00, Wed 10.00–20.00, Sun & public holidays 10.00–14.30. Fee. Metro Barceloneta. Bus 14, 17, 19, 36, 45. Shop. Rooftop café/restaurant. Wheelchair access. Walk 5. Interactive displays chart the history of Catalunya from prehistory to modern times. Temporary exhibitions.

Museu d'Història de la Ciutat, Plaça del Rei (☎ 93 315 1111, www.museuhistoria.bcn.es). Open Oct–May Tue–Sat 10.00–14.00, 16.00–20.00, Sun & public holidays 10.00–14.00; June–Sept Tue–Sat 10.00–20.00, Sun & public holidays 10.00–14.00. Fee. Free first Saturday of the month after 16.00. Metro Jaume I. Bus 16, 17, 19, 40, 45. Book and gift shop. Wheelchair access. Guided tours. Walk 2. The history of Barcelona is imaginatively explained in the evocative setting of the historic buildings flanking the Plaça del Rei. Part of the museum is in the Roman remains underneath the square. Temporary exhibitions.

Museu Egipci de Barcelona, Fundació Arqueològica Clos, C/Valencia 284 (☎ 93 488 0188, www.fundclos.es). Open Mon–Sat 10.00–20.00, Sun 10.00–14.00. Fee. Metro Passeig de Gràcia. Bus 7, 16, 17, 22, 24, 28. Shop. Café/restaurant. Wheelchair access. Guided tours. The Clos collection of archaeological finds is used to give an informative insight into the lives of the Ancient Egyptians. Temporary exhibitions.

Museu Etnològic, Passeig de Santa Madrona, Parc de Montjuïc (☎ 93 424 6402, www.museuetnologic.bcn.es). Open Tue & Thu 10.00–19.00, Wed, Fri, Sat, Sun & public holidays 10.00–14.00. Fee. Metro Espanya. Bus 55, 13. Bookshop. Guided tours. Walk 8. Exhibits from all over the world, with particularly good Moroccan and Latin American collections. Temporary exhibitions.

Museu Frederic Marès, Plaça de Sant Iu 5–6 (☎ 93 310 5800, www.museumares.bcn.es). Open Tue & Thur 10.00–17.00, Wed, Fri & Sat 10.00–19.00, Sun & public holidays 10.00–15.00. Fee. Metro Jaume I. Bus 17, 19, 40, 45. Shop. Café in summer. Wheelchair access. Guided tours. Walk 2. The extensive collections of sculptor Frederic Marès include sculpture from the pre-Roman period to the 19C, as well as jewellery, fans, toys and a wealth of personal belongings. Temporary exhibitions.

Museu Geològic del Seminari de Barcelona, C/Diputació 231 (☎ 93 454 1600, www.minerals.uv.es/mgsb). Open Mon–Fri 16.00–19.00 (prior notification by phone essential). Donation for guided visit. Metro Universitat. Bus any to Plaça Universitat. Founded in 1874, this important geological museum specialises in invertebrates and is also a research centre.

Museu i Centre d'Estudis de l'Esport Dr. Melcior Colet, C/Buenos Aires 56–58 (☎ 93 419 2232, http://cultura.gencat.es/esport/museu). Open Mon–Fri 10.00–14.00, 16.00–20.00. Free. Metro Hospital Clinic. Bus 6, 7, 14, 63, 67, 68. Walk 7. Permanent displays and temporary exhibitions related to the history of sport in Catalunya, housed in a building designed by Puig i Cadafalch.

Museu Marítim de Barcelona, Avinguda de les Drassanes (☎ 93 342 9920, www.diba.es/mmaritim). Open daily 10.00–19.00. Fee. Metro Drassanes. Bus 14, 20, 36, 38, 57, 59. Shop. Café/restaurant. Walk 5. Situated in the former Royal Shipyards, exhibits include navigation instruments, maps and models of ships. Temporary exhibitions.

Museu Militar, Castell de Montjuïc (☎ 93 329 8613). Open Tue–Fri 09.30–18.30, Sat & Sun 9.30–19.30. Fee. Shop. Café. Bus 50. Montjuïc funicular & cable car. Walk 8. Displays include weapons, maps, armour, model soldiers, paintings and archaeological exhibits.

Museu Monestir de Pedralbes, Baixada del Monestir 9 (☎ 93 203 9282, www.museuhistoria.bcn.es). Open Tue–Sun 10.00–14.00. Fee. Free first Sunday each month. Metro Maria Cristina. FGC train station Reina Elisenda. Bus 22, 63, 64, 75, 114. Bookshop. Wheelchair access. Walk 9. 14C monastery with superb Gothic cloister. Temporary exhibitions. Also houses Thyssen-Bornemisza Collection, which is listed above.

Museu Nacional d'Art de Catalunya (**MNAC**), Palau Nacional, Parc de Montjuïc (☎ 93 622 0360, www.mnac.es). Open Tue–Sat 10.00–19.00, Sun 10.00–14.30. Fee. Metro Espanya. Bus 9, 13, 30, 50, 55. Bookshop. Café. Wheelchair access. Walk 8. Outstanding collections of Catalan Romanesque and Gothic art. Temporary exhibitions.

Museu Picasso, C/Montcada 15–23 (☎ 93 319 6310, www.museupicasso.bcn.es). Open Tue–Sat 10.00–20.00, Sun 10.00–15.00. Fee. Free first Sunday of the month. Metro Jaume I. Bus 17, 19, 40, 45. Shop. Café/restaurant. Wheelchair access. Walk 3. The substantial collection concentrates on the earlier stages of Picasso's work. Temporary exhibitions.

Museu Taurí, Gran Via de les Corts Catalanes 749 (☎ 93 245 5803). Open Easter–Sept Mon–Sat 10.30–14.00, 16.00–19.00, Sun & before bullfights 10.30–13.00. Fee. Metro Monumental. Bus 6, 7, 56, 62. Shop. Walk 7. Located in the bullring, displays include posters from the 1920s onwards, photographs and bullfighting apparel.

Museu Tèxtil i d'Indumentària, C/Montcada 12–14 (☎ 93 310 4516,

www.museutextil.bcn.es). Open Tue–Sat 10.00–18.00, Sun & public holidays
10.00–15.00. Fee. Free first Saturday each month after 15.00. Shop.
Café/restaurant. Walk 3. The displays chart the development of textile production and decoration over the centuries, with 3C Coptic pieces from Egypt and
examples from the Al-Andalus kingdom in Spain. One section deals with leading fashion designers of the 20C.

Palau de la Virreina, La Rambla 99 (☎ 93 3017775). Open Tue–Sat
11.00–20.30, Sun & public holidays 11.00–15.00. Fee. Gift and bookshop.
Walk 1. Temporary exhibitions by major contemporary artists.

Galleries

The main area for established galleries is in the Eixample district around
C/Consell de Cent and cross streets, particularly the blocks between Passeig de
Gràcia and C/Muntaner. More traditional galleries are clustered in the Barri
Gòtic, particularly around C/Petrixol. For more avant-garde places, explore the
Born (Walk 3) and Raval (Walk 4) areas. The latter district has been attracting
new galleries since the opening of the MACBA museum in 1995. Galleries
usually open Tue–Sat 10.30–13.30, 17.00–20.30. Most close in August, and
maybe a couple of weeks either side as well. Look out for exhibition openings,
which usually take place on Thursday nights from 20.00–22.00 and are open
to anyone. Shows are listed in daily newspapers and in the Guía del Ocio (see
above).

BACKGROUND INFORMATION

A History of Barcelona

by Felipe Fernández-Armesto

On the ceiling of Barcelona's Llotja—an 18C Temple of Commerce—in a painting by Pere Pau i Montaner, a buxom figure of Prosperity clothes thankful Nakedness, while Poverty and Disaster are driven off with scourges. The image is typical of a tradition of civic propaganda, which can be traced back to the Middle Ages.

Yet poverty and disaster have never been effectively banished and an 'alternative' image of Barcelona has been nourished in the gutters and alleys. Jean Genet, picking the lice out of the trouser seams of his homosexual lovers in 1932, recorded memories of the city bespattered with every kind of bodily excretion. Picasso and Nonell painted brilliant portraits of sitters drawn from low life. The recurrence of disaster is documented in a long history, in overlapping phases, of plagues and social conflicts.

Out of the tension between these rival perceptions of the city—out of the efforts of the Barcelonese to re-mould Barcelona in their own image—extraordinary achievements have been wrought. In the Middle Ages, without a natural harbour, Barcelona became the centre of a great maritime empire. In modern times, without iron or coal, she led Spain's industrial revolution. Though her status as a national seat of government was extinguished in 1716, she has remained the capital and, in a sense, the embodiment—the 'head and hearth', as Catalans say—of Catalan culture. Today, by a fitful and fragile rise, she has become the centre of the biggest conurbation on the western Mediterranean seaboard.

Ancient and medieval Barcelona

The city's origins Visible to an explorer at street level, Roman graves line a 2C street under the Plaça de la Vila de Madrid. Along the Carrer dels Arcs, the towers of the 4C gates are revealed, abutted by what may be the remains of an aqueduct. Astonishingly, in the middle of a modern megalopolis, the Roman walls can be followed, not only in the street plan but also above ground in stretches and patches. In the Carrer del Call a Roman tower can be visited inside a draper's shop; the vast pillars of a temple grace the Centre d'Excursionistes in the Carrer del Paradis; and Roman floors and foundations can be viewed underneath the palaces of the medieval count-kings and early-modern royal lieutenants. These abundant, exciting remains of a remote past could easily mislead the visitor into supposing for Roman Barcelona a grandeur it never really possessed.

Although the Roman colony fed well off its 'sea of oysters' and served 'rich men' with such civilised amenities as porticoed baths and a Forum with seven statues, it was always a 'small town' of up to 10 or 12 hectares, dwarfed by nearby Tarragona and Empùries. For Catalan historians, it used to be a point of honour to imagine antique greatness stretching back to the supposedly autochthonous forebears of modern Catalans. But, although the whole plain of Barcelona was well populated from Neolithic times, and coins prove the existence of a pre-Roman urban civilisation, no evidence of continuous settlement of the central site of historic Barcelona, on Mons Taber, has yet been found earlier than the 1C AD. Pre-Roman 'Barcino' (named on coins) may have been on the hill of Montjuïc which the Romans inherited as a ritual centre. Finds from there include an impressive aedile's (magistrate's) seat, set ceremonially in the midst of the remains of a stone enclosure.

For half a millennium after the end of Roman rule, Barcelona's history remains sparsely documented. Of the occupiers of those years—the Visigoths, the Moors, the Franks—only the first seem to have esteemed the city highly. According to the 6C Gothic historian Jordanes, pity for the inhabitants of Hispania, smarting under the blows of less Romanised barbarians, moved Athawulf to seize Barcelona 'with his best men', leaving those 'less adept in arms' to occupy the interior. This suggests that Barcelona was thought particularly desirable, or particularly defensible, or both. Perhaps, as it was Visigothic practice to make the army a charge on conquered territory, Barcelona drew the 'best men' because it commanded the richest land. Narrators of the next century of Gothic history continue to associate Barcelona with politically important events: Athawulf's assassination and Amalaric's rise and murder, followed, in 540, by the meeting of a synod. The modest growth of the Visigothic period can be detected in excavations under the Palau Reial. Between the 4C and 6C, the *intervallum* (space between palisades) between the Roman building line and the ramparts was filled with new constructions. At the same time, streets were narrowed by building extensions. A building of noble proportions appeared on part of the present palace site: the written sources with their catalogue of royal assassinations seem to confirm that Visigothic Barcelona was sporadically a courtly centre.

The city was still without long-range commerce and, for the Moors and Franks, seems to have been significant only as a frontier garrison or *ville-carrefour*. Barcelona's potential for greatness only began to be realised when she was conquered, late in the 9C, by a fledgling state of regional importance, with heartlands close by: its granary in the plain of Urgell, its defences in the mountains. The warrior paladins of protean Catalunya adopted Barcelona as their favourite place of residence; they endowed religious foundations, which stimulated urban growth; they kept—and sometimes spent—their treasure there; and, as their state developed, they concentrated in Barcelona such permanent institutions—chancery, court and counting-house—as they created.

The Counts of Barcelona Of the man acclaimed as the founder of the House of the Counts of Barcelona little trace survives in the modern city: only the visitor brave enough to enter the dark alley of the Carrer d'Amargos, under straggling balcony-plants and dangling laundry, will find the painted ceramic plaque proclaiming almost certainly wrongly—that this was the limit of the palace of Wilfred the Hairy (d. 898). But by the early 10C Barcelona was already, in a sense, the 'capital' of a sovereign principality, which would come to be known as the **principality of Catalunya**. In about 911, Count Wilfred II chose a house of religion outside the walls for his mausoleum. His neglected grave, marked by an inscription discovered among rubble, deserved better treatment: the sort of patronage he conferred turned the former hick-town into a medieval metropolis.

For the next 200 years, Barcelona's wealth continued to come from farming and war, her urban character from her courtly status. The first known boom happened in the late 10C. Most historians have assumed that this must have been the result of commercially-generated wealth; but it is at least as likely that the presence of the knights, the court and the growing colony of clergy were the sources of stimulation. The growth of the cathedral chapter is the first clue to general growth: there were six canonries in 974, 17 by 1005. The canons were growing in sophistication as well as numbers: retiring to houses of their own; acquiring a reputation for erudition; building up libraries worthy, in one instance, of attracting a reader as famous for his learning as the future pope, Gerbert of Aurillac. They were not the only people building, and the first new burghs began to grow up outside the walls. In 989 Barcelona was a target of sufficient prestige to attract a raid by al-Mansur, the wide-preying vizier of Cordova. The raid inspired traditional lamentations, with lists of buildings destroyed and victims martyred. But, except for Sant Pere de les Puelles (burned with all the nuns), real losses appear to have been slight. By encouraging re-building, al-Mansur may have stimulated the boom.

Moorish hegemony only briefly survived al-Mansur's death in 1002. The empire of Cordova, enfeebled by squabbles at the centre and eroded by usurpation at the edges, collapsed in the 1030s. Like much of the rest of Christian Spain, Barcelona enjoyed a bonanza on the proceeds of booty, tribute, ransom, payola and the wages of mercenaries. An illumination in Barcelona's *Liber Feudorum* shows Count Ramon Berenguer I counting out coins from a lapful of gold for the price of the counties of Carcassonne and Beziers. The sort of expansion his forebears could contemplate only by conquest, he could undertake by purchase. In Barcelona, by the 1070s, 95 per cent of transactions were made in gold. To judge from the pattern of the circulation of coinage, even the Valencia of El Cid had less Moorish gold to mint than Barcelona.

A Maritime Power Some of this money was invested in a maritime vocation, which for the next 500 years supplied the city's wealth and formed its character. In 1060, although Barcelona was already a 'great town', according to the fastidious al-Bakrij the Barcelonese were still applying to Moorish ports to hire their galleys. By 1080 the counts possessed a fleet of their own, though it may not have been based in Barcelona. Two charters of Count Ramon Berenguer III (1082–1131) mention what sounds like substantial seaborne trade. In 1104 he refers to dues paid on 'all goods that come in on any ship in all my honour'; in the following year Jews were granted a monopoly of the shipping home of ransomed Moorish slaves. That some at least of this trade was going through Barcelona is suggested by the terms of privileges Ramon Berenguer granted to Genoa and Pisa in 1116. Despite the deficiencies of her shoaly harbour, Barcelona was the point of departure of a fleet big enough to attempt the conquest of Mallorca—500 vessels strong, according to the poet who accompanied the expedition. International commerce continued to develop gradually and in 1160 Benjamin of Tudela reported vessels of 'Pisa, Genoa, Sicily, Greece, Alexandria and Asia' off the beach of Barcelona.

Most of the buildings of this period were replaced in later eras of even greater prosperity: only Sant Pau del Camp, Santa Llúcia and the Capella d'en Marcús remain. For a flavour of what Catalunya was like in the 11C and 12C the visitor to Barcelona has to go to the Museu Nacional d'Art de Catalunya, where the collection of murals transferred from rural churches shows the high quality that Catalan money could buy, the search for Classical and Byzantine models by the artists: the wolf of Sant Joan de Boi bares predatory teeth as he stares around in a classical pose; the Seraphim of the apse with their feathery, eyed wings recall Byzantine mosaics. In the streets the explorer can match the map to documents that record the expansion of the 12C city. In 1160, Ramon Berenguer IV gave permission for a new public bath outside the city wall, where today the Carrer dels Banys Nous curls in the spectral shadow of lost ramparts: the profits of this enterprise were to be divided equally between the count and the Jewish investor.

Because of the winds and currents of the western Mediterranean, to become a great centre of long-range commerce, rivalling Genoa and Pisa, Barcelona needed to solve her problem of access to the Balearic islands. An illumination in Barcelona university library shows a leading merchant of the city, entertaining the count-king 'and the greater part of the nobles of Catalunya' in November or December 1228, and persuading them of the merits of conquering the islands. In his extraordinary *Book of Deeds*, Jaume I (1213–76) identified his own motives for launching the conquest as essentially chivalric: there was 'more honour' in conquering a single kingdom 'in the midst of the sea, where God has been pleased to put it' than three on dry land. To chivalric and crusading satisfactions, the nobles who took part added substantial territorial rewards. The Barcelonese, however, and the other merchant-communities of the Catalan and Provençal worlds, needed little inducement. Their participation is adequately explained by commercial motives: the anxiety to break the entrenched position of Moorish traders and their privileged partners from Genoa and Pisa.

A period of building Like so many imperial adventures, Barcelona's marked the apogee of her achievement and sowed the seeds of her decline. The marks of both are everywhere in the old city today, in the form of great churches begun in the 13C or 14C; in vast ritual and even industrial spaces that survive from that time, in building works slowed or halted in the 15C; and in decayed aristocratic streets of the late Middle Ages. The new walls of the reign of Jaume I enclosed an area ten times as big as those they replaced. The **cathedral** is the dominant monument of the 13C: the cloister portal, transitional in feel, with its carving of harpies and wild men dragging a half-naked, pudgy-faced warrior, contrasts with the elegant High Gothic of the interior. The early 14C, when the profits of empire were perhaps at their height, was a time of frenzied building. The Capella de Santa Agueda, in the Palau Reial, was built by Jaume II (d. 1327). The first stone of the church of El Pi was laid in 1322, that of Santa Maria del Mar, renowned for its glazing, in 1329. Not even the Black Death—which killed half of the city council and four of the five chief magistrates—could dent the city's confidence or interrupt the building boom.

Never was the city so spectacularly embellished as in the reign of Pere III (1336–87); he built the vaulted halls—more reminiscent of Italy than Spain— of the Saló del Cent in the town hall and the Saló de Tinell, with its martial wall-paintings, in the palace. He reconstructed the shipyards on a larger scale, where galleys from the Mediterranean war-effort had been built since the reign of Pere II (1276–85): the eight great bays can still be visited, on the frontier of the Raval and the port, housing the Maritime Museum. Of Pere's vastly extended walls, a fragment can still be seen near the foot of the Paral-lel. Private builders were also active. An example of late medieval 'urbanisation', the Carrer de Montcada, was driven through the old town in a broad, straight line and was promptly colonised by the aristocracy: the modern visitor, seeking the street for the sake of the Picasso Museum, runs the risk of being more impressed by the medieval architecture of the palaces in which it is housed.

The trading empire that paid for all this was essentially a western Mediterranean affair. The deeds of Catalans in the east—of mercenaries in Thrace and Athens, of merchants in Alexandria and Constantinople—are justly renowned. But they happened in the wings of the main theatre. The conquests of Mallorca (1229), Ibiza (1235), Sicily (1282), Sardinia (1324) and the series of treaties from 1271 that gave the count-kings something like a protectorate over a number of Maghribi ports: these were the landmarks of an empire of grain and gold, silver and salt.

Vicissitudes of a failing empire As the empire grew, its costs came to exceed its benefits. Mallorca proved a thankless daughter, sustaining a turbulent political relationship with the count-kings and using Catalan savoir-faire to set up shipping, arms and textile industries to rival Barcelona's own. The ambition to control the western Mediterranean sea-lanes caused wars with Genoa, which were wasteful because Barcelona never had sufficient resources to exploit her victories. Above all, Sardinia was Barcelona's 'Spanish ulcer'. The city seems largely to have borne the costs of conquest and defence by herself, with little support from the count-kings' other realms. Sardinian resistance lasted, intermittently, for a hundred years, and exhausted the over-committed conquerors. The empire that made a metropolis of Barcelona also sucked the rural life-blood of Catalunya: as the centre of gravity of the count-kings' realms moved towards the city, the balance of population shifted. By the eve of the Black Death, Barcelona contained twenty per cent of the population of Catalunya.

The countryside no longer had the means to keep the armies supplied with men or, perhaps, the city with food. In 1330 Barcelona experienced her first serious famine. Never was a city more obviously the victim of its own success. Barcelona evinced the classic symptoms of the monster: corpulence induced by over-feeding, tentacles stretched to uncontrollable lengths. Yet resolute civic spirit remained etched into the faces of the élite depicted, for instance, in Lluís Dalmau's *La Verge dels Consellers* (now in the Museu Nacional d'Art de Catalunya), painted in 1443 to project a magnificent image of the city magistracy in the intimate company of heavenly protectors.

Like the similar problem of the 'decline of Spain' in the 17C, that of the decline of Catalunya in the 15C has to be treated cautiously. Though it appears with hindsight that by the end of the century the centre of gravity of power in the Iberian peninsula had shifted forever towards Castile, Catalan experience seems too mottled with intermediate shades to justify the use of a sweeping term like 'decline' except in a relative sense. Especially in the late 15C, the neighbouring kingdoms of France and Castile were developing the means to mobilise unprecedented strength. Barcelona's 15C was at best an era of difficulties—progressive exhaustion and something close to ultimate prostration, redeemed only by the mental resilience of an indomitably optimistic ruling class. The city's predicament was compounded of social violence, demographic stagnation and economic constraint.

The uprisings of the 15th century In the century after 1360, not a decade went by without a recurrence of plague, sometimes accompanied by famine; from 1426, the yield of the customs and wool tax plummeted and did not recover until the next century. Hearth-counts suggest a modest increase of population until the cataclysmic civil war of the 1460s: that of 1500, showing 5765 hearths, probably represents the lowest tally since the Black Death. Protracted insecurity caused social tension. The first uncontrollable outburst was the pogrom of 1391, when the authorities were powerless to protect the Jews from massacre. In 1436 and 1437 popular agitations were effectively suppressed, but by the mid-century the failures of the city's natural rulers had attracted the sympathy of the city governor for a movement to democratise the municipal institutions or—at least—to enlarge the élite. The name of the incumbent party, the *Biga*, probably signifies a large beam used in the construction of a building; that of the challengers, the *Busca*, a piece of tinder or bunch of kindling. The names evoke the natures of the parties: the solidity of the establishment; the incendiary menace of its opponents.

Their conflict in the 1450s did not, in the long-run, unseat the traditional patriciate, but left it enfeebled and embittered against the Count-king Joan II (c 1458–79). His unpopularity grew as he tried to exploit Catalunya in what was felt to be a private attempt to meddle in Castile; he exacerbated his relations with his subjects by attempting to exclude his son and one of his daughters from succession to the throne; and by appealing to popular elements in the towns and to the peasants in the country he alienated the urban patricians and rural aristocrats alike. No part of Catalunya entered the rebellion of 1462 more wholeheartedly than Barcelona; none suffered so much from the long conflict and disastrous defeat. The insurgents' cause, never very promising, became desperate as each of the pretenders they put up to challenge the king died or dropped out in turn. The siege that finally ended resistance in 1473, followed by punitive measures, left Barcelona devastated. 'Today no trade at all is practised in this city', the consellers wrote. 'Not a bolt of cloth is seen. The workers are unemployed and the men of property are deprived of their rents and goods... And of all our troubles, the worst is this: for we see our city turning into something no bigger than a village on the road to Vic.'

The city in modern history

No visitor to Barcelona can fail to be struck by the relative dearth of great buildings of the Renaissance and Baroque. There are examples of grandeur: the Palau de la Generalitat hides its medieval core behind a Renaissance façade; and examples of charm: the Casa de l'Ardiaca in the Carrer de Santa Llúcia was decorated by a snobbish connoisseur, who was Archdeacon in the early 16C, as a setting for his antiquities and heraldic vanities. But most of what survives in the city from the 16C and 17C reflects private efforts, rather than public wealth, and a chequered history of slow recovery until 1640, when began the terrible era of war and unrest in which more was destroyed than built and which lasted until 1715.

Sixteenth-century Barcelona kept sufficiently closely in touch with fashion to earn praise from almost every visitor who left an account. With the unremitting confidence that has characterised them in every age, the city fathers poured money into the creation of an artificial port in an attempt to recover lost trade: the task would remain incomplete for 300 years, but was never abandoned. Private patrons like the Fiveller family could build splendid new palaces—theirs still stands in the Plaça de Sant Josep Oriol. The Carrer Ample (a straight gash across the view of the town by Philip II's official topographical artist, Anton van Wyngaerde) was opened as a gesture to Renaissance town planning, although it seems to have attracted few of the hoped-for noble residents. At the beginning of the century, a Florentine diplomat commended the city for beauty while lamenting the decline of its commerce; by the end, a measure of recovery can be detected in the terms of praise from Lope de Vega, the most renowned poet and playwright of the day: 'Just as a splendid façade enhances the value of a building, so great Barcelona stands at the entrance to Spain, like a portico framing a famous threshold.'

The significance of the Principality Barcelona's decline had coincided with the progressive loss of the courtly status which, before the rise of the city's commercial importance, had been the foundation of her fortune. After the extinction of the House of Barcelona in 1412, she had been ruled by a series of kings whose main interests were in Castile or Naples and who spent ever less time in Barcelona. For a while from 1479, and continuously from 1516, her counts were also kings of Castile and were mainly concerned with the affairs of that larger and fiscally more productive country. Yet the Barcelonese patriciate never lost their sense of ruling the capital of a sovereign principality—or even a quasi-polis, a city with the potential, at least, to be a city-state like Genoa or Venice. From inside the Spanish monarchy, Barcelona affected the status of a foreign power and her representatives swaggered like the emissaries of foreign potentates. When, for instance, a new viceroy of Catalunya was appointed in 1622, the congratulations of Barcelona were tendered by an ambassador, attended by 200 carriages, in what was rumoured to be the most magnificent procession ever seen in the streets of Madrid. Twenty years earlier, the city's representative at court was honoured with so much pomp that 'even the leading nobles of this court,' he reported, 'say that neither the *nuncio* of his Holiness himself, nor the envoy of the Emperor has ever been given such a reception ... and the Castilians are all amazed that an ambassador who is a vassal of the king should be received with so much honour.' A similar war of protocol was carried on inside the city, where the leading magistrates demanded the right to remain hatted in the king's presence and disputed seats of honour in church with the viceroy's wife.

This was more than play-acting. The 'privileges' (*privilegis*) and 'liberties' (*furs*) that meant so much to Barcelona were never systematically codified and are difficult to define. The Castilian models and the different nuances of Castilian thinking, which could not be translated into Catalan, tended to mislead policy-makers in Madrid into misapprehensions about the sort of traditions they had to deal with in relations with Barcelona. In Castile, civic liberties normally consisted in a charter granted by the king: they were a negotiable commodity, revered but not made sacred. Barcelona's identity, however, was bound up with the juridical status of the Principality of Catalunya as a distinct and equal partner in the Crown of

Aragon and separately, in the Spanish monarchy. She had liberties not granted by the prince as an act of grace, but governed by the *constitucions*—the statutes irrevocable except by the representative parliamentary assembly (the *corts*), which limited royal authority in the principality. The most important *constitucions* guaranteed fiscal exemptions. During the early 17C, when the Spanish monarchy was tottering from the inevitable effects of immoderate greatness, the growing need of money and manpower made the Catalans apprehensive of their immunities. At a time when to be 'a very good Catalan' was to be 'jealous of the country's privileges', the implicit constitutional conflict was bound to be noticed in Barcelona, where all the institutions of the statehood of Catalunya, inherited from the Middle Ages, were concentrated and where a large body of professional lawyers more or less lived by watching the *constitucions*. The costs of the Thirty Years War, and direct hostilities with France from 1635, brought the demands of the monarchy to a peak and the differences with the principality to a head. When Catalunya rose in revolt in 1640, Barcelona was the centre and sustainer of the rebellion.

Like the roughly contemporary rebellion in England, Catalunya's was reluctantly espoused. An anonymous but representative diarist in Barcelona blamed the king's bad counsel for 'the greatest sorrow this principality of Catalunya has suffered... May God and most holy Mary be pleased to return us to the grace of our father and lord, Philip.' But, like the English war, the Catalans' juggernaut rolled out of control. The élite of Barcelona had to share power with popular elements; Catalunya enfeoffed herself to Louis XIII of France, and 16 years of war devastated her land, depopulated her towns and despoiled her wealth. The **siege of Barcelona** in 1652 was one of the most desperate episodes of the war; it ended only when the citizens were 'reduced to eating grass'. Yet the king's commander, Don Juan José of Austria, was architect of a restoration that left the status quo unimpaired.

The War of the Spanish Succession The very success of this policy raised the danger of another round of similar conflict. In the second half of the century, Barcelona had little respite. Civic-minded optimists like Narcis Feliu de la Penya had hardly begun to revive the 'Catalan Phoenix' before the French wars of the 1680s and 1690s exposed her lands to more campaigns and the city to another siege. Barcelona had still not reconstructed her stake in stability when the War of the Spanish Succession plunged the entire monarchy into crisis. The Bourbon claimant, Philip V, arrived in 1702, scattering rewards and promises with a lavish hand; but he was suspected of an arbitrary disposition and absolutist plans—an impression confirmed by his failure to invite the chief magistrates to cover their heads in his presence. An insensitive viceroy, Francisco Fernández de Velasco, blundered into other infringements of the *constitucions*.

Despite the naturally peaceful inclinations of a mercantile élite, many of the leading members of Barcelonese society were willing to respond to Velasco's indelicate rule with violence. Many of them were the sons of fathers who had fought against Madrid in the 1640s and 1650s. They owed an obligation of honour to memories dating from those years. Psychologically inclined to fight, they were also ideologically equipped. It was an almost unquestioned assumption that Catalunya was a sovereign state with a right, in principle, to secede from a monarchy that was thought to be federative. Catalans' reading of their own history represented theirs as a contractual monarchy, in which the contract between people and prince, once broken, could be repudiated. By the end of the war, when Barcelona was fighting on alone, the inhabitants were inclined to blame the English for inveigling them into the fight with promises: the trick was performed, almost equally, with implicit threats. On 20 June 1705, when representatives of 'the most Illustrious, Famous and Renowned Principality of Catalunya' signed a treaty with England in Genoa, the guns of English ships could be heard in Catalan waters. Catalans came to see the episode as a typical instance of Albion's habit of acquiring by bribery or intimidation an ally whom she would later abandon. From their point of view, the sixth clause of the treaty was the most important, by which England guaranteed that 'now and in the future the Principality of Catalunya shall keep all the graces, privileges, laws and customs which severally and in common her people have enjoyed and do enjoy'.

In Barcelona, it seems, appetite for war *vient en mangeant* (goes with eating), and the Barcelonese, after their shy start, would become the most committed opponents of Philip V. They joined the allied cause in a calculating spirit but clung on when it was hopeless and all the other allies had withdrawn. They dared beyond hope, endured beyond reason and reaped the usual reward of that sort of heroism: defeat. The precedent of 1652 was fatally misleading: it encouraged the Barcelonese to believe that their liberties could be ventured again and that a hopeless resistance would save them. The final siege lasted from August 1713 until November 1714. The rule of visionary priests and populist fanatics throve on short rations. The 'repression' denounced by Catalan historians after Philip's victory was really rather mild: clerics and generals were its only individually targeted victims. But the *constitucions* were abolished; Barcelona was reduced to the rank of a provincial city in a unitary state and subjected to the indignity of a permanent garrison—an army of occupation overlooking the city from the new citadel. In this once grim symbol of oppression the present visitor can enjoy the delights of the zoo and the park.

The prosperous 18th century Defeat turned the energies of the citizens to a mood of *enrichissez-vous*. Though the city was prostrate and revival slow, the 18C as a whole was an era of forward-looking prosperity in which sustained economic growth began, thanks to new activities such as direct trade with the Americas and the beginnings of industrialisation based on American cotton. Some of the palaces and villas of the Bourbon collaborators can still be seen: the finest of them, the Palau Moja, houses the Generalitat bookshop in the Rambla; around the corner, the palace of the Comte de Fonallar enhances the grandeur of the expensive shops in the Carrer de Portaferrissa; a metro ride into the suburbs can be rewarded with the sight of the Can Carabass between the Carrer de Llobregós and the Carrer de Peris Mencheta. The ensemble that has most to say about Barcelona's 18C is the **Barceloneta district**, the first industrial suburb, begun in 1753 to house a population then beginning to burst out of a city diminished by the destructions and demolitions of the era of war. The tight, neat grid of its streets, the contrast with the traditional cityscape of Barcelona, make it one of the earliest surviving examples of 'enlightened' town planning in Europe. It was an attempt to put into reality the vision with which Pere Pau i Montaner decorated the ceiling of the Llotja—the headquarters of the merchant community—where crowned Prosperity clothes Nakedness, while

Industry and Commerce urge the scourging of Poverty and Disaster.

In the 'lost world' of pre-industrial Barcelona, manufacturing was a mainstay of the economy; but it was confined to the intimate society of the workshop and the master's home, regulated not by the impersonal 'market' but by the collective morals of powerful guilds. A visitor to the Museu d'Història de la Ciutat can see the sort of images that dominated the mental world of the guilds: their art reflected professional pride and devotion to the patron saints. The book of privileges of the shoemakers is decorated with a huge but elegant gilt-bronze slipper with tapering toe; the silversmiths' pattern books record, in meticulous detail, the masters' copyright to thousands of intricate designs. The market-gardeners' book of privileges, begun in 1453, is flanked by busts of their otherwise obscure patrons, Saints Abdó and Senen, and the gaudily painted coffer in which their relics were preserved. Everywhere the images of saints are reminders that the guilds doubled as devotional confraternities. Evidence of their prestige and wealth can be found around the city today: the shoemakers' palatial hall, for instance, in the Plaça de Sant Felip Neri, decorated with the lion of St Mark, who converted the first Christian shoemaker; the graves of the masters in the cathedral cloister, bearing the same emblem and the sumptuous premises of the silk weavers' guild in the Via Laietana.

The industrialisation of the city The beginnings of the conversion of Barcelona's economy to an industrial basis can be traced in the decline of the guilds. Eighteenth-century immigrants to Barcelona—most of them from communities in southern France, where languages similar to Catalan were spoken— 'preferred factory life to subjection under the oligarchy of guild-masters'. The bridle-makers had 108 members in 1729, 47 in 1808 and 27 in 1814; the decline occurred during a period when the population of the city trebled and was at its most acute at a time of war and high demand for harness. In the textile industry, which was directly affected by reorganisation into factories, the decline was even more spectacular. By 1825, the cloth-dressers had only three members left, who had neither studios nor workshops and were too old to work.

In the last quarter of the 18C a number of economic indicators seem to have accelerated. The rate of increase in wages between 1780 and 1797, for instance, was double that of Madrid. Manufacturers' profits, which had already doubled between 1720 and 1775, more than kept pace. When Joseph Townsend visited in 1786, he was particularly impressed by the Bernis factory, which employed 350 operatives making woollen cloth for America; the following year, Arthur Young could hear 'the noise of business' everywhere. The Napoleonic war and its aftermath interrupted progress. Amid post-war unemployment, after a terrible yellow fever epidemic in 1821, the city council of Barcelona lost its habitual optimism and publicly doubted whether the city would ever recover. In fact, though recovery was socially painful, it was complete: in 1836, the first steamship rolled off the slipway of Barceloneta; in 1848 Spain's **first railway** linked Barcelona to Mataró.

Working-class degradation and unrest accompanied economic change. The pattern of life in Barcelona in the mid-l9C was of fitful mass violence and intermittent plague. The horrific symptoms induced by the poisonous atmosphere of the mills were described by Jaume Salarich, a philanthropic physician, in 1850, and confirmed from personal experience by the literate worker, Ramon Simó. Ildefons Cerdà surveyed the working-class way of life in the 1850s and found that a diet of bread and potatoes, enhanced with the odd sardine, was all an average family could afford. Most observers blamed the cholera epidemic of 1854, which claimed nearly 6000 lives, on overcrowding in insanitary conditions. Disorder, incubated with **disease and riots**, were a regular feature of the long, hot summer. With increasing frequency these took on revolutionary proportions. The rioters' targets gradually changed: there had been disturbances in the 18C—in 1766, 1773 and 1789, when the targets had been grain speculators and the military service quotas. The insurgents of 1835 also attacked the steam-power factories, the representatives of the government and the houses of religion; the disturbances of 1840–42 culminated in a political revolution by a coalition of the disaffected whose only rallying-point was the call for protective tariffs: it was suppressed by a memorable bombardment. In 1854 a long series of strikes and Luddite outrages began, only to be deflected into political channels by the fall of a 'progressive' ministry in Madrid. The barricades of Barcelona had to be reconquered bloodily, in the worst scenes the city had witnessed since 1714. A conservative observer noted with satisfaction: 'The rebels were massacred as they were captured... The spectacle was magnificent.'

The authorities' conviction that the bourgeoisie would soon recover from this shock proved justified. The confidence of the burgeoning city was displayed in the competition, held in 1859, for a design for enlargement (*eixample*) of the city beyond the walls. The public exhibition attracted huge crowds. Antoni Rovira i Trias submitted a popular plan, sympathetically integrating the old town; Ildefons Cerdà's proposal looked more rigidly 'modern'. He made only minimal use of nodal piazze and surrounded the old town with a grid of boulevards and public gardens. Political controversy, caused by the Madrid government's determination to impose Cerdà's solution, delayed work while the case grew desperately urgent: in 1863, for instance, the rate of growth of the population of Barcelona was 27.42 per cent—three times the national Spanish average. The **Spanish revolution** of 1868, which swept the Bourbons from the throne, temporarily abated the differences between Barcelona and Madrid and in 1869 the laying out of the **Eixample** proceeded along the lines of the Cerdà plan. Despite the delayed start and the slow initial growth, Barcelona's boom in the late 19C was so rapid that the expectations of the plan were exceeded. In-filling robbed it of its best feature, the expansive parks and garden squares. The sudden grafting of a criss-cross of 19C branches onto the trunk of an ancient town created the view from Montjuïc—the image that defines the city's character, despite the subsequent (even greater) growth to this day.

The rise of Catalanism The era of the Eixample was accompanied by relative social peace. The political energies of the Barcelonese were deflected into Catalanism—the movement for the recognition of Catalunya's distinctive institutions and the conservation of her language and cultural heritage. Bourgeois life moved out of the cafés onto pavement terraces and out of the house onto the gas-lit streets that dazzled Hans Christian Andersen when he visited in 1862. The industrialisation of Barcelona swallowed up huge amounts of capital, scattered among too many under-funded firms. The 'gambler's synagogue'—the unofficial Bourse, where 'everybody played and won'— opened in 1858. Slack money and new money created a market for art and architecture that impressed Barcelona with the showy, experimental look that has characterised Barcelonese style ever since.

The symbol of this era of self-assurance was the **'Universal' Exhibition of 1888**. The idea originated with a Galician entrepreneur who had seen the Paris and Vienna expositions; the opportunistic Rius i Taulet took it up when he became mayor in 1885. When he summoned the world to Barcelona on 13 June 1887, everything had still to be extemporised. Not only did the citizens build on time the exhibition ground that sarcasts had deemed impossible, but also planted the Plaça de Colon with palms and drove the Rambla de Catalunya and the Paral·lel through suburbs where they had previously been thwarted. The Hotel Internacional was built in only 60 days and its five floors proved unequal to the demand. The exhibition opened ten days late, drew exhibitors from 20 countries and attracted nearly 2¼ million visitors. The young Puig i Cadafalch was inspired with a vision of a 'great Barcelona' that animated his later work as an architect and politician. The idea of Barcelona as a model of 'go-ahead hard work' entered popular fiction.

Rapid growth rarely happens painlessly. In 1860, Barcelona had less than 200,000 inhabitants. By 1897, when the city limits were redrawn to incorporate the towns of the immediate hinterland, the official figure was 383,908. By 1930, the conurbation contained well over a million people. Social conflict could hardly be avoided. When the rail link was completed, young French anarchists took the Barcelona Express and were frightened by the prostitutes on arrival; this was the character of the revolutionary anarchism that became the most potent force of Barcelona's political underworld: naïf and puritanical. In the 1890s, Barcelona was the 'city of bombs'; explosions detonated in the opera house, at a Corpus Christi procession and on a royal visit. In the early 1900s, while terrorism collapsed, the workers' movement was infused by anarchism: the **general strike of 1901–02** was Bakuninite in inspiration. The **Setmana Tràgica** (Tragic Week) of 1909, when a strangely self-disciplined mob systematically destroyed 70 buildings of religious orders while sparing other targets, was attributed to anarcho-syndicalism; the movement's spokesman, Francesc Ferrer, was executed for presumed complicity after a trial that shocked the world.

Some of these tensions were reflected in the work of the Modernista artists who gathered in the Quatre Gats café, (today expensively restored in the Carrer de Montsió). The most representative figure was **Ramon Casas**, whose father had made a fortune in the Indies and who, on his mother's side, was the heir to a textiles mill. His inheritance thus combined two typical sources of the wealth of Barcelona in his day. His best works were problematical genre-scenes, but his most memorable canvases, perhaps, were those in which the social commentary was most overt. *Barcelona 1902* is an extraordinarily dynamic composition, in which a mounted civil guard is about to trample a sprawling, dramatically fore-shortened worker in the foreground, while the crowd is cleared by the cavalry from a space which seems to grow before the onlooker's eyes. Casas' most famous work was *Garrote Vil* of 1893, recording the public execution of a 19-year-old who had cut the throats of his victim and accomplice for a gold watch. Some aspects seem ironic: the clergy are a corpulent contingent, under an enormous crucifix; the penitents' black conical caps prod towards the centre of the canvas like pitchfork prongs. The public loved the engaging horror more than they feared the social import; horror-paintings in Barcelona were always popular and frequently connected with the traditions of public scourging—common until the early 19C—and public execution, which continued until 1908.

The early 20th century From 1901 to the First World War, anarchism and anarcho-syndicalism, though conspicuous, did not command genuine mass allegiance. The political loyalty of the working class lay with the Andalusian demagogue, Alejandro Lerroux and his patriotic 'Republican Fraternities'. He was not above recourse to violence: in election campaigns he was escorted by intimidatingly grown-up 'schoolboys' and, in anticipation of rigged defeat, carried a pistol with two shots 'one for the returning officer and the other for myself'. Still, under his influence, bombing raids were succeeded by 'republican picnics' and a workers' press 'which sold like blessed bread' supplanted terrorism as a means of publicity.

The industrialist Gual Villalbí remembered the **First World War** as a time when it 'rained orders' in the factories and the streets were strewn with 'flowers of evil'—spies, deserters and refugees. It was a frivolous time—the Teatre Principal was enlarged with an American Bar and a casino—and a time of suspense, lived under the threat of an end to the boom. Cotton exports, which doubled during the war, plunged to little more than half their pre-war levels in the early 1920s. Wartime full employment, followed by post-war lay-offs, created ideal conditions for unions to breed. The anarchist C.N.T. had 15,000 members in Catalunya in 1915, and 73,860 in July 1918, 54,572 of them in the Barcelona branches. Conflictive strikes were at their height in 1919 and 1920, when 7.76 per cent and 8.4 per cent respectively of the working year were lost: the figure had never been more than 2 per cent before 1916.

Workers' issues, however, lost political prominence under the 'iron surgery' of General Primo de Rivera's dictatorship from 1923 to 1930, when the most urgent cause seemed that of Catalanism, ham-fistedly repressed. The unions generally held aloof from Catalanist politics, partly because many of their members were immigrants from other parts of Spain and partly because, as the workers' leader, Salvador Seguí, said: 'A problem of independence or autonomy doesn't exist in Catalunya because we, the workers from there, don't want any such problem and don't feel it!' Under a detested centralist regime, however, Catalanism was an issue that could unite all classes and during the transition to a republic in 1931–32 Catalan autonomy was cheered in the Plaça de Sant Jaume by workers and bourgeois, natives and immigrants alike.

Civil War That alliance was broken by the experience of the civil war. The anarchist revolution of 1936 made an enemy of anyone who wore a tie in the street. When Franco's troops marched in with the slogan 'Spain has arrived', a collaborationist bourgeoisie came out of the woodwork. Catalan culture went deeper underground than under Primo de Rivera. The monumental allegorical statue, *La Republica*, by Josep Viladomat (1899–1989) found an ignominious refuge among the packing-cases of the municipal storehouse. The big threat to Barcelona's identity under Franco came, however, not from repression but from economic growth. Three-quarters of a million immigrants, mostly from southern Spain, came to the city between 1950 and 1970. The case of the immigrant from Badajoz who in 1950 sold his house for 7000 pesetas to buy a cave in Sabadell for 3000, shows the scale of the opportunities that attracted them and of the degradation they underwent. It was easy for Francoism to 'buy' these people with job security and modest economic rewards, hard for Catalanism to win them with the blandishments of an alien tongue, an inhospitable culture and a mandarin creed. Yet when the exiled Catalan leader, Josep Tarradellas, appeared after Franco's death on the balcony of the Generalitat in the Plaça de Sant Jaume, he found the immigrants willing to vote for autonomy. His cry, '*Ja sóc aquí!*' ('Here I am at last!') contrasted with the 'Spain has arrived' of the Francoists. A survey found that many *soi-disant* Andalusians also considered themselves Catalans: but the main reason for favouring autonomy was rejection of Francoism, not Catalanist sentiment. The dictatorship's other legacy was a proletariat with drawn fangs. Communists took the lead in organising a clandestine union movement from 1963: by the 1970s it was strong enough to attempt political strikes. But, as it grew in numbers, it became ideologically diluted. The union elections of 1975 put apolitical leaders in control of most branches. 'Responsible' unionism has been dominant ever since.

The new constitution The Spanish constitution of 1978, which restored to Barcelona the autonomous government of the four provinces of the historic Principality of Catalunya, boosted demand and morale alike. Creative tension between the left-wing city government and right-wing Catalan government stimulated the flow of official funds into urban renewal and cultural programmes. Spanish membership of the EEC, with the prospect of the development of a genuine regional economy around the western Mediterranean seaboard, enhanced Barcelonese confidence in the future by promising to free the city from the traditional economic role of maker and purveyor of goods to a protected Spanish market. Then the choice of Barcelona as the site of the 1992 Olympiad brought a bonanza to the construction industry and embourgeoisement to neglected inner-city areas. Still the Barcelonese remain dissatisfied. The policy of 'coffee all round'—granting comparable levels of autonomy to all Spain's historic communities—has wounded Catalunya's sense of her own uniqueness. Barcelona's upstart rival, Madrid, whose rule the Barcelonese endured while convinced of their economic and artistic superiority, has caught up in terms of achievement as well as presumption and Barcelonese anxiety to cultivate a non-Spanish sense of identity—as Catalans, 'Mediterraneans' or Europeans—seems as strong as ever. To remain the 'head and hearth' of Catalunya, Barcelona has to Catalanise the huge numbers of Spanish-speaking immigrant workers who have filled the outlying districts in the last half-century. Civic patronage in recent years has taken on an increasingly desperate air, detectable in the bizarre postmodernist 'sculpture park' that stands outside Sants railway station or the oppressive cement monoliths that adorn the Plaça de la Palmera.

Thus Barcelona's achievements continue to incubate in frustration and, as they confront the challenges and opportunities of the 21st century, the Barcelonese merit as much as ever the characterisation of a Castilian humanist, 500 years ago: 'I now behold her citizens, triumphant despite their dearth of natural resources, and her people possessed of all world prosperity, thanks to their efforts alone.'

A chronology of the medieval rulers of Barcelona

Wilfred the Hairy	878–897
Wilfredo Borrell	897–911
Sunyer	897–947
Borrell II	947–992
Ramon Borrell	992–1017
Berenguer Ramon I	1017–1035
Ramon Berenguer I the Elder	1035–1076
Ramon Berenguer II	1076–1082
Berenguer Ramon II	1076–1096
Ramon Berenguer III the Great	1096–1131
Ramon Berenguer IV	1131–1162
Alfons I of Barcelona	1162–1196
Pere I the Catholic	1196–1213
Jaume I the Conqueror	1213–1276
Pere II the Great	1276–1285
Alfons II	1285–1291
Jaume II the Just	1291–1327
Alfons Ill	1327–1336
Pere III the Ceremonious	1336–1387
Joan I	1387–1396
Martín I the Humane	1396–1410
Ferran I of Trastámara	1412–1416
Alfonso IV the Magnanimous	1416–1458
Joan II	1458–1478
Ferran II the Catholic	1479–1516

Further reading

History and general background

Robert Hughes' *Barcelona* (Harvill, 2001) gives an excellent and comprehensive insight into the city's history and character.

Colm Tóibín's *Homage to Barcelona* (Picador, 2002) provides a more light-weight portrait of the city, but is highly readable.

A general work on Barcelona which combines beautiful literary evocation with penetrating analysis and insight is Manuel Vázquez Montalbán's *Barcelonas* (Editorial Empúries, 1990).

Felipe Fernández-Armesto's *Barcelona: a Thousand Years of the City's Past* (London, 1991, currently out of print) is stimulating, scholarly and delightfully perverse. A thematic rather than a straightforwardly chronological account, this broadly-based work skilfully interweaves political, social and cultural history.

George Orwell's *Homage to Catalonia* (Penguin Books, 2000) describes the author's experiences in Barcelona during the Civil War.

Art and architecture

Few other cities are so well served as Barcelona for architectural guides and surveys.

Numerous architectural and other guides to Barcelona are published by the Barcelona firm of Gustavo Gili. These include Raquel Lacuesta's and Antoni González's *Modernista Architecture in Catalunya* (Barcelona, 1995), a detailed but practically-sized guide to the numerous Art Nouveau buildings in Barcelona and its surroundings.

By the same authors is *Barcelona Architecture Guide 1929–2000*, the latest edition of a regularly-updated series that details the most significant buildings from the post-Modernista period to the present day.

Contemporary architecture is also dealt with in *Barcelona: A Guide to Recent Architecture* (Ellipsis London Ltd, 2001), by Suzanna Strum.

Barcelona Interiors (Loft Publications, 2001) features lavish photographs of houses, apartments and restaurants. *Barcelona Art Nouveau* (Rizzoli Publications, 1999), by Lluis Permanyer et al., contains excellent photographs of Modernista buildings.

The celebration in 2002 of 150 years since Gaudí's birth has given rise to many new books about the great architect. One of the most illuminating is Gijs van Hensbergen's *Gaudí: A Biography* (Harper Collins, 2001).

Among the general works on Catalan art and architecture, the best introduction in English to the early medieval paintings is Charles L. Kuhn's *Romanesque Mural Painting of Catalonia* (Cambridge, 1930).

John Richardson's masterly *A Life of Picasso, vol. 1: 1881–1906* (Jonathan Cape, 1991), the first of his four-volume biography of the artist, offers a much-needed reassessment of Picasso's earliest years, as well as a wealth of new information on the Barcelona of Picasso's youth. *Volume II 1907–1917* was published in 1997, followed by *Volume III* in 2001.

Theatre in Madrid and Barcelona 1892–1936 (University of Wales Press, 2002) provides a much-needed history of theatre design and development.

Food and wine

Colman Andrews' *Catalan Cuisine* (Grub Street, 1997) is the bible of Catalan food in English.

Also good for recipes is *The Catalan Cookery Book* (Prospect Books, 1998) by Irving Davies.

Desmond Begg's *Traveller's Wine Guide to Spain* (Aurum Press, 1998) has a good section on Catalunya.

More detailed information is provided in *The Wine Routes of Penedès and Catalonia* (International Wine Academy, 2000), by Alan Young.

Gourmet travellers should also try and find *Catalonia: Traditions, Places, Wine and Food* (Herbert Press, 1990) by Jan Read and Maite Manjon.

Literature in translation

Manuel Vázquez Montalbán's entertaining novels featuring the gourmet detective Pepe Carvalho give an accurate portrait of modern Barcelona. Several are published by Serpent's Tail, including *Southern Seas*, *The Angst-Ridden Executive*, *An Olympic Death* and *Off Side*.

Another Catalan writer of today whose works have dealt extensively with Barcelona is the novelist Eduardo Mendoza. His exceptionally lively and enjoyable novel *City of Marvels* (Harvill, 1989) provides a fantastical but solidly researched portrait of Barcelona between the World Exhibition of 1888 and the International Exhibition of 1929 (much of the research for this book was later re-used for his excellent work of non-fiction *Barcelona Modernista* (Barcelona, 1989), which he wrote with his sister Cristina). Some of Mendoza's other novels, including *The Year of The Flood* and *A Light Comedy* are also published by Harvill.

Juan Goytisolo's Juan the Landless trilogy (*Marks of Identity*, *Count Julian* and *Juan the Landless*) are published in English by Serpent's Tail. Although somewhat hard going, the books include fascinating cameos of Barcelona life. Goytisolo's autobiographical *Forbidden Territory* is published by Quartet Books.

Colm Tóibín's *The South* (Picador, 1992) is partly set in Barcelona with vivid evocations of the city's streets and hidden corners.

Mercè Rodoreda's *The Time of the Doves* (Graywolf Press, 1984) rates among the most popular novels set in Barcelona, with a wonderful portrayal of the Gràcia district. A book of her short stories, *My Cristina and Other Stories* (Graywolf Press, 1984), is also available in translation.

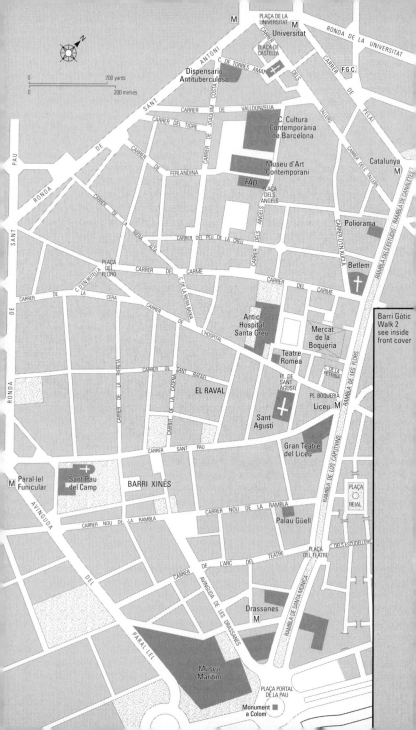

M PLAÇA DE LA
UNIVERSITAT M

RONDA DE LA UNIVERSITAT

Universitat

PLAÇA DE
CASTELLA

C. DE TORRES AMAT

CARRER ANTONI SANT

F.G.C.

CARRER DELS TALLERS

CARRER DE PELAI

Dispensario
Antituberculoso

CARRER DE JOAQUIM COSTA

CARRER DE VALLDONZELLA

CARRER DE

CARRER DEL TIGRE

C. Cultura
Contemporània
de Barcelona

CARRER DE FERLANDINA

Museu d'Art
Contemporani

Catalunya

M

FAD

PLAÇA
DELS
ANGELS

CARRER DE LA RIERA ALTA

CARRER DEL PEU DE LA CREU

CARRER DELS ANGELS

CARRER DELS ESTUDIS · RAMBLA DE CANALETES

Poliorama

CARRER D'EN XUCLÀ

RONDA SANT PAU

PLAÇA
DEL
PEDRÓ

CARRER DEL CARME

CARRER DE LA RIERA BAIXA

CARRER DEL CARME

Betlem

C. D'EN BOTELLA

CARRER DE LA CERA

CARRER DE L'HOSPITAL

Antic
Hospital
Santa Creu

Mercat
de la
Boqueria

CARRER DE LES FLORS

Barri Gòtic
Walk 2
see inside
front cover

CARRER DE LA RIERETA

CARRER DE SANT RAFAEL

Teatre
Romea

C. DE LA
PETXINA

CARRER DE LA CADENA

EL RAVAL

PL. DE
SANT
AGUSTI

PL. BOQUERIA

Liceu M

RONDA

Sant
Agusti

RAMBLA DE LES FLORS

M Paral·lel
Funicular

Sant Pau
del Camp

BARRI XINÈS

CARRER SANT PAU

Gran Teatre
del Liceu

RAMBLA DE LOS CAPUTXINS

CARRER NOU DE LA RAMBLA

PLAÇA
REIAL

AVINGUDA DEL

CARRER NOU DE LA RAMBLA

Palau Güell

C. DELS ESCUDELLERS

CARRER DE L'ARC DEL TEATRE

PLAÇA
DEL
TEATRE

PARAL·LEL

AVINGUDA DE LES DRASSANES

Drassanes

M

RAMBLA DE SANTA MÒNICA

Museu
Marítim

PLAÇA PORTAL
DE LA PAU

Monument
a Colom

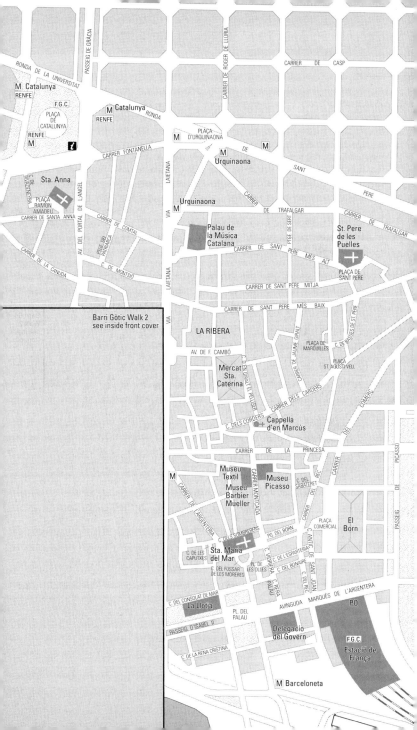

M Catalunya
RENFE

F.G.C.
PLAÇA
DE
CATALUNYA

RENFE
M

RONDA DE LA UNIVERSITAT

PASSEIG DE GRACIA

M Catalunya
RENFE

RONDA

CARRER DE ROGER DE LLURIA

CARRER DE CASP

CARRER FONTANELLA

PLAÇA
D'URQUINAONA
M

M
Urquinaona

M

DE

SANT

PERE

Sta. Anna
PLAÇA
RAMON
AMADEU

CARRER DE SANTA ANNA

CARRER DE LA CANUDA

AV. DEL PORTAL DE L'ANGEL

PGE. DEL PATRIARCA

C. DE MONTSIÓ

C. DE COMTAL

LAIETANA

M
Urquinaona

VIA

DE TRAFALGAR

CARRER

PIGE DE SER

CARRER DE SANT PERE MÉS ALT

Palau de
la Música
Catalana

St. Pere
de les
Puelles

CARRER DE TRAFALGAR

CARRER DE SANT PERE MITJÀ

PLAÇA DE
SANT PERE

CARRER DE SANT PERE MÉS BAIX

LA RIBERA

VIA

AV. DE F. CAMBÓ

LAIETANA

CARRER DE JAUME GIRALT

PLAÇA DE
MARQUILLES

C. DE BASSES DE ST. PERE

Mercat
Sta.
Caterina

EL DRET EL PELISSER

PLAÇA
ST. AGUSTÍ VELL

CARRER DELS CARDERS

C. DELS CORDERS

Cappella
d'en Marcús

CARRER

DE

LA

PRINCESA

CARRER

COMERÇ

M

CARRER DE L'ARGENTERIA

Museu
Textil
Museu
Barbier
Mueller

CARRER MONTCADA

Museu
Picasso

C. DEL
SABATERET

CARRER DE REC

PICASSO

PASSEIG DE

C. DELS SOMBRERERS

PG. DEL BORN

PLAÇA
COMERCIAL

El
Born

C. DE LES
CAPUTXES

Sta. Maria
del Mar

C. DEL FOSSAR
DE LES MORERES

C. VIDRERIA

C. DE L'ESPARTERIA

PL. DE
LES OLLES

C. DEL BONAIRE

C. REFA
PALAU

C. REFA
RIC

C. DE SANT JOAN

C. DEL CONSOLAT DE MAR

La Llotja

PL. DEL
PALAU

AVINGUDA MARQUÈS DE L'ARGENTERA

PASSEIG D'ISABEL II

Delegació
del Govern

PO

C. DE LA REINA CRISTINA

F.G.C.
Estació de
França

M Barceloneta

Barri Gòtic Walk 2
see inside front cover

THE GUIDE

1 • La Rambla

▸ Start from Plaça de Catalunya. See map on pp 84–85.

Soon after arriving in Barcelona, most visitors find themselves drawn into La Rambla, the main artery of the old town, and one of the most famous thoroughfares in the world. Though compressed between a picturesque variety of buildings, its essential character is derived from its central pedestrian area, which is shaded by rows of plane trees, and crowded by kiosks, stalls, buskers and a fascinating cross-section of the city's motley population.

Crowds are sucked into the upper end from the vast Plaça de Catalunya (p 174), and those who survive the whole course, about 1.5km, eventually emerge by the sea near the entrance to the old port. So much unfolds in the course of La Rambla's journey towards the sea that writers such as Manuel Vázquez Montalbán have been tempted to see in this thoroughfare 'a metaphor of life', the sea being the oblivion where all destinies are united.

The origins of La Rambla are in a seasonal torrent that was used as a road in the dry season. The actual name is from the Arabic word *raml*, which means sand. The torrent, converted after 1366 into a covered sewer, lay some distance to the west of the walls that contained the Roman settlement of Barcino. However, with the extension of Barcelona during the reign of the 13C ruler Jaume I, the torrent was lined with walls on its far side, and came to represent the western boundary of the city. These walls were to remain intact right up to the beginning of the 18C, despite the construction in the 14C of a new line of walls to the west, embracing the district known as the Raval.

Beginning with the building in 1553 of a Jesuit monastery, a large number of monastic institutions grew up on the western side of La Rambla, directly facing the 13C walls. Following the first stage in the demolition of these walls in 1704, La Rambla was slowly transformed into a proper street, acquiring palaces and a central row of trees. By 1781, when the earliest street lamps were put up, the thoroughfare had become a popular promenade, complete with seats for hire.

The fame of La Rambla spread widely and by 1845 the French writer Théophile Gautier was describing the place as one of the city's main attractions. George Sand, accompanied by Chopin, came here in 1838, and—as with so many later visitors to the city—was fascinated by the life on La Rambla. 'Isolated from the rest of Spain by banditry and civil war,' she wrote, 'the brilliant youth (of the city) stroll under the sun along La Rambla, a long avenue lined by trees and buildings, just like our boulevards. The women, beautiful, graceful and coquettish, are concerned with the arrangement of their mantilla shawls, and by the play of their fans; the men, occupied with their cigars, are smiling, speaking, casting oblique looks at the ladies, talking about Italian operas, and giving the impression of being largely uninterested in anything that happens outside the city.'

In terms of its future look and character, the most significant development in the 19C resulted from the disentailment of Spain's monastic institutions in 1836. Along La Rambla, this led to the creation of squares, tall residential blocks and such important buildings as the Teatre Liceu, Spain's most impressive opera house. Another development occurred with the popularisation of cast iron after 1860 and the subsequent construction in the middle of the promenade of flower stalls, urinals, newspaper kiosks and other such structures that today form such a major component of La Rambla.

Various other Catalan cities such as Girona attempted to emulate La Rambla, though no other city in Spain, and particularly not Madrid, can boast a promenade with such a great variety of diversions, from exotic birds to fortune-tellers and puppeteers. Writers have devoted a great deal of space to these diversions. Foreigners love to point out the wealth of books and foreign newspapers available at the kiosks, in the belief that this is indicative of the traditional cosmopolitanism and cultural sophistication of the Catalans. Visitors tend also to assume that the human spectacle to be observed here is a virtual 24-hour affair, though in fact life on La Rambla is relatively quiet after about one o'clock in the morning, a time when the streets of other Spanish cities are experiencing their greatest nocturnal animation.

La Rambla de Canaletes

La Rambla is often referred to as Las Ramblas and indeed is broken down unofficially into five distinct sections, starting with the La Rambla de Canaletes at the Plaça de Catalunya end, where our walk begins. We are going to walk down the Ramblas looking at the points of interest on the right-hand side, then walk back up concentrating on the other side.

The ancient spring of Les Canaletes survives in the form of a cast-iron fountain of the turn of the century (just to your right as you start walking down). 'To drink the waters of Canaletes' means to live in Barcelona and it is said that anyone who drinks from the fountain will return to the city.

The surrounding late 19C and early 20C buildings include at no. 129 an elegantly stuccoed structure of c 1850, housing on its ground floor the *Musical Emporium*, which has a fine glass portal of 1917, engraved with a Modernista design.

Rather more sophisticated is *Boadas*, on the corner of La Rambla with the Carrer dels Tallers. Founded in 1933 by Miguel Boadas, who grew up in Cuba with his Catalan parents, this is one of the city's better known cocktail bars. Now run by his daughter, Maria Dolores, it is a popular haunt of people returning from the Teatre Liceu, and is renowned in particular for its daquiris and dry martinis. Picasso, Hemingway and Miró were all regulars in their time.

La Rambla dels Ocells

Continuing down, you enter the **Rambla dels Estudis**, a vestige of the days when a university building once blocked off the top end of the street. The university, founded by Martí I in 1402, was closed down by Philip V at the beginning of the 18C, following a history of anti-Castilian activity, including supporting the Revolt of the Reapers in 1647.

In the absence of the university a more appropriate name for this stretch of La Rambla is the popular one of '**La Rambla dels Ocells**' ('of the birds'), a reference both to the numerous sparrows that haunt the plane trees, and to the permanent **bird market** here. This market, with its rows of cages containing a wide variety of exotic birds, fascinated the young Picasso who, newly arrived in the city, was regularly brought here by his father.

Most of the Rambla dels Estudis is now taken over by early 20C buildings, many of them housing hotels, and the inevitable bars and cafés. At no. 115 is the **Poliorama building**, designed by Josep Domènech i Estapà in 1883, with sculptures by Manuel Fuxà. The Poliorama cinema opened on the ground floor in 1906 and later became a theatre. During the Civil War, George Orwell was holed up on the roof here, which he recounts in *Homage to Catalonia*:

> *I used to sit on the roof marvelling at the folly of it all. From the little windows in the observatory you could see for miles around—vista after vista of tall slender buildings, glass domes and fantastic curly roofs with brilliant green and copper tiles; over to eastward the glittering pale blue sea... And the whole huge town of a million people was locked in a sort of violent inertia, a nightmare of noise without movement... Nothing was happening except the streaming of bullets from barricades and sandbagged windows. Not a vehicle was stirring in the streets; here and there along the Ramblas the trams stood motionless where their drivers had jumped out of them when the fighting started... Looking out from the observatory, I could grasp that the Ramblas, which is one of the principal streets of the town, formed a dividing line. To the right of the Ramblas the working-class quarters were solidly Anarchist; to the left a confused fight was going on among the tortuous by-streets.*

The building was remodelled in 1985 by the Bohigas, Martorell y Mackay architectural practice to become the home of the Josep Maria Flotats theatre company; it also houses the Academia de Ciencias y Artes.

The right side of the Rambla dels Estudis used to be occupied by a Jesuit College and Convent, but these institutions were destroyed shortly after the expulsion of the Jesuits from Spain in 1767. All that remains of this vast complex is the **former Església de Betlem** (Church of Bethlehem), at the corner of La Rambla and the Carrer del Carme.

Dating back to 1553, the church was burnt down in 1671 and rebuilt after 1680 to a plan attributed to Josep Juli. The construction work, supervised at first by the Jesuit priests Tort and Diego de Lacarre, was completed by 1732. The building, which combines a simple plan with exuberant decorative touches, is of interest today chiefly for its well-preserved exterior. Its long side façade, overlooking La Rambla, has a heavy, austere character, relieved only by two elaborate portals sculpted by Francesc Santacruz with representations of John the Baptist and the child Jesus. The six domes, covered with green tiles, must be the ones Orwell is describing above.

The magnificent **main façade**, on the Carrer del Carme, was completed in 1690 and is crowned by an undulating pediment adorned with finials. Its richly modelled frontispiece comprises a main portal flanked both by Solomonic columns (a characteristic feature of Catalan Baroque) and by dynamic statues of Sant Ignacio and Sant Francisco de Borja, attributed to Andreu Salà. Above the portal is a relief of the Nativity by Francesc Santacruz, who was also responsible for the statue of Sant Francis Xavier in the elaborate corner niche on the side of the façade bordering with the Carrer del Xuclà. The dark, single-aisled interior was once the most sumptuously decorated of all of Barcelona's churches, with marble marquetry and a wealth of gilded and polychrome fittings, including lattice-work screens in the gallery, which marked the area of the church reserved for the aristocracy. None of this remains, as the building was gutted during the Civil War.

At no. 24 Carrer del Carme is the **Lencería 'El Indio'**, a draper's shop founded in 1870 with a delightful Modernista exterior executed by the decorators Vilaró i Vals in 1922. Inside, the high-ceilinged shop is flanked by long counters, with a black marble floor. Originally, it sold clothes and was frequented by the great and good of Barcelona society, who came along with their seamstresses. It even published its own magazine each season, an enterprise thwarted by the Civil War.

La Rambla de les Flors

The most beautiful stretch of La Rambla starts below the Carrer del Carme and Carrer de la Portaferrissa, a stretch known sometimes as 'de Sant Josep' but more usually as 'de les Flors' ('of the flowers'). Markets have been held here since the 13C, but with the construction of the market of Sant Josep in 1836, most of the stalls were cleared from the street, leaving only the young women who sold flowers.

The market is in operation every day and the **flower stalls**, which share the street today with kiosks selling books and newspapers, provide La Rambla with a constant colourful spectacle which, to many of the city's visitors and inhabitants, has represented the essence of Barcelona's beauty. 'A week without seeing the Rambla of the Flowers,' sighed the writer Eugenio d'Ors, prevented once by a strike from coming here. The attraction of the area lay as much with the women who sold the flowers as with the flowers themselves, as is suggested by the light-hearted lyrics of a popular Barcelona song of the 1940s: 'How lovely is Barcelona/ pearl of the Mediterranean/ how lovely it is to stroll/ and watch the women/ on the Rambla de las Flores.'

The painter Ramon Casas was one of the many to have fallen in love with one of the street's legendary 'flower girls', the girl in question becoming first his favourite model and later his wife. The English travel writer H.V. Morton—who claimed that a summer evening spent on La Rambla was one of the highpoints of a tour he made of Spain in 1954—was also delighted by these women, and was prompted to reflect on how much London had been impoverished when it had cleared its own 11 flower girls from Piccadilly Circus at the end of the 19C.

At no. 99 is the grandest palace on the whole Rambla, the **Palau de la Virreina**, now a venue for exhibitions of contemporary art. *Open Tue–Sat 11.00–20.30, Sun 11.00–15.00; fee.* At the entrance there is an excellent bookshop and cultural information centre.

The palace was built in 1772–78 as a retirement home for Manuel Amat i Junyet, who had made a fortune while Viceroy of Peru, where he had achieved notoriety for an affair with an actress called Perricholi. He died a few years after moving into the palace, for which reason the place is known after his young widow, who had originally been betrothed to his nephew. The story goes that the former Viceroy, seeing this woman dressed up for her intended wedding to the nephew, said to her that he would have married her himself if he had not been so old. She is said to have replied that the walls and cloisters of the convent where she had been staying were older still and very much to her taste.

Manuel Amat i Junyet had a great knowledge of architecture, and it seems likely that he had a hand in the design of his palace, which was carried out under the supervision of the architect Josep Ausich i Mir and the sculptor Carles Grau. The powerful main façade, set back slightly from the street, comprises a rusticated basement supporting an upper level articulated by giant pilasters, the whole crowned by a parapet with finials. Lacking the classical French elegance of the nearby Palau Moja (see below), it has a characteristically Spanish top-heaviness, with elaborate detailing set against otherwise austere expanses of heavy masonry.

Behind the entrance vestibule you come to a patio impressively decorated with Corinthian columns and military trophies. A double-ramp staircase, with exquisite ironwork railings, leads to a series of rooms containing fragments of the original decoration, including painted Rococo allegories in the former dining room.

La Boqueria

Immediately below the palace was the convent of Sant Josep, which was demolished in 1836. This led to the creation by Francesc Daniel Molina of an arcaded market square inspired by the work of John Nash. The arcades remain but have been almost entirely hidden by an exuberant ironwork structure of c 1840 covering Barcelona's most famous and colourful market, La Boqueria.

The name comes from '*boq*', meaning goat butcher's, a reference to what was originally sold on the site. Just outside the walls, at a key entry point to the city, there has been a market of some sort here for at least 700 years. A stroll around La Boqueria provides a shocking reminder of what shopping and eating is really about. From the showy displays of exotic fruit at the entrance to the spectacular seafood section and the astounding Petrás mushroom stall at the back, this is a visual feast of the highest order.

A good way to appreciate the bustling life of this place is to have a drink and a tapa at the bar of the tiny kiosk inside known as *Pinotxo*, which is on the right as you enter (stall 66). A favourite place of the designer Mariscal, this bar is also mentioned in Raul Núñez's comic novel *Sinatra* (1984; translated into English as *The Lonely Hearts Club*), which is set around La Rambla: 'It was just a little bar with three or four stools, set into one wall of the market. It was enjoyable sitting there, drinking something and letting luck take care of the rest.'

Continuing down La Rambla, you come to the *Escribà patisserie*, known as the *Antiga Casa Figueres* (at no. 83 on the corner of the Carrer de Petxina). This Modernista shop of jewel-like beauty dates back to 1820 but owes its present appearance to a remodelling carried out in 1902 to a design by Antoni Ros i Güell, who worked mainly as a landscape painter and stage designer. He assembled a remarkably varied team of artists and craftsmen to carry out the decoration of the shop, which features metalwork by Vila i Domènech, mosaics by Merogliano, paintings by Boix, sculptures by Lambert Escaler and Bernadors and stained-glass windows by Granell Rigalt, who gave the interior a magical, multi-coloured glow. Dominating the exterior is a corner frieze by Escaler representing an allegory of a wheat harvest.

Further down the street, at no. 77, is the **former Genové pharmacy**, a fantastical Gothic structure designed by Enric Sagnier in 1911. The entrance arch features a keystone portraying the attributes of Asclepius, the Greek god of healing. It now houses municipal offices.

Just along from here is the main focal point of La Rambla, the **Plaça de la Boqueria**, which marks the site of the medieval gate of Santa Eulàlia. In medieval times, this gate was a favourite meeting-place for countryfolk and other visitors to the city, who attracted in their wake jugglers and professional gamesters. The bodies of executed criminals were also hung here as a warning to those among the city's newcomers who were contemplating crime themselves. Today, the numerous visitors who gather here are captivated by the pavement decoration by Joan Miró, who was born in the nearby Passatge del Crèdit (p 121).

The Teatre del Liceu

The **Rambla de los Caputxins** begins immediately below the Plaça de la Boqueria. The first building to your right, despite its deceptively modest façade, is one of the most important of Barcelona's institutions, the Teatre del Liceu. *Times of guided tours vary according to season.* ☎ *93 485 9900 for information. See p 49 for ticket information.*

In 1844, the Barcelona operatic society with the tortuous name of *Liceo Filarmónico Dramático Barcelonés de Su Majestad la Reina Doña Isabel II* applied for permission to build a theatre on the site of a Trinitarian convent that had been dissolved in 1835. Superstitious misgivings about building a place of entertainment on the site of a holy institution were voiced at the time, and were to be vindicated in the light of the building's subsequent troubled history. Work on the theatre was nonetheless begun the following year. The architect chosen, Miquel Garriga i Roca, based his designs on La Scala in Milan, which it almost equalled in size, becoming the second largest opera house in Europe, with a seating capacity of 4000. The building, inaugurated in 1847, was almost entirely destroyed by fire in 1861, but was rebuilt in the space of one year by Garriga's former collaborator, Oriol Mestres. There were to be several remodellings in later years, most notably by Pere Falqués i Urpí.

After 1882, the place became one of the main centres in Europe for the production of Wagner's operas, as the citizens of Barcelona were particularly enthusiastic about the works of this composer. The most notorious event in the theatre's history, however, occurred in 1893, and superseded in dramatic power anything that has been officially put on here. In September of that year, the anarchist Paulino Pallas, on the point of being shot for his failed assassination attempt on the Captain General of Catalunya, Martínez Campos, swore that his death would soon be avenged by his anarchist colleagues. That revenge came one month later, on 7 October, and was directed at the Teatre del Liceu, a symbol of bourgeois decadence. Halfway through the second act of Rossini's *William Tell*, the anarchist Santiago Salvador threw two bombs from the fifth-floor balcony of the theatre. The number 13 proved for once to be unlucky, for the bombs landed on the 13th row of the stalls, killing 20 people outright and wounding at least 50 others. Only one of the bombs had actually gone off, the other prevented from doing so by landing in the lap of a woman killed by the first one. It is now one of the more macabre exhibits in Barcelona's Museu d'Història de la Ciutat.

Salvador was not caught until several weeks later, by which time most anarchists had distanced themselves from him, refusing to provide this obvious psychopath with any more bombs. When in prison awaiting execution, he told the journalist Tomás Caballé y Clos how 'magnificent' the whole occasion had been in the theatre, and how much satisfaction he had received from witnessing the panic and confusion among the bourgeoisie. He also boasted of his enormous strength, for it had been no mean feat to throw a bomb as far as the 13th row. On 21 November, 1893, a large crowd came to see him being garrotted in the courtyard of the old prison on the Carrer d'Amalia. Excited by this audience, he shouted 'Long live anarchism!', and began singing an anarchist song while the metal around his neck tightened and silenced his voice for ever.

The Teatre del Liceu, with its associations with wealth and the establishment, has continued to provoke the wrath of left-wing fanatics. In 1977, shortly after the death of Franco, a group of militants stood outside the doors of the theatre to taunt and jeer at the well-dressed members of the public. As Vázquez Montalbán pointed out, these same people were unaware that one of the leading trade unionists of this time, José Luis López Bulla, was himself a fanatic of the opera, knowing several works off by heart, and believing, like Trotsky, that opera is the heritage not just of the middle classes but of humanity in general.

The theatre was completely overhauled by Ignasi de Solà-Morales as part of the 1992 celebrations. Tragedy struck just two years later, however, in 1994, when a spark from a blowtorch caused a fire that destroyed everything except the façade. Solà-Morales devised a plan to rebuild it, and the theatre reopened in October 1999. Although many of the original Neo-Baroque features have been recreated, the ceiling decoration was entrusted to the leading conceptual artist Perejaume. In 2001, the members of the private club known as the Cercle del Liceu reluctantly agreed to allow women to join their society for the first time.

Another survival of old Barcelona is the **Hotel Oriente**, which is situated just below the Liceu, at nos 45–47. The hotel, with its elegant pale yellow façade, and ground-floor Ionic arcade, was originally opened in 1845 on the site of the 17C Franciscan College of St Bonaventura. The present building was designed in 1882 by Eduard Fontseré and Juli Marial. One of those who stayed here during its heyday was Hans Christian Andersen. The public spaces of the hotel, with their gilded columns and grand 19C character, include obvious remodellings of the cloister and refectory of Pere Serra i Bosch's Franciscan College of 1652. Once a month, the hotel is the meeting place for the Narigut's Club, open to anyone with a prominent nose and regularly attended by local celebrities.

Adjoining the hotel, at no. 43, is the former theological College of Sant Angelo, dating back to 1593 and rebuilt in 1786–90. Occupied until 1985 by the Guardia Civil, the building retains its elegantly simple cloister and single-aisled Neo-classical chapel.

Palau Güell

Back on La Rambla, immediately to your right is the sombre and grimy Carrer Nou de la Rambla, which leads into the Raval, a part of Barcelona traditionally famed for drugs and prostitutes but now undergoing a far-reaching regeneration process. This district is explored in Walk 4, but it is worth making a short detour up the street now to see, at nos 3–5, the superlative Palau Güell, one of the most important of Gaudí's earlier works. *Guided tours only Mon–Sat 10.15–13.00 and 16.15–19.00. Fee. Free with Ruta del Modernisme voucher.*

Built in 1885–89 as the extension of the Rambla town house of the industrialist Eusebi Güell, the Palau Güell coincided in its construction with the intense and exciting years of architectural activity leading up to the Barcelona World Fair of 1888. Eusebi Güell, whom Gaudí had first met in 1878, supposedly said that he liked the building less and less the more it went up, to which the architect replied that he himself liked it more and more. If this is true, then Güell was almost certainly being flippant, for he was to remain the most faithful of Gaudí's patrons.

The family fortune had been initiated by Eusebi's father, Joan Güell i Ferrer, who had spent his early years in Cuba. With the vast amount of money that he had made there, Joan was later able to establish his own business in Barcelona. Between 1836 and 1860, he managed to revolutionise the local textile and metallurgical industries. He later developed an interest in agriculture and was able to take advantage of the phylloxera epidemic in France to build up Catalan viticulture. The finances and social position of the family were further improved when Eusebi married the daughter of another self-made man (the future Marquis of Comillas), and acquired for himself the titles of count, viscount and baron.

Eusebi, a major voice in Catalan politics, was also someone who exploited an interest in culture to further his aristocratic image. His palace on the Carrer Nou de la Rambla, which was joined by a gallery to the main family home on La Rambla itself, was intended not only as a guest annexe, but also as a place for social gatherings, private concerts and other cultural functions.

The Palau Güell, neglected even during Eusebi's lifetime in favour of the family's estate on the outskirts of Barcelona (p 208), was later donated to the city by Eusebi's descendants. During and after the Civil War, the building served as a police barracks and prison and numerous political prisoners and delinquents were detained and tortured in its basement. The place later housed the Centre of Theatre Studies, with a museum devoted to the history of the Catalan theatre. At the same time sinister, mysterious and exotic, the palace provided the perfect setting for one of the key scenes in Antonioni's atmospheric thriller, *The Passenger* (1977). In this scene, the main character, played by Jack Nicholson, first sets eyes on Marie Schneider, with whom he subsequently embarks on an affair that begins in glamour but ends sordidly and enigmatically.

Façade of Palau Güell

The palace was restored between 1989 and 1992 by Antoni González Moreno-Navarro and Pablo Carbó Berthold. Occupying a dark and cramped site, the white stone façade looks distinctly forbidding. The use of colour—such an important feature of Gaudí's later work—was limited to the exuberant ceramic decoration on the twisted chimneys, which are only just visible from street level. The most exciting features of the exterior are the two large parabolic arches that form the entrance. Gaudí loved this geometrical form, which clearly illustrated his expressive and highly personal interpretation of the Gothic style. Also of interest is the portal's elaborate and rather aggressive ironwork, in which the initials of Eusebi Güell can clearly be made out, as can a medieval-inspired heraldic motif that reinforces the fortress-like nature of the façade.

From the moment you enter the darkened vestibule, you find yourself in a world where a suggestive use of light and space has taken over from rational, symmetrical planning, and the experience is in itself a highly theatrical one. A central ramp winds down to the bare brick basement. Originally used for horses and carriages, for a short time after the Civil War this became a much-feared place of detention. A wall remained standing until quite recently that was covered all over with graffiti scrawled by detainees of that period.

The interconnected main-floor rooms, where the public life of the palace took place, have dark wooden surfaces, Moorish-style screens, medieval-inspired coffering and exquisitely wrought ironwork highlighted in gilding. The central feature is a towering salon, surrounded by screened galleries, which extends up three floors to a dome pierced by holes as in a Moorish bath. The rooms above the main floor were used as bedrooms, while at the top of the house are the unornamented servants' quarters. It is well worth taking the guided tour just for the chance to walk around the roof terrace to see the tiled chimneys and views. The chimneys, which had lost their ceramic decoration, were restored by the architects and a team of specialist artists.

The *Hotel Gaudí* opposite the palace stands on the site of the notorious night club known as the *Eden Concert*.

> Specialising in French-style cabaret, in the early years of the 20C it acquired a reputation no more salubrious than that of the famous 19C *café-cantante* that it replaced, the Café de la Alegría. The Catalan writer Josep Maria de Sagarra recalled in his memoirs that the *Eden Concert* was the only place that you were banned from mentioning in polite society. If you wished to refer to someone of certain standing who had gone down in the world you need only to have said that 'he had been seen in the Eden' or was 'frequenting the Eden'. One of its habitués was Picasso who, on returning from Paris to Barcelona in January 1902, hired a studio next door (at no. 10), which he shared with the sculptor Angel Fernández de Soto and the painter Ramón Rocarol. The seedy low-life of the surroundings was a great influence on the development of his Blue Period.

Those interested in the bohemian Barcelona of old might like to visit the tiny *Bar London*, at Carrer Nou de la Rambla 34 (open from 19.00), which has an unmodernised interior of 1910. Favoured by young musicians during the Franco era, this place now attracts aging hippies and intellectuals, who mingle with a younger, largely foreign crowd.

Returning to the Rambla, next you come to the **Plaça del Teatre**, named after the **Teatre Principal**, which stands on the site of a wooden theatre dating back to 1597. The present classical structure is mid-19C, but has been remodelled several times owing to fires. After being used as a storeroom for the Liceu for a few years, it was revamped in 1997 and is now used to stage contemporary and classical plays. Below the theatre is the arch marking the entrance to the dark and narrow Carrer del Arc del Teatre.

Rambla de Santa Mònica

The stretch of La Rambla below the Plaça del Teatre is known as the Rambla de Santa Mònica.

This was once the smartest section of the whole Rambla, and the first to be dignified with the name of '*paseo*' or 'promenade'. In the 18C, aristocrats used to parade here in their carriages, and this was also one of the most exclusive residential districts in the city. After a long period of extreme seediness, this stretch has been cleaned up to provide relatively safe access to the waterfront.

At no. 4 of Carrer de Santa Mònica, which leads off to the right, is the infamous *Pastís* (open from 19.30), a tiny, dark and musty survival of the 1940s, when French-style bars were still the fashion. Its evocative decoration of old bottles and pictures continues to acquire further layers of dust and grease, while the ever more creaking sounds of Edith Piaf, Maurice Chevalier and other French classics are still played on its gramophone.

The oldest surviving structure on the whole thoroughfare is the former **Convent of Santa Mònica**, of which only the severe cloister and church tower remain. Dating back to 1626, and founded by the Discalced Augustinians, this convent was taken over in the late 19C by the 'Circ Barcelonès', a theatre that hosted Spain's first Workers' Congress in 1870. The structure was restored and revamped by Helio Piñón and Albert Viaplana as a contemporary art venue, the Centre d'Art Santa Mònica, which stages major international exhibitions as well as showcasing cutting-edge Catalan artists. *Open Mon–Sat 11.00–14.00 and 17.00–20.00, Sun & public holidays 11.00–15.00. Free.*

The Rambla widens into the Plaça Portal de la Pau, dominated by the monument to Columbus (p 149) at the point where it meets the sea. The Maritime Museum on the right is discussed on p 150.

After a break to gaze at the sea and have a drink, we start walking back up the other side of the Rambla. The building immediately to the right at **no. 2** used to be the Banco de Barcelona. The sculptures, by Venanci Vallmitjana, represent Commerce and Industry. Two hundred years ago, however, it was a foundry where cannons were made. The building is now used by the army as offices.

A little further up is a stately marble building erected in 1867 as the headquarters of the Compañía General de Crédito al Comercio (accessed via the Passatge de la Banca). It now houses the **Museu de Cera** or Waxwork Museum. *Open Oct–June Mon–Fri 10.00–13.30, 16.00–19.30, Sat, Sun and public holidays 11.00–14.00, 16.30–20.30; July–Sept daily 10.00–22.00. Fee. Bus Turístic discount.* Certainly the best in Spain, this is well worth a visit for the architecture alone. It retains much of its original character, complete with a striking grand staircase and a patio glazed with stained glass.

The idea of a waxworks museum in Barcelona was initially that of Nicomedes Méndez, an executioner who had been responsible for the garrotting of a number of famous anarchists and murderers, including Salvador Santiago of Liceu fame. Méndez, noting the enthusiastic audiences who had attended each of his executions, had originally planned to create a pavilion filled with wax representations of Barcelona's most notorious criminals. In the end he did not get permission to do this, and the museum that was eventually created concentrated on foreign criminals, its directors preferring to show the people of Barcelona in a positive light.

The present museum includes a combination of world-famous Spanish and Catalan personalities, including Salvador Dalí. Among the tableaux are the infirmary of a bull-ring, a typical Catalan rural interior, a gypsy cave and a room in the Liceu, the latter enhanced by the recorded voices of the famous opera stars who have sung there.

Of particular interest to children are the science fiction tableaux called 'Space Capsule' and 'War of the Galaxies', the inevitable Chamber of Horrors (with spiders' webs, bats and monsters), and the so-called 'Fiction Journey', which is advertised as a journey by 'underwater craft' to a 'Submarine tunnel' and 'Ship-wrecked Galleon'. The *Bosc de les Fades* café is done out like a grotto and invariably delights adults as well as small children.

At this point on the Rambla there is a drinking water fountain which is one of twelve presented to the city by the British philanthropist Richard Wallace in 1888. A number of 18C houses survive along this stretch. By far the most impressive is the **Palau March** at no. 8, which was built in 1775–80 by Joan Soler i Faneca for the March family from Reus, and has an elegantly simple façade, with rustication in shallow relief and a frontispiece articulated by giant Ionic pilasters. Acquired in 1892 by the Bank of Spain, the building belongs now to the Generalitat and houses the Conselleria de Cultura. The salmon-pink house next door was one of the first to be put up following the initial stage in the demolition of the medieval defensive walls. Now the headquarters of the UGT (General Workers' Union), the building previously housed the Catalan Trade and Industry Centre. In 1934 it was bombed by the army when the Catalan government tried to make the region an independent republic.

No. 16 was the family home of the photographer Antonio Napoleón Fernández, who also had his studios here and installed Barcelona's first cinema in 1896. It was later converted into pelota courts and the facilities were modernised in 1992 for the Olympic Games, when pelota was one of three show sports.

The **Universidad Pompeu Fabra**, at nos 30–32, opened in the 1990s following the restoration of the Hotel Falcón, which dated back to 1775 and was used by the POUM (*Partido Obrero de Unificación Marxista*). In *Homage to Catalonia*, George Orwell describes it as 'a sort of boarding-house maintained by the POUM and used chiefly by militiamen on leave'. The Universidad Pompeu Fabra was created by the Catalan Parliament in 1990 with the aim of providing a new role for disused historic buildings in the city centre.

Arriving back at the Plaça del Teatre, on the right is a delightful monument of 1900 commemorating a man regarded as 'the founder of the Catalan theatre', **Frederic Soler** (1839–95), who was popularly known as Serafí Pitarra. Designed by the architect Pere Falqués i Urpí, and sculpted by Agustí Querol Subirats, this work in marble and dark stone represents a wonderful compromise between a Modernista and Neo-Baroque style. Pitarra is shown seated nonchalantly on top of a huge volute that rises up like a wave on the point of breaking.

The **Carrer dels Escudellers** leads off the Plaça del Teatre. At **no. 8** is a magnificent Modernista restaurant, the **Grill Room**, which was founded in 1902 by Flaminio Mezzalama and designed by Ricard de Campmany. In the same year, they also created the celebrated **Café Torino**, one of the most fashionable Barcelona cafés at the beginning of the 20C. The original Café Torino, which was situated on the Passeig de Gràcia, no longer exists but has been recreated at no. 59. A good idea of its decoration can be had from the Grill Room, however, which has remained virtually unchanged over the years. The exterior comprises a flamboyant frontage in wood and stained glass, while the interior has a painted panelled ceiling, metalwork lamps and a dazzling series of ceramic wall tiles. **La Fonda**, next door at no. 10, is one of a tremendously-successful chain of restaurants that serve good food in elegant surroundings at astoundingly cheap prices.

La Rambla de los Caputxins and Plaça Reial

Back on the Rambla, the Hotel les Quatre Nacions was built in 1849 and for many years was the city's most important hotel. Three arches mark the entrance to the **Plaça Reial**, a large traffic-free square built on the site of the Capuchin monastery from which this stretch of La Rambla takes its name. Designed in 1848 by Francesc Daniel Molina, its architecture was inspired by the formal public squares of Napoleonic France. The arcading that surrounds the whole square supports an elegant stucco frontage articulated by a giant order of pilasters, the tall attic level above being crowned by a white balustrade. Tall palm trees, placed at regular intervals in the stone pavement, give the square a certain look of Nice, and the French character of the place is reinforced by the central **Fountain of the Three Graces**, which is a standard late 19C model provided by the Parisian firm of Duresne. Unmistakably Catalan, however, are the splendid Modernista **lampposts** on either side of the fountain. Designed by **Gaudí** in 1878, they are this architect's first known works.

Benches and numerous café tables make the square a popular place both day and night. A **stamp market** is held on Sundays under the arcades. From the late 1960s onwards, the square came to attract hippies and other Bohemians, and it was here, during the period of the avant-garde comic magazine *Rollo Enmascarado* (the early 1970s), that the designer Mariscal and the painter Miquel Barceló lived with the artist Nazareño, who was the creative force behind the magazine. Tramps, alcoholics and drug-addicts, rollicking on the benches in the square's centre, followed suit. Despite restoration and the constant presence of tourists, the square is still a place to keep a tight grip on your bag.

Traditionally, the Plaça Reial had been the haunt of **bootblacks**, who until comparatively recently had a group of stands under the square's northern arcade. Bootblacks had been working here from the 1840s onwards, the earliest and most famous one being Fructuòs Canonge, one of the more popular Barcelona personalities during the reign of Isabel II. As well as cleaning shoes, Canonge was an organiser of carnival festivities and a magician with such a reputation for supernatural powers that he came to be known as the 'Spanish Merlin'.

The Taxidermista

The Plaça Reial no longer has its Canonge, or the so-called Museu Pedagógico de Ciencias Naturales, a bizarre shop and taxidermist establishment situated at no. 8, on the corner with Carrer del Vidre, which exuded a strong magical aura.

Now a lively bar and restaurant which has kept the name, the *Taxidermista*, as well as the sign above the window, this unusual 'Natural History Museum' was founded in 1889 by Lluís i Pujol, and moved to this site in 1926. The painter Joan Miró regularly visited the shop during the many years that he lived at the nearby Passatge del Crèdit (p 121) but, being a very shy person, never asked for anything, and merely contented himself with staring at the exotic showcases. Miró also had a great love for the Plaça Reial itself, and claimed to have been influenced in his work by the shapes created both by the water splashing from the *Fountain of the Three Graces* and by the branches of the palm trees.

Shortly after the Civil War, Salvador Dalí went into the shop to demand 200,000 ants, and over the years asked to have a lion, a tiger and even a large rhinoceros stuffed. Dalí insisted that the rhinoceros should be carried out on wheels into the Plaça Reial so that he could have himself photographed seated on top of it. On another occasion, Dalí asked the proprietors to make him a walking stick with a handle incorporating two live snakes, but as this proved impossible, he had to make do with two stuffed snakes instead. Another client was Ava Gardner, who came here once with the bullfighter Mario Cabré and requested the owners to stuff the head of a bull that he had dedicated to her in a fight.

Leave the Plaça Reial via the **Carrer del Vidre**, the alley leading off the square by the Taxidermista. Here, at no. 1, there is a fascinating survival from the mid-19C, a herbalist known officially as the *Antigua Herboristería Ballart*. The tiny shopfront comprises panes of glass set in a Neo-classical framework but with Gothic detailing. Presiding over the interior is a marble fountain crowned by a bust of the naturalist Linnaeus, whose features have frequently been mistaken for those of Charles III, thus giving rise to the shop's popular name of 'L'Herbolario del Rei'.

The alley leads to Carrer de Ferran (p 121), where at no. 7 is *Wolf's*, a shop with an exuberant Modernista façade which is a fine survivor of the street's early 20C heyday. Turn left back to the Rambla.

At no. 74 is the *Café de l'Òpera*, which was founded in 1929 and is one of the few places from this period where the decoration has remained unchanged. The constantly packed interior is panelled, mirrored, gilded and decorated with cheerful linear designs in a pseudo-classical style. Built initially to serve the Liceu, and still experiencing a great rush of clients during the intervals at that theatre, the place later developed a slightly Bohemian character and came to be filled in the 1970s with many of the more disreputable-looking types from the nearby Barri Xinès. Today, the café is particularly popular with foreigners, with the consequent increase in prices and lowering of standards.

The *Xancó* shirt shop, at no. 80, right by the Plaça de la Boqueria, was founded in 1820. On the ground in front of the shop is a plaque, designed by Enric Satué, which is awarded to traditional shops and is inscribed with the symbols of cutlers, shirtmakers, fishmongers and cobblers. Around the corner is the Boqueria Fountain, installed in 1828. Another landmark of the present-day square is the recently restored *Casa Bruno Quadros*, at no. 82. Now occupied by a bank, this former shop was decorated in 1883–85 in a Neo-oriental style, complete with a famous Chinese dragon that supports both a lantern and an umbrella.

Further along the street, the white shopping complex was designed by the Martorell, Bohigas, Mackay practice in 1992. The first floor of the next building houses the **Museu de l'Eròtica**, which charts the development of erotica over the centuries by means of paintings, photographs and sculptures. *Open daily 10.00–24.00. Fee. Bus Turistic discount.*

La Rambla de les Flors

Heading back up the Rambla de les Flors, **nos 110** and **116** feature 19C sgraffito decorations, which have recently been restored. The elegant Palau Moja next door at no. 118 is a classical French-inspired structure built in 1774–89 to the designs of Josep Mas i d'Ordal.

> The exterior had Neo-classical painted decorations by Josep Flaugier and Francesc Pla, but these were destroyed in a series of mysterious fires. At the end of the 19C, the building came into the hands of the Marquis of Comillas, whose guests here included Alfonso XII and the poet Jacint Verdaguer. While under the Marquis's patronage, Verdaguer wrote his celebrated epic, *Atlàntida*, which shows how Columbus' discovery of America restored the cosmic order upset by the disappearance of Atlantis.

The building has now been extensively restored and adapted for use by the Cultural Department of the Generalitat de Catalunya, but has retained inside a number of Pla's original fresco decorations. These include the splendid cycle of allegories and mythological scenes that cover the walls and ceiling of the two-storeyed Grand Salon. However, only the bookshop on the ground floor is open to the public. It is a good hunting ground for material about Catalunya, with some books in English.

The main entrance to the building is on the attractive pedestrian street of the Carrer de la Portaferrissa, which leads to the Cathedral (p 106), and features a number of tall and dignified 18C and early 19C palaces. Today, the shops here are given over mainly to clothes, but at the beginning of the 20C included one of the most influential of Barcelona's private art galleries. Known as the Dalmau Gallery, it was run by Josep Dalmau, whom Miró once described as 'a sort of genial fool who managed to exploit artists and look after them at the same time'.

A favourite meeting-place for artists and critics, the gallery introduced Barcelona to some of the leading figures of the French and foreign avant-garde. Of particular importance was an exhibition of Cubist art, held here between 20 April and 10 May in 1912.

Further on La Rambla, the *Café Moka* (at no. 126), though radically modernised, is the same establishment mentioned by George Orwell in *Homage to Catalonia* as the scene of a shoot-out involving the various rival groups comprising the Republican forces. These included the anarchists, the communists, POUM (*Partido Obrero de Unificación Marxista*) and the guards of the Generalitat. Next door, now the Hotel Rivoli, was the POUM headquarters, and a plaque on the façade commemorates the organisation's secretary general, Andreu Nin, who was last seen there before being tortured to death in 1937.

Turn right down Carrer de la Canuda. At **no. 6** is the palace built in 1796 for Josep Francesc Ferrer de Llupià, baron of Sabassona.

> This austere Neo-classical building, which has retained inside several of its ceiling paintings by the leading late-18C painter Francesc Pla ('el Vigatà'), was extended and remodelled in 1907 after becoming the seat of the important cultural institution known as the Ateneu Barcelonès. Founded in 1836 as the 'Ateneu Català', this institution played a central role in the history of the Catalan revival, acquiring special notoriety after an inaugural speech given provocatively in Catalan by Àngel Guimerà in 1895. The painter Antoni Tàpies, in his autobiography, *Memoria Personal* (1977), recalls how as a young boy he saw little of his father, who spent much of his time attending meetings and discussions at the Ateneu. His family home at the time was at 39 Carrer de la Canuda, where Tàpies was born on 13 December, 1923.

From here, either return to Plaça de Catalunya or start exploring the Barri Gòtic, which is discussed in the next walk.

2 • The Barri Gòtic

▶ Start at Plaça de l'Àngel. See map on inside front cover.

The Barri Gòtic or 'Gothic Quarter'—a term coined only in 1927—refers only to the area within the boundary of the Roman city, which is a small part of the extensive surviving medieval quarter.

> Like the Iberian settlement that preceded it, Roman *Barcino* grew up on the gentle elevation known as Mons Taber. Its highest point was marked by the Temple of Augustus, a few columns of which have survived behind the medieval Cathedral.
>
> Up to the time of Jaume I (1213–76), Barcelona did not extend beyond the Roman city, an oval-shaped area bordered by the present Carrer Banys Nous and Carrer d'Avinyó, and the surviving stretch of walls extending—with long interruptions—between the Plaça Nova and the Carrer Correu Vell. This has always been the administrative heart of Barcelona, and in the Middle Ages also became very much of a showpiece, its streets lined with elegant palaces that reflected the great wealth which poured into the city from the 13C to 14C.

Wandering around what was formerly known as the Barri de la Catedral or de la Seu, you sometimes have the feeling of being in some medieval mock-up rather than a real city. It seems almost too well preserved, with every corner of this dark but tidy maze of streets prettified by noble and picturesque masonry.

An appropriate and convenient place for beginning a tour of the Barri Gòtic is the **Plaça de l'Àngel**, which stands on the site of one of the gates of the Roman city, a short distance away from the principal remains of Roman Barcelona.

The site, probably lapped by the sea in ancient times, was, at least as far back as the 10C, the scene of one of Barcelona's liveliest markets, which specialised in cereal products after the 12C. Known at one time as the Plaça del Blat or 'Wheat Square', the place acquired its present name after one of the various legends connected with Barcelona's patron saint, Santa Eulàlia.

In 878 the remains of the saint were discovered in the old church of Santa Maria del Mar and were subsequently transferred in a solemn procession from the church to the Cathedral. When they reached this gate, however, they became so heavy that no one was able to carry them any further. Finally, an angel appeared, pointing an accusing finger at one of the Cathedral's canons, who had to confess that he had removed one of the saint's toes. The toe was put back in its rightful position and the procession was able to continue. To commemorate this event, the statue of an angel was erected above the gate, and in 1616 this was replaced by a bronze figure surmounting an obelisk. The obelisk was pulled down by the revolutionary town council of 1823, but a copy of the statue survives in a niche on the building at nos 2–3 (the original is in the Museu d'Història de la Ciutat).

The city walls

The construction after 1908 of the Via Laietana (p 129), which cut a great swathe through Barcelona's old quarter, radically changed the character of the Plaça de l'Àngel, turning it into what is now a noisy junction. However, two long and impressive stretches of Barcelona's defensive walls have survived on either side of the square, running parallel with the busy Via Laietana. The stretch below the square towards the sea is on the Carrer del Sots-Tinent Navarro and above the square the wall rises above a narrow group of gardens stretching all the way to the Plaça Nova in front of the Cathedral.

By far the most impressive view of the walls is from the Plaça de Ramon Berenguer, a verdant square immediately above the Plaça de l'Àngel. The square, planned in 1922, features cypresses and a central equestrian bronze of *Ramon Berenguer III*, a work executed by Josep Llimona in Rome in 1888. The tall and picturesquely uneven walls that loom up behind the statue reflect a complex constructional history dating back to the 4C AD, when the walls were first erected. The Roman walls, built of huge blocks of stone to a height of 9 metres and a width of 3.56 metres, were given a special elegance by supporting a cornice. Large fragments of this have survived, as have many of the tall, cube-shaped watchtowers that were built at regular intervals above it.

The walls remained untouched until the extension of the city in the 13C, after which Jaume I gave permission for houses to be built against them. The towers overlooking what is now the Plaça de Ramon Berenguer were joined together and made to buttress the chapel of Santa Agüeda and other structures on the Plaça del Rei (see p 103). The arches on the lower level of the walls mark the site of the various medieval buildings that were attached to either side of the walls and thus helped to preserve the Roman masonry.

Studied in 1837 by the classical scholar Mestres i Bernadet, the walls were restored in the second quarter of the 20C. Red brick was deliberately used to replace the sections where the masonry had disappeared, rather than attempting to replicate the original structure.

The straight **Carrer de Jaume I** runs towards the Rambla from the Plaça de l'Àngel. Together with its continuation, the Carrer de Ferran, it divides the former Roman city in two. Designed in 1820–23 and constructed in 1849–53, it is lined mainly with late 19C buildings.

From the Plaça de l'Àngel, walk up the parallel **Carrer de la Llibreteria**, which is much narrower and older and also links the Plaça de l'Àngel with the Plaça de Sant Jaume.

At no. 7 on the right is the *Cerería Paulino Subirà*, a candle shop founded in 1761. One of the oldest shops in Barcelona, it has a beautiful interior of 1843 featuring columns, an upper gallery and a double-ramp staircase of great lightness and elegance. Further up on the left at no. 16 is the charming *Mesón del Café*, an establishment dating back to 1909 with a façade in the form of a tiny white house which seems to be taken directly from a fairy tale. This cosy and always crowded café reputedly serves the best coffee in Barcelona.

Walk back down Carrer de la Llibreteria and turn left up the short Carrer del Veguer. On the right is the entrance to the Museu d'Història de la Ciutat.

Museu d'Història de la Ciutat
The museum is housed in the Casa Clariana Padellàs, a Gothic merchants' palace of 1497–1515 with a simple main façade supporting a small upper gallery. Originally situated in the Carrer de Mercaders, this building was reconstructed in its present position in 1930–31, following the creation of the Via Laietana. *Open June–Sept, Tue–Sat 10.00–20.00, Sun & public holidays 10.00–14.00; Oct–May, Tue–Sat 10.00–14.00, 16.00–20.00, Sun & public holidays 10.00–14.00; fee. Free first Saturday of the month. Bus Turístic and Barcelona Card discounts. Book and gift shop.*

The museum contains numerous maps, diagrams, models and photographs relating to the history of the city. Among its more interesting objects are a 14C volume listing the privileges of the city (the so-called *Llibre Verd*), and a clock of 1575 said to be the largest of its kind in the world (it was designed for the Cathedral by the Flemish clockmaker Simon Nicolau). There is also a virtual reality show of the city's history. Temporary exhibitions are also mounted.

A lift takes you down to a large underground complex built below the Plaça del Rei, where the results of excavations begun in 1931 and continued and completed in 1960–61 are exhibited. A fascinating section of the **Roman city** has been uncovered, comprising streets, columns, baths, the foundations of houses and shops and huge urns used for the storage of wheat, wine and oil. In Visigothic times this area was built over and used as a burial ground, a large model of which is on display. Beyond the excavations you enter two barrel-vaulted rooms forming part of the basement of the Palau Reial Major and further still is an excavated passage directly underneath the Carrer dels Comtes. On display here are the remains of both a Visigothic palace and a 4C Christian basilica. A final attraction of the museum is that it gives access to the apse of the Capella de Santa Agüeda (see overleaf), providing a close-up view of the magnificent altarpiece by Jaume Huguet. The main body of this chapel can be entered from the Plaça del Rei, but is separated from the apse by a glass screen. From the top of the museum there is a wonderful view of the Plaça del Rei.

Plaça del Rei

An abstract sculpture by the contemporary artist Eduardo Chillida marks the entrance to the remarkable architectural ensemble constituting the Plaça del Rei, a square more like a stage set than a real urban space.

Though formerly the courtyard of the royal palace, for 300 years it was also a straw, hay and flour market, and locksmiths exhibited their wares here until their expulsion in 1387. In 1403 Marti I planned to have the square enlarged to the same size as the Born (p 138), but in the 16C the square was reduced to its present proportions by the construction of the Palau del Lloctinent.

One side of the square (the continuation of the museum complex) is taken up by the **Capella de Santa Agüeda** (Chapel of St Agatha).

This former palace chapel, built during the reign of Jaume II, was begun in 1302 under the direction of Bertrán Riquer and completed by Pere d'Olivera in 1411. As with the Sainte Chapelle in Paris, this was a reliquary chapel, housing in this case the stone tablet on which the severed breasts of Santa Agatha had been placed. Used as a workshop in the 19C, the building was later converted into an archaeological museum, and now is an exhibition venue.

The exterior is dominated by a tall octagonal tower built over one of the defensive towers of the Roman walls. The building is accessed via the elegant rounded flight of steps in the top right-hand corner of the square. The very theatrical nature of this great sweep of steps might perhaps account for the tradition that it was at the top of this staircase that Ferdinand and Isabella greeted Columbus on his return from America in June 1493. A year earlier, a peasant by the name of Canyamas attempted to cut Ferdinand's throat here. The tall and narrow single-aisled chapel features Gothic arches supporting a polychrome wooden ceiling. The apse contains the coats of arms of Jaume II and his wife Blanca of Anjou. The high point of the chapel is undoubtedly the **retable** above the High Altar, one of the most outstanding paintings to be found in any of the city's churches. It was commissioned from Jaume Huguet in 1465 by Pere, Constable of Portugal, who was briefly king of the Catalans during the war against Joan II. A very decorative work in the International Gothic tradition, with extensive gold highlighting, the retable comprises a central scene of the *Adoration of the Magi*, flanked by scenes of the *Annunciation*, *Nativity*, *Resurrection*, *Ascension*, *Pentecost* and *Assumption of the Virgin*.

Adjacent to the chapel on the Plaça del Rei is the main façade of the **Palau Reial Major**. The seat first of the counts and then the kings of Catalunya, this palace dates back at least to the end of the 10C, and possibly occupies the site of the city's centre of political power in Roman and Visigothic times. The present structure dates essentially from the late 14C onwards, but incorporates masonry and other elements from earlier periods, such as the elegant triple openings on the main façade, which are from the time of Pere II the Great (1276–85).

Plaça del Rei

The buttressing of this façade and the upper row of rose windows date from the reign of Pere III the Ceremonious (1336–87), and resulted from the creation behind this wall of the ceremonial hall known as the Saló del Tinell, which was commissioned from Guillem Carbonell in 1359. Rising above the side of this façade is the **Mirador del Rei Martí**, which is in many ways the most distinctive feature of the whole square. Built by Antoni Carbonell in 1555, this is a tall rectangular tower comprising five superimposed galleries, the arches of which are sprung from Doric pilasters. The geometrical simplicity of this tower gives it an almost modern character, recalling the arcaded fantasies of the Italian painter De Chirico, or even the fascist structures put up by Mussolini.

The steps up to the entrance to the Capella de Santa Agüeda also take you to the Romanesque door that leads to the ante-room of the **Saló del Tinell**. Completed in 1370, the Saló del Tinell has been put to a variety of uses in the past, even serving between 1372 and 1377 as the seat of the Catalan Parliament. In 1479, the curious funeral rites of Joan II were celebrated here, when the king's embalmed body was placed on a lavish catafalque in the centre. The destruction in 1715 of the Ribera district of Barcelona to make way for the Ciutadella (p 161) led to the demolition of a Clarissine Convent, whose nuns were subsequently offered the hall and adjoining Reial Audiencia (see overleaf) as compensation.

Transformed by the nuns into a Baroque church, the hall was later considered to have been lost forever. Investigations carried out in 1934 revealed that the structure had survived almost intact underneath the Baroque overlay; subsequently purchased and restored by the municipality, the hall is used today for temporary exhibitions.

Of vast dimensions, the hall comprises enormous rounded arches supporting a timber roof. A fresco of c 1300, representing a military procession headed by a king and bishop, has been placed against the inner north wall.

Opposite the Capella de Santa Agüeda on the Plaça del Rei is the **Palau del Lloctinent**, which was built by Antoni Carbonell in 1549–57 as a residence for the viceroy of Catalunya. From 1836 to 1994 it housed the Archives of the Crown of Catalunya, which were then transferred to a purpose-built premises (p 104). To get a glimpse of the interior, turn right out of the square along the narrow Bajada de Santa Clara, and take the first turning to the right, the Carrer dels Comtes. The entrance, at no. 2, leads to a fine Renaissance patio, with a tall upper arcade supported by the large basket arches so typical of Catalan architecture. An ancient vine runs up one of the patio's corners, while off the left-hand side is a staircase vaulted with a magnificently elaborate wooden ceiling.

Museu Frederic Marès

Continuing up the Carrer dels Comtes, you come immediately to the tiny Plaça de Sant Iu. Facing you is the Museu Frederic Marès. *Open Tue & Thur 10.00–17.00, Wed, Fri & Sat 10.00–19.00, Sun & public holidays 10.00–15.00. Fee. Barcelona Card discount. Guided visits. Shop. The **Café d'Estiu** in the courtyard is open in summer.*

The museum is housed in the former Bishop's Palace of the early 13C. Acquired by Jaume II (1291–1327) as an extension of the royal palace, this building was used in 1487 by the notorious tribunal of the Inquisition. In 1542 it became the seat of the Reial Audiencia (Royal Law Courts), and in 1544–45 was extended and remodelled by Antoni Carbonell. Clarissine nuns occupied the complex from 1715 up to their expulsion in 1936, after which it was thoroughly restored.

Shortly afterwards it was adapted for its new use as a museum, which was officially inaugurated in 1948.

Marès (1893–1991), a wealthy sculptor who had studied at the Llotja and in the workshop of Eusebi Arnau, was a passionate collector, scholar and traveller. His collections are particularly rich in Spanish sculptures from ancient times up to the Renaissance. Iberian objects include a group of bronzes from Jaén province and an impressive series of 13C polychrome crucifixions. The basement contains medieval tombs and architectural fragments, most notably a splendid Romanesque portal from the Huesca village of Anzano.

On the first floor is a superb polychrome relief by Juan de Oviedo (1565–1625) of the *Adoration of the Shepherds*, originating from the Andalusian town of Cazalla de la Sierra, as well as a scattering of 15C paintings, including a heavily gilded and embossed *Calvary Group* by Jaume Huguet.

The second and third floors are taken over by what is known as the **Museu Sentimental**, which contains the more ephemeral objects amassed by Marès, dating mainly from the 18C and 19C. Of greater historical than artistic interest, this section of the museum charms largely by its dazzling variety of objects, including cribs, scissors, pipes, ceramics, photographs, toy soldiers, fans, dolls, playing cards, ashtrays, clocks, buckles and opera glasses. There is even the much-travelled, label-encrusted suitcase that Marès had used to assemble much of this loot.

The Carrer dels Comtes is flanked on the other side by the Cathedral. If you head back down the street and turn right into the Carrer de la Pietat, you skirt the building's apse. Before visiting the Cathedral, turn left into the dark alley of the **Carrer del Paradís** where, at no. 10, there is a much restored medieval palace occupied today by the Centre Excursionista de Catalunya, a mountaineering organisation founded in 1876, which was responsible for introducing skiing to Catalunya.

However, the reason most people come here has nothing to do with either skiing or mountaineering, for in the building's small glazed courtyard there are four tall Corinthian columns which originally formed part of a Roman Temple, popularly known as the **Temple of Augustus**, situated at the highest point of the Mons Taber. *Open Tue–Sat 10.00–14.00, 16.00–20.00, Sun 10.00–14.00. Free.*

At one time this temple was popularly thought to have housed the tomb of Hercules, the mythical founder of Barcelona, but is believed today by most scholars to have been dedicated to Augustus. Originally dominating the forum of Roman Barcino, the structure later stood in the middle of the garden which gave the street its name of Paradise. The 18C scholar Antonio Ponz described the temple at length in Volume XIV of his *Journey through Spain* (1788), and hoped that the surrounding late medieval walls would be pulled down so that the monument could once again enjoy the prominent position worthy of its importance.

The Cathedral

The tawny-gold mass of the Cathedral today dominates the Barri Gòtic, its tall octagonal towers and openwork spires pushing their way high above the narrow surrounding streets and alleys that congest this area. *Open Mon–Fri 08.00–13.30, 16.00–19.30; Sat & Sun 08.00–13.30, 17.00–19.30. Cloister daily 09.00–13.30, 16.00–19.00. Museum daily 10.00–13.00. Fee to enter museum and choir.*

The origins of the Cathedral go back to a three-aisled palaeochristian basilica of the 4C or 5C, the foundations of which can be seen in the basement of the Museu d'Història de la Ciutat. Destroyed by the Moorish leader Al-Mansur in 985, this was replaced in 1046–58 by a Romanesque structure commissioned by Ramon Berenguer I the Elder. The present Cathedral was begun in 1298, during the bishopric of Bernat Pelegri and the reign of Jaume II. The unknown first architect was succeeded in 1317 by the Mallorcan Jaume Fabre, who remained in charge of the works until his death in 1339, bringing to completion the apse, ambulatory and crossing. From 1358–88 the construction of the building was taken over by Bernat Roca or Roquer, who laid out most of the nave and initiated the construction of the cloister. Arnau Bargués, who was director of works after 1397, planned the magnificent chapter house, which was built in 1405–15. The choir, in the middle of the nave, was completed c 1460, after which the fabric of the Cathedral was little altered until the 19C.

In 1820 a modern solution was proposed for the Cathedral's unfinished west façade, but Richard Ford reported more than twenty years later that nothing had been done to this façade despite the fact that 'the rich chapter have for three centuries received a fee on every marriage for this very purpose of completing it...'. Financed by the banker Manuel Girona, Josep Oriol Mestres finally built the west façade in 1887–90, basing his design very closely on one that had been drawn up in 1408 by the French architect Charles Galtes (who is known in Catalan as Carli). Leading the team of sculptors working on the façade was Agapit Vallmitjana i Barbay.

Work on the Cathedral was begun, unusually, at the south transept and the oldest feature of the exterior is the Romanesque portal overlooking the Plaça de

Sant Iu. The portal, carved in marble and Montjuïc stone, is flanked by panels with inscriptions recording the commencement of work in 1298. Above these are carvings of a man with a griffin and a man battling with a lion, while in the tympanum itself is a figure believed to be St Iu (Ivo).

The finest statuary on the exterior is the **wooden relief** contained within the tympanum of the Portal del Pietat, which leads into the cloister. Attributed to the German artist Michael Lochner, this angular and expressive late 15C work represents the *Pietà*, the diminutive figure at Christ's feet being Canon Berenguer Vila.

The Cathedral

Among the most striking architectural features of the exterior are the two octagonal towers—dating from the 1380s—that rise above the transepts. The late-19C west façade is in a style more indebted to Northern European architecture than to Catalan Gothic, not only because of the soaring proportions, but also owing to the elaborate and intricate overall decoration, which is in sharp contrast to the ornamental restraint characteristic of most medieval Catalan exteriors. Three openwork spires punctuate the skyline of this façade, the enormously tall central one being reminiscent of those of Ulm and Freiburg.

Interior The three-aisled interior, with its blind triforium and tiny rose windows in the clerestory, is spacious and atmospheric. Large bosses decorate the Gothic cross-vaults, while a colonnade of tall piers forms a particularly elegant ambulatory. Rose Macaulay, in *Fabled Shore* (1949), described the Cathedral as a 'triumph of Catalan Gothic magnificence', but added that 'it is outside my scope and power to emulate the guidebooks in their persevering, detailed and admirable accounts of church interiors'. She was perhaps right in skimping on the detail, for the initial impact of the interior is more memorable than most of the individual features and furnishings. As the interior was constantly guarded by the Generalitat during the Civil War, it is one of the few in Barcelona to have escaped the attentions of the anarchists. You cannot help thinking, however, that the destruction of the 17C and 18C altarpieces that decorate many of the dark chapels of the nave and ambulatory would not have been such a great artistic loss.

By far the most impressive of the **chapels** is the one at the west end of the south aisle. Covered with an elaborate star-shaped vault richly adorned with bosses, this was originally the chapter house built in 1407 by Arnau Bargués. Following the canonisation in 1676 of the 12C Bishop of Barcelona, Ollegarius, it was transformed into a memorial chapel to the saint, and the partition walls that once made the place accessible only from the cloister were pulled down.

Later, the chapel was dedicated to the Christ of Lepanto in honour of its carved image of the Crucifixion, which is said to have been carried by Don John of Austria in the Battle of Lepanto, where it was placed on the prow of his flagship *La Real*.

Directly opposite the chapel, in the first bay of the north aisle, is the **baptistery**, where a plaque records the baptism of the six native Americans brought back by Columbus from the New World in 1493. The stained glass above, representing Christ and Mary Magdalene, was executed by Gil Fontamet to designs by the great artist Bartolomé Bermejo from Cordoba.

The central enclosed **choir**, which was begun after 1390, features some of the most impressive sculptural work to be found in the Cathedral. The original stalls were the upper ones, which were completed by Pere ça Anglada in 1399. The elaborate canopies, with rich Plateresque decoration, were added in the late 15C by Michael Lochner and Johann Friedrich. Also added later were the coats of arms painted on the stalls by Juan de Borgoña on the occasion of the celebration here, in 1519, of the first and last chapter of the order of the Golden Fleece. The meeting, presided by the Emperor Charles V—the Grand Master of the Order—was attended by the kings of England, Poland, Portugal, Denmark, Hungary and France. The coat of arms of England's Henry VIII is immediately to the right of the Emperor's, facing the high altar.

The lower stalls, of less artistic interest, were executed by Macià Bonafè in 1456–62. Attached to the choir is a dazzlingly elaborate wooden **pulpit** of 1403 by Pere ça Anglada, reached by an early-15C stone stairway built by Jordi Johan and adorned with a traceried ironwork balustrade incorporating lily motifs. The splendid Renaissance **choir-screen**, or retrochoir, was begun in 1519 by Bartolomé Ordoñez (assisted by the Italians Simone de Bellano and Vittorio de Cogono), and completed in 1564 by Pedro Villar. Ordoñez himself was responsible for the exquisitely worked Italianate reliefs of Sant Sever, Santa Eulàlia and the scenes of Santa Eulàlia's proclamation of her faith and martyrdom at the stake. Between the choir and the presbytery are steps leading down to the **crypt chapel**, where the most venerated object in the Cathedral is to be found: a sarcophagus containing the remains of the 4C co-patroness of the city, Santa Eulàlia.

Santa Eulàlia

This virgin daughter of wealthy merchants from Sarrià (which is still a very prosperous district of Barcelona), was so shocked by the corruption of the Roman city that she was converted to Christianity by the age of 12. Described by one of her early chroniclers as being 'extraordinarily beautiful', she has inspired a great number of legends, many of which relate to her gruesome sufferings at the hands of the Roman governor of Barcelona, Dacian. Aged only 13, she was forced by Dacian to worship the false idols in the Temple of Augustus, to which she responded by throwing a handful of sand at the altar. Thrown into a tower next to the Call district (p 118), she was then subjected to a series of progressively crueller tortures the nature of which the Marquis de Sade would have greatly approved. Eventually she was killed at the stake, some say on the site of the Boqueria Market, others at the Plaça de l'Àngel or the Plaça de Sant Pere. Doubts about the existence of the saint have frequently been voiced, and some even claim that she was a Catalan appropriation of the Merida saint of the same name.

Whatever the authenticity of the contents, the **Sarcophagus of Santa Eulàlia** is a particularly fine alabaster work of 1327, intricately carved by a Pisan artist who clearly had a close knowledge of the work of Giovanni Pisano. The previous sarcophagus—made immediately after the discovery of the remains in 877—has now been placed on the wall at the back of the crypt. Radiating like a sun in the middle of the star-shaped vault is a huge boss of 1371, carved with a relief of Santa Eulàlia and the Virgin and Child. Altogether, the crypt provides the Cathedral with the note of climax that is at present so lacking in the raised presbytery above.

The **presbytery** was radically altered in 1970, when the 14C Bishop's chair was moved from the side to a central position at the rear. To accommodate this change the 14C gilded reredos above the High Altar was taken away to the church of San Jaume, leaving as the main embellishment of the presbytery today an uninspired bronze by Frederic Marès of the *Exaltation of the Holy Cross*. Placed above the south wall of the ambulatory are the wooden sarcophagi of Ramon Berenguer I (d. 1035) and his wife Almodis. The third apsidal chapel contains a retable of 1450 by Bernat Martorell, with heavily gilded scenes representing the Life of Christ. Until the late 1980s, a cardboard Moor's head hung under the 16C organ in the north transept. Known as the *carassa*, on certain feast days it used to eject sweets from its mouth.

For many visitors, the greatest pleasure of a tour of the Cathedral comes from the **cloisters**, which are off the south transept. Though begun by Bernat Roca in the late 14C, they were not completed until late in the following century, and have much Flamboyant Gothic detailing, such as the ironwork grilles entwined with floral motifs. The luxuriant character of the cloisters is due above all to the rich vegetation in the centre, featuring orange-trees, aloes and palms hovering over a large pool and fountain. However, unusually for places such as these, the cloisters cannot be described as a haven of peace, not only because of the large crowds of tourists, but also because of the squeals made by the geese that have been kept here over the centuries. Originally 13 in number, these geese (now thankfully reduced to six) are thought to have had a symbolic significance, though this has yet to be satisfactorily explained. Richard Ford believed that the canons of the Cathedral, inspired by the geese on the Roman Capitol, installed the geese here as a reminder of the greatness of Barcelona in Roman times. Though Ford's explanation makes you wonder why no such animals are to be found today in Tarragona—a far more important Roman city than Barcelona—it has been widely accepted, and there are several guidebooks that continue to refer to the Cathedral's 'Capitoline geese'.

The fountain that feeds the Cathedral's pond is protected by a mid-15C tabernacle decorated inside with a boss representing St George and the Dragon. The **Cathedral museum** (*open daily 10.00–13.00*), situated off the north side of the cloisters, partially occupies the chapter house, and features numerous silk altar frontals and many indifferent religious paintings and sculptures. Two 15C works stand out, however, one being a **retable** by Jaume Huguet painted for the Guild of Esparto Workers (*Gremio de Esparters*). The other, and more impressive of the two, is Bartolomé Bermejo's signed and dated *Pietà* of 1490, which was formerly in the chapel of the nearby Casa de l'Ardiaca (Archdeacon's House). Bermejo, a Cordoban-born artist who worked mainly in Catalunya and Aragón, is regarded as one of the greatest painters of the so-called Hispano-Flemish School. His superb *Pietà* reveals strong Flemish influence in the wealth of naturalistic detail to be found in the extensive landscape background. The angularity, harsh realism and expressiveness of the whole is inherently Spanish, however.

Leaving the Cathedral by the west portal you will find yourself in the Plaça de la Seu, where every Sunday from about 12.00 to 14.00 a small band provides the music for the Catalan national dance known as the **Sardana**. In its stateliness and complete absence of sensuality, the *Sardana* is comparable to the English Morris dance. Anyone can join in, but before doing so you would be well advised to read John Langdon-Davies's scholarly and entertaining study, *Dancing Catalans* (London, 1929), which gives a detailed description of the movements.

The square itself was formed in 1421–22 by the demolition of houses belonging to the deacon and canons, and of a section of the Roman wall. A stairway was created leading down to the Carrer de la Corribia, a street that has now been replaced by the modern and bustling Avinguda de la Catedral. Later in the 15C, the Casa de la Pia Almoina was erected on the site of one of the destroyed buildings on the north-east side of the square. The heavily-restored structure now houses the **Museu Diocesà**. *Open Tue–Sat 10.00–14.00, 17.00–20.00, Sun 11.00–14.00. Fee. Shop.* The displays include textiles, ceramics, paintings and sculpture from Barcelona churches. Exhibits include a 13C polychrome figure of the Virgin of Santa Maria de Toudell and a 15C altarpiece by Bernat Martorell from the church of Cabrera de Mar. Temporary exhibitions highlight different aspects of the collections.

Further changes to the square were made in 1943 and involved the demolition of other houses facing the Cathedral. One of these, which belonged to the medieval guild of shoemakers, was subsequently rebuilt in the nearby Plaça de Sant Felip Neri. From the Avinguda de la Catedral and the adjoining Plaça Nova, there is a good view of both the west front of the Cathedral and the long section of Roman wall attached to the back of the Casa de l'Ardiaca (Archdeachon's House; see below).

Before resuming a tour of the Barri Gòtic, you should take a look at the tall modern block at no. 5 **Plaça Nova**, which was built by Xavier Busquets i Sindreu in 1958–62. This dreary and incongruously situated structure—a sad advertisement for the **Collegi d'Arquitectes de Catalunya** which it houses—is of interest largely for the long frieze inscribed with linear childlike murals designed by Picasso and executed in 1960 by the Norwegian Carl Nesjar, an expert in the then new technique of sandblasting. The original idea was to commission Miró, but Picasso poured scorn on this plan, saying that he would give them a Miró if they wanted, and quickly sketched a typical Miró sun on a piece of paper. The authorities disliked the murals at first, and used to cover them with a Catalan flag at every opportunity. They came round, however, following a phone call from the Japanese consulate, saying that their tourists were complaining about not being able to photograph them.

There are two further Picasso murals inside, one of which represents the *Sardana*. Architectural enthusiasts might also like to visit the college's outstanding **bookshop**, which is housed in the basement, along with an excellent **restaurant** (p 34).

The large bronze letters spaced out along Plaça Nova are the work of Joan

Brossa, the brilliant conceptual artist who died in 2000, and spell out the word 'Barcino', the Roman name for Barcelona.

From the Plaça de la Seu in front of the Cathedral, turn right down the Carrer Santa Llúcia, passing to your right the **Casa de l'Ardiaca** (Archdeacon's House), which houses the Historical Archive. Built in 1479–1512, and partially remodelled in 1548–59, the house was adapted in the early 20C for use as a Barristers' College by the leading Modernista architect Lluís Domènech i Montaner. The street façade is marked by an elegant Renaissance portal of c 1510–12, to the right of which is a delightful letterbox designed by Domènech i Montaner in 1902. The swallows and tortoise that decorate the box are thought to be a reference to the slow pace of either Spain's postal service or its legal system. Behind the portal is a charming small patio comprising a fountain and arcades of basket arches.

On the other side of the street, attached to the Cathedral's cloisters, is the small **Capella de Santa Llúcia**, which was built in 1257–68 during the bishopric of Arnau de Gurb. *Open Mon–Fri 08.00–13.30, 16.00–19.30; Sat & Sun 08.00–13.30, 17.00–19.30.* Possibly intended as the chapel of the neighbouring Bishop's Palace, it was soon afterwards incorporated into the Cathedral complex. The façade has the characteristic severity of the Catalan Romanesque, with the ornamentation concentrated solely on the portal, which is decorated almost entirely with vegetal and geometric motifs. One of the capitals has worn carvings of the Annunciation and Visitation. The dark barrel-vaulted interior features the late-13C sepulchre of Bishop Arnau de Gurb (protected today by a glass panel), and a floor extensively paved with tomb slabs.

At the end of Carrer de Santa Llúcia, directly in front of you in the tiny Plaça Garriga i Bachs that opens out on the Carrer del Bisbe, is the **Palau Episcopal** or Bishop's Palace, which dates back at least to the time of the Bishop Arnau de Gurb, but was extensively remodelled after 1681. The surviving and much restored parts of the original Romanesque palace are visible in the entrance courtyard off Carrer del Bisbe, and include an arcade of elegantly ornamented arches, with rows of paired and triple openings on the second floor. The façade of the palace overlooking the Plaça Nova is a Neo-classical work of 1784 by the brothers Mas, while that on the Plaça Garriga i Bachs was added as late as 1928.

The **Plaça Garriga i Bachs** was created in 1929 with the demolition of the houses separating the palace from the Palau de la Generalitat. On one side of the square, attached to the side façade of the church of Sant Sever (see overleaf) is a monument of 1929 to the city's victims of the Napoleonic wars. It features bronze and stone figures executed respectively by Josep Llimona and Vinçens Navarro, as well as ceramic tiles reproducing a series of early-19C historical prints.

Before making your way to the Palau de la Generalitat, turn off the square along the dark and alley-like Carrer Montjuïc del Bisbe, which was originally a path leading to the cemetery of that name. Although the cemetery has gone, the former solemn nature of the street is recalled in a couple of shops that specialise in religious objects. In place of the cemetery is the small and shaded **Plaça de Sant Felip Neri**, which appears to be a particularly atmospheric and well-preserved corner of the old town, though in fact is largely a modern sham incorporating older elements.

The Irish heroine of Colm Toibin's novel *The South* (1990) finds herself one night in this square and believes that she has stumbled at last on the 'real Barcelona': 'I had been in Barcelona for about a week and suddenly I felt as though I had found the place I had been looking for: the sacred core of the world, a deserted square reached by two narrow alleyways, dimly lit, with a fountain, two trees, a church and some church buildings.'

The only two buildings actually to have been intended for the square are the **former Residence of the Secular Priests of the Oratory** (the Filipenses) and the attached **Church of Sant Felip Neri**. The former, founded in the late 17C, was austerely remodelled in the second half of the 18C. The present church, begun in 1721, was not completed until 1751. Its severe exterior, with its flanking giant pilasters and crowning rounded pediment, is one of several in Barcelona inspired by that of the Ciutadella church. The single-aisled interior, featuring interconnected side chapels and a dome above the crossing, is of a type derived from the Gesù in Rome.

The pock-marked masonry on the lower level of the church's exterior is a result of the bomb that was dropped on the square during the Civil War. In the course of the square's subsequent restoration, two fine Renaissance buildings were brought here from other parts of the city. Next to the church is the much-travelled **Casa del Gremi de Calderers**, originally situated on the Carrer de la Boria. After being removed to the distant Plaça Lesseps in 1911—following the creation of the Via Laietana—it finally ended up on its present site. The elegant Renaissance detailing on its exterior dates from the time that this former private house was acquired by the Guild of Coppersmith Workers.

The Guild of Shoemakers was responsible for the construction in 1565 of the adjacent Cases del Gremi dels Sabaters, which was one of the houses taken down in 1943 during the relaying of the area in front of the Cathedral's west façade. On its façade is a relief of the lion of St Mark, the patron of shoemakers. The building now houses the **Museu del Calçat**, an entertaining collection of Catalan shoes from the medieval period up to the present day, as well as equipment and footwear worn by famous people. *Open Tue–Sun 11.00–14.00. Fee.*

Heading down the short Carrer de Sant Felip Neri, you come to Carrer de Sant Sever, a charming and quiet street lined with modest 17C and 18C houses. Turning right, the street becomes the Bajada de Santa Eulàlia, where the saint was supposedly rolled naked in a barrel filled with pieces of glass. On the left, a mosaic incorporated into a small tabernacle commemorates this event.

Walking back up Carrer de Sant Sever to the Plaça Garriga i Bachs, you come to the **Església de Sant Sever** on the left on the corner of the square. Built in 1698–1705 to the designs of Jaume Arnaudies, the decoration on the modest façade is limited to the portal, which supports a niche containing a statue of Sant Severus made by Jeroni Escarabatxeres in 1703. Little hint is given by this façade of the rich interior which, though simple in plan, contains some of the most elaborate Baroque decoration to be seen in Barcelona. As with the Cathedral, the church was spared by anarchists during the Civil War, thanks to the constant vigil of the Generalitat. The decoration of the three-aisled interior is comparable to that which once adorned the Betlem church on La Rambla (p 88), and includes a richly sgraffitoed vault and elaborate gilded screens in the galleries. The dazzlingly sumptuous high altar, set in front of an apse painted with illusionistic architecture, was designed by Escarabatxeres. The church is rarely open, but you may gain access by calling at the house at no. 9 Carrer Sant Sever.

Walk down Carrer del Bisbe towards the Plaça de Sant Jaume. As you make your way along this narrow and elegant pedestrian street, you flank the side of the enormous palace of the Generalitat on your right and pass under a Neo-Gothic bridge which connects it to the **Cases dels Canonges**. This rambling complex was formed by the joining together of a group of canons' houses dating back to the 14C. Used today as the official residence of the Presidents of the Generalitat, the buildings were heavily restored in 1924–25, three years before the construction of the bridge. Beyond the bridge on the right is the magnificent medieval entrance to the Palau de la Generalitat.

The Generalitat

Open on 23 April (St George's Day) and some other public holidays, and for guided tours usually on alternate Sundays. Free. ☎ 93 4024600 for details, or ask at the entrance or the tourist office.

The Generalitat, or Government of Catalunya, has its origins in the *Corts Catalanes* (Catalan Parliament) founded during the reign of Jaume I (1213–76), the monarch who was also responsible for making St George (Sant Jordi) the patron saint of Catalunya. St George achieved this honour after the king was impressed by his performance at the siege of Mallorca in 1229, when the saint made a posthumous appearance in order to lead the Catalans to victory. The effigy of this mythical saint was later to be the principal ornamental and symbolic motif of the Palau del Generalitat.

In 1283 Pere II the Great restructured the *Corts Catalanes*, dividing it into bodies representing the clergy, army and citizenry. The committees created by this parliament in 1289 to collect the royal taxes formed the basis of the Generalitat de Catalunya, which were given permanent status in 1359 by Pere III the Ceremonious (1336–87).

Under Pere III, the Generalitat became an administrative council for Catalunya, comprising three deputies from each of the three bodies that made up the Parliament. Though one of the first governing bodies in Europe with the authority to mitigate the absolutism of a sovereign, it was not given its own premises until the early 15C. These premises—the nucleus of the present palace—were created in 1403–34 by the joining together of a group of houses on the Carrer de Sant Honorat that had been confiscated from wealthy Jews. The principal architect in charge of the works was Marc Safont. The acquisition of another house early the following century led to the extension of the palace to the north. The works were mainly carried out by Tomas Barsa and Pau Mateu, who built the original Pati dels Tarongers (Courtyard of the Oranges). Pere Ferrer extended this courtyard northwards in 1570–91, and in 1610–30 Pere Pau Ferrer provided the building with its present north façade overlooking the Plaça Garriga i Bachs. The most important of the later additions was the Hall of St George, which forms the building's main façade and was originally conceived as a new chapel to accommodate the ever-growing cult of St George.

In 1714, following Catalunya's support for the Habsburgs during the Spanish War of Succession, the Generalitat was suppressed by the Bourbon monarch Philip V. The palace was turned into the city's Law Courts and remained as such until 1908. During this period it saw the trials of most of Barcelona's notorious anarchists, including Santiago Salvador (the man responsible for the Liceu attack, p 91), and Joaquín Miguel Artal, who was condemned in 1904 to 17 years' imprisonment for his assassination attempt on the minister Antonio Maura. On his arrival at the Law Courts, he received a clamorous ovation from a group of anarchists standing outside. Among those sentenced to death here was the murderer Isidro Monpart, whose sentence was carried out in 1892 by the infamous Nicomedes Méndez, who was able to use for the purpose a special garrotte which he had invented himself but had not yet been able to try out. The garrotting was later the subject of a popular painting by Ramon Casas.

After serving after 1908 as local government offices, the palace became once again the seat of the Generalitat with the restoration of this institution in 1931. The first President of the new Generalitat was Francesc Macià, who in 1934 was succeeded by Lluís Companys. A Statute of Autonomy issued by Macià gave Catalunya its own Parliament, judicial administration and police force. After the Civil War, the Generalitat was once again outlawed and went into exile. Companys—sent back to Spain by the government of Vichy France—was executed in 1940, but was replaced as 'President in exile' first by Josep Irla and later by Josep Tarradellas. Tarradellas, together with the Generalitat, was able to return to Catalunya following the death of Franco in 1976. A new Statute of Autonomy, passed in 1979, greatly increased the power of the Generalitat by making Catalunya one of the three Spanish regions known as 'historical autonomies' (the other two being Galicia and the Basque Country). Since 1980 the Generalitat has been led by the appropriately named Jordi Pujol, whom some like to compare to the pugnacious St George, but he has announced that he will stand down at the next elections.

The entrance to the Palau del Generalitat on the Carrer del Bisbe is that of the medieval palace, and was built by Marc Safont in 1416–18. The low exterior wall, which shields the smaller of the old palace's two courtyards, is distinguished by an exquisitely worked Gothic parapet, lined with gargoyles, topped by finials, and incorporating an outstanding carved roundel of St George by the sculptor Pere Joan. The Generalitat was apparently so pleased with this work that the sculptor was paid twice the amount that he had asked for. The early-17C façade on the Plaça Garriga i Bachs is in an austere classical style inspired by that of Juan de Herrera, while the late-16C main façade, on the Plaça de Sant Jaume, recalls Michelangelo's design for the Palazzo Farnese in Rome. Two later additions to the latter façade were the statue of St George (a modern work by the sculptor Andreu Aleu), and the balcony, which was added in 1860. From the balcony Francesc Macià proclaimed the short-lived Catalan Republic in 1931 (it lasted one day!), while Josep Tarradellas, on his return to Catalunya in 1977, greeted the crowds with the memorable words, '*Ja sóc aquí!*', 'Here I am at last!'

On St George's Day (23 April, see p 116), when the rich and wonderfully varied interior of the palace is officially open to the public, the patios are filled with roses, and popular Catalan songs are played continuously on the palace's bells.

Guided tour The excellent tour of the palace begins with the medieval palace, which is one of the best-preserved civic buildings of its period in Europe. The core of the medieval building is the **Inner Courtyard**, where a staircase sprung at a daringly low angle leads up to a Gothic arcade of exceptional lightness and elegance, dating from 1425. Above this is an upper arcade of basket arches crowned by finials and gargoyles attributed to Pere Joan. The two Corinthian columns supporting the arch at the top of the staircase have finely carved banding of classical inspiration. Directly in front of these is the entrance to the **Chapel of St George**, which was built by Marc Safont in 1432.

The entrance itself is one of the most elaborate and exuberant examples of the Gothic style in Catalunya, with pinnacles and ogee arches, and a riot of tracery which extends up from the portal and flanking windows to cover the whole wall and cornice. Such flamboyance is in marked contrast to the austerity of the Catalan Gothic in general. The chapel itself was altered and extended in 1620 and given a cupola decorated at each corner with four suspended capitals, a feature peculiar to Barcelona. The furnishings are particularly fine and include numerous scenes of St George and the Dragon, among which are a late-15C altar frontal embroidered in relief by Antoni Sadurni, and an Italian silver reliquary of c 1500 featuring the first known representation of the saint on foot.

Attached to the northern side of the inner courtyard's Gothic arcade is the long **Courtyard of the Oranges**, the southern end of which was begun by Pau Mateu in 1532. This end is given a brilliant colouring not only by its orange trees but also by the pink columns with Renaissance capitals that support the lower Gothic arcade. The narrower northern end, dating from the late 16C, is far more austere, but has been made to harmonise with the other half by carrying through the whole length of the courtyard a Gothic upper arcade of basket arches, gargoyles and finials. Among the rooms off this courtyard is the so-called **Gilded Hall**, which is named after its gilded ceiling of 1578, a resplendent coffered structure from which are suspended two 18C Murano chandeliers. The walls are lined with 16C Flemish tapestries representing allegorical scenes from Petrarch. Nearby is a small room containing early 20C frescoes by Torres Garcia that were originally painted for the Hall of St George. These classical allegorical

Courtyard of the Orange Trees, Palau Generalitat

works, full of overtones of the art of the French Symbolist painter Puvis de Chavannes, are typical examples of so-called Noucentisme. More recent art to be found in the palace includes a room with walls adorned with bizarre post-modern reliefs by the present-day sculptor Josep Maria Subirachs. Another room is decorated by Tapiès.

The tour of the building ends in the **Hall of St George** (Saló de Sant Jordi), the church-like interior of which—complete with central dome—is a reminder that this reception hall was originally planned as a replacement to the chapel of St George. The decoration, comprising heavy gilding and conventional historical scenes, was executed in 1928 during the dictatorship of Primo de Rivera, which explains why most of the scenes depicted are of Spanish rather than specifically Catalan subject-matter.

St George's Day

The Plaça de Sant Jaume is undoubtedly seen at its most animated on St George's Day (23 April), when stalls of books are laid out around it, and crowds queue up to buy roses from the courtyard of the Palau de la Generalitat. This feast-day in honour of Catalunya's patron saint was instigated in 1436 (later than in either Valencia or Mallorca), and coincided with another popular festivity of 15C origin, the Festival of the Roses. The old custom of men presenting women with roses on this day is still enthusiastically maintained, and has been enhanced by the rather more recent tradition of women giving books to the men in exchange. This goes back only to 1926, when St George's Day was chosen additionally as the Day of the Book, in commemoration of the death of Cervantes.

Plaça de Sant Jaume

The symbolical heart of Barcelona, and by far the largest square of the old town, the Plaça de Sant Jaume dates back to Roman times, when it marked the junction of two roads. However, from the Middle Ages onwards, most of the area that it now covers was occupied by the church of Sant Jaume and a building known as the Bailia, which was where taxes on goods imported into the city were administered. The destruction by fire of the church of Sant Jaume in 1822 provided the impetus for the creation of the present square, which was laid out by 1850 and given a predominantly classical look. This is not today a square where people generally come to linger, as there is constant traffic and nowhere to sit, though the inevitable *Sardanas* are danced here on Sunday evenings (19.00–21.00).

Casa de la Ciutat

On the opposite side of the square, directly facing the Palau de la Generalitat, is the city's other main civic building, the Casa de la Ciutat (City Hall), the main seat of the *Ajuntament* (City Council). *Open Sat & Sun 10.00–14.00. Free.* ☎ 93 402 7000 for information.

Whereas the Generalitat is responsible for administering the whole of Catalunya, the *Ajuntament* deals purely with the city of Barcelona, though in practice there is a certain degree of confusion concerning their respective spheres of influence. This situation has been complicated by the present political confrontation between the two institutions, the former being essentially right-wing, and the latter being much more to the left, many of its supporters being found among the city's large colonies of Andalusian workers.

Despite the importance of medieval Barcelona, its citizens were not given the right to elect their own councillors and aldermen until as late as 1249, when a constitution of civilian rights was introduced by the enlightened Jaume I. The subsequently formed municipal assembly, which later developed into the *Consell de Cent* (Council of One Hundred), met up to begin with in various places, and did not have a permanent home until the construction by Pere Llobet in 1373 of the Saló de Cent, which was the nucleus of the present city hall. Between 1399 and 1402 Arnau Barguès, with the assistance of Francesc Marenya, extended the building through the creation of the façade on the Carrer de la Ciutat. A large courtyard was created in the 1550s, although the present façade on the Plaça de Sant Jaume was built in 1830–47, while the square itself was being relaid.

The visit of Isabel II to the city in 1860 led to the construction of a new sessions chamber and the extension and redecoration of the original Saló de Cent. Numerous other changes and additions have been made to the building since then, including work executed by Domènech i Montaner in preparation for the World Exhibition of 1888, when the City Hall came also to serve as a royal residence. The Exhibition of 1929 inspired a further series of major works, including an ambitious redecoration campaign involving an iconographic programme drawn up by the historian Duran i Sanpere. A large modern extension was added in 1958, and in 1982 the courtyard and vestibules were adorned with modern sculptures.

The City Hall's main façade on the Plaça de Sant Jaume is a grand but brutally austere Neo-classical structure by Josep Mas i Vila. A typical work of the progressive Barcelona government of the 1820s, it aroused enormous controversy in its day, and certainly forms a dramatic contrast to the surviving parts of the Gothic building which it so incongruously shields. Most visitors today are somewhat surprised and relieved when they discover, on the adjacent Carrer de la Ciutat, Arnau Barguès' Gothic façade of 1399–1402, a quaintly irregular work with delicate tracery in the arches and parapet. The Gothic court-yard and arcades to be found inside the building are largely 19C and 20C work, but there survives here a Gothic loggia of the mid-16C. Members of the public are allowed freely to wander around this area, which contains sculptures by Francesc Marès, Josep Clarà, Joan Miró and others.

The parts of the **interior** open to the public have an altogether dark and heavy character and lack the immediate appeal of the rooms of the Palau del Generalitat. A late-16C portal of Solomonic columns leads into the late-14C **Saló de Cent**, a vast heavily restored hall in the style of the Saló del Tinell, with enormous round arches supporting a wooden beam ceiling. Two of the arches were added in 1848, while the Neo-Gothic furnishings are of 1914. The present council chamber, dating from the reign of Isabel II, is a gloomy panelled structure with dark oak seating arranged in a hemicycle. The most outstanding of the building's decorations are those by Josep Maria Sert decorating the **Saló de Les Cróniques** (Hall of the Chronicles). These enormous murals, painted on canvas in Paris in 1928, were among the palace's many decorations executed for the Exhibition of 1929 and represent scenes of Catalan exploits in 14C Greece and Asia Minor.

Sert (1876–1945), who is not to be confused with the architect of this name, enjoyed a deservedly large international reputation in the 1920s, when he received such prestigious commissions as the decoration of the Palace of the League of Nations, and of New York's Waldorf Astoria. Largely because he supported Franco, he went out of fashion after the Civil War, and was an almost completely forgotten figure after his death in 1945. The murals he executed in the Saló de les Cróniques are painted solely in ochre, gold and sepia, and show a compositional and illusionistic bravura worthy of his great idol, the Venetian 18C painter Giovanni Battista Tiepolo.

The Call

Beyond the Plaça de Sant Jaume is a district known as the Call, which extends all the way to the street marking the western boundary of the Roman city, the Carrer dels Banys Nous. The name *Call*, first mentioned in a document of 1241, is derived from the Hebrew word *quahal*, which means a meeting-place. Up to 1492 this was the centre of Barcelona's thriving and distinguished Jewish community.

The Jewish community in Barcelona

Though Jews had probably settled in Catalunya by Roman times, the earliest mention of them here is a document of 889 attesting to their presence in Girona. The Barcelona community had become firmly established in the Call by the 11C and experienced its heyday between the 12C and 14C. As well as playing a leading role in the commercial history of Catalunya, the community also became the country's undisputed centre of learning and culture, boasting most of the great doctors of the time.

For a long time, the **Jewish College** was Catalunya's only institution with the character of a university. Among the more celebrated figures of the community were the poet Ben Ruben Izahac, the astronomer Abraham Xija ('Hanasi') and the philosophers Abraham Ben Samuel Hasdai, Rabbi Salomon Arisha and Bonet Abraham Margarit.

Enclosed by the Roman wall to the west and to the east by a wall that ran parallel to the present Carrer Sant Honorat, the Call was turned into a **ghetto** in 1243, the entrance to which was on what is now the Plaça de Sant Jaume. With the creation of this ghetto, laws were issued preventing Christians from entering here other than on days when goods were displayed on its streets. Furthermore, the Jews were forced to wear long capes and hats, and to place red or yellow bands around their heads. Jaume I, who had been responsible for these segregation laws, was also one of the Jews' great benefactors, and he offered them special privileges in return for their financial support. Royal favour and protection—implemented in Barcelona by the *Consell de Cent* (Council of One Hundred)—were to be extended to the Catalan Jews up to 1400, eventually being undermined by growing anti-Semitism.

The first attacks on the ghetto were recorded at the very end of the 13C, but it was not until 1391 that the Jewish community came seriously under threat. A wave of anti-semitic rioting spread that year from Seville to Valencia and eventually to Barcelona, where the *Consell de Cent* organised a force of 1000 men to defend the Call. This force was in place by 17 July, but, believing after about a fortnight that the danger had passed, was unprepared for the attack on the Call made on 5 August, when men bearing torches put fire to the houses, and killed everyone they found in the streets.

Orders given by the *Consell de Cent* to execute ten of those responsible for the outrage only increased the fury of the mob, and in a subsequent attack 300 Jews were reputedly murdered in the space of an hour. Joan I ordered the execution of 15 more of the offenders, and arranged that taxes should be paid to the surviving Jews for a period of 30 years. However, the ghetto had by now been effectively destroyed, and was to survive for only a short time afterwards. The smaller of its two synagogues was turned into a church in 1395, and in the following year the remaining one was rented out to a stone-mason.

All Jewish synagogues and cemeteries in Catalunya were suppressed in 1401, and the stones acquired from these places were later used for such buildings as the palaces of the Generalitat and Lloctinent. Expelled from the Call in 1424, the remaining Jewish families were to stay on in Barcelona until 1492, when they were thrown out of Spain itself. Jews only began returning in significant numbers to Barcelona after 1930, the number of Jewish families increasing from 400 at the beginning of the decade to 5000 by 1935. In 1931 the first Jewish synagogue since the 15C was opened in Barcelona (situated in the Eixample, at the corner of the Carreres de Balmes and Provença). The triumph of Franco during the Civil War, however, led to a further Jewish exodus, and the Barcelona synagogue was not to be reopened until 1948.

The attractive dark and narrow streets comprising the present-day Call feature a number of 14C to 16C buildings, and a jumble of antique shops. From the north-west corner of the Plaça de Sant Jaume, walk along the winding **Carrer del Call**, which was the main street of the Jewish ghetto. A mosaic plaque at no. 14, above an ironmonger's, records the site of the shop founded in 1591 by the printer and bookseller Cormellas. This establishment, which was mentioned in Cervantes' *Don Quixote*, achieved particular renown through its late-16C commemorative edition of Ovid's *Metamorphoses*, a work referred to in the façade's sgraffitoed decoration of 1780.

Turn around and turn left into the **Carrer de Sant Domènech del Call**, which was where the main Jewish synagogue was situated. The house at **no. 5**, occupied by a pension, has retained much of its 13C to 15C structure, and has a delightful small courtyard decorated with ceramic tiles designed in 1900 by the Modernista architect Antoní Maria Galissa Soqué. The *Vinateria del Call*, at no. 9, is a pleasant traditionally decorated wine bar renowned for its selection of wines and tapas. At no. 15 a plaque records the site where St Dominic of Guzmán founded the first Dominican monastery in Barcelona in 1219. Arriving at the Placeta Manuel Ribe, turn left then left again down Carrer Arc de Sant Ramon del Call.

Just around the corner of Carrer de Marlet, on the left at **no. 1**, is a 19C house bearing a stone of 1314 with the enigmatic inscription in Hebrew, 'Holy Foundation of Rabbi Samuel Hassardi, whose life is never-ending' (implying that his holiness was immortal). This stone, which features the date 692 of the Jewish calendar, possibly came from the nearby former synagogue, and is the sole remaining testimony to the Jewish presence in the Call in medieval times.

Continuing down Carrer Arc de Sant Ramon del Call brings you back to Carrer del Call. Turning right, you come to the junction with the **Carrer dels Banys Nous**, the name of which (the New Baths) refers to the Jewish baths that were founded here in 1160. At no. 20 of Carrer dels Banys Nous on the right is the barrel-vaulted *Bodega Portalón*, one of the finest of Barcelona's few surviving traditional wine cellars.

Walk back down to the crossroads and turn right into Carrer de la Boqueria, a street originally lined with butchers, and now featuring a number of modest 16C, 17C and 18C houses. No. 12, now the *Pension Dalí*, is an 18C building with a delightful early 20C portal in a Flamboyant Gothic vein.

The Pi area

You are now in the Pi district, an area of ancient origin that grew up outside the Roman walls. The name derives from the great pines that once grew here. Arriving at the Rambla, turn right into Carrer Cardenal Casañas, which brings you to Placita del Pi, one of three interconnecting squares surrounding the large church of **Santa Maria del Pi**.

This impressive building, erected on the site of a much earlier church, was begun in 1322, but not completed until the late 15C, under the supervision of the master mason Bartolomeu Mas. One of the most characteristic examples of the Catalan Gothic, this is a box-like structure notable for its austerity and great width. The west façade, on the Plaça del Pi, is articulated by two prominent string courses, which give it a pronounced horizontal character. Above the portal is a vast rose window, said to be the largest in the world. The echoing single-aisled interior was gutted in 1936 and lost most of its original stained-glass windows, which were subsequently replaced by rather brash copies.

The squares surrounding the building, marking the site of two cemeteries, are among the most pleasant in Barcelona's old quarter. Street artists, musicians and other performers gather here and a **produce market**, selling cheeses, sausages and other local produce, is held on Thursdays, Fridays and Saturdays. The large and solitary pine at the centre of the Plaça del Pi, though planted comparatively recently, is a reminder of a famous, ancient tree which once stood here. The house at no. 3 (originally the premises of the Guild of Retailers) is covered with sgraffito decorations dating back to 1685.

There are few better places in the city centre to sit outside than the café tables belonging to the popular *Bar del Pi*, on the west side of the shaded Plaça Sant Josep Oriol. On Carrer del Pi, one of the streets leading off the square, is the **Cercle Artístic de Sant Lluc**, an art academy which was founded at the beginning of the 20C in opposition to the prevailing radical tendencies of the time. Its founder members, of strong symbolist and mystical tendencies, included Gaudí and the sculptor Josep Llimona. During the First World War Joan Miró studied drawing here, finding himself in the same class as the ageing Gaudí. Towards the end of the street, at no. 16, is the *Xarcutería la Pineda*, a famous delicatessen and bar dating back to the early 20C.

Running off the Plaça del Pi is the narrow **Carrer de Petritxol**, its old houses adorned with balconies overflowing with plants. Though widely admired today for its shops and general prettiness, this street was not so fondly remembered by the Madrilenian playwright and poet of the Romantic era, Leandro Moratín (1760–1828). This Francophile writer stayed here at a squalid pension, which he described in a letter of 18 July 1814: 'I am staying at a terrible lodging-house in an alley called the "Carrer de Petritxol"; this house, with service, bed, breakfast, lunch and dinner, costs me three pesetas, and from this you can infer that the food is quite evil; but it's time to make economies.'

Living here in somewhat grander style later in the 19C was another playwright and poet, Angel Guimera (1849–1924), who wrote in Catalan and was named in 1877 the *mester en gai saber* (master troubadour) in the Jocs Florals. His house, marked by a plaque, is the elegant early 19C building at **no. 4**. The Jocs Florals were originally medieval poetry festivals, which were revived in 1859 with the revival of interest in the Catalan language and traditions. At no. 5 is the **Sala Parès**, which was founded in 1840 as the city's first art gallery and is owned by the children of the poet Joan Maragall. *Open Mon–Sat 10.30–14.00, 16.30–20.30, Sun 11.30–14.00. Jun–Sept closed Sun.*

In 1901, the 20-year-old Picasso exhibited a series of pastels here that had mainly been executed in Paris. The exhibition met with an enthusiastic response from his circle of friends at Els Quatre Gats (p 128), and led to an article on the artist by Miguel Utrillo. Nowadays, locals flock to the street to drink thick hot chocolate and eat cakes at the traditional establishments known as *granjas*. *La Pallaresa* and *Granja Dulcinea* are two of the best, but be prepared to queue as they are always busy.

Returning to the Plaça Sant Josep Oriol, walk through to Carrer Alsina and Carrer d'en Rauric, which bring you to **Carrer de Ferran**, the animated street that connects the Rambla with the Plaça de Sant Jaume. Designed by Josep Mas i Vila in 1820–23, in connection with the re-laying of the Plaça de Sant Jaume, in the late 19C it became one of the most fashionable of Barcelona's streets.

The **Església de Sant Jaume**, halfway along Carrer de Ferran on the south side, was founded for converted Jews in 1394 on the site of the smaller of the Call's two synagogues. The much-restored portal is of 1398, but the appearance of the interior is due largely to remodelling carried out between 1866 and 1880 by Josep Oriol Mestres. The high altar bears today a magnificent retable of 1357 commissioned by Pere III for the Cathedral.

Beyond the church towards Plaça de Sant Jaume is the **Passatge del Crèdit**, an elegant passage built by Magi Nus i Mulet in 1875–79, which features cast-iron columns and girders in imitation of fashionable Parisian shopping arcades.

The painter **Joan Miró** (1893–1983) was born at an apartment at no. 4, where his father had a successful jewellery shop. The apartment remained in the family's possession until 1944, and Miró had a studio here for much of this time, working apparently in such cramped conditions that he had to crawl on his stomach under the stacks of canvases. The artist is commemorated here by a mosaic plaque erected in 1968 on the occasion of his 75th birthday.

Palau district

Walking through the Passatge del Crèdit brings you into the Palau district, a quarter of quiet and narrow streets bordered by the Carrer d'Avinyó and the Carreres Ciutat and Regomir. The name is derived from the medieval Palau Menor (Lesser Palace), which was built on the site of a large Roman fortress, and occupied by the queens of Catalunya. The palace was demolished in 1858, and only its **chapel** remains, at no. 4 of the Carrer d'Ataulf (immediately below the modern extension of the Casa de la Ciutat). This much altered chapel, remodelled in the mid-16C, has a 19C façade incorporating a 13C side portal.

The Passatge del Crèdit leads to the Baixada de Sant Miquel. Facing you to the left at no. 8 is the fine **Palau Centelles**, a partial compensation for the destroyed royal palace. Built c 1514 for Lluis de Centelles, in the mid-19C the palace came into the possession of Maria Pignatelli, a descendant of the Gonzagas. It is now owned by the Generalitat. Though the interior cannot be visited, you are allowed to wander around its beautiful small courtyard, which mingles Gothic and Renaissance elements, and has an open staircase supporting a slender arcade.

Turning right down the Baixada de Sant Miquel, you come to **Carrer d'Avinyó**. Now enjoying a renaissance with an increasing number of funky boutiques and bars, the street is lined with imposing 17C and 18C palaces that bear witness to an earlier fashionable era, before it went into a sharp decline towards the end of the 19C.

The building at **no. 27** marks the site of a well-known brothel frequented by **Picasso**, who was possibly referring to this street in the title of his pioneering Cubist work *Les Demoiselles d'Avignon* (others believe that this title derived from a ribald suggestion that the Avignon grandmother of the poet Max Jacob had posed for one of the figures).

In 1899, a year before his first trip to Paris, the 19-year-old Picasso had a studio at no. 1 of the parallel street to the west of the Carrer d'Avinyó, the dark and narrow Carrer dels Escudellers Blancs. This studio was a small room in the apartment of the brother of the young sculptor Josef Cardona. Other rooms in this building were used in Picasso's time as workshops for the making of ladies' underwear. Jaume Sabartés, Picasso's friend and secretary and founder of the Picasso Museum (p 134)—whose first meeting with Picasso took place here—recalled how the artist, 'in his idle moments, entertained himself by making eyelet holes in the corsets with the appropriate machines'.

Walking down Carrer d'Avinyó, you pass on your left, near the street's far end, the entrance to the short Carrer de Milans, an impressive example of town planning conceived in 1849 by Francesc Daniel Molina. Near its centre the street swells out into a tiny round space (known as Plaça dels Lleons) before changing course and heading east, the overall effect resembling a snake which has swallowed a large object.

Continuing along Carrer d'Avinyó, the next street to your left is the Carrer d'en Gignàs, where *Agut*, one of the city's best-known restaurants, opened at no. 16 in 1924. Over the years, this family-run place has maintained a reputation for excellent food, remarkably modest prices and increasingly long queues to get inside.

The Carrer Avinyó ends immediately below this street, at the junction of the long Carrer Ample.

The word *ample* means 'wide' in Catalan, and this street was known as such because it was wide enough for horses and carriages to parade along. This was once the most aristocratic street in Barcelona, and a remarkably distinguished group of people have lived or stayed here, including the kings of Hungary and Bohemia, the Emperor Charles V and his wife Isabel of Portugal, the viceroys of Catalunya, and the future wife of Charles VI of Germany, Isabel Cristina of Brunswick (the mother of Maria Theresa). From the mid-18C onwards the street became the favourite residential district of the city's upper middle classes, but decline set in with the construction of the Eixample in the mid-19C.

This whole area lying behind the Passeig de Colom has today a rough but lively character, with much animation provided by the wealth of bars providing a great variety of wines and tapas. This is a popular district for a tapas crawl, and in the evenings is filled with people moving from one bar to another.

Turning right along Carrer Ample from Carrer d'Avinyó, on your left is the former monastery church of **La Mercè**, the façade of which overlooks the elegant Plaça de la Mercè.

Founded by the Mercedarians in 1267, the monastery was dissolved in 1835, and its main building was taken over as the premises of the Capitania General (p 154). The present church, which now serves the parish, was built in 1765–75 by Josep Mas d'Ordal, with sculptural ornamentation by Carles Grau. Its most remarkable feature is the façade, which, though restrained in its decoration, is the only one in the city to employ the theatrical and characteristically Baroque device of placing curved walls on either side of a straight frontispiece.

The square which it faces was created in 1982 with the demolition of a group of houses in the centre, and the placing here of a 19C fountain of Neptune, originally from the port.

Retrace your steps along Carrer Ample. Beyond the junction with Carrer d'Avinyó, on your right at no. 28, is the finest of the street's remaining 18C and early 19C palaces, the **Palau Sessa Larrard**, now a Piarist school. Built in 1772–78 for the Viceroy of Catalunya, the Duke of Sessa, it was acquired only a year after its completion by the banker and Danish consul, J.A. Larrard. The architects were Josep Gaig and Joan Soler, who worked to a plan drawn up by Josep Rivas i Margarit. The building displays a late Baroque classicism similar to that of the Palau de la Virreina (p 89), and is distinguished, on its main façade, by an elegant portal comprising Corinthian columns supporting a superlative ironwork balustrade, executed, like the surrounding sculptural ornamentation, by Carles Grau.

Continuing along the Carrer Ample, on the right is Carrer de la Plata, the street where Picasso had his first studio in 1898. Although it was thought that this studio was situated on the fifth floor of the house at no. 4, some experts believe that the room was located in the basement of no. 5.

Regomir district

Further along the Carrer Ample, turn left into the picturesque **Carrer del Regomir**, which is also the name of the surrounding area and is derived from a certain Count Rego Mir, who built an irrigation canal here in the 10C. Up to the 13C, it was one of the *vilanoves* or new towns at the edge of Barcelona.

Nos 11–19 house the quaintly irregular complex forming the 14C **Casa dels Gualbes**. Elements of the original structure have survived, but the most impressive feature of this building is the early 18C portal at no. 13, a Baroque structure of an elaborate kind rare in Barcelona. For many years the building has been used as a studio by one of the most successful of Catalunya's sculptors, Josep Maria Subirachs.

Further along, also to the right (at no. 5), is the **Chapel of Sant Cristòfol**, which was built in 1530, but given a Neo-Gothic interior by Joan Martorell in 1899. Every year, on St Christopher's Day (10 July), cars queue up along the already congested street to be blessed outside the chapel by the patron saint of travellers and drivers. Originally the chapel was attached to a 15C palace, the decayed and much altered remains of which can be seen by turning right into the narrow Carrer de Sant Simplici. At the end of this alley is an arch marking the entrance to the palace's courtyard, known today as the **Pati d'en Llimona**, one of the more evocative hidden corners of old Barcelona.

The courtyard's outstanding feature is a late 15C gallery supported on corbels carved with a number of life-like heads. The building is now a community centre. When the conversion work was under way in 1991, remains of one of the Roman gates to the city were uncovered. A section of the wall and a tower are still standing nearby on Plaça Traginers, just east of here.

Sant Just district

Walk back down to Carrer del Regomir and turn right into Carrer Cometa, which was named after the sighting of Halley's Comet in 1834. You come out at the lower end of the **Carrer de Lledó** in the district of Sant Just, which is quieter and more sophisticated than Regomir, but similarly decayed. If you want to see the section of wall and tower, turn right here down the Baixada Viladecols.

The narrow Carrer de Lledó dates back to the 13C, when permission was given to build alongside the Roman walls. It was one of the wealthiest and most aristocratic streets of the late medieval city and is surpassed only by the Carrer de Montcada (p 133) in evoking what Barcelona must have been like in its medieval heyday. In contrast to the latter street, however, its appearance today is characterised by an overall shabbiness, and though it has miraculously retained a remarkable number of palaces of medieval origin, these have been much altered and poorly maintained.

The palace at **no. 13**, remodelled in the mid-19C, has kept on its façade two fine Renaissance medallions of female heads (and another one inside, which you can see through the window).

Further up, at **no. 11**, is an 18C palace (now occupied by a college of Carmelite nuns) with an unusual open staircase in the courtyard. The columns of this staircase are truncated in a way that leaves their upper section suspended in mid-air. The architect might just have been showing off, but in any case the idea for these columns certainly derives from the suspended capitals to be found elsewhere in Barcelona (for instance in the Palau de la Generalitat).

The oldest of the street's palaces date back to the 14C and are concentrated at the street's upper end, beginning with the one at **no. 7**, which was largely remodelled in the 18C. Marginally better preserved is the palace at **no. 6**, which is claimed to have belonged to Queen Elionor of Sicily for no other reason than that it adjoins the street of this name. On the side façade is a Renaissance window with an architrave supported by tiny carved corbels. Inside is a Gothic gallery.

The neighbouring palace, at **no. 4**, has a rundown courtyard with a Gothic window featuring further corbel figures, possibly the work of a follower of Pere Joan. In the late 14C this was the palace of Joan Fiveller, a town councillor of legendary character whose intransigence was such that he is supposed to have compelled King Ferdinand of Antequera to pay a municipal tax on fish consumed by his retinue. Another celebrity associated with this street was the court poet and translator Joan Bosca Almugaver (1487?–1542), who was born here. Bosca, an important force in the introduction to Spain of the literature and ideas of Renaissance Italy, was the Spanish translator of Castiglione's *The Courtier*, a work to which he had been introduced by his poet friend Garcilaso de la Vega.

The street ends at the small and charming **Plaça de Sant Just**, at the entrance to which is a fountain donated to the city in 1367 by Joan Fiveller. The fountain, which was not operational until 1427, was given a Neo-classical remodelling in 1831. The square itself was created in the early 19C following the closure of the small remaining section of the ancient cemetery of Sant Just, which was reputedly the burial place of Barcelona's first martyrs. The **church of Sant Just** has the reputation of being the oldest church in the city.

According to legend, the church of Sant Just has its origins in a 4C temple erected by Christians above the ruins of a Roman amphitheatre. The documented history of the church, however, begins only with its reconstruction by Louis the Pious in 801. This royal church was made a dependency of the Cathedral in 965, and, from then up to the 15C, its rectors automatically became archdeacons of the Cathedral. The former importance of this church was shown by the special privileges that were bestowed upon it in the early Middle Ages. The most significant of these was the Right of Sacramental Wills, which allowed Barcelona citizens anywhere in the world to make a valid will—orally and without the presence of a notary—simply by getting a witness to come to this church within six months and validate the will's contents in front of the altar of Sant Feliu. This right, reputedly instituted by Louis the Pious, is first known to have been used by one Berenguer Sendret in 1082. Remarkably, it still remains in force, and more than 100 people have had recourse to it since 1939.

The present church, generally attributed to Bernat Roca, was begun in 1342 and completed up to the fourth bay of the nave by 1363; the last bay was not finished until the late 15C. The austere façade is largely due to restoration and remodelling carried out after 1883 by Josep Oriol Mestres, who, with a view to enlarging the square in front of it, demolished various structures that had been added to the façade, most notably the parish archives. The semi-octagonal belltower was built in 1559–72 by Pere Blay and Joan Safont.

The single-aisled interior features on the nave vault a series of 14C polychrome bosses carved with scenes of the Life of Christ and the Virgin. The Neo-classical high altar of 1832 incorporates an image of the Virgin of Montserrat, who is reputed to have paid a visit to the church before appearing in the mountain which bears her name. By far the most remarkable of the church's furnishings is the **altarpiece** to be found in the **Chapel of Sant Feliu**, which is situated at the far left-hand side of the nave. The work was commissioned in 1525 by Joan de Requesens, who had been given permission to be buried here on the condition that he decorated the chapel. Comprising a central panel of the *Pietà*, this altarpiece was painted by the Portuguese artist Pero Nunyes. The intricate framework was the work of the Flemish craftsman Joan de Bruseles.

On the other side of the square is the late 18C **Palau Moixó**, which is richly sgraffitoed with garlands and putti. From here the Carrer del Bisbe Caçador leads down to the main entrance of the **Palau Requesens**, which was the largest private palace in medieval Barcelona. Dating back to the 13C, it incorporated on its eastern side the stretch of Roman wall that extends down the Carrer del Sots-Tinent Navarro. The palace was greatly extended during the 15C, when it belonged to Galceran de Requesens, Count of Palamos, and Governor General of Catalunya. Its wonderful courtyard, which retains windows and masonry from the original 13C structure, has an open staircase leading up to a delicate 15C arcade. Since 1970 the palace has been the seat of the Academy of Fine Arts.

North of the Plaça de Sant Just you rejoin the Carrer de Jaume I and the Plaça de l'Àngel.

3 • The Barris de Santa Anna, Sant Pere and El Born

▶ Start from Plaça de Catalunya. See map on pp 84–85.

The extension of Barcelona's walls during the reign of Jaume I embraced an especially large area to the east of the Roman city. This area, comprising the districts of Sant Pere and El Born, has a similar wealth of narrow medieval streets as the Barri Gòtic, but without either the latter's museum-like character or the overall seediness of other parts of medieval Barcelona. It is lively and busy, its streets filled with artisans, shoppers and schoolchildren. In recent years, the Born in particular has become a favourite haunt of creative types, which has led to the appearance of numerous galleries, bars, restaurants and boutiques.

Leave the Plaça de Catalunya by the Carrer de Rivadeneyra (next to the Rambla), and turn left into the Placeta Ramon Amadeu. You might be surprised to come across, incongruously hidden behind the modern blocks, an enclave of cypresses and flowers enclosing one of the city's oldest churches. This is the former monastery church of **Santa Anna**, which was founded by the Knights Templar shortly after their arrival in the city in the early 12C. The building was much altered and extended in later periods, most notably in the 15C, when the monastery was merged with that of Montsió.

The single-aisled church, entered through a 13C portal, is in the shape of a Greek cross, and has an interior of exceptional simplicity and austerity, which was made more apparent through the loss of most of its furnishings during the Civil War. The main survivals of the Romanesque structure are the barrel-vaulted square apse and transepts. Modern restoration has replaced some of the original stone masonry with brickwork. The nave was revaulted and extended in the 14C, while the crossing dome is a modern reconstruction of an unfinished 15C structure. The elegant two-storey Gothic **cloister**, which has been greatly enhanced by the luxuriant group of palms and other trees in its centre, was begun in the 15C but not completed until c 1590. Adjacent there is a former **chapter house** (now a chapel), also dating from the 15C. The rest of the monastic complex fell into ruin shortly after the monastery's dissolution in 1835.

All that remains is a 15C door that once marked the entrance to the whole precinct, which has been preserved on the Carrer de Santa Anna. Leaving via this door, turn right and walk down to **no. 21**, which is a fine Modernista block of 1907, designed for Elena Castellano by Jaume Torres i Grau. The exterior features exuberant floral motifs, while the vestibule is especially lavish, with stucco, stained glass, ceramic and sgraffito decorations.

Retrace your steps along the Carrer de Santa Anna to the **Avinguda Portal de l'Àngel** and turn right. This busy shopping thoroughfare marks an old route that headed north from the city's 13C walls. The street significantly narrows towards its lower end, and eventually reaches an octagonal fountain that dates back to 1356 but was remodelled in the 19C and given a ceramic coating in 1918 by Josep Aragay.

On the left is **nos 20–22** is the ostentatious and eclectic façade of the Catalana de Gas i Electricitat, which was built in 1893–95 by the Modernista architect Josep Domènech i Estapa. Take the next left into the quiet and narrow Carrer de Montsió.

On the corner of the Pasatje Patriarca on the left is the **Casa Martí**, which houses the former artistic tavern of *Els Quatre Gats*, the famed haunt of the city's avant-garde at the beginning of the 20C.

The building was the first work in Barcelona by the leading Modernista architect Josep Puig i Cadafalch. Built in 1895–96, it has a striking brick exterior, imitative of a medieval palace, but wholly fantastical in its overall effect. Certain elements such as the arcaded top-floor gallery recall Catalan Gothic architecture, but the Flamboyant Gothic windows below, as well as the pinnacled oriel window on the side façade, are of North European derivation. The virtuoso carvings are by Eusebi Arnau and include a coat of arms formed by the emblems of the textile industry, and—on the large corbel at the comer of the building—a lively carving of St George and the Dragon, a motif which features on nearly all of subsequent Puig i Cadafalch's works and serves almost as the architect's signature.

Manuel Ballarín was responsible for the splendid ironwork balconies on both the main façade and the gate closing off the lane in between this building and the one at no. 5 Carrer de Montsió (a structure of 1906 attributed to Puig i Cadafalch). The floral and other ornamental details of the ironwork are inspired by the railings in the cloister of the Cathedral.

In recent years the original decoration of *Els Quatre Gats* has been recreated, and a bar and restaurant have been installed here, of distinctly un-Bohemian character. Clean, smart and moderately expensive, it is frequented largely by a combination of tourists and office-workers. A visit here will at least give you some idea of the look if not the character of the place that Utrillo had described as a 'Gothic beer hall for lovers of the north, and an Andalusian patio for amateurs of the south, a house of healing'.

The bright ceramic decoration on the walls, evocative of the south, competes with elements of northern medieval inspiration, such as the heavy wooden beam ceiling and the wooden chandeliers, the latter becoming a hallmark of Catalan Modernisme. The wooden chairs, benches, long tables and other furnishings are reproductions of designs by Puig i Cadafalch. The walls have been decorated with copies of the works by Rusinyol and Casas that once hung here (the originals are now in the Museu d'Art Modern in the Ciutadella Park). Among these are a series of portrait sketches of the regular associates of the tavern (including Picasso), a large picture of Rusinyol swinging on one of the chandeliers and a mural-sized canvas of Casas and Romeu riding through Barcelona on a tandem (in 1900 this work had been replaced by a portrait of the pair in an automobile).

Els Quatre Gats

This famous Barcelona institution was essentially created by four individuals who had spent much time in Paris, where they had taken an enthusiastic part in the Bohemian life of Montmartre. Two of these figures were the painters Ramon Casas and Santiago Rusinyol. Another was Miquel Utrillo, who had gone to Paris in 1880 as an engineering student, but had found himself drawn to the artistic circle which had gathered in a well-known Montmartre café called *Le Chat Noir*. There he met the artist and model Suzanne Valadon, by whom he was to have an illegitimate child who grew up to be the painter Maurice Utrillo. He also acquired at this café a taste for shadow-puppet theatre, which was then very much in vogue in Montmartre.

While still in Paris, Utrillo worked as a puppeteer with an eccentric and flamboyant compatriot, Pere Romeu. Romeu, who was later to manage *Els Quatre Gats*, appears to have begun his career as a painter, but was later consumed by a dual passion for bicycling and cabaret. An enormous inspiration to him was the infamous cabaretier Aristide Bruant whom he was to emulate both in his behaviour and attire, going around Barcelona dressed in a long waistcoat and flat-brimmed hat.

On his return to Barcelona, Romeu founded a gym that was attended by both Utrillo and Ramon Casas, who appear to have been more interested in the conversation than the physical exercise. When Rusinyol joined their group, the enthusiasm for the gym waned and they decided to set up an artistic tavern instead. Remarkably, financial backing for this rather unworldly new project was provided by Manuel Girona, the banker who had sponsored the construction of Barcelona Cathedral's west façade. This may have had something to do with the fact that Romeu's sister-in-law had been a cook in his household.

Els Quatre Gats opened on the ground floor of Puig i Cadafalch's newly completed Casa Martí on 10 June 1897. The name Four Cats alluded not only to the Chat Noir in Paris, but also to the tavern's four founders. The Catalan phrase *quatre gats* has the additional meaning of 'a handful of people', which aptly conveyed the minority nature of Barcelona's Modernista circles. As a tavern, *Els Quatre Gats* was famously informal, providing the city's cultural and intellectual élite with an environment far less sophisticated and elegant than that of other fashionable institutions of the time such as the Café Torino.

Although it promoted its high-quality French and Catalan food, in fact it appealed less as a restaurant than as a meeting-place for a late-night crowd composed largely of writers, journalists, artists, actors and musicians. These were people who talked far more than they consumed, but this appears not to have unduly worried Romeu.

One of the visitors to the tavern in 1899 was the Nicaraguan poet Rubén Darío, who later wrote of this place that it was packed to capacity, and that 'a residual note of elegance was provided by a handful of young ladies—intellectuals, we were told—but these were types neither from Botticelli nor Aubrey Beardsley, for neither their clothes nor the way they wore their hair betrayed the slightest snobbery'. The place, he continued 'abounded in artistic types straight from the Boul' Mich; young, long-haired, with 1830-style cravates, and other types of cravate... '

The importance of *Els Quatre Gats* in the history of Catalan culture is due above all to the many and varied functions that were organised there. These included poetry recitals, musical performances (given by the likes of Albéniz and Granados), meetings of the newly-formed Wagnerian Society and shadow-puppet shows put on by Utrillo.

Following on from the example of Le Chat Noir in Paris, the tavern even came to publish its own art journal, which was eventually succeeded by the influential *Pel i Ploma*, edited by Utrillo and Casas. Perhaps the most significant aspect of the place's activities was the holding of art exhibitions, its main room providing young artists with an informal alternative to the Sala Parès, which up to then had been the only private exhibiting institution in the city. The first of its exhibitions, held only one month after the tavern's opening, was devoted to the work of four of the younger generation of Modernistes: Nonell, Canals, Mir and Ramon Pichot. A later exhibitor was the young Pablo Picasso.

The tavern, though enormously influential, was only to survive for six years. In July 1903, following the departure of Rusinyol to Paris, Romeu closed the place to devote himself wholly to his passion for the bicycle. He died a few years later, a victim of poverty and tuberculosis.

Ironically, the tavern's premises were subsequently taken over as the headquarters and exhibition gallery of the Cercle Artístic de San Lluc (p 120), the members of which were politically conservative and deeply opposed to the atheist, left-wing tendencies associated with the tavern's previous habitués.

Walk up the Passatge Patriarca by the side of the café, passing under a Modernista mosaic bridge, to the **Carrer de Comtal**, a lively pedestrianised shopping street. The ceramic plaque on this corner commemorates the monks who used to live here. They wore sack-like habits, which they would shake out every morning over the street to keep them clean.

Among the varied shops on Carrer de Comtal is *La Casa de Bacalao* (no. 8), which specialises in different cuts of dried and salted cod, all of which are displayed as if they were goods in a high-class confectioner. The house at **no. 3** (and not at no. 2, as a plaque indicates) was the birthplace of the influential Catalan essayist and philosopher, Eugeni d'Ors y Rovira (1882–1954), the leading spokesman of the Noucentisme movement.

At its eastern end the Carrer de Comtal emerges into the **Via Laietana**, a busy thoroughfare that runs from the Eixample all the way south to the port, cutting a great swathe through the medieval city. The street was conceived in 1868, but the construction work did not go ahead until 1907, amidst enormous protests from conservationists. As with Madrid's Gran Vía, with which it is almost contemporary, the street is lined with a number of tall blocks inspired by the Chicago School, a pioneering example of which is the one at **no. 17**, built by Albert Joan i Torner in 1918–28.

The most eccentric of its modern buildings is the **Caixa de Pensions per a la Vellesa i d'Estalvis**, which rises up to your left as soon as you enter the street from the Carrer de Comtal. Built by Enric Sagnier i Villavecchia in 1917–18, this structure was a self-conscious reaction to the emergent American influences of the time, and harked back to the Neo-medievalism of Modernisme. Its main façade, at the corner of the Carrer de les Jonqueres, features a soaring, pinnacled spire which was intended to give the building the look of a Cathedral, in this case a Cathedral to money.

On this same side of the street, but directly facing the entrance to the Carrer de Comtal, is a solitary survival from an earlier century, the **Casa Gremial Velers** (no. 50). Built by Joan Garrido i Bertran in 1758–63 as the headquarters of the silkworkers' guild, its ostentatious sgraffito decoration of caryatids, columns and putti testifies to the former economic and political power of the city's guilds. With the construction of the Via Laietana this building was almost pulled down, but was saved after being declared a national monument in 1913. It was extensively restored in 1928–31.

Turn left by the Casa Gremial Velers into the Carrer de Sant Pere Més Alt. In front of you is the Palau de la Música Catalana, the supreme expression of Catalan Modernisme, and certainly one of the most seductive and entertaining concert halls in the world.

Palau de la Música Catalana
Guided tours in English at 10.00, 11.00, 13.00, 14.00 & 15.00. Fee. Ruta del Modernisme, Bus Turístic and Barcelona Card discounts. Times may change according to concerts, ☎ *93 2957200. Tickets sold at adjacent museum shop in Casa Gremial Velers building.*

The history of this building goes back to the foundation in 1891 of the private musical society known as the Orfeó Català. In 1904 the society commissioned Lluís Domènech i Montaner to design a building that would serve both as their headquarters and as a large concert hall. His brief was to design a 'Temple of Catalan art, a palace to celebrate its renaissance'. The first stone was laid in 1905, but already by October of the following year funds were running dangerously low, and a public appeal had to be made. This appeal, which played heavily on nationalist sentiments and Catalan pride, was enormously successful, and in February of 1908 the building was finally inaugurated. The place won for its architect the municipal prize for the best building of 1908, but by the late 1920s there was already much talk of pulling it down or at the very least of completely remodelling its interior. Architectural critics considered it to be a decadent work, and one of them even wrote that it was 'a monument to the ostentatious vanity of an age filled with illusions'.

The building, which managed fortunately to survive unscathed the critical onslaught of the 1920s, has been enhanced by an excellent modern extension containing offices, dressing-rooms, a library and rehearsal rooms. Built by Oscar Tusquets and Carles Díaz in 1982–90, this extension was conceived as part of these architects' remodelling of the adjoining church of San Francesc de Paula. In the Palau de la Música, Domènech i Montaner made the most of a cramped and awkward site by placing the auditorium on the first floor and turning the ground floor into a large vestibule which is linked to the street by a spacious arcade. The use of space is suggestive and fluid, with a brilliant play of light and shade, and a lack of rigid division between exterior and interior. Of more obvious appeal is the building's stunning decoration, which involved several of the finest craftsmen of the day, including the sculptors Miquel Blay and Pau Gargallo, the mosaic artist Lluís Bru and the designer of stained glass, Antoni Rigalt.

The mauvish-red brick exterior is crowned on its façade by a frieze of allegorical mosaics, below which, suspended in niches recalling the arcades of the Mosque at Cordoba, are busts of Palestrina, Bach and Beethoven. Further down is a forest of polychrome columns with exuberant floral capitals whose elaborate forms are taken up in the abstract decoration featured in Tusquet and Diaz's extension. Especially remarkable is the sculpted group by Blay at the corner of the façade, a frothing mass of stone from which a knight in armour and a woman billow forth to proclaim an allegory of popular Catalan music.

Within the auditorium itself all the stops of Modernisme are pulled out in the creation of a spectacular ensemble of breathtaking richness and colour, glowing under a great ceiling of stained glass. Waterlilies and nymphs provide some of this room's principal decorative motifs, but the most memorable features of the ornamentation are Gargallo's massive sculptural groups flanking the stage. The group to the left, lyrical in tone, features a bust of the Orfeo's founder, Josep Clavé, basking under the luxuriant shade of the Tree of Life. The righthand group, incorporating a bust of Beethoven, shows with exceptional drama and a frightening degree of realism the horses of the Valkyries making a massive leap in the direction of the audience, an excellent device for keeping awake any somnolent listeners.

Barri de Sant Pere

From the Palau de la Música, continue along the Carrer de Sant Pere Més Alt, which will plunge you into the medieval heart of the Barri de Sant Pere. At **no. 24** is an 18C house that was remodelled by Puig i Cadafalch in 1924. The Neo-classical building at **no. 27** on the left is the former Ateneo Polytechnicum, a workers' educational institution. Near the end of the street at **no. 49** is the birthplace of the outstanding muralist Josep Maria Sert (1874–1945), whose many works include decorations in the Casa de la Ciutat (p 116). The house is marked by a plaque in the Passatge Sert, where his family had a carpet factory, one of many such businesses in the textile district.

Beyond this you come to an attractive small square dominated by the church after which this district is named, **Sant Pere de les Puelles**.

This former monastery church, one of the oldest surviving monuments of the city, was founded for the Benedictines in 945 by the Counts of Barcelona on the site of a Visigothic church dedicated to Sant Saturninus. Destroyed by Al-Mansur in 985 and again by the Almoravids in the early 12C, the church was rebuilt and reconsecrated in 1147. The building experienced various other changes before being gutted by fire in 1909 and again in 1936.

The fortress-like main façade is a medieval pastiche of 1911, its only earlier feature being the 15C portal. The interior has preserved its 12C Greek plan, but owes its appearance largely to modern remodelling. A large fragment of the 12C cloisters—which were pulled down in 1873—can now be seen in the Museu Nacional d'Art de Catalunya in Montjuïc (p 196).

The Carrer de Sant Pere Més Alt is the highest of three parallel ancient streets that converge at their eastern end on the Plaça de Sant Pere. The street below is the Carrer de Sant Pere Mitjà, while further south is the **Carrer de Sant Pere Més Baix**, an especially lively shopping street lined with numerous old houses of medieval origin.

A 16C nobleman's house near the far end of this street (at **nos 7–9**) housed up to 1986 the pioneering Institut de Cultura i Biblioteca Popular per a la Dona.

> This institution, founded by Francesca Bonnemaison de Verdaguer in 1909, was the first cultural society and library in Spain intended solely for women. On the ceiling of its main reading-room was a quotation by the medieval Catalan philosopher Ramon Llull: '*Tota dona val mes quan letra apren*' (every woman is worth more if she knows how to read). As well as its books, the institution also offered conference rooms, a restaurant, a hairdresser's and—another novelty in pre-First World War Spain—showers. After the Civil War this former progressive institution was taken over briefly by the Female Section of the Falange before being incorporated into the Library of Catalunya. It is now a drama school.

At **no. 46** is a 15C building with deteriorated 18C sgraffito decoration, featuring different landscapes on each floor, framed by curtains. The two consoles on the first-floor balcony survive from the original building, as well as a doorway on the Carrer dels Mestres Casals i Martorell.

Another 16C building on this street, at **no. 52**, houses the former Farmàcia Pedrell, a Modernista pharmacy of 1890, with a remarkable stained glass frontage by Juan Espinagosa. A plaque next door at **no. 50** marks the birthplace of the Impressionist artist Isidre Nonell.

Walk back along Carrer de Sant Pere Més Baix and turn right down the Carrer Basses de Sant Pere (also marked in Spanish as Calle Balsas de San Pedro), which widens into a quiet and picturesquely irregular small square, the Plaça Marquilles. From the Middle Ages up to the early 19C, this space was occupied by artificial ponds or *basses*, serving a group of textile mills. At the lower end of the square on the left at **no. 4** is a modest 14C building where, according to popular tradition, Christopher Columbus was once imprisoned.

Beyond this the Carrer Basses de Sant Pere reaches the decayed Plaça de Sant Agustí Vell. Bear right and head south-west down the Carrer de Carders. On the right is the Carrer Sant Jaume Giralt, where the great Catalan poet Joan Maragall (1860–1911) was born and grew up. The exact house of the poet's birth is not known, and claims have been made for nos 5, 7 and 4. The street is recalled in one of Maragall's poems: 'When I was a boy/ I lived huddled/ in a dark street./ The walls were damp/ but the sun was joy.' Another inhabitant of this same street was the actress Margarita Xirgu (1888–1969), who lived as a child at **no. 36**. One of the greatest Spanish actresses of her day, Xirgu is best remembered today for her association with García Lorca, which began with a production of *Mariana Pineda* in 1927.

Continuing down the Carrer dels Carders, you reach, at no. 2 on the left, a tiny Romanesque chapel of the 12C, the **Capella d'en Marcús**. Built between 1166 and 1188, this is the sole survival of the Hostal de la Bona Sort, which was founded on the initiative of the merchant Bernat Marcús in 1147, and served both as a travellers' hostel and hospital for the poor. The chapel, which is rarely open, was gutted by fire in 1909 and 1936, and has little of interest inside.

On the other side of the street is the Carrer Giralt i Pellisser, which leads to the large and lively **Mercat de Santa Caterina**. This covered market, which stands on the site of a Dominican monastery, was founded in the early 19C but rebuilt in 2001. Back on Carrer dels Carders, turn left by the chapel. You come almost immediately to the top end of the Carrer de Montcada.

Carrer de Montcada

The finest of all Barcelona's medieval streets was created in 1148 by Ramon Berenguer IV and named after the merchant Guillem Ramon de Montcada in recognition of his efforts to raise funds to win back the city of Tortosa.

The street was originally the main route between the important commercial district of the Bòria and the ancient port of Vilanova de la Mar. Wider and straighter than the streets of the old walled city, in the 15C it became the favoured residential street of aristocrats and wealthy merchants. The maritime decline of Barcelona from the 16C onwards, the transference of the port to the south-western side of the city after 1768 and the creation of the Eixample in the late 19C all contributed to the gradual decay of the street.

Saved from further deterioration by being listed on the national monument register in 1947, it was gradually restored by the city council after 1953, and in the process several of its finer palaces were adapted as museums and other cultural institutions. Whereas the surrounding district has maintained a lively residential character, the Carrer de Montcada has been turned into a show-piece, and is noticeably quiet on Mondays, when its museums and galleries are closed.

The Carrer de Montcada is intersected by the long **Carrer de la Princesa**, which was built after 1853 as the final phase of the plan conceived in 1820–23 to link La Rambla with the Ciutadella. At the time of its construction the Carrer de la Princesa was regarded as a marvel of modern town planning, and for a short while was one of the most fashionable addresses in town. The city's chronicler at that time, Josep Coroleu, wrote of the street that 'it is one of the best and largest that have been built in Barcelona this century. This spacious thoroughfare…has got rid of a large number of gloomy and insalubrious alleys'.

The painter Santiago Rusinyol was born here in 1861, at the height of the street's fashion. His family home, situated above the shop of his father's textile factory, was at **no. 37** (near the intersection of the Carrer de Montcada); the birthplace is marked today by a plaque.

The outstanding section of the Carrer de Montcada begins immediately below the Carrer de la Princesa. From here all the way down to the Born, the street is lined with a near uninterrupted series of medieval palaces. Much of the Gothic detailing has been lost on the façades through later remodelling (particularly in the 17C), but many of the buildings have retained their original courtyards. The street is now a cultural hub, its buildings housing a series of museums, galleries and shops.

Museu Picasso

On the left, five adjoining palaces form the Museu Picasso. *Open Tue–Sat 10.00–20.00, Sun 10.00–15.00. Fee; free first Sunday of the month. Barcelona Card discount. Café, shop and library.*

The first building is the **Palau Berenguer d'Aguilar**, which dates back to the 13C. Among the fragments discovered here of the original structure was a series of murals depicting the conquest of Mallorca (these are now in the Museu Nacional d'Art de Catalunya; p 196). The palace was entirely remodelled in the 15C, and features a magnificent Gothic courtyard comparable to the inner courtyard by Marc Safont in the Palau de la Generalitat, and possibly by the same architect.

From 1970 up to 1981 the premises of the museum were gradually expanded to include the two adjacent structures: the **Casa del Baró de Castellet**, an 18C building with 15C fragments, and a sumptuously decorated Neo-classical salon, and the **Palau Meca**, an 18C remodelling of a 14C structure. In 1999, the museum was substantially extended with a new series of rooms in the next two mansions, the 17C **Casa Mauri** and the **Palau Finestres**, parts of which date back to the 13C. This section was remodelled by architect Jordi Garcés and is used for temporary exhibitions.

Thanks to Sabartés' persistence, this museum was finally opened in the Palau Berenguer d'Aguilar on 9 March 1963. Sabartés, in declining health for several years, had been unable to attend the opening, and died five years later. As a commemorative gesture to his old friend, Picasso presented 58 works to the museum in 1968, including a famous series of paintings and oil sketches relating to Velázquez's *Las Meninas*.

In 1970 the museum was further enhanced when Picasso donated an enormous group of works that had been executed in his youth, which had been kept over the years in his sister's flat on the Passeig de Gràcia. After the artist's death in 1973, his heirs, carrying out the conditions of his will, gave a large body of his graphic work to the museum. In 1981, a collection of 141 ceramics owned by his widow Jacqueline was also donated.

For all the donations that it has received over the years, the perpetually crowded Museu Picasso can barely compete in the number and range of its works with the Musée Picasso in Paris. Its great strengths lie in its exceptionally beautiful setting—an imaginative blending of the old and the new—and its unrivalled holdings of the artist's early works. Academic drawings carried out as a child in Malaga and La Coruña put to the test the artist's later boast that he could draw like Raphael at the age of ten.

You can also appreciate here the close similarities between the works of his early years and those of his Barcelona circle, in particular Nonell. Experiments with Impressionism, Pointillism and Symbolism gave way after c 1901 to the development of a more personal style first in the Blue Period and then in the Rose Period. Both these periods, which are excellently represented in the museum, drew inspiration from scenes of poverty and hardship, observed in the streets of both Paris and Barcelona. Several of the Blue Period works were executed in his studio at no. 10 Nou de la Rambla (p 94), situated on the edge of Barcelona's notorious Barri Xinès.

Pablo Picasso

Born in Malaga in 1881, Pablo Picasso spent three years as a child in the Galician town of La Coruña, where his father taught at the local art school. In 1895 the father was appointed Professor of Fine Arts at the Academy of Art in Barcelona (La Llotja), and the family moved here from Galicia in September of that year, staying apparently to begin with at a pensión at no. 4 Passeig d'Isabel II (p 154). In the summer of 1896 the family settled in an apartment on the Carrer de la Mercè, in a building which was recently pulled down to make way for the Plaça de la Mercè (p 123).

Already having his own studio by 1896 in the Carrer de la Plata, Picasso later worked at no. 1 Carrer dels Escudellers Blancs, where, in 1899, he had his first meeting with the man who was later to found this museum, Jaume Sabartés i Gual (1881–1968). The myopic Sabartés, who was to be Picasso's life-long friend and future secretary and collaborator, was the constant Barcelona companion of the artist during the years when they frequented *Els Quatre Gats* (p 128). Picasso, followed shortly by Sabartés, went to Paris in 1900, but was back again in Barcelona in 1902, working first at no. 10 Nou de la Rambla, and later at no. 28 Carrer del Comerç. These were the years of the artist's Blue Period.

Picasso settled permanently in France in 1904, and subsequently made only the occasional short visit to Barcelona, where his parents continued to live. One of these visits—in the company of Diaghilev and the Ballets Russes—was in 1917, following a five-year absence from the city. His father had died in the meantime, and his mother had moved in with her daughter Lola and son-in-law Juan Vilato to a house on the Passeig de Gràcia. Picasso, who stayed on that occasion in a hotel on the Passeig de Colom, was warmly received by his friends and admirers, who put on numerous parties for him, and took him to flamenco sessions held in the music halls of the Paral·lel.

On that same visit, Picasso showed a large oil painting entitled *The Harlequin*—a work clearly inspired by the world of the Ballets Russes—at an exhibition organised by the city council. Two years later this painting would be the first of his works that he was to present to the city of Barcelona.

Many years later Barcelona's Museu d'Art Modern—to which *The Harlequin* had been given—created a Picasso room, incorporating a further donation from the artist in 1937, as well as works from the important Plandiura and Garriga i Roig collections, acquired respectively in 1932 and 1953.

For most of the Franco period, Picasso had little contact with Spain, and was unresponsive to the attempts made by the Spanish Government to lure him back to the country at the beginning of the 1960s, when there was a lessening of the official hostility towards him. The Government was at one time even willing to accept his controversial painting of *Guernica*, but the artist was resolute in not allowing this work to be shown in Spain until the return of democracy there.

Picasso was rather more flexible in his dealings with Catalunya, however, regarding this region as a country in its own right, and harbouring a particular affection for Barcelona. In 1962 he accepted an invitation from a group of young Barcelona architects to produce designs for their new

College of Architecture (p 110). He also gave full support to Sabartés when he proposed to offer his extensive collection of the artist's work to Barcelona on the condition that a Picasso Museum was established here.

The museum's holdings of later stages in Picasso's art are far from being representative, with only a *Head* of 1913 to testify to the Cubist years. Apart from the superb *Harlequin* of 1917—a work heralding the onset of his classical phase—the high point of the later collections is the series of 44 interpretations of Velázquez's *Las Meninas*. Picasso's fertile imagination and creative energy are fully revealed as he explores all the compositional possibilities of Velázquez's multi-faceted painting, making you see the work in a completely new light.

On the other side of the street is the excellent Textile and Costume Museum, the **Museu Tèxtil i d'Indumentària**. *Open Tue–Sat 10.00–18.00, Sun & public holidays 10.00–15.00 Sun & public holidays. Fee. Free first Saturday in the month after 15.00. Barcelona Card discount. Shop. Café. The shop is good for unusual gifts and the café is a great place for a drink or meal even if you are not visiting the museum.*
The museum is situated in the Palau de los Marqueses de Lló, a palace of 14C origin with a combination of Gothic and Renaissance windows and a Baroque entrance portal. The building was restored and remodelled in 1969 to house the museum.
The textile collections include 3C Coptic fabrics, Moslem pieces from Al-Andalus, 16C Flemish tapestries and modern Catalan embroideries. There is a large group of liturgical vestments from the 13C to 20C. The costume collections were mainly the legacy of Manuel Rocamora i Vidal, and comprise a wonderfully varied representation of male and female wear from the 16C up to the present day. Exhibits include designs by Cristóbal Balenciaga (who was born in the Basque Country), Paco Rabanne and Azzedine Alaia.

On the other side of the courtyard, the Palau Nadal houses the **Museu Barbier-Mueller de Arte Colombino**. *Open Tue–Sat 11.00–18.00, Sun & public holidays 10.00–15.00. Fee. Barcelona Card discount. Free first Saturday in the month after 15.00. Shop.*
The museum presents the artistic legacy of the societies that occupied Meso-America, Central America, the Central Andes and the lower Amazon regions before the arrival of the Europeans. This important collection of Pre-Columbian art, which includes sculpture, textiles, ritual objects and ceramics, was donated by the Barbier-Mueller Museum in Geneva. Exhibits include a Mayan jade pendant (500–900 AD); a funeral mask from Guatemala (400–500 AD); a fragment of a cotton tunic from Nazca, Peru (200 BC–600 AD), and a Peruvian mural tapestry decorated with animal figures (12–13C AD).
Another part of this building houses one of the many exhibition halls run by the Fundació Caixa de Pensions, the **Sala Montcada**, which holds outstanding temporary exhibitions by mainly contemporary Spanish and international artists.
On the other side of Carrer de Montcada, at no. 25, is the **Maeght Gallery**, housed in the early 16C Casa Cervelló Giudice, the only palace on the street to have retained its original façade and entrance portal. The gallery is run by the ·

same art dealers who created the famous modern art foundations at St Paul de Vence in southern France. *Open Tue–Sat 10.00–14.00, 16.00–20.00. Free.*

On the right, at no. 20, is the **Palau Dalmases**, part of which is now an opulently-decorated bar. Though featuring fragments of the original 15C structure, its present appearance is essentially due to a late-17C remodelling. The courtyard has an impressive open staircase with Solomonic columns and an elaborate balustrade.

In 1699 the Catalan cultural society known as the *Academia dels Desconfiats* (literally the 'Academy of the Mistrustful') was founded here, and held its meetings in the building during the early years of the 18C. Since 1962, the palace has housed the Omnium Cultural, which was founded by Félix Millet in 1961 and is likewise devoted to the promotion of Catalan culture.

Near the end of the Carrer de Montcada, turn right into the Carrer Sombrerers, which runs alongside the church of **Santa Maria del Mar**.

This magnificent church of Cathedral-like proportions is one of the most eloquent examples of the Catalan Gothic style. It was erected during Catalunya's heyday as the hub of an empire, in the heart of the maritime quarter. The origins of the building are traditionally thought to be in a temple built to house the remains of Santa Eulàlia, though the first documented mention of the church dates back only to 988. It served at first as the parish church of an outlying district composed mainly of fishermen, but was later made the church of an archdiocese following the extension of the city's walls in the 13C, and the arrival here of numerous noble families, wealthy shipbuilders and merchants. The present structure, attributed to Berenguer de Montagut, was initiated by Canon Bernat Llul, who in 1324 was appointed archdeacon of Santa Maria. Building began in 1329, and this imposing building was completed in under 50 years, which helps to explain its remarkable unity.

No other Catalan church of its size has such a perfectly preserved exterior, which, furthermore, encapsulates the essential characteristics of the Catalan Gothic style, such as a preference for horizontal proportions and large areas of unadorned masonry. Two tall octagonal towers flank the west façade, at the centre of which is a portal decorated with statues of St Peter and St Paul, and a tympanum representing Christ between St John and the Virgin. The rose window above is a mid-15C replacement of a window destroyed in an earthquake in 1428.

The interior was gutted by fire during the Civil War and lost its central choir and many of its furnishings, a loss that at least had the advantage of making you appreciate all the more the extraordinary harmony and spaciousness of the architecture. Without transepts, and with aisles of almost the same height as the exceptionally wide nave, the interior closely resembles that of a hall church.

In the apse, the slender piers form an arcade of stunning elegance that makes the apse of Barcelona's Cathedral seem clumsy by comparison. The beauty of the interior is enhanced by the wealth of 15C to 18C stained glass, including a scene of the Coronation of the Virgin in the rose window of the central façade.

The surroundings of Santa Maria del Mar include some of the more picturesque corners of the old city. The intimate **Plaça de Santa Maria** was created in 1807 on the site of one of the church's two cemeteries. The tiny *Vinya del Senyor* bar is a good place to sample Catalan wines, and at weekends the outdoor tables provide an ideal vantage point for observing the succession of wedding entourages entering and exiting the church. At the top end is a Gothic fountain built by Arnau Bargués in 1402, and restored in 1962. Behind this runs the diminutive **Carrer de les Caputxes**, one of the most toy-like of Barcelona's medieval streets, complete with archways, timber beams, overhanging eaves and projecting floors supported by columns, the whole forming a quaintly asymmetrical ensemble.

Through the archway at the southern end of the street you will emerge again at the Plaça Santa Maria. Heading east from here along the south side of the church, you will come immediately to the **Fossar de les Moreres**, which marks the site of a cemetery where those who defended Barcelona in the siege of 1714 were buried. The place inspired some famous lines dedicated by the 19C poet Pitarra to the 'martyrs of 1714':

Al Fossar de les Moreres
no s'hi enterra cap traidor
Fins perdent nostres banderes
sera l'urna de l'honor

(At the cemetery of the Mulberries
no traitor is buried.
Even though losing our flags,
their tomb will be an honourable one.)

In 1989, the Fossar de les Moreres was turned into a small square by the pulling down of a number of decrepit buildings attached to the side of Santa Maria. As with so many of Barcelona's recent public spaces, this square features a large expanse of brickwork tilted at a slight angle. At the end, just beyond the apse of the church, you reach the long rectangular square known as El Born, the name of which is derived from the Catalan word for tournament.

El Born

From the 13C to the 17C, this was the nerve centre of the city, a place where jousting tournaments were held in the Middle Ages—and also executions during the era of the Spanish Inquisition. Later, it was the scene of carnivals, processions and evening promenades, which wealthy merchants, shipowners and aristocrats watched from the balconies of the grand palaces that flanked the square. The glass and metal markets were enthusiastically described by the 17C Madrilenian dramatist Tirso de Molina.

As with La Rambla, which eventually superseded it in importance, El Born came to be synonymous with Barcelona, and gave rise to a well-known saying, 'Roda el món i torna al Born' ('Go round the world and come back to the Born'). The buildings that surround this pleasantly shaded square date mainly from the late 18C and early 19C, the one survival from the Middle Ages being the heavily-restored 14C house at **no. 17**. Near the stone benches in the middle of the square, look out for some large iron balls and a trunk, which actually form an artwork by the renowned sculptor Jaume Plensa. The piece was installed in 1992.

Little of the district's past grandeur remains today. After a couple of hundred years in the doldrums, a magnificent iron structure was built in 1874 to house a fruit and vegetable market, a move that led to the regeneration of the whole area. This pioneering building was designed by Josep Fontseré, who was also responsible for the construction of the flanking commercial buildings. When the market moved to modern premises outside the centre in 1971, however, the quarter once again slipped into decline. A project is underway to create a library for the province of Barcelona in the structure.

Beyond the market runs the Passeig de Picasso, which skirts the Parc de la Ciutadella (p 161). A line of trees overlooking the park shades a row of pools centred on a controversial **Monument to Picasso** by the contemporary artist Antoni Tàpies. This remarkable monument comprises a large glass box in which old furniture and other objects have been placed. Jets of water shoot up against the glass sides, obscuring the contents. The water was in fact added later as a cooling device, as the original box cracked under the heat.

Returning to the Passeig del Born, you cannot fail to notice how the area is buzzing with galleries, quirky cafés and funky boutiques. This renaissance began in the 1980s when the creative community began to move into the abundance of abandoned warehouses.

Walking up the Carrer del Comerç, which leads north from the market, you reach the **Museu de la Xocolata** at no. 36. *Open Mon, Wed–Sat 10.00–20.00, Sun & public holidays 10.00–15.00. Fee.* Opened in 2000 in the former Convento de San Agustín, the exhibits chart the history of chocolate, its arrival in Europe and how it came to be so popular.

Emerging from the museum, turn right then immediately left into Carrer del Rec, a narrow street that used to be a stream, complete with mill-lined banks. Now, it is a mixture of galleries, workshops, bars and antique shops. Cutting along the tiny Carrer Sabateret brings you to the parallel Carrer dels Flassaders. At no. 40 is the **Casa de la Seca**, with the Bourbon coat of arms on the portal, where coins were minted from 1441 to the mid-19C. On the corner with Carrer Mosques, look up to see a stone face on the side of the building. Such sculptures used to be common in these back streets, but now very few survive. For people who were unable to read, they advertised the location of brothels.

Crossing the square again and continuing down Carrer del Rec, you will see a curious group of dilapidated, houses with flower-filled terraces supported by stone columns. These are some of the oldest structures in the neighbourhood, dating back to the 15C.

An old greengrocer's is still going strong on the corner with Carrer Esparteria, named after the artisans who used to make baskets and mats from esparto grass in workshops along the street. Rec and the adjoining streets used to be lined with fishmongers selling fresh and salted fish. On the corner of Carrer Bonaire you can still see the faded lettering of **Salazones Izomar**, advertising its salted tuna and mackerel.

Turning right here brings you to Plaça de les Olles, a pretty pedestrianised square with a string of pavement cafés. If you are passing at lunchtime, stop at Cal Pep, an extremely popular seafood bar, where you just follow the waiters' advice about to have. The square is named after the potters who had their workshops here. Neighbouring streets similarly reflect the craftsmen formerly working there: Carrer Espaseria was home to the swordmakers, glassmakers were based along Carrer Vidriera and silversmiths on Carrer Argenteria.

The arches spanning the narrow streets leading off the square are a characteristic feature of the area. In medieval times, space was at such a premium that someone came up with the idea of building in the gaps between the houses, leaving a passage at ground level for through traffic.

Turning right out of the square brings you back to Santa Maria church. Leave the area by walking up the diagonal Carrer Argenteria, which brings you back to the Via Laietana.

4 • The Raval

▸ Start from Plaça de la Universitat. See map on pp 84–85.

The area known as the Raval lies between La Rambla and the circuit of avenues to the west. The word *raval* comes from *arrabal*, meaning outside, and this was originally an outlying district with a scattering of hospitals and religious institutions set among fields and orchards. In the 14C it was embraced by the third and final extension of the city walls. Up to the late 18C it continued to be an area especially favoured by hospitals, charitable institutions and other such buildings, but its present-day character is due largely to radical redevelopment in the 19C, when it became the cradle of industrial Barcelona. An extensive improvement programme has been underway since the late 1990s, aimed at cleaning up the area, which is very seedy in places. Whole blocks have been demolished to create broad boulevards and let light in to previously dank, dark streets. The opening of the MACBA contemporary art museum in 1995 was the catalyst for an upturn in the area's fortunes, and galleries, boutiques and bars are now springing up everywhere.

The northern and more respectable part of the Raval is sometimes referred to as the Raval de Ponent. An excellent description of this area in the 1950s and early 1960s is to be found in *El día que murió Marilyn* (*The Day that Marilyn Died*), a semi-autobiographical novel by Terenci Moix, who was brought up here. Leading writer Maruja Torres also spent her childhood in this district, in her case in the streets just off the Rambla behind the Liceu, which she recreated in her funny and evocative novel *Un Calor Cercano* (*A Warmth Close By*).

From the Plaça de la Universitat, head down the Carrer dels Tallers, the name of which is a reference to the slaughterhouses that were situated here from the 12C onwards (cutting meat was not allowed within the city walls). The street leads shortly to the Plaça de Castella, with the former monastery church of **Sant Pere Nolasc** on the right.

The Paulist monastery to which this belonged was converted in the early 19C, first into a tobacco factory and then into a military hospital serving French troops. Only the church survived when the complex was pulled down in 1943.

Built in 1710–16, this Baroque structure has been given a dreary Neo-classical look in the course of numerous remodellings and alterations. The most interesting feature is the dome, decorated inside with a scene of the Coronation of the Virgin by Joseph Flaugier (1757–1813), a pupil of David.

Behind the building, on the Carrer Torres i Amat, is the pale pink block of the **Dispensario Antituberculoso** (Tuberculosis Clinic), one of the more important early examples of Rationalist architecture in Spain. Commissioned in 1934 by the Generalitat as part of their pioneering scheme to nationalise hospital and other social services, the building was designed by the Le Corbusier-inspired architectural team known as GATCPAC, whose main members were Josep Lluis Sert, Josep Torres i Clavé and Joan Baptista Subirana.

The building, described by the Spanish architectural historian Oriol Bohigas as 'the masterpiece of our Rationalism, and one of the most important buildings of its kind in Europe', was completed at the height of the Civil War and thus little appreciated in its time. After the war, GATCPAC was dispersed, and all Modernist trends in architecture came to be regarded as ideologically suspicious. The building was restored between 1982 and 1992 and is now a health centre.

The Carrer Torres i Amat leads to the Carrer de Joaquim Costa. On the corner is the Centro Aragonés, built in 1916 as a meeting place for the substantial Aragonese community, who had come to Barcelona from the neighbouring region in search of work.

Known to the older members of this district as the Carrer de Ponent, the **Carrer de Joaquim Costa** is one of the liveliest and best preserved streets in the Raval de Ponent, and is lined on both sides by tall 19C tenements adorned with metalwork balconies. The writer Terenci Moix was born at **no. 37** on the right. The ground floor of the building houses the *Granja de Gavá*, a friendly café where exhibitions are also held.

As you walk down the street, on your right is the Carrer del Tigre, where at no. 27 is a famous and very popular dance hall known as **La Paloma**. Founded in 1904, it has retained its original interior by Salvador Alarma, and features a long and profusely gilded hall, surrounded by balconies on all sides, with elaborate ceiling decorations and a central chandelier. It is still going strong, popular with old and young alike, with a range of music and dance styles from the traditional to the most avant-garde.

Another traditional establishment is the *Casa Almirall*, a wonderfully old-fashioned bar (*open from 19.00 onwards*) situated at the junction with the Carrer de Ferlandina. Founded in 1860, the place was used in 1966 as the setting of José María Nunces' film, *Noches de Vino Tinto* (Nights of Red Wine). A little further down on the right at no. 30 is the *Casa Riera*, which is a very cheap place to eat and has a changing menu that includes Indian vegetarian dishes.

Museu d'Art Contemporani de Barcelona

Turning down Carrer de Ferlandina into the Plaça dels Àngels, you enter a part of the city that has undergone radical redevelopment in recent years. The sleek white building on the left is the Museu d'Art Contemporani de Barcelona, known as the MACBA. *Open late June–late Sept Mon, Wed & Fri 11.00–20.00, Thur 11.00–21.00, Sat 10.00–20.00, Sun & public holidays 10.00–15.00; late Sept–late June Mon, Wed–Sat 11.00–19.30, Sat 10.00–20.00, Sun & public holidays 10.00–15.00. Fee. Half price Wed. Free with Articket, Barcelona Card and Bus Turístic discount. Guided tours. Book and gift shop. Café.*

The museum was designed by the American architect Richard Meier. The circular foyer opens onto a glass and enamelled metal atrium with ramps linking the three floors and the basement. Selections from the permanent collection are

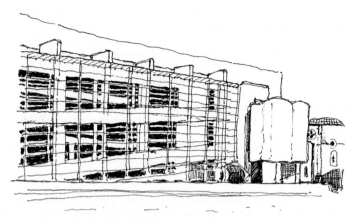

Museu d'Art Contemporani de Barcelona

displayed on a rotational basis on the ground floor, and the next two floors are used for temporary exhibitions.

The collection concentrates on art from the second half of the 20C onwards, with an emphasis on Catalan and Spanish artists. Artists represented include Joan Miró, Alexander Calder, Paul Klee, Modest Cuixart, Lucio Fontana, Antonio Saura, Antoni Tàpies, Robert Motherwell, Jorge de Oteiza, Dau al Set, Manuel Millares, Robert Rauschenberg, Pablo Palazuelo, Cy Twombly, Joan Brossa, Bruce Naumann, Mario Merz, Gerhard Richter, Francesc Torres, José Maria Sicilia, Antoni Miralda, Frederic Amat, Miquel Barceló, José Manuel Broto and Perejaume.

The MACBA site and the square in front of it were created following the demolition of part of the **Casa de La Caritat**, which was founded in the 14C as a convent for Franciscan nuns. In 1592 it was converted into a Tridentine seminary, and from 1803 to 1957 was used as a hospice. The oldest surviving parts of the building date from the 18C, and include the long façade on the Carrer de Montalegre (turn left out of the square) and the Pati Manning, a two-storey courtyard built in 1743 and containing charming ceramic decoration on the upper level. This courtyard now belongs to the cultural department of the Diputació (access via Carrer de Montalegre 7, next door up from the CCCB).

Some of the remaining sections of the structure have been drastically remodelled to house the CCCB, or **Centre de Cultura Contemporània de Barcelona** (Carrer de Montealegre 5). *Open mid June–late Sept Tues–Sat 11.00–20.00, Sun & public holidays 11.00–15.00; late Sept–mid June Tues, Thu & Fri, 11.00–14.00, 16.00–20.00, Wed & Sat 11.00–20.00, Sun & public holidays 11.00–19.00. Fee. Guided tours. Book and gift shop. Café.*

The centre, which opened in 1994, is situated around the 19C Pati de les Dones, or Women's Courtyard. The north side of the space was rebuilt to house the exhibition areas, designed by Helio Piñón and Albert Viaplana. The glass façade tilts outwards on the upper level, reflecting the surrounding buildings. The other three sides of the courtyard were restored in the original style.

Although it has only been open a few years, the centre has gained a reputation for staging innovative and stimulating exhibitions, and usually has three shows running concurrently.

We now return to the Plaça dels Àngels, the name of which derives from the former **Convent dels Àngels**, a Dominican monastery that moved to the Raval in 1497. The monastery church is a late Gothic structure of 1562–66. From 1906 to 1978 the church and adjoining buildings were used as an arms store-room by the former Francoist mayor Miquel Mateu. The structures have since been controversially converted by Carles Díaz and Lluís Clotet for use as the head-quarters of the Foment de les Arts Decoratives (FAD), a prestigious Catalan organisation that promotes design and the decorative arts. Its annual awards are regarded as the benchmark of the Catalan design industry. The complex includes the Forum dels Àngels, a shop, bar and restaurant open to the public.

Antic Hospital de la Santa Creu

Leave the square by turning down the Carrer dels Àngels, by the side of the convent. You shortly come to the lively Carrer del Carme, and facing you is the Antic Hospital de la Santa Creu.

> The complex dates back to 1402, when the Consell de Cent decided to rationalise the city's hospital system and bring together all the city's hospital institutions on one site. In 1629 the city councillors laid the first stone of the Casa de Convalescència within the precinct of the hospital, and in 1760 the Colegi de Cirurgia (College of Surgeons) was established alongside.

Walking through the entrance arch, the **Colegi de Cirurgia** is on the left. This is the only part of the complex that still has a medical role, as it has housed the Royal Academy of Medicine since 1929. At the time of writing, the building was being restored and was not open to the public. Designed by the great Neo-classical architect Ventura Rodríguez, it has an exceptionally severe exterior, with mould-ings and window frames of great simplicity and a virtual absence of decoration. The structure is articulated by bare pilasters, niches and blind windows. The design is centred on two large windows that give light to the Anatomy Theatre.

This oval room, which is the outstanding feature of the interior, was used initially for the training of students and now as a ceremonial hall. The gilded Rococo decoration features a bust of *Charles III*, a marble dissecting table and a Venetian crystal chandelier presented in 1929 by Alfonso XIII.

The eastern façade of the building overlooks a tiny garden named after the Scottish discoverer of penicillin Sir Alexander Fleming, whose memory is commemorated in virtually every Spanish town and village. A bust of him, with the inscription '*Barcelona a Alexander Fleming*' is attached to the wall.

Walking into the complex is like entering an Oxford or Cambridge college, and you find yourself in a peaceful enclave that seems far removed from the bustling city outside. The strong university character is largely explained by the fact that the Casa de Convalescència (on the right as you enter) and the Hospital de la Santa Creu (on both sides of the courtyard) now house the **Institute of Catalan Studies**, the **Library of Catalunya** and the **Escola Massana**, a design school that is part of the university.

The construction of the Casa de Convalescència, though begun in 1629, was delayed by a fire in 1638, the War of the Harvesters of 1641–53 and epidemics of plague and famine in 1650–54. Under the supervision of Andreu Bosch and Josep Juli the building was eventually completed in 1680.

The vestibule is richly decorated with ceramic scenes of the life of St Paul executed by Llorenç Passoles between 1679 and 1682. At the end of the vestibule you emerge into a splendid Renaissance-style courtyard dominated by a statue of *St Paul* sculpted in 1678 by Lluís Bonifaç. The same sculptor was also responsible for the gargoyles above the courtyard's upper arcade, an ornamental feature that harks back to the Gothic period. Staircases adorned with ceramic fruit and flowers by Bernat Reig lead to the upper floor, the main attraction of which is the profusely decorated chapel. The ceramic murals are attributed to Josep Bal and Llorenç Passoles, and the gilded altarpiece, with Solomonic columns, is thought to be the work of Lluís Bonifaç.

The upper floor also gives access to the three surviving wards of the former Hospital de la Santa Creu, which are now used as library halls. The vast wards, which date back to the 15C, are typical structures of the Catalan Gothic, with large pointed arches supporting timber roofs (visits by appointment only, ☎ 93 317 0778).

The **main courtyard** is a beautiful space, shaded by orange trees, and incorporates at its northern end three wings of an early 15C cloister by Guillem d'Abiell. A Baroque cross stands on the site of the cloister's south wing, which was demolished in 1509 in order to extend the space. The southern half of the courtyard is made up of a variety of interconnected structures dating from the 16C to the 19C. The whole was extensively restored after 1930, when the place was finally abandoned as a hospital.

Through the arch at the southern end of the courtyard you emerge on the Carrer de l'Hospital, a narrow but busy commercial street. The entrance to the hospital from this street is marked by a curious Renaissance portal featuring a tympanum incorporating the arms of the hospital within the scallop shell of St James.

Turning left, you come to the former hospital chapel, built as an independent structure in 1406–44 and extensively remodelled in the 18C. The dark and simple barrel-vaulted chapel is now the Lacapella exhibition centre.

Continuing down the street, on your right is the Plaça de Sant Agustí, on which stands the former **Augustinian Monastery of Sant Agustí**. The Augustinians were given this site following the demolition of their previous monastery to make way for the Ciutadella (p 161). The church, designed by Pere Bertran and Pere Costa, was begun in 1728 and is an example of the Catalan Baroque at its most austere. Especially impressive is the unfinished west façade, which features a porticoed atrium articulated by giant Ionic columns. The interior, heavily remodelled in the 19C, lost most of its original decoration as a result of a series of arson attacks.

Heading back up the Carrer de l'Hospital, you pass *Curtidos Pinos* at no. 79, a traditional cobbler's where you can have shoes, belts and gloves made. Further up on the right, the Carrer de la Riera Baixa is an example of the area's emerging fashionable status. Lined with boutiques, second-hand shops and record shops, it is particularly lively on Saturdays when the shopkeepers move their stock outside to create a street market.

Just beyond the junction with the Carrer de la Riera Baixa, the narrow Carrer de l'Hospital opens up, the result of bulldozing entire streets. Before strolling down the Rambla del Raval, as the new boulevard leading south is called, walk the short distance to the end of the Carrer de l'Hospital.

You come out at the Plaça del Pedro, a small square formed by the intersection of the Carrer de l'Hospital and del Carme. Between the two streets is the Romanesque **Capella de Sant Llàtzer**, which originally belonged to a lepers' hospital that Bishop Guillem de Torroja had had built on the outskirts of the city in 1141. The chapel, which was deconsecrated in 1913, has been largely engulfed by the surrounding dwellings, but some have been demolished to reveal the apse. The interior of the chapel was considerably modified in the 18C and has recently been restored.

At the centre of the square is a famous statue of *Santa Eulàlia*, which was commissioned in 1670 by the Consell de Cent to commemorate the site where, according to tradition, the saint's tortured body was laid out. The original statue, in wood, was replaced in 1687 by a stone monument by Lluís Bonifaç. The revolutionary municipal government of 1823 wanted to demolish the statue, but a public outcry led to its being saved, and three years later a fountain was erected at its base. The work was extensively damaged by anarchists in 1936, but its head was saved by two brothers who later presented it to the Museu d'Història de la Ciutat. The figure was reconstructed by Frederic Marès in 1952.

Taking the left fork from the square, Carrer de la Botella, brings you shortly to the Carrer de la Cera, which is one of the main streets associated with the city's **gypsy** population. The restaurant *Can Lluís* (no. 49) has been popular over the years with artists and writers. It looks rather smart, which is somewhat surprising considering the surroundings, but is actually very reasonable, particularly the fixed-price lunch.

Retrace your steps to the Rambla del Raval. The area between here and the port used to be described as the largest red-light district in Europe, but is gradually being cleaned up. Referred to increasingly by the innocuous name of the Raval de Sant Pau, it is popularly known as the Barri Xinès (Chinatown), a name that has traditionally inspired a mixture of fear, revulsion and fascination.

The Rambla del Raval is crossed by the long Carrer de Sant Pau, which runs all the way from La Rambla to the western boundary of the Raval. This is the main artery of the Barri Xinès, though its character is changing in line with the great changes that are happening to this district.

At the Ramblas end of the street is the *Hotel Espanya* (nos 9–11). This architectural jewel was once a luxury hotel that later went slightly to seed as a result of its situation in the Barri Xinès. It is now a reasonably priced place with a pleasantly intimate character.

The hotel dates back to the late 19C, but owes its architectural distinction to reforms carried out on the ground floor by Domènech i Montaner in 1902–03. The outstanding features of the interior are the two dining rooms, both of which have retained much of their original Modernista furnishings, including elaborate ironwork candelabra. One of the rooms has extensive ceramic decorations, while the other has curious classical-style murals of mermaids by Ramon Casas, as well as an interesting frieze of ceramic roundels inset in a wooden framework imitative of bamboo-work. The small hotel bar has suffered the most from insensitive remodelling in the 1950s, but is nonetheless worth visiting for its magnificent fireplace, which was expressively sculpted by Eusebi Arnau (with the assistance of Pau Gargallo), with allegorical figures and the coat of arms of Spain. The amusing details include a cat making its way to the fender.

Barri Xinès

The term 'Barri Xinès' was coined in the 1920s to describe the small district between the Carrer Nou de la Rambla and the Carrer Portal de Santa Madrona. Later, the term came to be loosely applied to the entire seedy area to the south of the Carrer de Hospital. This red-light district, serving Barcelona's port, has nothing to do with the Chinese, but appears instead to owe its name to the writer Miguel Toledano, who wrote under the pseudonym Manuel Gil de Oto.

Following a journey to the United States in 1924, Toledano wrote a colourful book entitled *Los Enemigos de América* (*The Enemies of America*), which included a lurid description of the Chinatown of some North American city. A young journalist called Angel Marsá, reporting on a den of thieves to be found on the Carrer del Cid, remembered Toledano's book and likened the surrounding area to a 'Chinatown'.

The squalid and corrupt aspects of the area attracted the Bohemian elements in Barcelona society, and the place has always held a strong romantic fascination for foreign visitors to the city. The French writers Georges Bataille and Jean Genet were the authors of some of the most vivid descriptions of the area, most notably Genet in the powerful opening pages of his *Thief's Journal*.

More recently the area has been described at length by the Barcelona-born writer Juan Goytisolo, whose self-confessed 'fervour for slum areas' undoubtedly developed as a result of having been brought up in the smarter middle-class areas of the city. Lengthy accounts of Goytisolo's youthful experiences in the Barri Xinès feature in his controversial book, *Forbidden Territory*:

Alone or with Carlos, I carefully explored the bars and dives on the back streets between Conde de Asalto (Nou de la Rambla) and Atarazanas: the Criolla had disappeared after being frequented by the author of Thief's Journal, *but other haunts exuding filth and dirt still justified the reputation of that Barcelona opposed forever to the homogeneous, paternalist, limp ideal of its petty bourgeoisie and the magnetic attraction the city held for writers like Genet or Bataille. Cigarette girls, blackmarketeers, cripples, dope peddlers, vile, ill-lit bars, adverts for permanganate baths, contraceptive shops, grotesque sights from the Bodega Bohemia, rooms let by the hour, six-peseta brothels, the entire Hispanic court of miracles imposed a brutal reality that burst the bubble around me with one blast. The public whore houses of Robadors and Tapias (Carrer de les Tàpies), the opulent, sometimes obese shapes of the women queuing on the benches, their legs wide apart, half-naked, preoccupied, in a posture of innocent bestiality, attracted me not only because of a consciously perverse Baudelairean aesthetic but because of their tangible, disturbing promiscuity.*

Typical Modernista pharmacy

At no. 65 of the Carrer de Sant Pau is the **Bar Marsella** (*open only from 22.00 onwards*), which opened in 1820 and was once a notorious haunt of Barcelona low-life, bohemians and artists. Picasso and Gaudí were regulars in their time. It is now favoured increasingly by foreigners with a yearning for the Barri Xinès of old. As its name suggests, this spacious wood-panelled bar was created in imitation of a typical bar of Marseilles, where the founder was from (another such establishment is the nearby **Pastís**; p 95). The particular attraction of the Marsella is its absinthe.

At the other end of the street is the former monastery of **Sant Pau del Camp**, the most important of Barcelona's surviving Romanesque monuments. The writer Vázquez Montalbán, who was born in Barcelona, commenting on this monastery's unexpected presence within the Barri Xinès, likened the building to 'an abandoned Christian mission'. Today, however, the incongruity of its situation has been somewhat lessened by the pulling down of neighbouring slum dwellings and houses of ill-repute to make way for a large park and sports centre.

A tombstone of 912, and Visigothic capitals on the portal of the monastery church, indicate that the foundation of Sant Pau del Camp dates back at least to the beginning of the 10C. Possibly destroyed by Al-Mansur in 985, it was almost certainly set fire to by the Almoravids in 1114–15, for the place was refounded by the viscounts Geribert and Rotlandis in 1117. In 1528 the monastery was taken over by friars from the Chapel of Montserrat, and in 1672 was turned into a Benedictine noviciate. During the Peninsular War it served as a hospital and shelter for Royalist troops, and following a fire in 1835, the monastery buildings were converted into a barracks, while the church was temporarily designated as parish of the Raval.

The demolition of the whole complex was later prevented through the intervention of the Associació Catalana d'Excursions, who, with the support of the politician Victor Balaguer, obtained national monument status for it in

1879. Restoration work was begun in 1896, and renewed in 1922 and 1930. In the course of the last two restoration campaigns, Baroque and later structures were demolished in order to expose the Romanesque church and cloister, which now stand within a small garden.

Entering the precinct of the former monastery, on your right is the much restored 14C **Abbot's House** (now the rectory), which is joined to the 12C church by a brick school building of 1932. The exterior of the church, decorated with Lombard arcades, has a portal incorporating marble capitals from an earlier structure, and corbels and reliefs crudely carved with the emblems of the Evangelists. A Latin inscription on the lintel refers to Sts Peter and Paul, and also to the unidentified Renardus and Raimunda.

The church, shaped like a Greek cross, has an octagonal crossing tower crowned by an 18C belfry. The simple, barrel-vaulted interior was largely refaced following damage caused during the 'Tragic Week' of 1909 (see p 78). A door through the south transept leads into the early 14C **Chapter House** (now a chapel), with the tomb slab of the early Catalan leader, Guifre Borrell (947–992), on the east wall.

From here, you can enter the tiny **cloister**, one of the more enchanting corners of old Barcelona. Centred around a garden and fountain, this Romanesque structure of the 13C has arcades of Moorish-inspired polyfoil arches, the capitals of which are decorated with vegetal and grotesque motifs.

Just beyond Sant Pau del Camp, the Carrer de Sant Pau reaches the western boundary of the Ciutat Vella (Old Town), marked today by the junction of the Ronda de Sant Pau with the long, wide and ugly Avinguda del Paral·lel. The surrounding district, with its various nightclubs, music halls and other places of entertainment, enjoyed its heyday in the early 20C, when it was regarded as the Barcelona equivalent of Montmartre.

Facing you across the square is a celebrated nightclub dating back to 1909 and at one time referred to as the *Moulin Rouge*. Although closed at the time of writing, it may well reopen in a new guise in the future. A little further down the Avinguda del Paral·lel you come to the Plaça Raquel Meller, named after a popular singer of the early 20C who made her debut in 1911 at the Arnau music-hall, which is on the left of the square. At the entrance to the Carrer Nou de la Rambla, a full-length statue of the singer, by Viladomat, shows her in the pseudo-rustic costume appropriate to the type of song that made her famous, the *cuplé*.

This end of the Carrer Nou de la Rambla has been particularly affected by the programme of urban renewal. The infamous *Baghdad* survives at no. 103, however, a place which has had the reputation for many years of putting on one of Europe's most pornographic shows, featuring live sex acts and audience participation.

From the Plaça Raquel Meller, you could take the old funicular that climbs up the hill of Montjuïc (p 193). Alternatively, you could continue walking down the Avinguda Paral·lel until you reach the stretch of the city walls attached to the Museu Maritim Drassanes (p 150).

5 • The Waterfront

▸ Start from Plaça Portal de la Pau. See map on pp 150–51.

One of the much-repeated sayings about Barcelona was that after its maritime heyday in the Middle Ages the city had turned its back on the sea. Now it has one of the finest seafronts of any European city, as the situation was dramatically reversed by the radical urban transformation of Barcelona in preparation for the 1992 Olympic Games. Elegant promenades were created and the beaches were reclaimed, cleaned up and provided with a wealth of facilities. Although this waterfront development is still expanding, it has already acquired its own distinctive character and is a very welcome addition to the city's attractions.

The Plaça Portal de la Pau is a large seaside square created in 1849 by the opening of the stretch of medieval walls that blocked off the end of La Rambla. At the centre of the square is the 60m-high **Monument a Colom** (Monument to Columbus). *Open Mon–Fri 10.00–13.30, 15.30–18.30, Sat, Sun & public holidays 10.00–18.30. Fee. Bus Turístic and Barcelona Card discounts.*

Although this is the most prominent and popular of the city's commemorative monuments, there is a certain irony in the fact that such a work should celebrate the man whose achievements effectively demolished Barcelona's maritime economy by diverting trade to Seville.

The idea for a monument commemorating Columbus's alleged visit to Ferdinand and Isabella in Barcelona in 1493 came from local merchant Antoni Fages i Ferrer, who obsessively pursued this idea with the authorities. Eventually the project was taken up by the mayor, Rius i Taulet, who claimed it as his own, and in May 1881 set up a commission to raise funds and organise a competition to decide on the architect. After initially failing to find a suitable candidate, the competition was won in September 1882 by Gaietà Buïgas i Monravà, who proposed a cast-iron column resting on an elaborate stone plinth. While cast-iron columns of this sort had been relatively common since the time of the July Column in Paris, Gaietà Buïgas had the novel idea of creating a lift-shaft within the monument.

Construction of the monument was delayed for several years until the finance was found, but eventually work began. The State donated a number of old cannons from the castle at Montjuïc that were melted down to provide more than 30 tonnes of bronze. The column was finally inaugurated on 1 June, 1888, shortly before the opening of the first World Exhibition. Extensive restoration has been carried out in recent years.

A group of bronze lions surround the base of the monument. Behind them are eight copper reliefs of scenes from Columbus' life, four of which are by Josep Llimona and the rest by Antoni Vilanova. Placed in front of the buttresses of the plinth are stone figures by Carbonell, Gamot, Atché and Carcasso representing the kingdoms of Catalunya, Aragón, León and Castile. The bronze detailing on the plinth is by Rossend Nobas and includes decorative forms featuring the figure of Fame and the prow of a caravel. Representations of the Four Continents by Francesc Pastor decorate on the capital of the column, and the whole is crowned by a massive crown supporting a bronze statue by Rafael Atché of Columbus pointing to the sea. You can take a lift right up to the base of the crown, but the views are somewhat obscured by the ironwork.

Museu Marítim

The far side of the Plaça Portal de la Pau (towards Montjuïc) is occupied by the extraordinary former shipyards known as the Drassanes, which now house the Museu Marítim. *Open Tue–Sun 10.00–19.00. Fee. Bus Turístic and Barcelona Card discount. Shop. Good café.*

These are the most important medieval shipyards to have survived anywhere in the world, but have been extensively altered in the course of many centuries of use. The royal shipyards were the place where the galleys of the Crown of Aragón and later of Spain were not only built and repaired, but also put into dry dock. The yards were first mentioned in 1243, but it was not until 1284, during the reign of Pere II the Great, that they were built on their present site. Their subsequent history is exceedingly complex, and it is not easy today to sort out the various phases in their construction, particularly as the same building system seems to have been favoured over the centuries.

This system appears to have been evolved during the reign of Pere II's great-grandson, Pere III the Ceremonious, who in 1378 decided to alter and enlarge the shipyards through the creation of eight parallel aisles formed of rounded arches supporting pointed roofs. These aisles both extended the yards to the north and covered part of the large open courtyard comprising the nucleus of the original structure. By the early

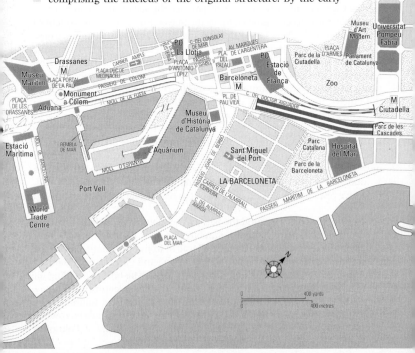

17C, this courtyard had been almost entirely covered by additional aisles, and in 1613–18 three further ones were built to the east. The façade of the building overlooking the sea was created in the early 18C, and at the same time the two central aisles were joined together to form a large single one.

The decline of the shipyards set in during the 17C, culminating with the dissolution of the royal galleys in 1748. The building, which had already served as an ammunition store, barracks and fortress during the War of the Harvesters, was eventually taken over entirely for military purposes. In the late 19C numerous plans were proposed entailing the demolition of the building, and it was not until the 1920s that the future of this remarkable complex was finally assured, thanks to a large extent to an eloquently persuasive article written in 1926 by an artillery colonel called Joaquín. This article, which appeared in the newspaper *La Vanguardia*, referred to the shipyards as a 'priceless jewel that is completely unknown'. In 1936 plans were made to transform the oldest part of the yards into a Maritime Museum, which was finally opened in 1941.

Seen from the Plaça Portal de la Pau, the shipyards could almost be mistaken for a vast 19C warehouse were it not for the odd medieval tower peering over the sea of long parallel roofs. The side of the building overlooking the Avinguda del Paral·lel is in fact attached to the longest surviving stretch of the city's 14C to 15C defensive walls.

The museum is the finest of its kind in Spain, with a no less impressive setting. With its forest of enormous arches and columns, the building could almost be described as a secular version of the Mosque at Cordoba. It is especially memorable if visited at dusk, when the dramatic spotlighting of the museum's exhibits, contrasted with the cavernous gloom of the vast surroundings, creates mysterious chiaroscuro effects of a Piranesi-like character.

Following an intelligent revamp in 1995, this is now a lively, popular museum with lots of interactive exhibits. The permanent displays begin with exhibits charting Barcelona's relationship with the sea over the centuries and the history of the Royal Shipyards. Other sections include the development of the shipbuilding and fishing industries. The **Image of the World** deals with the search for new trade routes from the 15C to the 19C. There are models of the three ships that made the first voyage to America, together with the navigation instruments used. The revolution brought about by steam in the mid-19C is illustrated by exhibits on Barcelona's two major shipping lines, the *Compañia Transatlántica* and the *Compañia Transmediterránea*.

Visitors wear headphones (English commentary available) when moving through **The Great Sea Adventure**, which highlights the most significant events in Catalunya's martitime history and takes you on simulated voyages aboard a steamboat and submarine.

On the quayside of the Plaça Portal de la Pau is the pompous **Aduana** (Customs House), a Neo-Renaissance structure articulated by a giant order of columns and crowned by a row of griffins, which was built in 1895–1902 by Enric Sagnier i Villavecchia and Pere Garcia Faria i Monteys. The ornate cream and grey building opposite is the **Puerto Autónomo** (Port Headquarters), designed by Juli Valdés in 1907.

Nearby is the landing-stage of the *Golondrines*, pleasure boats that take people around the harbour or down to the Port Olímpic. Evocative descriptions of the now rapidly changing port are to be found in Juan Goytisolo's autobiographical work, *Forbidden Territory* (English translation, 1989), and in his short story, *Otoño, en el Puerto, cuando llovizna* (*Autumn, in the port, in the drizzle*).

Facing the sea, leading out to sea to your right is the **Moll de Barcelona**, where a selection of cruise liners are usually docked. The circular building is the **World Trade Center**, designed by I.M. Pei, Cobb, Freed & Partners, which opened in 1999. Development is still underway along the quay, which will reinforce the waterfront as Barcelona's new business and leisure hub.

The spectacular timber **bridge** that links the Plaça Portal de la Pau with the Moll d'Espanya was designed by Helio Piñón and Albert Viaplana in 1994. Called La **Rambla del Mar**, it has indeed become an extension of the Ramblas, delivering thousands of visitors every day to *Maremàgnum*, a complex of shops, bars, restaurants and clubs. Also designed by Piñón and Viaplana, the complex is extremely popular, particularly in the evenings.

Alongside it on the quay there are multiplex and Imax cinemas, and also the **Aquarium**. *Open July & Aug daily 9.30–23.00; Sept–Jun Mon–Fri 9.30–21.00; Sat, Sun 09.30–21.30. Fee. Bus Turístic and Barcelona Card discounts.* Specialising in the Mediterranean, this excellent modern aquarium appeals to both children and adults with the chance to view sharks close-up and try out the interactive exhibits.

Walk back over the bridge to the Plaça Portal de la Pau. The quayside from here to the Port Vell marina is known as the **Moll de la Fusta**, and was the first part of the area to be developed. *Fusta* means 'wood', a reference to when this part of the harbour was used by the timber industry. Behind it runs the Passeig de Colom, which leads to Plaça d'Antonio López.

In the 1920s the waterfront was shielded from the Passeig de Colom by a group of drab warehouses serving the port. Despite numerous public protests, these structures were not finally to be taken down until the 1960s, and it was not until 20 years later that a new scheme for improving this whole area finally came to be implemented.

Built in 1983–87 under the supervision of Manuel de Solà-Morales, the wide thoroughfare of the Moll de la Fusta was designed to provide Barcelona with a dignified maritime façade and also to alleviate traffic congestion. There are two parallel promenades. The one nearest the sea is at a lower level and lined with rows of palm trees. A dual carriageway, partially covered by the upper promenade, separates the two levels and is spanned by two colourful red drawbridges inspired by Van Gogh's *Bridge at Arles*.

The upper promenade originally housed five bars, which were very fashionable until the mid-1990s. The most famous was *Gambrinus*, created in 1988 by the architect Alfredo Arribas and the designer Javier Mariscal. The sculpture of a gigantic, smiling prawn waving from the roof of the bar featured in dozens of articles about the new Barcelona, becoming a symbol of the city's innovative design scene.

Ironically, the demise of these bars was caused by the runaway success of Maremàgnum and the Port Olímpic. After they closed down in 2000, some were occupied by squatters. In 2001, the whole stretch was redeveloped and the existing premises were demolished to make way for two new bars and municipal buildings.

At the end of the Moll de la Fusta, where it meets the Moll d'Espanya, there is a large sculpture by Roy Lichtenstein called *Barcelona Head*.

The broad Passeig de Colom was created following the demolition of a large section of the medieval walls in 1878–81. Located in what was once the aristocratic part of Barcelona, it became the city's main thoroughfare during the World Exhibition of 1888. At this end once stood Domènech i Montaner's extraordinary Hotel International, which was built specifically for the Exhibition and taken down soon afterwards. Built in 53 days with the help of a daily workforce of up to 2000, it daringly featured foundations floating on water, an aspect of the building that led to numerous cartoons in the press, most notably of the whole structure sailing out to sea.

The buildings along the Passeig today are heavy, unimaginative structures of the late 19C and early 20C. Halfway along on the left is the Plaça Duc de Medinaceli, a small landscaped square that featured in Pedro Almodóvar's Oscar-winning film, *All About My Mother* (1999). The square was laid out in 1844 by Francesc Daniel Molina on the site created by the demolition of the Convent de Sant Francesc. Molina, together with Lluís Rigalt, was also responsible for the design of the memorial column to the Catalan admiral *Galceran Marquet* in the middle of the square, surrounded by tall palm trees. The memorial, executed in

1851, was sculpted by Damià Campeny, and was the first commemorative monument in the city to use cast iron.

On the corner of the square and Carrer Ample a plaque marks the birthplace in 1824 of Josep Anselm Clavé, who founded the Catalan choral associations.

Further down the Passeig de Colom, at no. 14, is the **Capitanía General** (Military Headquarters), which occupies the former Mercedarian Convent, the church of which adjoins the Carrer Ample (p 122). The building, constructed by Jeroni Santacana in 1605–53, was transformed into the Capitanía General in 1846, and given its present façade by Adolf Florensa i Ferrer in 1926–29. This colossal and overwhelmingly pompous classical façade was built as part of the city's preparations for the Exhibition of 1929, and was clearly influenced by the architecture of Mussolini's Italy. Florensa also remodelled much of the interior, but fortunately left untouched the magnificent 17C **cloister**, which is comparable to that of the contemporary Casa de Convalescència (p 143) and is likewise richly decorated with ceramics.

The fine 17C Renaissance house with corner towers at **no. 6** Passeig de Colom was remodelled in 1997 by Rafael de Cáceres to house the *Sociedad General de Autores de España*, which deals with publishing rights and authors' royalties.

Architecturally less interesting is the 16C house at **no. 2** (at the very end of the avenue, overlooking the Plaça d'Antoni López), which is known as the Casa Cervantes owing to the belief that the author of Don Quixote stayed here.

The Plaça d'Antoni López marks the chaotic junction of the Via Laietana with the Passeig de Colom and its continuation, the Passeig d'Isabel II. The square is dominated by the **Edificio de Correos** (Central Post Office), a modest building in comparison with that of Madrid, but exceedingly grand by any other standards. Designed in 1914 by Josep Goday i Casals and Jaume Torres i Grau (but not constructed until 1926–29), this massive classical structure features a central frontispiece articulated by giant Corinthian columns supporting four allegorical figures by the Noucentiste sculptor Manuel Fuxà. The Noucentiste painters Josep Obiols, Francesc Labarta, Francesc Canyelles and Francesc Galí were responsible for the classical, Puvis de Chavannes-inspired frescoes adorning the lunettes of the building's echoing main hall, though these works are now so darkened and gloomily lit as to be barely decipherable.

The broad but short Passeig d'Isabel II, which joins the Plaça d'Antoni López with the Pla de Palau, was created after 1835, following the first stage of the demolition of Barcelona's maritime defensive walls. The left side is occupied by **La Llotja** (Stock Exchange), the Neo-classical exterior of which blends well with the neighbouring ensemble of grand early 19C structures.

In 1339 the Consell dels Vint—a group of 20 merchants under the direction of a *cónsol* or judge—acquired a plot of land in the district of Ribera del Mar with the intention of erecting a building where all commercial transactions could take place. The money for its construction was to be raised by the levying of a 3 per cent tax on all goods entering and leaving the city. The original structure, built by Pere Llobet in 1352–57, appears to have been a simple porticoed structure, where the merchants carried out their business under the arches of the loggia. The building, which had been damaged both by the sea and by an attack carried out by the Castilian Navy in 1359, was replaced in 1383 by a new structure commissioned by Pere III the Ceremonious from

Pere Arbei. This new Llotja, apparently inspired by the one in Valencia, comprised a courtyard and a large hall, which is the only part to have survived to this day.

By 1764 a large section of the building was threatening to collapse and, soon afterwards, a commission of works was established with a view to transforming the place into the seat of the Barcelona Chamber of Commerce. The remodelling was entrusted to Joan Soler i Faneca, who destroyed all but the hall, which he encased in a large Neo-classical block. Soler supervised the work until his death in 1794, after which he was replaced by Joan Fàbregas and Tomàs Soler, who constructed the imposing pedimented façade on the Pla de Palau. After the dissolution of the Chamber of Commerce in 1847, part of the building was handed over to the Barcelona School of Fine Arts, which was based here until comparatively recently, and still has a small museum of academic works in the building. Picasso's father, José Ruíz Blasco, taught at the School at the end of the 19C, and Picasso himself was a pupil here. Joan Miró also studied here at the beginning of the 20C.

When I last visited the building was being restored and was not open to the public. Ask at the entrance on the street behind the building, Carrer Consolat del Mar, in case the situation has changed and you are allowed into the **Gothic Hall**.

This superlative if misleadingly named structure was built by Pere Arbei in the late 14C as the *Saló de Contractacions* (Trading Hall). Impressively spacious, it is divided into three aisles by exceptionally tall and elegant arcades formed not of pointed but rounded arches, the whole covered by a wooden beam ceiling. Part of the fascination of this hall is that it was used almost continuously for trading activities, and was the Stock Exchange until 1994, when the institution moved to the Passeig de Gràcia.

Facing the Llotja are the **Porxos d'en Xifré**, a porticoed Neo-classical block formed of five houses, one side of which faces the Pla de Palau. Promoted by Josep Xifré i Casas, a Catalan merchant who had made his money in America, it was built in 1836–40 by Josep Buixareu and Francesc Vila. Articulated by a giant order of pilasters, it is richly decorated with terracotta and other reliefs attributed to Tomàs Padró, a pupil of Campeny. Whereas the three upper floors of the building were intended as homes, the rooms off the ground-floor arcade were used as commercial establishments.

One of these, at **no. 14**, survives to this day, although it was extensively restored in 1980. This, the *Set Portes*, opened in 1838 and is one of Barcelona's most famous restaurants. It has been patronised by such diverse personalities as Picasso, Einstein and Ava Gardner, and was the subject of a book by José María Carandell.

When Picasso's family arrived in Barcelona in 1895, they lived in a basement apartment at Passeig d'Isabel II no. 4, but moved shortly afterwards to a second-floor apartment at the back of the Porxos d'en Xifré. This apartment was situated at Carrer Reina Cristina no. 3, a street that today has been turned into a great discount electronics bazaar. Incongruously situated amidst all this is the *Xampanyeria* (at **no. 7**), a bodega specialising exclusively in cava, the Catalan version of champagne.

The large Pla del Palau, laid out by José Massanés in 1836, constitutes one of Barcelona's grandest and most harmonious ensembles of early 19C buildings, even though it has lost the Palau dels Virreis, the royal palace that gave the place its name, which burnt down in 1875.

At the centre of the square is the *Font del Geni Català* (Fountain of Catalan Genius), which was designed by Francesc Daniel Molina in 1825, but not executed until 1855. The sculptors responsible were two Italians resident in Barcelona, Fausto and Angel Baratta. The work commemorates the Marquis of Campo Sagrado, who brought water to the city from Montcada. The central figure is an Allegory of Catalan Genius, while below are four seated figures representing the four Catalan provinces, the main rivers of which (the Llobregat, Ter, Ebre and Segura), are suggested by the four jets of water at their feet.

In the lower part of the square, near the Set Portes, there are four granite triangles by the German artist Ulrich Rückriem. This work is part of a series commissioned for the Port Vell area in 1992, more of which we will see presently.

At the junction of the square and the Avinguda Marquès de l'Argentera (the continuation of the Passeig d'Isabel II) is the former **Duana Vella** or Custom House, which was built in 1790–92 to replace a previous custom house which had burnt down in 1777. Designed by the versatile Count of Roncalli, then Minister of Finance, this cheerful stucco-coated structure is articulated by pilasters simulating coloured marble. The building, transformed in 1902 into the seat of the Civil Government, has retained sumptuous and extensive Neo-classical decorations by Pere Pau Montañà. Since 1997 it has been the headquarters of the Delegation of the Spanish Government.

Opposite is the *Hotel Park*, designed in 1950–54 by Antoni de Moragas and Francesc de Riba, a rare example of 1950s' architecture in Barcelona with a distinctive staircase and mosaic bar. Further along the Avinguda Marquès de l'Argentera is the enormous **Estació de França**, an enormous railway station built in 1926–29 as part of the city's urban improvements in preparation for the International Exhibition of 1929. It replaced a station of 1848, which was the first in Spain. The structure has a classical elegance in keeping with the tenets of Noucentisme. The most striking feature is the vestibule—decorated by Raimon Duran i Reynals and Salvador Soteras i Taberner—which is covered by three coffered shallow domes. Following extensive restoration and remodelling, the station reopened in 1992, but is no longer a major terminal. Part of the premises has been turned into bars and clubs.

Opposite the station is the Born district, explored in Walk 3, and just beyond it is the Parc de la Ciutadella, discussed in Walk 6.

Museu d'Història de Catalunya

Return to the Pla de Palau, turn left and walk down to the adjoining Plaça de Pau Vila. The enormous structure between the square and the marina is the Palau del Mar, now the Museu d'Història de Catalunya. *Open Tue, Thur, Fri & Sat 10.00–19.00; Wed 10.00–20.00; Sun & public holidays 10.00–14.30. Fee. Bus Turístic discount. Shop. Rooftop café has terrace with panoramic views.*

The building was originally a warehouse and was designed in 1894–1900 by the engineer Mauricio Garrán. In 1993 the structure was remodelled by Laurence Halprin, Edmund Berger and Eberhart Zeidler to house government offices and restaurants as well as the museum.

The museum, which opened in 1996, was designed by Josep Benedito and

Agustí Mateos and occupies one half of the building. Arranged in eight main sections on the second and third floors, the permanent displays chart the history of Catalunya from prehistoric times to the present day, using a wide range of imaginative and stimulating devices to engage visitors of all ages.

The first section, **Roots**, contains tools, vessels and other objects from from the Palaeolithic, Phoenician and Punic periods, moving on to exhibits relating to Roman, Visigoth and Moslem domination in the region. **Birth of a Nation** includes examples of Romanesque art and models of castles, palaces and chapels. **Our Sea** deals with Catalunya's varying fortunes as a trading nation under the crown of Aragon, the union with Castile and the discovery of America. There are models of the shipyards and the church of Santa Maria del Mar. Artworks include a fragment of a 15C retable by Pere Garcia de Benavarri. **On the Periphery of the Empire** charts Catalunya's links with the Habsburgs in the 16C and 17C, leading up to the War of Succession and the abolition of the Constitutions of Catalunya. The **Bases of the Revolution** deals with the economic success brought about by agricultural development and the textile industry. **Steam and Nation** explores the growth of the industrial society and the parallel cultural developments. **The Electric Years** explains both techno-logical and political changes in the early 20C, leading up to the Civil War. Finally, **Defeat and Recovery** deals with the crisis faced by Catalunya after the war and during the Dictatorship. The displays conclude with the re-establishment of the Catalan government and the first democratic elections.

On the ground around the Palau del Mar, look out for another of the 1992 street artworks. *The Windrose* was created by Lothar Baumgarten and consists of the names of winds spelt out in huge bronze letters set into the pavement in the direction in which each wind blows.

Running parallel to the quay along the marina is the Passeig de Joan de Borbó, forming one of the boundary lines of the triangular Barceloneta neighbourhood, which is discussed a little later on. At no. 43 of this street is the **Casa de la Marina**, designed in 1951–54 by José Antonio Coderch and Manuel Valls Vergès. With its asymmetrical lines and slatted wooden blinds alternated with ceramic facings, this is one of the best 1950s' buildings in the city. It was restored in 1991–92 by Gustavo Coderch, Carles Fochs and Jaume Avallaneda.

Continuing down the quayside, by the junction of the Passeig de Joan de Borbó and Carrer de l'Almirall Cervera, look out for the street sculpture by Mario Merz, which comprises neon figures set into the ground. Further on to the right is the **Torre del Rellotge** (Clocktower), which was originally a lighthouse and dates back to the end of the 18C. It was turned into a clocktower when the harbour was extended in the 19C.

The Plaça del Mar is a little square at the apex of the Barceloneta triangle where the long stretch of beach begins. The art installation here is called *A Room Where It Is Always Raining* and was created by Juan Muñoz, one of Spain's best conceptual artists who died suddenly in 2001 at the age of 48.

The bunker-like strucure facing you is the **Club Natació Atlètic Barceloneta**, a municipal pool and sports complex. *Open Mon–Sat 10.00–22.30, Sun & public holidays 10.00–16.30. Fee.*

Designed by José Antonio Martínez Lapeña and Elías Torres Tur in 1992–97, the main pool on the first floor has an open-frame wooden ceiling and a panoramic window, so that when swimming you look out onto the sea. The building stands on the site of the San Sebastian Baths, which opened in 1928 and also offered beach facilities and watersports, thereby creating a new summer leisure culture. This development led to the proliferation of makeshift bars and seafood restaurants along the beach. These shacks became a much-loved Barcelona institution and there was strong local resistance to their demolition as part of the 1992 revamp.

Just beyond the baths is the lowest of the two tall and flimsy-looking ironwork structures which support the **Transbordador Aeri cable-car** linking Barceloneta with the hill of Montjuïc. The cable-car was devised by Carles Buïgas in 1926 with a view to providing the city with another means of access to the site of the International Exhibition of 1929. Financial backing for the venture was however not found until 1928, and the cable-car scheme was not completed until two years after the Exhibition closed. This tower, the **Torre de Sant Sebastià**, resembles an old-fashioned oil rig, and features a lift that takes you to an upper platform from where the journey by cable-car begins. The whole system seems so antiquated that you might feel as if you are taking your life in your hands. You hover high above the port, passing at a height of more than 100 metres the top of the **Torre de Jaume I**, the more elegant of the two towers. Comparable in its design to the Eiffel Tower in Paris, tapering ironwork supports hold up an octagonal platform. The future of the cable-car is in doubt, however, owing to the development underway in the port area.

Barceloneta

The triangle of land between the marina and the beach is occupied by the popular maritime district of Barceloneta, which was built to replace the swathe of the Ribera district that was pulled down after 1714 to make way for the Ciutadella (p 161). Work did not begin, however, until 1753, and in the meantime many of the people who had lost their homes lived in makeshift shacks on the beach.

The construction of the new neighbourhood was masterminded by the Marquès de la Mina, using a grid scheme devised by Juan Martín Cermeño and Francisco Paredes, who were military engineers. The grid was divided into short narrow blocks both to enable natural light to reach the streets and to provide every house with windows overlooking the street. The original houses were only two storeys high, but most were extended to four or five floors in the 19th century. Examples can still be seen, however, at **no. 6** Carrer de Sant Carles and **nos 30–32** Plaça de la Font (alongside the market).

Nearby, on Plaça de la Barceloneta, is the parish church of Sant Miquel del Port, a late Baroque structure of Roman inspiration which was designed by Damià Ribas in 1753–55.

Until the development of the waterfront, Barceloneta was rather cut off from the city centre and very rundown. Now, however, properties in this prime location are increasingly in demand and the future looks promising. Despite the dilapidated state of the area in recent decades, it was always a popular place to come and eat with many excellent seafood restaurants. Two of the best are *Can Solé* (no. 4 Carrer Sant Carles) and *Can Majó* (no. 23 Carrer Almirall Aixada).

There are also some wonderful tapas bars, including *La Cova Fumada* near the market (no. 56 Carrer Baluard).

Along the Promenade to the Port Olímpic

The Passeig Marítim runs alongside the strip of beaches from Barceloneta to the Port Olímpic and beyond. It is still being extended, and by 2004 will reach the vast complex being built for the Universal Forum of Cultures to be held in that year. All the beaches have Blue Flag status. Palm trees have been planted, showers installed and of course, this being Barcelona, there is no shortage of stylish bars and restaurants. The promenade is very popular all year round for strolling, cycling, rollerblading and skateboarding, and has become such an established feature of the city that it has been dubbed the 'Copacabana of Barcelona'.

At the beginning of Barceloneta beach, there is a sculpture by Rebecca Horn. *Homage to Barceloneta* (1992) commemorates the seafood shacks that lined this stretch of sand before the seafront was redeveloped. The long, low building on the left (nos 25–29) is the **Hospital del Mar**, designed in 1989–92 by Manuel Brullet Tenas and Albert de Pineda Alvarez. The building is actually a remodelling and extension of the Hospital de Infecciosos, built in 1925 and extended in 1973. Inside, light materials have been used to create large, open spaces, making the most of the natural light and seafront location. The Modernista **watertower** with ceramic decoration that is visible behind the Hospital del Mar was designed by Josep Domènech i Estapà in 1905 and restored in 1982.

The Passeig Marítim continues to the **Port Olímpic** marina, which has become the focus of the Vila Olímpica. Once an industrial semi-wasteland of gasometers, railway shuntings and warehouses, the apartment blocks built to house the athletes during the 1992 Olympic Games have now become a coveted residential area.

> The creation of this new maritime district was proposed by Mayor Narcís Serra following the city's decision to put itself forward as a candidate for the 1992 Olympic Games. Pasqual Maragall, who succeeded him as mayor in 1982, keenly championed the idea, and in 1985, at a time when it was still not known whether or not the city would host the Games, the architects Martorell, Bohigas, Mackay and Puigdomènech were commissioned to devise the overall scheme.
>
> Apart from providing residential and other facilities for the Games, the project was intended to transform the industrial district of Poblenou, known as the 'Catalan Manchester', which had fallen into decay as the factories became obsolete. Popular with artists and designers, the area is now very much back on the map.

The Port Olímpic is dominated by Spain's two highest skyscrapers (both 153.5 metres), which have become prominent landmarks of modern Barcelona. The first one is the *Hotel Arts*, designed by Bruce Graham and the architectural practice of Skidmore, Owings & Merrill. With 45 floors, it is one of the most luxurious places to stay in the city. The amazing bronze fish sculpture in front of the hotel is the work of Frank Gehry. The other tower is the headquarters of the *Mapfre* insurance company and was designed by Iñigo Ortiz and Enrique de León. The marina has become as renowned for its nightlife as its yachts, with dozens of bars and clubs that stay open all night in the summer months.

The apartment blocks and other buildings in the Vila Olímpica were designed by architects who had won the prestigious FAD (Foment de les Arts Decoratives) Architecture Prize, which is awarded annually in the city. Among the most interesting buildings are the curving structures on the Plaça Tirant lo Blanc, by José Antonio Martínez Lapeña and Elías Torres, and Ricardo Bofill's apartments on the corner of Carrer Doctor Trueta and Carrer Arquitecte Serte. The entrance to the district is marked by the **Central Telefónica building** on the Avinguda d'Icària (at the crossroads with Carrer Joan Miró), which was designed by Jaume Bach Núñez and Gabriel Mora Gramunt. The two volumes on either side of the street—one elliptical and the other prismatic with a rectangular plan—are linked by a bridge with a sloping floor. Adjacent is the **Eurocity 1** office building, by Roder Amadó Cercós and Lluís Domènech Girbau, which acts as an entrance arch to Carrer Joan Miró. Only the top two floors, in glass and granite, house offices, while the support structure contains lifts and atriums.

The tree-like metallic sculptures in the middle of Avinguda d'Icària are by Enric Miralles and Carme Pinós. The next block of the avenue (alongside Carrer Rosa Sensat) is occupied by the **Eurocity 2, 3 and 4** complex, designed by Helio Piñón and Albert Viaplana. Faced in marble, the three volumes are structured in graded sections, like inverted steps, forming bridges across the street.

At the end of the avenue is evocative and decayed **Cementiri del Poblenou**, situated at the end of the Avinguda d'Icària. Founded by Bishop Climent in 1773, the cemetery was totally destroyed by the French in 1808 and rebuilt in 1818–19 by the Italian architect Antoni Ginesi. This symmetrically arranged Neo-classical complex, featuring an entrance portal flanked by obelisks, mausolea in the form of pyramids and a pedimented chapel reminiscent of Hansen's cathedral at Copenhagen, was an expression of the Enlightenment ideals of the city's planners of the early 19C.

On the crossroads at the entrance to the cemetery is the **Sant Abraham church**, designed by Josep Benedito and Agustí Mateos and built in 1990–92. The curved lines of the structure form the shape of a fish. During the Olympic Games, services were held for all the main religions of the participants, and it now serves as the Catholic parish church for the new residential and business community.

Poblenou

Beyond the Vila Olímpica is what remains of the district of Poblenou, which dates back to a 13C port and emerged in the 19C as the main industrial suburb of Barcelona. As mentioned above, the character of the neighbourhood is changing fast, sandwiched as it is between the 1992 transformations and the urban development spreading up the coast in the first decade of the 21C.

The long Carrer Bac de Roda leads up from Mar Bella beach, through a mixture of 19C and 21C buildings. The extensive and superficially rundown industrial complex on the adjoining Carrer Pellaires (no. 6) is a group of fashionable design studios, known collectively as *Palo Alto* and instigated by Pierre Roca in 1989. These include the headquarters of one of Barcelona's leading personalities of today, Javier Mariscal.

Born in Valencia in 1950, Mariscal moved to Barcelona in 1971 to study graphic design at the Escuela Elisava, and began making a name shortly afterwards as a comic illustrator, most notably in his undergound magazine *Rollo Enmascarado*, founded in 1973. Exhibitions held in the Sala Vinçon of his witty and curious designs and objects helped greatly to further his career, but his real breakthrough came in 1988, when he designed the 1992 Olympic mascot—a cheeky-looking dog called Cobi.

Another watertower still stands just beyond the far end of Carrer Pellaires, one of the few vestiges of Poblenou's industrial past. The **Torre de Les Aigües** was built in 1883 by Pere Falqués, and was part of the Can Girona factory, which closed in 1992.

The area immediately beyond the tower down to the sea has been redeveloped as **Diagonal-Mar**, which includes Catalunya's largest shopping centre. Beyond this, the waterfront is being transformed by the leading Swiss architects Herzog & de Meuron in preparation for the Universal Forum of Cultures in 2004.

6 • From La Ciutadella Park to Plaça de les Glories Catalanes

▶ Start at park entrance on the corner of Passeig de Picasso and Avinguda Marquès de l'Argentera. See map on pp 162–63.

La Ciutadella is Barcelona's oldest municipal park and the site of the World Exhibition of 1888.

The park has its origins in a notorious fortress commissioned by Philip V in 1715, following his successful siege of Barcelona in September of the previous year. His attack on the city had been made through an opening in the medieval wall, a section that for many years had been considered a potential military weakness. From the middle of the 17C onwards the army had been pressing for the construction of a citadel here to counterbalance the hilltop castle of Montjuïc, on the other side of the city.

Philip V's decision to build the citadel was taken for vindictive rather than military reasons, however, as he wanted to punish Barcelona for supporting the Habsburgs during the War of Succession. His plans initially entailed the destruction of the entire Ribera district, though in the end only the northern half was pulled down. Even so, no fewer than 61 streets disappeared completely, and the owners of 1262 houses and churches were forced to demolish their properties at their own cost and without any form of compensation.

The demolition of this half of the Ribera was carried out in 1715–18, and work on the new citadel was begun in 1716. The design of the fortress was entrusted to Prosper Verboom, who produced a star-shaped plan inspired by Vauban. The construction of the project was supervised by Verboom himself, together with Alexandre de Retz. The walls and defensive ditches were completed by 1719, but work on the buildings within the citadel continued until 1727, and was never entirely finished, as the plans to construct a hospital, a barracks and an artillery foundry were eventually abandoned. The place never functioned as a true fortress, and was captured with considerable ease by the French in 1808. It was later used as a prison and execution ground for political criminals, acquiring a special notoriety during both the Napoleonic occupation and between 1828 and 1830, the worst years of Ferdinand Vll's anti-Liberal reprisals.

No other place in Barcelona aroused such popular hostility as the Ciutadella, which became the supreme symbol of the oppression of the Catalan people and numerous attempts were made to have it pulled down. During the Regency of General Espartero in 1840, the city's specially created Civilian Guard began its demolition on the pretext that the place might have been appropriated by those members of the army taking part in the anti-Espartero revolt of 1841. The crushing of this revolt, and the Spanish Government's threat to bombard the city if the Ciutadella were taken down, led not only to the demolition work being abandoned but also to the reconstruction of those parts that had been destroyed.

With the decision in 1858 to pull down the remaining city walls and create

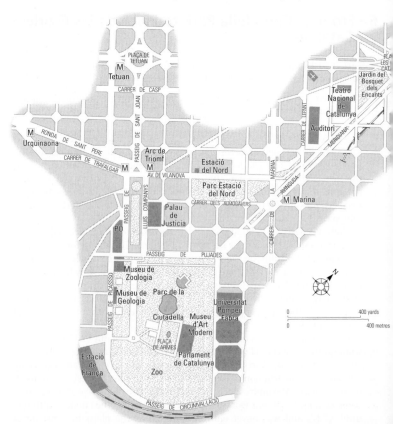

the Eixample, the Ciutadella lost all possible military significance. Nonetheless, it was not until the fall of Isabel II in 1868 and the instigation of the revolutionary government of General Prim that permission was finally given to demolish this hated monument once and for all.

The Ciutadella was handed over by the Spanish Government to the Barcelona City Council, and numerous plans were proposed for the development of the site, all of which were forced to include some provision for a public park. Eventually, after a protracted competition, the Council decided to adapt a scheme proposed by Josep Fontseré, who rejected the idea of creating any residential blocks on the site, and concentrated his plan entirely on the park, which he believed would stimulate the renewal of the old city. In his own words 'gardens are to a city what lungs are to the human body'. Work on the park was begun in 1872, but the 1885 decision to hold the World Exhibition within its grounds entailed considerable modification of the architect's original plans. Fontseré protested strongly to Barcelona's newly appointed mayor, Rius i Taulet, and in consequence found himself sacked for supposedly misappropriating funds. He was replaced as director of works of the park by his long-standing enemy Antoni Rovira i Trias. Meanwhile, the design of the Exhibition grounds was entrusted to Elies Rogent. There is a lively and excellently researched account of the transformation of the once dreaded Ciutadella into the grounds of the World Exhibition in Eduardo Mendoza's fantastical novel, *The City of Marvels* (English translation, 1989).

The World Exhibition was officially inaugurated on 20 May 1888, and was closed on 9 December of the same year. Two of its main structures—Vilaseca's Arc del Triomf and Domènech's Café-Restaurant—were retained, but plans for the park itself were gradually neglected. The municipal authorities became more interested in Montjuïc, the proposed site of the International Exhibition of 1929. A revival in the Ciutadella's fortunes came in 1932, when the former arsenal here was adapted as the seat of the Catalan Parliament. Although this function ceased in 1939, the Parliament was reinstalled here in 1980.

Entering the luxuriantly verdant Parc de la Ciutadella from the Passeig Marquès de l'Argentera, head straight down the broad alley. This leads to an equestrian monument to **General Prim**, executed in 1882–87 by Lluís Puiggener. The monument was destroyed in 1936 and reconstructed in 1945 by Frederic Marès. Beyond this are the main survivals of the original Ciutadella, beginning with the **chapel**, an austerely simple structure of 1718–27 by the military engineer

Alexandre de Retz. Inspired in its restrained classical detailing by the architecture of the French late Baroque, the building in turn influenced a number of later Barcelona churches, in particular in the use of a rounded pediment on the west façade (see for instance the Betlem church on La Rambla, p 88). The place is still used by the army for services. Adjoining the chapel is the former **Governor's Palace**, which was built by Prosper Verboom in 1716–27 and is now the premises of a school. As austere and French in its architecture as the chapel, it is surmounted by the Bourbon coat of arms.

Immediately beyond the two buildings is the former parade ground or **Plaça d'Armes**, which in 1916–17 was landscaped in a formal French style by the distinguished and appropriately named French landscape designer Jean C. Forestier. His classically simple arrangement of hedges and flowerbeds centred around an oval pool is fully in the spirit of Noucentisme, reinforced by the beautiful white sculpture by Josep Llimona which lies in the centre of the pool, surrounded by water-lilies. Entitled *Desconsol* ('Disconsolate'), this marble sculpture is a 1984 reproduction of the 1917 original, which in turn was based on a model of 1903, and is of a recumbent female nude staring at the water in a pose reminiscent both of Narcissus and the repentent Magdalene.

The pool and its sculpture form an elegant foreground to the **former arsenal**, which now houses the Catalan Parliament and the Museu d'Art Modern. Designed by Prosper Verboom in 1716–27, the palatial aspect of this building is the result of a remodelling in 1889–95 by Pere Falqués, who added the grand, pedimented frontispiece as part of a scheme to adapt it as a royal residence. Further changes to the building, including the addition of two wings, were made in 1904–15, when the place was converted to house the combined collections of Barcelona's museums of fine arts and archaeology.

These collections were transferred to Montjuïc in 1934, when the former arsenal was turned into the seat of the Catalan Parliament. After 1939 the place served as a barracks before being transformed, in 1945, into the Museu d'Art Modern. As a result of the return here of the Catalan Parliament in 1977, the building was divided into two sections to accommodate its dual purpose.

Museu d'Art Modern
Open Tue–Sat 10.00–19.00, Sun & public holidays 10.00–14.30. Fee. Discount with Ruta del Modernisme voucher and Barcelona Card; included on Articket.

The name is misleading, as the museum deals principally with Catalan art from the beginning of the 19C to the 1930s, with the emphasis on artists associated with Modernisme and Noucentisme. The institution has its origins in the Museu Municipal de Belles Arts, which was founded in 1891 with a group of works acquired during the World Exhibition of 1888, as well as paintings and sculptures executed by artists who had received bursaries from the municipality to visit Rome.

The holdings of medieval, Renaissance and Baroque art formed the basis of the Museu Nacional d'Art de Catalunya, which opened in 1934 in the Palau Nacional in Montjuïc. The post-18C collections—mainly composed of the works of Catalan artists from the Romantic period up to the early 20C—had several homes before being brought together in 1945 to create the Museu d'Art Modern. The museum is set to move again, however, once the remodelling of the Palau Nacional in Montjuïc is complete, to create a comprehensive museum of Catalan art.

The collection begins with Neo-classicism and Romanticism. The Reus-born Marià Fortuny (1838–74) is treated here as a precursor of Modernisme. In terms of subject-matter, Fortuny was little different from the academic artists of his time, his greatness as a painter lying essentially in the vividness of his technique, which comprises rapid brush-strokes and brilliant colouring. The first Catalan artist to achieve a truly international reputation, he spent much of his working life in Italy, dying in Rome at the age of 36. The museum to him in Venice is housed in his beautifully preserved studio in the 18C Palazzo Pesaro degli Orfei. Works include the enormous scene of the *Battle of Tetuan*, a minutely detailed work which takes up almost an entire wall and powerfully conveys the dust and chaos of war.

Realism is a category composed mainly of Catalan artists active in Paris, Barbizon and Rome in the late 19C. Among the works here are paintings by Antoni Caba and Ramon Martí i Alsina. **Landscape painting** is represented by Joaquim Vayreda and Modest Urgell.

The **Modernisme** displays start with the principal artists of the first generation of the movement, Ramon Casas (1866–1932) and Santiago Rusinyol (1861–1931). Works by Casas include those that decorated the famous artistic tavern of *Els Quatre Gats* (p 128), most notably a series of pencil portraits of the tavern's associates (including the young Picasso), an oil sketch showing Rusinyol suspended from one of the tavern's wooden chandeliers, and the no less celebrated double portrait of Casas himself riding a tandem with Pere Romeu. The most important of Casas' paintings were his large oils of contemporary political and social events, all of which were painted with a vivid life-like technique which combined compositions inspired by photography with a startling fluency of brushstroke derived from his experiences as a *plein-air* landscapist. In the richly-detailed *Corpus Procession Departing from the Church of Santa Maria del Mar*, the photographic boldness of Casas' compositions and his painterly fluency are shown by the feathered plumes of the soldiers' helmets, which stand in isolation in the painting's left-hand corner.

Rusinyol, while occupying a central position in the history of Modernisme through his organisation of the 'Festes Modernistas' at his house in Sitges (p 230), was a less powerful and original artist than Casas. His reputation as a painter lies mainly with his charming landscapes and genre-like portraits, of which the Museu d'Art Modern has a particularly fine selection. Some of the best were executed during his first stay in Paris in 1889, particularly the two scenes set in the famous Montmartre Beer Garden of the Moulin de la Galette. One of these is a view of the garden from the kitchen, while the other is a full-length portrait of his Catalan friend and colleague Miquel Utrillo. Whereas Renoir in the 1870s had portrayed the Moulin de la Galette with vibrant colour, Rusinyol represented the place in a more sober way, with an overall grey tonality inspired by the art of Bastien-Lepage, whose works were then at the height of their popularity. After flirting with Symbolism on his return to Catalunya (a phase in his art which can only be appreciated in the museum at Sitges), Rusinyol considerably brightened his palette and came to devote himself largely to the portrayal of gardens. These scenes, which tend towards the facile and sentimental, ensured Rusinyol's popular appeal, if not his critical reputation.

Modernista sculpture is represented by Josep Llimona, whose works here include a smaller version of his *Desconsol* (1907), that we saw outside.

Following the important 'Modernismo en España' exhibition, held here in 1970, the Museu d'Art Modern acquired a collection of **furniture, jewellery and architectural furnishings from the Modernista period**. These are excellently displayed in the next series of rooms, though it has to be said that many of the works can only be appreciated fully when seen in the original architectural context for which they were created. Among the exhibits are decorative elements from buildings by the great Modernista trio, Domènech i Montaner, Puig i Cadafalch and Antoní Gaudí. Domènech i Montaner designed the Casa Lleo Morera (p 177), on the Passeig de Gràcia, but the interiors were the work of Gaspar Homar. Much of the furniture from the drawing room is displayed here, some of which features magnificent marquetry.

Puig i Cadafalch was responsible for the decoration as well as the design of his Casa Amatller (p 177), various elements of which are displayed here. Gaudí is represented by ironwork railings from his Casa Vicens (c 1883–1885) in the Carrer Carolines (p 213) and also by furniture from the Casa Batlló (p 178).

One of the highlights of this section is a superb **oratory** by Joan Busquets, from the Casa Cendoya. Francesc Gimeno (1858–1929), whose work is shown in the next room, is misleadingly referred to as a Catalan Impressionist. He painted ochre-coloured landscapes of great expressive power and technical freedom, in particular his scenes set in and around the mountain village of Torroella de Montgrí. Also displayed here are paintings by his contemporaries Joaquín Sorolla, José Gutiérrez Solana and Darío de Regoyos. These figures are considered to hold an intermediary position between the first and second generations of Modernista artists.

The second generation displays include works by Hermenegildo Anglada Camarasa and Josep Maria Sert. The works of Ricard Canals (1876–1931) reflect the influence of Degas and, above all, Renoir. Joaquim Mir (1873–1940), the leading figure of the so-called **Olot School** of landscape artists, painted in a colourful decorative manner akin to that of Vuillard, and is also represented in the museum by a seductive stained glass window which he designed.

The most original of all these artists was **Isidre Nonell** (1873–1911) who, inspired by a combination of Daumier and Japanese prints, achieved effects of decorative simplification and luminous colouring. Among the many works of his in the museum are some near abstract still lives (executed in the last years of his short life) and a series of huddled gypsy women that appears to have strongly influenced Picasso in his Blue and Rose Periods.

The next section contains works by artists associated with **Noucentisme**, a movement initiated in 1906 by the writer and philosopher Eugeni d'Ors. Noucentisme, which was to be the prevalent Catalan style right up to the 1930s, represented both a return to classical models and a reaction against the stylistic eccentricities of Modernisme. One of its leading associates was the sculptor Josep Clarà (1878–1958), whose classically simplified and smoothly modelled female nudes closely recall the works of Aristide Maillol. The leading painter of the movement was Joaquim Sunyer, whose art combines the linear grace of Matisse with the colouring, composition and faceting technique of the great Noucentiste hero, Paul Cézanne.

Other key figures were the sculptor Manolo Hugué (1872–1945), a regular at **Els Quatre Gats** who later lived in Paris, and the painter Xavier Nogués (1873–1941). Nogués is represented here by a series of murals he painted for the Galerías Layetanas, a meeting place for Noucentiste artists.

The last section works by some of the more avant-garde artists working in Catalunya in the second and third decades of the century, including Josep de Togores, Josep Mompou, Leandre Cristòfol and Julio González. Particularly remarkable are the playful sculptures of Pau Gargallo (1881–1934), which include a caricature stone head of **Picasso** (1913) and **Great Dancer**, a lively metal cut-out made in 1929. There is also a portrait of mesmerising power by the young Salvador Dalí. It represents—without recourse to Dalí's later surrealistic devices—the artist's father, Salvador Dalí i Cusí, whose stern forbidding features express the scorn which he is known to have felt for his son's activities.

Leaving the museum and turning left, you skirt the part of the arsenal which is now occupied by the Catalan Parliament (restricted opening hours). Turning left again brings you to the entrance to the **Zoo**. *Open May–Aug 9.30–19.30, April and Sept 10.00–19.00, Oct–Mar 10.00–18.00. Fee. Bus Turístic and Barcelona Card discounts.*

Founded after the Civil War, the zoo is laid out on the pioneering principles of England's Whipsnade, with moats rather than cages separating the spectators from the elephants, bears, lions and other animals. Its attractions include a whale and dolphin show, and a series of glass panels where these mammals can be seen swimming under water. But for many years the zoo's greatest claim to fame has been Copo de Nieve (or Snowflake in English), the only known albino gorilla in the world and now of venerable age. Snowflake was captured in Equatorial Guinea and arrived at the zoo in 1966. He has six offspring, who live in the same quarters.

For the cultural tourist the zoo offers the delightful attraction of Joan Roig i Soler's sculpture of 1885 entitled **Lady with Umbrella**, an evocative survival from the time of the World Exhibition.

Returning to the former arsenal, immediately beyond the Plaça d'Armes you reach an artificial lake with a grotto on its far side. The lake and monumental cascade, created by Josep Fontseré between 1875 and 1881, were closely inspired by a Neo-Baroque complex (the Chateau d'Eau) designed in the 1860s by H.J. Esperandieu for the grounds of the Palais Longchamp in Marseille. The monumental cascade, which has recently been restored, has as its centrepiece a triumphal arch raised high above the ground, flanked by great sweeps of steps and adorned and surrounded by an abundance of statuary, including works by most of the leading Catalan sculptors of the day. A gilded bronze **Chariot of Aurora** (by Rossend Nolas) crowns the central arch, while below is a beautiful group designed by Venanci Vallmitjana of **Venus and the Naiads**. There are also works by Francesc Pagès, Josep Gamot, Manuel Fuxà, Joan Flotats and Rafael Atchè, the whole forming a composition which was criticised at the time for being ludicrously crowded.

Though the static and conventional overall design was by Fontseré, the boulders and the animated decorative detailing in the ironwork and elsewhere are often attributed to the young Antoni Gaudí, who, while still an architectural student, is known to have worked for Fontseré.

Gaudí, who is also thought to have been responsible for the ironwork gates at the two entrances to the park, certainly had a hand in the design of the building enclosing the original water supply for the cascade. This brickwork structure, erected in 1874–77, overlooks the edge of the park flanked by Carrer de Wellington. The story goes that Gaudí was asked by Fontseré to do the technical calculations for this building. Afterwards Fontseré showed these to Joan Torras, a professor of structural engineering in the School of Architecture where Gaudí was studying. Torras was apparently so impressed with the student's work that Gaudí passed his course without having to attend a single class.

West of the cascade is the **Monument to Bonaventura Carles Aribau**, which was erected in 1884 and features a statue of the poet by Manuel Fuxà (replaced by a bronze copy in 1934) and an eclectic pedestal designed by Josep Vilaseca, possibly with the help of Antoni Gaudí.

Four important 1880s buildings line the border of the park that overlooks the Passeig de Picasso. The earliest is the **Museu de Geologia**. *Open Tue, Wed, Fri, Sat & Sun 10.00–14.00, Thu 10.00–18.30. Fee.*

The structure was built in 1879–82 to house an important geological collection presented to the city by an amateur archaeologist and naturalist with the appropriate name of Martorell i Pena (the second of his names means 'stone'). Josep Fontseré was originally chosen to design the building, but his 1874 scheme was later turned down in favour of one by Rovira i Trias, who had attacked Fontseré for not having had an academic architectural training.

The building is a worthy but unexciting Neo-classical structure, comprising two long wings flanking a colonnaded frontispiece. The displays include exhibits on the different landscapes of Catalunya, mineralogy and palaeontology, with fossils from various parts of the region.

Standing facing the building, adjacent to the left is the glasshouse known as the **Umbracle**, a work of 1883–84 by Josep Fontseré. Its monumental side façades are of bare brick, while the main area features ironwork columns, steel beams and wooden louvres.

On the other side of the museum is another glasshouse, the **Hivernacle**. This light and elegant ironwork structure was built by Josep Amargós i Samaranch in 1884–88, and differs from the English prototypes established by Paxton in having an open central aisle. Part of the structure is now a very pleasant café where jazz and classical concerts are regularly held.

Next to the Hivernacle in the corner is the park's largest and most interesting structure, now the **Museu de Zoologià**. *Open Tue, Wed, Fri, Sat & Sun 10.00–14.00, Thu 10.00–18.30. Fee. Barcelona Card discount.*

The structure was built by Domènech i Montaner in 1887–88 to serve as the café-restaurant of the World Exhibition. With its large expanses of bare, undecorated brickwork, and its undisguised framework in laminated steel, this building occupies a pioneering position in the history of Functionalist architecture, anticipating by more than ten years Berlage's Stock Exchange building in Amsterdam. As with Modernisme in general, however, the building combines daring modernity with a fantastical medieval element. Its corner towers, crenellations, Mudéjar-style windows and upper row of ceramic plaques imitative of medieval shields (executed by Joan Llimona,

Josep Lluis Pellicer and Alexandre de Riquer), give the building the look of a fortress dreamt up by some science fiction illustrator. In its day the building came to be known as the Castell dels Tres Dragons (The Castle of the Three Dragons), after a popular contemporary play by Pitarra. Furthermore, in the course of its construction, jokes appeared in the local press suggesting that the waiters who were to work there would have to wear chain mail and armour.

As it happened, the building was not completed in time for the World Exhibition, and so never functioned as a café-restaurant. Instead, on Domènech's suggestion, the place was made to house not only his own architectural studio but also what were among the earliest craft workshops in Europe dedicated to the revival of traditional ceramic and ironwork techniques. These workshops were to play a vital role in the renaissance of the Catalan decorative arts at the turn of the century.

The building has housed the Zoological Museum since 1917. The displays of insects and stuffed animals include a comprehensive collection of Catalan fauna. Much of the original interior decoration has disappeared, including most of the painted ceiling panels, and all the stained glass.

The Zoological Museum

Leaving the Ciutadella by the gates adjacent to the museum on the Passeig de Pujades, in front of you is a long and broad landscaped promenade named after Lluís Companys, the **Passeig de Lluís Companys**. This dates back to the end of the 18C, but was transformed in the late 19C as one of the two main approaches to the World Exhibition. The promenade used to have mosaic pavements and ironwork lamps by Pere Falqués, but these were inexcusably removed during the construction of a large underground car park.

The promenade's main monuments have been kept, however, including—directly in front of the Ciutadella's entrance gates—an obelisk designed by Falqués in 1897 to commemorate the mayor who promoted the World Exhibition, Francesc de Paula Rius i Taulet. The sculptural elements, including a bronze bust of the mayor, and allegorical figures of Fame, Science and Art, are by Manuel Fuxà. On either side of the obelisk are statues of the medieval hero *Roger de Llúria* and the Baroque painter *Antoni Viladomat*, the work respectively of Josep Reynés (1888) and Torquat Tasso (1880).

As you walk up the promenade, you pass to your right the massive **Palau de Justicia**, a heavy eclectic structure in grey Montjuïc stone designed in 1887 by Josep Domènech i Estapà and Enric Sagnier i Villavecchia, and completed in 1908. The exterior has fantastically complex sculptural decoration and

Arc de Triomf

exuberant ironwork detailing, while inside are some early mural decorations by Josep Maria Sert.

Josep Vilaseca's superb and highly original **Arc del Triomf** dominates the top end of the promenade, and was built as a monumental entrance to the World Exhibition. In his creation of a triumphal arch appropriate to the modern age, Vilaseca radically departed from classical prototype, and produced a structure of which John Ruskin would have approved, achieving effects of monumentality through the use of such a humble building material as brick.

Though Vilaseca was prevented by Elies Rogent from carrying out his initial plan of placing crenellated towers at either side of the arch, the work still manages to have more of a medieval than classical character, the elaborately detailed brickwork recalling the techniques of the medieval Moorish craftsmen known as the Mudéjars. The sculptural decoration, executed by Josep Llimona, Josep Reynés, Torquat Tasso and Antoni Vilanova, has as its theme the welcome extended by the city of Barcelona to those participating in the Exhibition, and features a matronly figure handing out emblems representing the various Spanish provinces.

On the left, on the corner of the Passeig de Lluís Companys and the Ronda de Sant Pere, is a **monument to Lluís Companys**, president of the Catalan government, who was shot by Franco's soldiers in 1940, by Francisco López (1998). It features a girl holding a handkerchief and a rose, which she received as a gift from Companys in return for a poem she sent him when he was imprisoned. He used to wear it in the breast pocket of his jacket.

Nearby is the ***Bar Trole*** (Passeig de Lluís Companys 23), which occupies the ground floor of a black and white building designed in 1993 by Tusquets & Díaz. The bar is a new version of a popular café called Trolley, which opened in 1896 and got its name from being alongside the tramstop. Just beyond the arch on the right, at no. 6 Passeig de Sant Joan, is the Modernista **Casa Estapé**, which was designed by Jaume Bernades in 1906 and features a dome decorated with blue, green and white tiles.

Turn right from the arch into the Avinguda de Vilanova. At **no. 12** (at the junction with the Carrer de Roger de Flor) is one of the most important works by Pere Falqués, now the headquarters of the ***Catalan Electricity Company***. Built in 1897 as an electrical plant, this brick and ironwork structure was closely inspired both in its detailing and use of materials by Domènech i Montaner's Editorial Montaner i Simón (p 178). The original design included two large pyramids on the roof, but these were not built. The structure was restored for its current use in 1980.

Blocking off the end of the Avinguda de Vilanova is the former **Estació del Nord**. Dating back to 1861, this railway station was remodelled by Demetri Ribes Marco in 1912–13 and given its splendid Modernista ironwork. Abandoned as a station in 1972, the building was saved from decay in 1992 by being transformed into a sports centre and Barcelona's main bus station. A park has been laid out to the right of the building, featuring sloping lawns and sculptures by Beverly Peppers.

Turn right at the top of the park, then left into the Avinguda Meridiana. The grey modern building on the corner on the left is the **Archive of the Crown of Aragon**, designed in 1993 by Lluís Domènech Girbau (grandson of Lluís Domènech i Montaner) and Roser Amadó.

A few minutes later, you come to the **Auditori**, Barcelona's principal concert hall, which was designed by Rafael Moneo and opened in 1999 (see p 49 for information). The plain exterior makes it look like an office building, but the interior is faced with Canadian maple and contains the main auditorium with a capacity for 2340 people, as well as a chamber music hall and rehearsal studios.

Next on the left is the rather more grandiose **Teatre Nacional de Catalunya**, which was designed by Ricardo Bofill and opened in 1997 (p 50). Fronted by a lawn planted with olive trees and a monumental flight of steps, the Neo-classical building resembles a Greek temple and comprises an outer glass shell with a concrete inner structure, the whole flanked by colonnades.

Immediately beyond the theatre is a park called the **Jardin del Bosque del Encants** (Garden of the Enchanted Forest), which was named by local school-children. The park is gradually being taken over by the overspill from the nearby **flea market, Els Encants**, situated on the other side of the enormous Plaça de les Glòries Catalanes, a major traffic intersection. The market (*open Mon, Wed, Fri & Sat 09.00 until about 16.00*) sells clothes, bikes, furniture and all manner of bric à brac and is remarkably untouristy. There are plans, however, to move it to a new location. Also on this crossroads is a vast shopping centre, **Barcelona Glòries** (between Diagonal and Gran Via) and the **Farinera del Clot** cultural centre (between Gran Via and Avinguda Meridiana, *open Mon–Fri 10.00–22.00, Sat 10.00–14.00. Free*), where temporary exhibitions are held.

At this point, you are close to both the Sagrada Família cathedral (p 185) and the bullring (p 191). You could also venture further to the entertaining **Parc del Clot**, just beyond the shopping centre on Carrer dels Escultors Claperós. This immensely lively park, animated in the late afternoons by musicians and other performers, was built by Daniel Freixes and Vicente Miranda on the site of a former railway works.

Incorporated alongside the park's pools, lawns and grassy mounds are sections of the original brick and ironwork industrial complex, including chimney stacks, and a row of arches that resembles an aqueduct and supports a conduit of cascading water.

Worth seeing now you have come this far is the **Pont Bac de Roda**, designed by Santiago Calatrava. Either jump on the metro for two stops up to Navas station or from the end of the park continue up the Carrer dels Escultors Claperós to Carrer d'Aragó, turn right for three blocks, then left into Carrer Bac de Roda. The bridge is between Carrer del Clot and Carrer de València.

Built by Santiago Calatrava in 1984–87 to span the railway tracks, this magnificent white structure in chrome, metal and concrete features balustrades that are tilted inwards at the same angle as the outer piers. The lightness and dynamism of the whole inspires an enormous sense of elation in those crossing the bridge, which must surely be one of the most beautiful of its kind in Europe. However, as with so many of Barcelona's more recent new features, the beauty of the bridge is at variance with its present surroundings, the landscape immediately below being a semi-wasteland populated by the odd gypsy and beggar. On the north side of the bridge an attempt at urban improvement was made with the creation of the Plaça del General Moragues, a bleak sloping square in brick, adorned with an enormous metal sculpture by Ellsworth Kelly.

7 • The Eixample

▶ Start from Plaça de Catalunya. See map below.

This walk covers a large area, and there is a lot to see and visit. You may want to break it up into shorter stretches, taking more than one day.

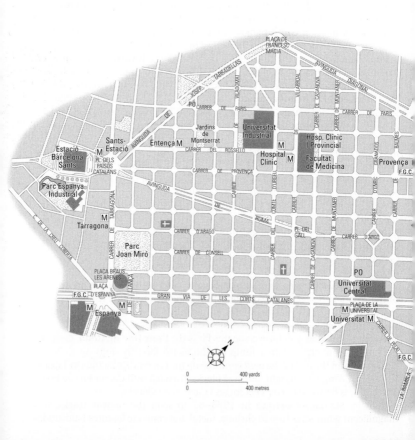

By the early 19C Barcelona was almost literally suffocating within its medieval enclosure. Various attempts were made to take this down so that the city could expand freely towards the mountains, and finally, in 1846, the municipal government put forward a draft plan for demolishing the walls and creating what was to be known as the 'Enlargement' or *Eixample* (*Ensanche* in Spanish). The Spanish Government hesitated for many years over whether to give permission for such a plan, and it was not until the late 1850s that a municipal competition was held to decide on the architect who would draw up the final scheme.

The competition was won by Antoni Rovira i Trias, whose radial plan had a visionary grandeur and offered an intelligent solution to the problem of linking the old and new towns of Barcelona. Unfortunately, the choice of the municipality was rejected by the Spanish Ministry of Works, who approved instead a strictly rectangular grid-plan devised by Ildefons Cerdà. The rejection of the Rovira plan by the Madrid authorities is frequently taken as yet another example of the way in which Catalan individuality has been squashed by Spanish centralism.

Cerdà's plan, which was comparable to the contemporary plan for the expansion of Madrid, featured regular blocks of 114 square metres, and streets that were 20 metres wide, the whole crisscrossed by vast avenues and scattered with gardens. In the end the gardens were never built, the spaces that had been reserved for them falling victim to the ruthless property speculation which ensued immediately after work on the Eixample had begun in 1860. An exciting and cruelly satirical account of the planning and creation of the Eixample is to be found in Eduardo Mendoza's novel, *The City of Marvels* (English translation, 1989).

Many of Barcelona's inhabitants feel that the spacious and elegant Eixample constitutes the city's main attraction, and this feeling is likely to be shared by anyone with a passionate interest in Gaudí and Modernista architecture. For the general sightseer, however, the Eixample can be a daunting prospect owing to the sheer monotony of the layout and the great distances separating its innumerable monuments of interest. Most tourists tend to limit their visit to the Eixample to a walk along the Passeig de Gràcia, and a journey by bus, metro or taxi to the outlying Sagrada Família. Any fuller tour of the district, such as the one outlined below, requires considerable energy and dedication, particularly if undertaken entirely on foot.

However much time you decide to devote to the Eixample, your starting point is likely to be the vast **Plaça de Catalunya**, which has its origins in a field between the Rambla (p 86) and the future Passeig de Gràcia.

Rovira planned a monumental esplanade for here—800 metres long and 200 metres wide—which he gave the impressive name of 'Forum de Isabel II'. This space would have been at the very centre of his radial plan of Barcelona and would have provided a suitably grand approach to the medieval cathedral.

Cerdà had more modest plans for this space, and simply intended to extend the Rambla and link it to a square attached to the end of his projected Passeig de Gràcia. General resistance to the Cerdà plan, combined with lingering nostalgia for the rejected project of Rovira, led eventually to a compromise solution being adopted. The work was however delayed for many years and necessitated the demolition of various structures that had been put up here in the interim by private developers.

The definitive project, based on designs put forward by Puig i Cadafalch between 1915 and 1922, was drawn up in 1925 by Francesc de Paula Nebot, Pere Domènech, Antoni Darder, Fèlix d'Azua and Enric Catà.

The square, which was inaugurated on 2 November 1927, is surrounded by pompous and uninspiring buildings, and is centred around a circular garden with fountains, rings of trees, statuary and an overall desultory character. Among the sculptures are Pau Gargallo's **Shepherd with a Flute** and at the bottom of the square, a replica by Ricard Sala of a kneeling female nude entitled *Goddess*, the original of which, by Josep Clarà, is now in the courtyard of the town hall (p 116).

None of the buildings that surround the square—most of which are the headquarters of banks—are of especial architectural interest, though readers of Orwell's *Homage to Catalonia* should cast a glance at the **Banco Español de**

Crédito at the square's top end. Formerly the Hotel Colón, it served during the Civil War as the headquarters of the socialist group known as PSUC, and its façade—as Orwell describes—was covered with portraits of Marx, Lenin and Stalin. Underneath the square are train and metro stations, as well as the **main tourist office**.

El Corte Inglés, the department store on the right of the square, was remodelled by Elías Torres Tur and José Antonio Martínez Lapeña in 1990–94, when the building was also substantially extended by Albert Puigdomènech and the Martorell, Bohigas, Mackay studio. The rooftop cafeteria provides a good vantage-point from which to observe the hectic life of the Plaça de Catalunya.

On the corner wih Carrer de Pelai at the bottom of the square is the *Triangle* shopping mall, which incorporates a reconstruction of one of Barcelona's great institutions: the *Café Zurich*. Originally the bar of a railway station, Zurich was founded in 1920 by a Catalan who had lived in Switzerland. The establishment was at one time popular with writers, and in its heyday international chess championships were held here, some of the contestants even taking part by telephone from Latin America. The décor of the new café is faithful to the original, and it continues to be a popular place for meeting friends and people watching.

Running north from the top left-hand corner of the Plaça de Catalunya is the Rambla de Catalunya, which, beyond the Gran Via de les Corts Catalanes, has a pedestrian central alley lined with rows of lime trees. **Markets** are occasionally held here, most notably a poultry market at Christmas-time and a market selling palm branches three days before Palm Sunday.

Passeig de Gràcia

Running parallel to the Rambla de Catalunya, from the top right-hand corner of the Plaça de Catalunya, is the city's most elegant thoroughfare, the famous Passeig de Gràcia.

The Passeig de Gràcia has its origins in the road leading from Barcelona to the former village of Gràcia (p 212). In 1827 it was converted into a wide tree-lined promenade, which was illuminated by gas lamps after 1853, and provided with horse-drawn trams after 1871. With the development of the Eixample, the Passeig de Gràcia replaced La Rambla as the fashionable promenade for the city's aristocracy and upper middle classes. It also became the central artery of the luxury district of the Eixample, which came to be known as the **Quadrat d'Or** (Golden Square), a district formed by the hundred or so blocks contained within the area bordered by the Carrer de Aribau and the Passeig de Sant Joan on either side, and to the top and bottom by the Avinguda Diagonal and the 'Rondes'.

The earliest buildings here were two- or three-storey one-family dwellings with gardens, but from the 1890s onwards these came to be replaced by apartment blocks for the wealthy middle classes. Over the years, the whole area was transformed into a densely-populated residential and commercial district.

From about 1925, the ground floors of many of the buildings along the Passeig de Gràcia were let out to retailers, and the street soon emerged as the foremost shopping thoroughfare of the city with numerous boutiques. The upper floors of most of the former residential buildings along this street have now been taken over by offices. The Quadrat d'Or has the reputation of having the largest concentration of Art Nouveau buildings in the world, among which are several of the most famous masterpieces of this style.

We begin our tour by walking the whole length of the Passeig de Gràcia. Starting from the Plaça de Catalunya, the Passeig de Gràcia is marked on the right by the Neo-Gothic corner tower of the **Casa Pascual i Pons** (nos 2–4), which was built by Enric Sagnier i Villavecchia in 1890–91. Next along the street, also on the right-hand side (at nos 6–14), with distinctive copper domes, come the group of buildings known as the **Cases Rocamora**, an imposing and elaborate Modernista ensemble of 1914–20, designed by Joaquim and Bonaventura Bassegoda Amigó and featuring elements derived from French Gothic architecture.

Further up, at no. 11 on the left (at the corner with the Gran Via de les Corts Catalanes), rises Lluís Bonet's *Banc Vitalici d'Espanya* of 1942–50, an American-style skyscraper with conventionally classical decorative detailing. The building typifies the reaction that had set in after the Civil War to the progressive Modernism of the 1930s, an excellent example of which can be seen on the other side of the Passeig de Gràcia, at **no. 18**. This, the jewellery shop known as the *Joieria Roca*, is a Functionalist work of 1934 by Josep Lluís Sert. The flat continuous façade in glass and finely polished stone, smoothly rounded at the corner with the Gran Via, has been excellently preserved even down to its Art Deco lettering, but the interior was much altered after the shop was extended in 1964 by Marcelo Leonori. This shop, however, replaced the exquisite *Café Torino*, designed by Gaudí. The café has been recreated in name further up the street at no. 59.

Continuing up the Passeig de Gràcia, on the left at **no. 21** is the pompous French-style corner building designed by Eusebi Bona i Puig in 1927 as the headquarters of the insurance company *La Unión y el Fénix Espanol*. The building is closely similar to this company's former headquarters in Madrid, which forms one of the most prominent landmarks of the Gran Vía.

One block further up you come to the junction of the Carrer de Consell de Cent, where, on turning right, at the corner of the intersection of the street with the Carrer de Roger de Llúria, you come to the earliest buildings to have been constructed in the Eixample, the **Casas Cerdà**. These buildings of Neo-classical simplicity were built by Antoni Valls i Galí in 1862–64 on a site owned by the designer of the Eixample, Ildefons Cerdà.

Another survival from the early days of the Eixample is the **Passatge Permanyer**, a passage dividing in two one of the blocks situated immediately to the south of the Cerdà buildings (the alley can be entered either from the Carrer Roger de Llúria or the parallel Carrer de Pau Claris). This and the handful of other remaining passatges in the Eixample mark the spaces that Cerdà had originally intended as gardens, but that soon came to be covered with terraces of houses. The Passatge Permanyer is flanked by two particularly harmonious rows of terraces, built by Jeroni Granell i Barrera in 1864 in what was described at the time as '*a l'Anglesa*' (English style), each of the two-storey houses having its own front garden with railings.

It is worth continuing two blocks further east down the Carrer del Consell de Cent to the corner with the Carrer de Girona, to see a charming Modernista baker's and pastry shop, the *Forn Sarret* (now sadly defaced with graffiti). Dating back to 1906, it features particularly splendid façades created out of expressively undulating wooden forms.

Returning to the Passeig de Gràcia and continuing upwards, immediately to your left is a block comprising the most famous ensemble of Modernista buildings in Barcelona. The block is known by the punning name of **Manzana de la Discordia**, '*manzana*' being the Spanish name for both 'block' and 'apple'. The '*discordia*' (discord) here is a reference to the disparate and dashing Modernista styles represented by this group of buildings. The phrase 'Apple of Discord' comes from the Judgement of Paris in Greek mythology. Although most urban names are now given in Catalan in Barcelona, the pun only works in Spanish. Given the zeal to catalanise everything, however, the phrase is now often corrupted as '*Mançana de la Discòrdia*', which makes it sound a bit more Catalan.

The first of the buildings, at **no. 35** (at the corner with the Carrer de Consell de Cent), is the **Casa Lleó Morera**, which dates back to a house of 1864, one of the earliest to have been erected on the Passeig de Gràcia. Completely remodelled between 1902 and 1906 by Lluís Domènech i Montaner, the present building is generally regarded as one of the latter's greatest residential works, and certainly an example of Modernisme at its most florid, with a profusion of floral decorative motifs and an overall *horror vacui*.

The building remained in the possession of the Lleó Morera family until 1943, when its upper floors were sold off as offices, and its ground floor acquired as a shop for the luxury retailers *Loewe*. In the creation of this tastelessly decorated shop, the ground floor of the building was entirely mutilated, thus depriving the façade of one of its richest layers of ornamentation.

Adjoining the Casa Lleó Morera, at Passeig de Gràcia **no. 37**, is the **Casa Mulleres**, a relatively austere structure built in 1906 by Enric Sagnier i Villavecchia and decorated with a combination of classical and discreetly rococo elements. Yet more severe and conventional is the next building, the **Casa Bonet**, which was designed by Jaume Brossa in 1901. The ground floor houses a jeweller's that also contains the **Museu del Perfum**. Exhibits include some 5000 perfume bottles from all around the world, from ancient civilisations to the present day. *Open Mon–Fri 11.00–13.30, 16.30–20.00, Sat 10.30–13.30. Free.*

The Manzana de la Discordia regains its architectural distinction with the **Casa Amatller** (**no. 41**), which is now the headquarters of the **Centre del Modernisme**. *Open Mon–Sat 10.00–19.00, Sun & public holidays 10.00–14.00.*

The centre holds exhibition and provides information on Modernista architecture. Also available are tickets for the **Ruta del Modernisme**, which is a suggested route around the principal buildings, undertaken independently, with discounted or free entrance. The very reasonable price includes a useful book.

A remodelling of an earlier structure, this was carried out by Puig i Cadafalch in 1898–1900 for the chocolate manufacturer Antoni Amatller and was the first of the buildings constituting the Manzana de la Discordia to be completed. The eclectic façade, so characteristic of this architect who was also a historian, archaeologist and politician, brings together elements from secular and religious buildings, as well as from the Catalan Gothic and Northern architecture. This latter influence is particularly apparent in the enormous stepped gable, which seems derived from some fantastical vision of Holland. The architectural historian Cirici Pellicer described the building as the 'apotheosis of the Decorative Arts', and the façade is certainly remarkable for its decorative richness, with star-like ceramic plaques studding the gable, geometrical sgraffito decoration above the upper gallery, elaborate wrought-iron balconies, stained glass, ceramic tiles by Manuel Ballarín and intricate and deeply modelled statuary by Eusebi Arnau and Alfons Juyol. The interior, which houses the **Institut Amatller d'Art Hispànic** (an institution founded in 1942 by Antoni Amatller's daughter Teresa), features further statuary by Arnau and a heavy, Nordic-style hall by Gaspar Homar.

The neighbouring **Casa Batlló**, by Antoni Gaudí, completes the Manzana de la Discordia, and brings the row to a suitably fantastical climax. As with the other structures on the block, this was a remodelling and extension of a previous structure, the architect's brief being in this case to add two floors, produce new front and back façades, and create an entirely new main floor. Gaudí carried out the work between 1904 and 1906. The front façade, exemplifying his love of melting amorphous forms, is encrusted all over with blue ceramic decorations—resembling strange subaqueous forms—by his usual collaborator Josep Maria Jujol.

Its most striking feature is its undulating, ceramic-tiled roof, the design of which took into account the steep gable of the adjoining Casa Amatller, while revealing to the full the greater dynamism of Gaudí's architecture in relation to that of Puig i Cadafalch. The actual shape of the roof was almost certainly intended to suggest the figures of St George and the Dragon, the saint being represented by the turret crowned by a cross, and the dragon wittily evoked through ceramic tiles and ribs that appear respectively to be the animal's scales and bones.

The back façade, which can be seen from an alley leading off the adjacent Carrer d'Aragó, is much more sober, though it does have a colourful upper level resplendent with ceramic floral decorations. The interior decoration of the main floor rooms has been excellently preserved, and opened to the public in spring 2002. The small entrance lobby contains a curious staircase well, which was designed to create an illusion of deep recession, an effect achieved through tapering walls, and blue ceramics that become increasingly pale in hue the nearer they reach the skylight.

From the Casa Batlló, turn left into the Carrer d'Aragó to visit the **Fundació Antoni Tàpies** at no. 255. *Open Tue–Sun 10.00–20.00. Fee. Free with Ruta del Modernisme voucher and Articket. Barcelona Card discount. Bookshop.*

The building is the former Editorial Montaner i Simon, designed by Domènech i Montaner in 1879 for his brother, who was a partner in the publishing company **Montaner i Simon**. Built between 1880 and 1885, it is regarded as a key work in the early history of Modernisme, the building expressed Domènech's belief in a rational architecture involving the latest technologies, and was the first building in Barcelona other than a market or railway station to take the form of an ironwork structure clad in brick. The element of fantasy so necessary to Modernisme was provided by the actual brickwork, which was inspired by the techniques of the Mudéjars.

In 1987, under the architectural direction of Roser Amadó and the appropriately named Lluís Domènech, work was begun on the transformation of the building as the seat of the Tàpies Foundation, which was opened in 1990 and is now one of the more popular of the city's recent attractions. Antoni Tàpies

Fundació Antoni Tàpies

himself boldly embellished the façade with a crowning sculpture entitled *Chair and Cloud*, an expressively untidy aluminium mesh resembling a large piece of steel wool that has been torn at by a madman.

The **interior**, with its original ironwork columns and beams, has been strikingly modernised. The upper part is divided between a specialist library of modern art and a gallery where selections of the foundation's large bequest of Tàpies' paintings, sculptures and graphic work are shown. The main works owned by the foundation, however, as with those by Miró in the Miró foundation on Montjuïc, date from the artist's more recent years, and perhaps do not represent the best of his art. The lower floor is used for temporary exhibitions.

Back on the Passeig de Gràcia, walk up another two blocks to the Carrer de Mallorca and turn right. On the right at **no. 278** (at the corner with the Carrer de Roger de Llúria), is the **Casa Montaner**, the family home of the Montaner family of the *Editorial Montaner i Simon*. It was begun in 1885 by Josep Domènech i Estapà, who had previously built a nearby (and no longer extant) palace for the Montaners' partners, the Simons. For reasons that are not known the architect was replaced in 1891 by the owner's cousin, Lluís Domènech i Montaner, who completed the building in 1896.

The first two floors of the exterior are by Josep Domènech and in their sober eclecticism differ markedly from the crowning floor added by Lluís Domènech, a work of great ornamental richness featuring mosaic decorations designed by Gaspar Homar. Lluís, aided by two other of his usual collaborators, the sculptor Eusebi Arnau and the stained-glass artist Rigalt, was responsible as well for the magnificent vestibule, with its brilliantly coloured stained-glass skylight and its grand staircase profusely carved with motifs of Baroque and Plateresque inspiration. Since 1980 the palace has housed the *Delegaciò del Govern a Catalunya*.

Further along the Carrer de Mallorca, on the opposite side of the street, is yet another work by Lluís Domènech i Montaner at **nos 291–93**, the **Casa Thomas**, now the *BD Ediciones de Diseño* shop. This was built in 1895–98 as a two-storeyed building as a home and workshop for the Thomas engravers, further relatives of Domènech. In 1912 it was given an additional three floors by Domènech's son-in-law, Francesc Guàrdia Vial, who respected the intricately ornamental nature of the original façade, and probably worked in collaboration with his father-in-law.

The entrance at **no. 293**, which leads today to a lawyer's office (occupying the upper part of the building), takes you into a beautiful small vestibule decorated with ceramic tiles, stained-glass windows and elaborate carvings. The ground floor and basement (entered through the door at no. 291) comprise what was originally the Thomas's workshop and were sensitively transformed in 1979 for the leading Barcelona design firm *BD Ediciones de Diseño*.

> *BD* was founded in 1972 by Oscar Tusquets, Lluís Clotet, Pep Bonet and Cristià Cirici, all of whom had studied architecture together at the Escuela Técnica Superior de Arquitectura de Barcelona. On graduating from this institution in 1965 they had set up the *Studio Per* architectural practice. In an article on *Studio Per* written in 1969, Alexandre Cirici Pellicer identified this group with the youth generation of the 1960s, 'incorporating themselves into active life at the moment of the consumer boom, of the sexual revolution and the youth movements of Paris, Amsterdam and Berkeley.'

La Pedrera

Returning to the Passeig de Gràcia, turn right to reach Antoni Gaudí's secular masterpiece, the **Casa Milà**, better known as La Pedrera, the massive curved façade of which spreads around to the Carrer de Provença. *Open Mon–Sun 10.00–20.00. Guided tours Mon–Fri 18.00, Sat, Sun & public holidays 11.00. Fee. Included on Articket; Ruta del Modernisme, Barcelona Card and Bus Turístic discounts. Rooftop also open July–Sept daily 21.00–24.00, with live music and a bar. Shop and café.*

Built in 1905–10, when Gaudí was at the height of his fame and at work both on the Sagrada Família (p 185) and the Park Güell (p 217), the Casa Milà was a residential and commercial block commissioned by the local businessman Pere

La Pedrera (Casa Milà)

Milà i Camps. The building, with its sinuous façade centred around the corner of two streets, breaks away from the rigid geometry of Cerdà's Eixample, and can almost be regarded as a work of sculpture. Revealingly, shortly after work on the building had begun, Gaudí adapted his original plans as a result of a scale plaster model commissioned from Joan Beltran.

The façade, made of Montjuïc limestone, appears to have been modelled rather than designed. It has been frequently likened to an abandoned quarry-face, thus giving rise to the building's nickname of 'la Pedrera', which means 'the Quarry'. The rippling and smoothly eroded forms are also reminiscent of waves, an image reinforced by the extraordinary ironwork balconies by Josep Maria Jujol, which give the impression that the building has been covered in seaweed.

The originality of the building is not simply limited to the exterior but also permeates the **interior**, the complex arrangement of which is centred around two undulating and irregular courtyards adorned with ceramics and traces of murals. Gaudí was also responsible for the interior decoration of the first-floor rooms where Milà and his family lived, but this was stripped shortly after Milà's death by his wife Roser Segímon i Artell.

The building was acquired in 1986 by the *Caixa de Catalunya* bank, which embarked on a thorough restoration campaign, which included the cleaning of the façade and the removal of later structural alterations on the upper floor.

The visit starts with **El Pis de la Pedrera** (the Pedrera Apartment), where an exhibition shows how the city, society and industry were developing at the time Gaudí was working. The apartment retains many original features and is decorated and furnished in the typical style of a bourgeois family in the early 20C.

You then continue upstairs to the **Espai Gaudí** exhibition space in the attic. This space amd the roof terrace were restored and remodelled in 1991–96 by Francisco Javier Asarta and Robert Brufau, under the direction of Enric Mira and advised by the art and architecture historian Raquel Lacuesta.

The Espai Gaudí, designed by Daniel Giralt-Miracle, Fernando Marzá and Laura Baringo, charts Gaudí's life and career in a highly informative and original way, from his earliest projects to the Sagrada Família, documented by photographs, plans, models, charts and audiovisuals.

The highpoint of the tour, however, is undoubtedly the visit to the fantastical **rooftop**, with its strange twisted chimneys and ventilation shafts, which are coated with fragments of pottery, marble and glass. The straight and undecorated chimneys were later additions, as were the safety railings. Gaudí was reluctant to install railings, believing that these detracted from the wild mountain-top character of the roofline.

He had originally intended to add a sculptural group to this surrealistic landscape. More than four metres high, this would have represented either the Virgin of La Gràcia (the name of the former township which began at the Carrer de Provença) or the Virgin of Roser (in honour of his patron's wife). Milà, however, in view of the anarchist disturbances of the time, thought it unwise to crown the building with such a prominent Catholic symbol, and Gaudí had to content himself with the cross-like shape of the central chimney. From the roof there are panoramic views of the city from Tibidabo mountain down to the sea.

On the way out, you can also visit an exhibition space on the first floor, where temporary exhibitions are held.

Almost adjoining la Pedrera, at **no. 96** Passeig de Gràcia, is Barcelona's most progressive and influential store, *Vinçon*, situated in the palatial Casa Casas. This was built by Antoni Rovira i Rabassa in 1898–99 as the residence of the painter Ramon Casas, and for many years Casas' friend and colleague Santiago Rusinyol had an apartment on the third floor. Elements of the original interior decoration by Josep Pascó i Mensas have survived, including—on the main floor—a magnificently elaborate fireplace.

Founded on the present premises in 1940 by Jacinto Amat, *Vinçon* was originally a shop specialising in the import and sale of German porcelain. In the 1960s, under the direction of Jacinto's son Fernando, the shop expanded into gifts and office and shop equipment, soon achieving a reputation as Spain's leading showcase of modern furniture. Fernando Amat was influenced to a certain extent by the British store *Habitat*. Unlike the latter's founder, Terence Conran (whom he met in 1974), however, he resisted the temptation to develop his shop into a large chain, and was thus able to keep a much closer eye on the quality of the goods and design. By giving priority to objects that he preferred rather than to what the market wanted, Amat's store took on an increasingly avant-garde character, as exemplified in the activities of its special exhibition hall, the **Sala Vinçon**. This hall has been the setting of performance art, installations, lectures on everyday objects, conceptual art and exhibitions of avant-garde furniture and design. Its first major show in 1973 was of the Post-Modern tables of film director Bigas Luna. Amat's best known discovery was the designer of the Olympic logo, Javier Mariscal (p 161), who has been closely associated both with the store and the Sala Vinçon since his student days in the early 1970s.

There are lots of good bars, cafés and restaurants in this area. If you go back down the Passeig de Gràcia and turn right into Carrer de Provença, you reach, at the corner with the Rambla de Catalunya, the basement bar known as *La Bodegueta* (Rambla de Catalunya no. 100). This narrow and intimate bar, which is a popular meeting-place for people going to the many surrounding cinemas, is one of the Eixample's rare survivals from the 1940s. Its décor of marble tables, wooden panelling and packed shelves of bottles has barely changed since the place opened in 1949. It stocks a good selection of wines, served with *bocatas*, or small sandwiches.

Another traditional Eixample establishment is the adjoining *Saló de Te Mauri* (at Rambla de Catalunya no. 102), a lavishly decorated confectioner's and tea-room (with a pseudo-Baroque ceiling painting and an elaborately carved wooden counter), frequented by Barcelona's old families and those recuperating from an afternoon's shopping.

You can return to the Passeig de Gràcia along the Passatge de la Concepció, which runs parallel to the Carrer de Provença and is another of the Eixample's surviving passages lined with late-19C family houses. At no. 5 is the smart and fashionable restaurant called *Tragaluz* (opened in 1990), which has an interior decoration by Sandra Tarruella and Pepe Cortés, and graphic designs by Mariscal.

The main restaurant occupies a conservatory-like space on the first floor, and is still one of the top places to eat in Barcelona, with respect to both food and atmosphere. The Japanese restaurant opposite is run by the same team. The owners of the restaurant had made their name with the nearby **Mordisco** restaurant (at Carrer del Rosselló no. 265, the street parallel to the north), an informal place also designed by Sandra Tarruella, and popularised by the famous, including artists such as Mariscal and the painter Miquel Barceló.

Also on the Carrer del Roselló (at no. 208) is the first of Barcelona's designer bars to achieve a truly popular success, **Nick Havanna**, the name of which is derived from a fictitious cowboy hero of the West. It was designed in 1985 by Eduard Samsó, who created a great variety of spaces, each intended to appeal to a particular clientele. Although out of vogue for much of the 1990s, the bar is now once again a happening venue. You can wander from a standing area overlooked by a wall of videos to a sumptuous seating area with armchairs designed by the fashionable French artist Philippe Starck. A giant pendulum provides another of the many distractions, but the real surprises are to be found in the toilets, which were among the first in Barcelona to be designed with a view to being a talking-point in their own right. The basins are treated almost as shrines, and the urinals as a cascading, mirrored waterfall.

One block further up, the Passeig de Gràcia crosses the wide Avinguda Diagonal before coming to an end in a small stretch enclosing a verdant garden—called the **Jardins de Salvador Espreu**. At no. 113 is the **Casa Bonaventura Ferrer** (1905–6) by Pere Falqués i Urpí, the architect responsible the distinctive combined bench and streetlight design along the Passeig de Gràcia. At the top righthand corner of the square is Lluís Domènech i Montaner's **Casa Fuster** (at no. 132), a structure of 1908–10 featuring one of this architect's characteristically varied and richly-ornamented façades. In this case, classical elements mingle with others inspired by both the Venetian and Catalan Gothic.

Walk back to the junction of the Passeig de Gràcia with the Avinguda Diagonal and turn left. Almost immediately to your left, at no. 442, is the **Casa Comalat**, a fine Modernista structure built in 1909–11 by Salvador Valeri Pupurull, and featuring an expressively undulating crowning-piece with a green-tiled dome. This building is even more unusual in that it also has a notable rear façade, which gives onto Carrer de Còrsega and has mosaic decoration and elaborate carpentry. The building was restored in 1987.

Museu de la Música
On the other side of the street at no. 373, on the corner with Carrer del Rosselló, is the Museu de la Música. *Open mid June–mid Sept Tue–Sun 10.00–14.00, Wed 10.00–20.00; mid Sept–mid Jun Tue, Thu–Sun 10.00–14.00, Wed 10.00–20.00. Fee. Free with Ruta del Modernisme voucher; Barcelona Card discount.*

The museum is housed in the Palau Quadras, a former residential block which was transformed by Puig i Cadafalch in 1904–06 as a palace for the Baron of Quadras. The main façade is distinguished by a projecting gallery with exquisitely elaborate carvings of Gothic Plateresque derivation, executed by Alfons Juyol to the designs of Eusebi Arnau. The vestibule and main rooms have been well preserved, and include stained-glass windows, ceramic decorations and an intricately carved fireplace.

The museum is therefore worth visiting for the interior alone, even if you think you have no interest in musical instruments. This is however a fascinating collection of unusual instruments from all over the world, as well as numerous personal mementoes of Pau Casals, Albéniz and Granados. Exhibits include stringed instruments from countries including China, Japan, Equatorial Guinea and Afghanistan, from the 16C–19C. The guitar collection is rated as one of the best in the world. There is also a section on castanets from different parts of Spain. Sometime in the future, the museum is set to transfer to the Auditori concert hall.

On the other side of Avinguda Diagonal (nos 416–20) is Puig i Cadafalch's best known building, the **Casa Terrades** of 1903–05. This large residential block, resembling a fantastical Gothic fortress, is generally known as the **Casa de les Punxes** from the 'witch's hat' spires that crown its turrets. The rear façade, which gives onto Carrer de Rosselló, features a large ceramic plaque of St George and the Dragon which bears the slogan 'Patron Saint of Catalunya, give us back our freedom'.

Two blocks further down, the intersection with Carrer de Girona is marked by a sculpture entitled *Ictíneo*, made by Josep Maria Subirachs in 1963. The piece commemorates the Catalan submarine of that name, which was invented by Narcís Monturiol in 1861.

Turning down Carrer de Girona, on the corner with Carrer de Mallorca you come to the green Modernista façade of the *Puigoriol pharmacy*, installed in the ground floor of the **Casa Sofia García**. The building, designed by Juli Maria Fossas in 1912–14, combines the more classical elements of the original Eixample buildings with Modernista details. Is is worth having a look inside the pharmacy to see the ornate lamps, carpentry and marblework.

Turn left into Carrer de Mallorca and walk along one block to Carrer de Bailén, passing a string of Modernista apartment blocks. Turning right into Carrer de Bailén, at **no. 113**, at the intersection with the Carrer de València, is a cream residential block with pink sgraffito decoration. Known as the **Casa Llopis Bofill**, this was built in 1902 by Antoni M. Gallissà i Soqué, an architect who had worked with Domènech i Montaner, and had been in charge of the crafts workshop that the latter had instigated in the café-restaurant of the World Exhibition (p 163). Gallissà's close collaboration with craftsmen such as stuccoists and ceramicists is evident in his few known buildings, of which this is the most important, a sensual Neo-Moorish structure clearly inspired by the Alhambra in Granada.

Turn left into Carrer de València and walk along to the junction with the Passeig de Sant Joan. Facing you is a former **Salesian Monastery and church**, an elaborate Neo-Gothic complex built in 1882–85 by Joan Martorell i Montells, who was very much influenced at the time by the ideas of Ruskin and Viollet-le-Duc. The church, now the parish church of Sant Francesc de Sales, has elaborate sculptural decoration in the presbytery by Enric Monserdà.

Adjacent at no. 98 of the Passeig de Sant Joan, on the corner of Diagonal, is one of Barcelona's more unusual museums, the **Museu del Clavegueram**, or Sewer Museum. *Open Tue–Fri 10.00–13.00, 16.00–18.00, Sat & Sun 10.00–14.00. Fee.* The displays chart the history and development of sewers over the centuries, with comprehensive exhibits on Barcelona's system. At weekends or by appointment, visitors can also visit the very real sewers underneath the museum.

On the other side of Diagonal, Passeig de Sant Joan is adorned with bosky central gardens, overlooking which, at **no. 108**, is the **Fundació la Caixa Centre Cultural**. The centre closed in spring 2002, when its important collection of contemporary art was transferred to CaixaForum, the foundation's new venue at the base of Montjuïc (p 199). There are plans to move the Science Museum (also run by La Caixa, see p 221) here while its Tibidabo premises are being refurbished from September 2002 to October 2003. A long-term future use for the building had not been decided upon at the time of writing.

Designed by Puig i Cadafalch in 1901, this was originally a family house, known as the Casa Macaya. The white stuccoed façade features detailing of late Gothic inspiration, with intricate carving by Eusebi Arnau. Inside is a fine Gothic-inspired courtyard complete with gargoyles and an open staircase, but the rest of the interior has lost its original appearance.

Continuing down the Avinguda Diagonal, the next building of note is the **Casa Planells** at no. 332 at the junction with the Carrer de Sicilia. Built in 1923–24, this curiously undulating structure in the form of a truncated triangle is the work of Josep Maria Jujol, Gaudí's most faithful collaborator. Although clearly displaying Modernista features, the building also heralds the trend towards Functionalism. Inside, some of the apartments are arranged over two floors, a technique considered avant-garde at the time.

Temple de la Sagrada Família

Turning left here along the Carrer de Sicilia, after two blocks you come to the most important and notorious work of Gaudí himself, the Temple de la Sagrada Família. *Open Apr, May, June, July, Aug Mon–Sun 09.00–20.00; Mar, Sept, Oct Mon–Sun 09.00–19.00; Jan, Feb, Nov, Dec Mon–Sun 09.00–18.00. Fee. Ruta del Modernisme, Barcelona Card and Bus Turístic discounts. Guided tours. Shop.*

Contrary to popular belief, the Sagrada Família was never intended as Barcelona's new cathedral, but was originally planned instead as a church to house a copy of the Holy House of Loreto. The idea for such a building had been formed during a visit made in 1869 to the Italian town of Loreto by Josep Maria Bocabella, the founder of a religious society devoted to the cult of St. Joseph. One of the main aims of this society was the bridging of the ever-widening gulf between workers and employers. A suitable site for the church was acquired by the society, and work on the building was begun in 1882 under the direction of Francesc de Paula de Villar. Villar planned a structure inspired by a Gothic cathedral, but disagreements with Bocabella led to his dismissal after only a small section of the crypt had been completed. On 3 October, 1883, the task of completing the building was entrusted—on the advice of the architect Joan Martorell—to the 31-year-old Antoni Gaudí.

Using as his starting point Villar's original plan, Gaudí evolved a project of ever-increasing originality, ambitiousness and scale. While respecting the Gothic cathedral plan of ambulatory, transepts and five aisles, he intended the building to be 60 metres wide at the crossing and have a central nave 95 metres long. The massive transept façades were to have four towers of an average height of 100 metres, while four more towers would surround a crossing tower no less than 170 metres high.

The originality of Gaudí's projected church lay not simply in its remarkable size and the bizarre nature of the forms, but in such novel features as an exterior ambulatory which was to have surrounded the whole building and to which Gaudí gave the misleading name of *claustre*. Gaudí was involved in the construction of the building for the rest of his life, refusing to take on any other architectural commissions after the death in 1914 of his close friend and collaborator, Francesc Berenguer i Mestres. Those who worked on the building were paid the most meagre of wages, including Gaudí himself, who in the end was able to renounce all payment thanks to the money he had made on other works. Suffering from poor health from 1910 onwards, Gaudí spent his last years living unwashed and unkempt in a worker's shack on the site. He was not destitute, as was believed until recently, but had become so absorbed in his work that he was totally uninterested in material things and chose to live a frugal life.

At the time of Gaudí's death in 1926, all that had been completed of the building was the crypt, the apse and part of the transept façade of the Nativity. The latter façade was still missing three of its four projected towers, but these were erected soon afterwards by Domènec Sugrañes Gras.

George Orwell, describing the church during the Civil War, at a time when both Gaudí and Modernisme in general had reached the nadir of their popularity, greatly regretted that the main body of the building had escaped the attentions of the anarchists, thinking it 'one of the most hideous buildings in the world... [with] four crenellated spires exactly the shape of hock bottles'.

Work on the building was renewed in 1952 and has been continuing ever since. Using modern production methods, it might be possible to complete the building by 2020, though there are many people who believe that the place should have been left as a monumental shell commemorating Gaudí's visionary but wayward genius. The absence of any detailed plans indicating exactly what Gaudí had intended, combined with Gaudí's tendency constantly to alter his ideas at construction stage, certainly provide insuperable obstacles for those attempting to complete the building in as faithful a way as possible. Funds for the completion of the church continue nonetheless to pour in, and, as with 'Mad Ludwig' of Bavaria's Neuschwanstein, the enormous investment that has been put into the building will almost certainly be recouped hundreds of times over through the place's sheer importance as a tourist attraction.

The architectural magnificence of the Sagrada Família in its present state is due mainly to the dynamic and sculpturally-conceived **Nativity façade**. Dedicated to the Nativity of Christ and executed between 1893 and 1904, it features three portals in the shape of Gaudí's adored parabolic arches. The portals, representing (from left to right) Hope, Charity and Faith are encrusted with a struggling mass of naturalistic statuary, some of the figures made from life casts. The strange oozing forms surrounding the figures give a grotto-like character to the portals, a character that accords well with the tapering crenellated towers above, the shape of which was inspired by the curiously eroded peaks behind the monastery at Montserrat. The expressively twisted tops of these towers are decorated with polychrome mosaics.

You can climb by lift to the base of the towers, and from there wind your way up each of the openwork spires, a disorientating experience likely to induce claustrophobia, agoraphobia and vertigo, all at the same time.

Interior Entering the main body of the building through the Nativity transept, you see to your right the wall of the apse, which was one of the earliest parts of the church to be completed, and also the dullest, being an unremarkable Neo-Gothic work. The transept in front of you was built entirely after 1952 and has a façade that acts as a grey, concrete travesty of that of the Nativity transept. Called the **Passion façade**, the sculptural decoration—representing, as Gaudí had intended, the Passion and Death of Christ—was executed by Josep Maria Subirachs. A **museum** relating to the history of the building is situated in the crypt, which was restored by Quintana i Vidal in 1939–50, follow-

Sagrada Família

ing extensive damage caused during the Civil War. The displays include photographs showing the construction process, models of various parts of the structure and plans of the ongoing work.

Leading north from the Sagrada Família is the remodelled Avinguda de Gaudí, an elegant sloping thoroughfare covered in café tables, and decorated near its centre with **ironwork street-lamps** by Pere Falqués i Urpí of c 1900.

Hospital de la Santa Creu i de Sant Pau

Whereas the Sagrada Família provides an outstanding vista looking towards the sea, a scarcely less remarkable vista to the north is supplied by the Hospital de la Santa Creu i de Sant Pau, the most ambitious undertaking of Domènech i Montaner.

Pau Gil i Serra, a Catalan banker resident in Paris, bequeathed a large sum of money in his will for the creation of a model hospital complex in Barcelona, designed on the lines of the then fashionable garden cities. The hospital's functions were to be divided between different pavilions, some of which were to be joined by underground galleries. In 1891, the executors of the will acquired 30,000 square metres of land for this purpose, and entrusted the overall design of the complex to Domènech i Montaner.

The foundation stone of this hospital—which by the terms of the will had to bear the name of Gil's patron saint, Paul—was laid on 15 January, 1902.

By 1911, however, when funds had run out, only eight of Domènech's projected 46 pavilions had been erected, and none of these was as yet in a suitable state to be used. The executors were forced to enter into negotiations with the administrators of the Hospital de la Santa Creu in the Raval (p 143), an institution which at the time was greatly in need of space to enlarge and modernise its premises.

Eventually it was agreed that the two institutions would be joined together, the Hospital de la Santa Creu being transferred to the site of the Hospital de Sant Pau. New funds for the completion of the complex subsequently became available, and the site was extended to a total of 145,470 metres. Lluís Domènech's son, Pere Domènech i Roura, came to the assistance of his father, and was responsible for the design of many of the later pavilions. The complex was finally completed by the beginning of 1930, and officially opened on January 16 of that year by Alfonso XIII. Insensitive modernisations were carried out in later years and, though the complex continues to function as a hospital, a large section of it has been left to ruin.

The Hospital de la Santa Creu i de Sant Pau, Barcelona's most extensive Modernista complex, is a fascinating if melancholy place to visit, with a haunting, dream-like atmosphere, particularly if seen on a winter's evening. The brick pavilions, with their medieval and Byzantine overtones and colourful ceramic-tiled roofs, are remarkable for their variety and overall fantasy, the ones that have been abandoned providing an element of the macabre. Essentially this is a place simply for wandering around, but one building in particular deserves special attention: the **Administrative Pavilion**, which was built by Lluís Domènech in 1905–10, and stands at the entrance to the complex, directly facing the northern end of the Avinguda de Gaudí. The brick and stone façade, which brings together elements from Byzantine architecture and the Catalan Gothic, has a steepled frontispiece rising up on steps, and is adorned with statuary by Pau Gargallo and his studio.

As in all his buildings, Domènech worked closely here with a great number of craftsmen, and the interior is of particular ornamental richness, aglow with ceramic decorations and stained glass, hung with elaborate ironwork lamps, and richly carved throughout. As you walk up one of the grand flights of steps which lead off from the large vestibule, the overall effect is particularly dramatic, with star-shaped vaulting coming suddenly into view above you, giving you the impression that you are entering some fantastical cathedral-like structure. From the windows of the upper hall there are outstanding views looking all the way down the Avinguda de Gaudí to the Sagrada Família.

Walk back to the Plaça de Gaudí and head down the Carrer de Marina. Cross the Avinguda Diagonal to reach, two blocks further down, the **Plaça de Toros Monumental** (or take the metro to Monumental, or bus 10 down Carrer de Lepant, getting off at the intersection with the Gran Via).

Built in 1915–16 by Ignasi Mas Morell and Domènec Sugrañes Gras, this is claimed to be the only Modernista bullring in the world, and is certainly a most curious building, with huge ceramic-coated eggs, in blue and white, crowning brick towers perforated by parabolic arches. This is the only one of Barcelona's two bullrings still to be used for bull-fights (see p 48 for details) and features a small **Museu Taurí**. *Open only during the bullfighting season, Easter to Sept Mon–Sat 10.30–14.00, 16.00–19.00, Sun, & before bullfights 10.30–13.00. Fee*. Exhibits include posters, costumes, capes and photographs, as well as documentation relating to the career of the legendary bullfighter Manolete, who was killed in the ring of the Andalusian town of Linares in 1947.

The bullring overlooks the wide Gran Via de les Corts Catalanes. At **nos 798–814**, just beyond the junction with Carrer de Lepant, is the apartment complex known as the **Casa de los Toros**. Designed by Antoni de Moragas Gallissà and Francesc de Riba Salas in 1960–62, the reinforced concrete blocks look quite normal, but were pioneering structures in their day, and have an unusual feature in that the roofs of the balconies are decorated with photographs of bullfights by the renowned photographer Francesc Català Roca. All the images were taken at the Monumental bullring, which the architects attended regularly.

Turn back along the Gran Via towards the Plaça de Tetuán, in the middle of which stands the **Monument al Doctor Robert**. This was originally situated in the Plaça de la Universitat, but was dismantled in the Civil War in the belief that it would be a rallying point for nationalist Catalan rebels. It was brought here in 1979. Commemorating the popular mayor of Barcelona, Dr Bartolomeu Robert (1842–1902), it was sculpted by Josep Llimona in 1910, and is the most remarkable Modernista commemorative monument in the city.

A stone bust of Dr Robert being kissed by a woman representing Fame surmounts a tapering stone base adorned with eight allegorical and realistically modelled figures in bronze. Much of the pictorial power of this monument is derived from the contrast between bronze and stone. The undulating base, which seems to have been removed from the façade of La Pedrera, has often been attributed to Gaudí, who was a close friend of Llimona's.

Gaudí was fatally injured one block further along, at the intersection of the Gran Via and Carrer de Bailén. It was here, on 7 June, 1926, that he was run over by a tram. His body was subsequently mistaken for that of a tramp. He died three days later in the Hospital de la Santa Creu i de Sant Pau, and was buried in the crypt of the Sagrada Família.

Turn left down Carrer de Bailén and right into Carrer de Casp one block down. On the left, at no. 48, is the **Casa Calvet**, the most restrained of the three residences created by Gaudí for the Eixample, which is now a restaurant. Built in 1898–99 as a store and residence for a textile merchant family, the Calvets, it features a flat, rusticated façade crowned by two undulating pediments, the whole revealing the strong influence of the Catalan Baroque. If you are fortunate enough to pass by when the concierge is not around, have a look at the tiny vestibule, which has ceramic decoration and a Gaudí-designed lift. The furniture Gaudí created for the Calvet store and office was his first to reveal strong naturalistic inspiration. These pieces can now be seen in the Museu d'Art Modern in the Ciutadella (p 164).

Further along Carrer de Casp at nos 24–26, on the corner with Carrer de Pau Claris, is the **Casal Sant Jordi**, a former commercial and residential block built in 1929–31 by Francesc Folguera Grassi. A three-sided block of great simplicity, this is generally regarded as one of the finest examples of the progressive,

Rationalist tendencies within the architecture of the Noucentisme movement.

Turning right into Carrer de Pau Claris, immediately on the left is the *Laie bookshop*, which opened in 1980. Gabriel García Marquéz is just one of the writers and artists who buy their books there when in Barcelona. The large upstairs café is a great place for a coffee and a rest.

Continuing along Carrer de Casp, on the left at no. 6 is the **Teatre Tívoli**, a grand cinema built by Miquel Madorell i Rius in 1917–19. Arriving back at the lower end of the Passeig de Gràcia, turn right and immediately left into the Gran Via de les Corts Catalanes.

On the right is the imposing **Cine Coliseum**, an example of Noucentiste architecture at its most pretentious, in this case taking its inspiration from Charles Garnier's Opera House in Paris. It was built in 1923 by Francesc de Paula Nebot i Torrens. One block further on is the **Edifici de la Universitat**, the main building of Barcelona University.

The origins of the university are in the Estudis Generals, a college situated at the lower end of the Rambla. After this was suppressed in 1717, the role of a centre of Catalan higher education was taken over by the University of Cervera, which was transferred to Barcelona in 1842 and temporarily housed in the former Carmelite convent on Carrer del Carme. The present building, designed by Elies Rogent in 1859–62, takes the form of a vast Neo-Romanesque block inspired by the monastery of the Catalan village of Poblet. Inside, Neo-Romanesque elements are contrasted with detailing of Byzantine and Islamic inspiration, as is particularly evident in the splendid Assembly Hall. With the expansion of Barcelona University in recent times, most of the faculties were moved to the campus near the Palau Reial on the Avinguda Diagonal.

The remaining attractions of the Eixample are more scattered. Continuing down the Gran Via de les Corts Catalanes, on the left on the corner of Carrer de Villaroel is the **Casa Francisco Farreras**, designed by Antoni Millàs Figuerola in 1902. The corner building actually comprises three apartment blocks with different decoration on the Montjuïc stone façades. The windows on the right-hand corner (as you face the building) are decorated with columns featuring female figures. The chemist's on the ground floor retains many original Modernista features.

Three blocks further on the right, on the corner of Carrer de Viladomat, is the fascinating Modernista house known as the **Casa Golferichs**. One of the first and most important buildings of Gaudí's assistant Joan Rubió Bellver, this was built in 1900–01 near the edge of the Eixample, at a time when there was still room for family homes to have small gardens, although this was an unusual feature even then. A brick structure combining influences from William Morris and Islamic architecture, the house features exceptionally wide wooden eaves, and a Neo-Gothic corner room, in which members of the family used to sit and watch the parading carriages in the street. In a ruinous state by the mid-1980s, the house was almost pulled down by the notorious property speculator Núñez y Navarro, but was saved and restored by the city council. It is now used as a college. An annexe to the rear houses the **Espai de Fotografia Francesc Català-Roca**, a foundation that holds exhibitions in the main building. If there is a show on, go and have a look as you can also see some of the interior decoration. Some of the original features have survived, most notably around the large and impressive stairwell, which is decorated all over with green embossed patterns, and the coffered ceiling in the main salon.

A few doors further down, at nos 475–77, is the **Casa de Lactància**, which was built in 1908–13 by Pere Falqués i Urpí and Antoni de Falguerra i Sivilla. The façade, of late Gothic inspiration, is crowned by an elaborate parapet containing a large central relief sculpted by Eusebi Arnau. The relatively sober exterior contrasts with the covered courtyard. This light and colourful space is glazed with stained glass and features bricks painted a pale blue and a first-floor gallery adorned with green ceramics. The building is now an old people's home.

The Gran Via de les Corts Catalanes continues to the Plaça de Espanya, which is discussed on p 194. On the last street on the right before the square, the Carrer de Llançà, is an interesting Modernista apartment block built by Josep Graner Prat in 1912. The building, at no. 20, is known as the **Casa de la Papallona** (House of the Butterfly) because of the butterfly-shaped crowning-piece adorning the otherwise sober façade. Although the colours have faded, this extraordinary feature, covered all over with an abstract decoration in blue, green, white, red and yellow ceramic fragments, gives a good idea of the extent to which Joan Miró was influenced by his city's Modernista past.

The street runs alongside **Les Arenes bullring**, which was built by August Font i Carreras in 1899–1900. It is in the pseudo-Islamic style characteristic of many of Spain's bullrings, and has as its main source of inspiration the Great Mosque at Cordoba. Bullfights are no longer put on here and the site is currently being remodelled by Richard Rogers as a leisure and entertainment venue. In 1906, a crowd of people waved handkerchiefs in the air in the ring in protest against a new law, an event claimed to be the first political demonstration in Europe. The Beatles gave their first performance in Spain here in 1966, an event that is often regarded as a key moment in the gradual liberalisation of the country during the last years of Franco's rule.

Walking up Carrer de Llançà or Carrer de Tarragona on the far side of the bullring brings you immediately to a large formal park named after the artist Miró, the **Parc Joan Miró**, which was planned in close collaboration with him. A competition held in 1981 to design the park was won by Andreu Arriola, Beth Galí, Màrius Quintana and Antoni Solanas. Interestingly, a project put forward by the leading Post-Modernist architect Ricardo Bofill was turned down by Miró on the grounds that the classical temple that it featured was 'antiquated and dehumanised', a throw-back to the Franco days. Miró himself was to have provided a 'forest of sculptures', but died after completing only one, a massive concrete phallic-like object, covered in brightly-coloured ceramics. Called *Dona i Ocell* (*Woman and Bird*), the work was unveiled in 1983, the year the artist died. The park also contains a library for children, attractively situated among ramps and ponds.

Beyond the park, the boundary of the Eixample is marked by the **Estació Barcelona Central-Sants**, which is reached either by walking up Carrer de Tarragona or taking the metro from Plaça de Espanya or Tarragona stations.

Sants is the main and most modern railway station of Barcelona, and its interest for the sightseer lies essentially in the surrounding urban spaces comprising the **Plaça de los Països Catalans** and the Parc de l'Espanya Industrial. The former, built in 1981–83 by Helio Pinón and Albert Viaplana, was the prototype for the many bleak squares that have mushroomed in Barcelona in recent years.

Intended to tidy up what had previously been a chaotic intersection, the square was created on a space—above the station's sunken tracks—which could not support the weight of any buildings, soil or trees.

The architects conceived the square as a vast sculpture. The bare expanses of pavement are articulated at wide intervals by canopies, poles and other apparently abstract forms that are meant to be full of playful figurative references. A long canopy with a wavy roof is said to suggest the smoke of a moving train. The average visitor is unlikely to appreciate these subtleties, or to comprehend the design historian Guy Julier's description of the place as a 'lyrical Minimalist essay which ensured its revival as a viable aesthetic beyond Postmodernism'.

Far more entertaining, if similarly ugly, is the **Parc de l'Espanya Industrial**, which has been extravagantly described as a 'mixture of Disney and Gaudí'. Built in 1984–86 by the Santander architect Luis Peña Ganchegui, it has the conventional attractions of trees, fountains and a large lake, but is likely to be remembered not for these but for a row of large lookout towers that resemble lighthouses but serve no apparent function. Various sculptures adorn the park, the most memorable—for children at least—being Andrés Nagel's enormous work in coloured metal representing *St George and the Dragon* (1985), which doubles as a slide.

Leave the Plaça de los Països Catalans via Carrer de Josep Tarradellas and take the first turning on the right, Carrer del Roselló. Walk along to the block between Carrer de Viladomat and Carrer d'Urgell to reach the main entrance of the complex comprising the **Universitat Industrial de Barcelona** (or take the metro from Sants to Hospital Clínic). This technical college, dating back to 1908, was created on a site previously occupied by the Batlló textile mills, of which a tall brick chimney of 1868 survives. The main buildings of the college were built in 1927–31 by Joan Rubió Bellver, and include a large residential block to which is attached a fascinating chapel supported inside by giant parabolic arches.

At the top end of the complex, turn right from Carrer de'Urgell into Carrer de Paris, then turn left after two blocks into Carrer de Casanova. Near the junction of the latter street with the Avinguda Diagonal is the charming **Casa Companys** (at no. 203, on the corner of Carrer de Buenos Aires), a white chalet-like structure built by Puig i Cadafalch in 1911 for Pere Companys. The building belongs to the architect's so-called 'white period', and its cheerful simplicity is often interpreted as symptomatic of the transition between Modernisme and Noucentisme. Under the eaves of its steeply-pitched roof is a sgraffitoed decoration of the Assumption of the Virgin. The bright interior, adapted in 1940 as a surgery for Dr Melcior Colet, retains elements of the original ground-floor decoration, including some fine stained-glass windows in the hall. The building has recently been restored to house the **Museu i Centre d'Estudis de l'Esport Dr Melcior Colet**, an undeservedly little visited museum hosting simply displayed exhibitions relating to the history of sport in Catalunya. *Open Mon–Fri 10.00–14.00, 16.00–20.00. Free.*

Turning right down the Avinguda Diagonal, on the corner of Carrer d'Enric Granados on your right you reach the **Casa Sayrach** (nos 423–25), a large residential block built by Enric Granados in 1915–18. The sinuous roof-line clearly reflects the influence of Gaudí's Casa Milà, and the entrance hall features elaborate Modernista decoration. The first floor houses the sumptuous *La Dama* restaurant.

One block further down Diagonal is the junction with Carrer de Balmes, where, at no. 161, is one of Barcelona's most extravagant designer bars, *Velvet*. Designed by Alfredo Arribas in 1987, this is one of the few survivors of the period. Inspired in its lurid sensuality by David Lynch's film *Blue Velvet* (1987), it features a great ramp that takes you down into a world described as a 'delirium of total design', created out of brick, steel, glass, slate, velvet, wood, stone, and a myriad of sensuous forms and lush, decadent colours.

Continuing down Diagonal, you shortly come to Puig i Cadafalch's **Casa Serra**, at the intersection with the Rambla de Catalunya. This structure of 1903–08 resembles a fantastical late-Gothic palace. Recently restored to house the main seat of the *Diputació de Catalunya*, it is adorned outside with elaborate sculptures by the ubiquitous Eusebi Arnau. Immediately beyond the building you arrive back to the upper end of the Passeig de Gràcia.

8 • Plaça d'Espanya and Montjuïc

▶ Start from Plaça d'Espanya. See map on p 195.

Montjuïc hill covers a large area, so you may prefer to use the bus to get around. (Bus Turístic or regular service no. 50).

Whereas the Ciutadella evokes the World Exhibition of 1888, the Plaça d'Espanya and the park of Montjuïc are essentially the legacy of the International Exhibition of 1929.

Plans for a sequel to the World Exhibition of 1888 were first formulated in 1907 by a group composed of councillors and representatives of the city's main businesses. The decision was made to hold the exhibition in 1914 on the mountain of Montjuïc, the landscaping of which had already been proposed in the 1890s. Work on the projected Exhibition was abandoned almost immediately, and was only taken up again five years later, as a result of pressure exercised by the young and rapidly expanding electrical industry. The new plans for the Exhibition involved postponing the event until 1917 and dividing it into two separate parts: an international exhibition on the theme of electricity and a general exhibition devoted mainly to Spanish arts and crafts.

Puig i Cadafalch was entrusted with the overall design of the Exhibition, while the French landscapist Jean Forestier was commissioned to transform the slopes of Montjuïc into a lush park. Forestier, one of the leading landscapists of his day, had worked extensively in Spain, and was laying out the magnificent Maria Luisa park in Seville at the time that he received the Barcelona commission.

Economic and political crises led to further postponements of the Exhibition, while the coming to power of Primo de Rivera in 1923 resulted in the downfall of Puig i Cadafalch as both a politician and the Exhibition's main architect. The dictator's political ambitions provided another powerful motive for the Exhibition, which was finally opened by Alfonso XIII on 19 May 1929. Though based to a large extent on Puig i Cadafalch's initial designs, the Exhibition was far more ambitious than the original project, and comprised four main sections devoted respectively to the industries in general, the arts in Spain, agriculture and sports.

After the closure of the Exhibition at the end of 1929, the permanent structures were put to a variety of different uses, the ones at the foot of Monjuïc remaining to this day the venue of trade exhibitions. Some of the buildings on the mountain itself, including the main pavilion or Palau Nacional, were turned into museums, while another—the former Palau de l'Agricultura—has been converted into a theatre. Barcelona was also left with a large sports stadium and the Poble Espanyol, a walled village made up of buildings representing all the different Spanish regions.

By the early 1980s, the park of Montjuïc still remained one of the main recreational centres of Barcelona, but the whole area lacked coherence and many of its structures were in a decayed and neglected state. With the choice of Montjuïc as the main sports area for the 1992 Olympics, the mountain was given a new lease of life. Buildings were restored, road access greatly improved and spectacular new structures erected. An extensive programme of improvements began in 2001 and will continue until at least 2011.

Plaça d'Espanya

In Cerdà's 1855 plan for the expansion of Barcelona, the Plaça d'Espanya featured as an irregular space at the junction of the Gran Via de les Corts Catalanes and the old road to Madrid. The grand, semicircular square of today was planned by Puig i Cadafalch as the monumental approach to both the International Exhibition and the park of Montjuïc. In the words of the architect Rubió i Tudurí, the space was intended to become the 'nerve centre of Barcelona'. The various postponements of the Exhibition led to work on the square being delayed until the mid-1920s, and it was still not complete by the time the Exhibition opened in 1929.

The **large fountain** in the middle, commissioned as late as 1928 to mark the entrance to the Exhibition, was designed by the former collaborator of Antoni Gaudí, Josep Maria Jujol. In this work, Jujol departed radically from his previous Modernista style to create a pedantic classical structure in keeping with the Noucentiste spirit of the Exhibition. Inspired by the fountains of Baroque Rome, it has as its centrepiece a triangular-shaped structure formed of three Corinthian columns flanking niches adorned with statuary by Miquel Blay. The fountain was intended as a celebration of water, and the sculptural groups in the niches represent the three seas that surround the Spanish peninsula. Three winged Victories by the sculptor Llovet rise above the entablature, while at the base of the fountain are groups by Miquel and Llucià Oslé portraying Navigation, Public Health and Abundance.

The broad and landscaped **Avinguda de la Reina Maria Cristina** joins the square with the park of Montjuïc and was built as the main thoroughfare of the Exhibition. The buildings that line the avenue are still used for trade fairs, and include two enormous pavilions with curved colonnaded façades overlooking the south side of the Plaça d'Espanya. One of these (to your left as you approach the avenue) is the restored **Palau del Treball**, which was built in 1927 by Josep Maria Jujol and André Calzada Echevarría. The other is the contemporary **Palau de Comunicacions i Transports**, the work of Fèlix d'Azua and Adolf Florensa. Between the two buildings, at the very entrance to the avenue, stand two tall towers built by Ramon Reventós in 1927 and inspired by the campanile of St Mark's in Venice.

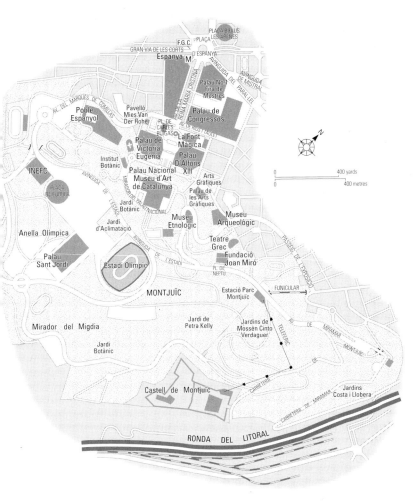

Walking down the avenue towards the looming mass of the Palau Nacional, you pass to your left the Plaça de l'Univers, which was laid out originally by Forestier, but was remodelled in 1985 by Pep Bonet i Bertran. In the centre of this largely bare space is a sculpture by Josep Llimona entitled *Forjador* (The Foundry Worker), which was donated by the artist to the city on the occasion of the May Day celebrations of 1930.

The Avinguda de la Reina Maria Cristina emerges at a grand square directly at the foot of Montjuïc, named after the engineer responsible for the ingenious electrical installations of the International Exhibition, Carles Buïgas. One of Buïgas' most successful creations was his *Magic Fountain* or *Font Màgica* of 1929, which dominates the square. It was intended as the centrepiece of an electrical show involving beams projected from behind the Palau Nacional, large lamps placed the whole length of the Avinguda de la Reina Maria Cristina, and an obelisk fitted with coloured lighting. The fountain, with its central jet shooting more than 50 metres into the air, is sometimes illuminated to the accompaniment of music. This popular and entertaining show is well worth seeing. *It lasts 15 minutes and takes place from late June to late September Thu–Sun every half hour from 20.00–24.00, and Fri & Sat 19.00–21.00 during the rest of the year. (Check with the tourist office for changes to these times.)*

A monumental flight of steps climbs from behind the fountain towards the Palau Nacional, and is flanked by the twin pavilions of Alfons XIII and Victòria Eugènia. These were built in 1923–28 using the designs of Puig i Cadafalch, and feature ornamental elements derived both from the Baroque and the Viennese Secession. Escalators on either side of the steps ease the climb up to the Palau Nacional, which since 1934 has housed the outstanding Museu Nacional d'Art de Catalunya.

Museu Nacional d'Art de Catalunya (MNAC)

Open Tue–Sat 10.00–19.00, Sun & public holidays 10.00–14.30. Fee. Included on Articket. Barcelona Card and Bus Turístic discounts. Book and gift shop. Café. The Palau Nacional was conceived by Puig i Cadafalch as a vast domed building to act as the dominant element of the monumental vista leading from the Plaça d'Espanya down the Avinguda de la Reina Maria Cristina. His basic intentions were respected, though the building itself was not to be built until 1926–29, using the designs of Enric Català i Català and Pedro Cendoya Oscoz. The end result was an eclectic structure of remarkable heaviness and pomposity, with elements derived from Spanish Baroque and Neo-classical architecture.

The central hall was originally used for the official ceremonies connected with the International Exhibition. Its dome is painted with frescoes by Francesc Galí, Josep de Togores and Manuel Humbert, with sculptural decoration by Enric Casanovas and Josep Dunyach. The rest of the structure had been planned by Puig i Cadafalch to display exhibits celebrating electricity, originally the main theme of the exhibition. The redesigned building was to house instead the sections of the International Exhibition relating to art and archaeology.

The desire to create in Barcelona a museum devoted to the fine arts goes back to the late 19C and was realised on the basis of works amassed during the World Exhibition of 1888. Founded in 1891, this museum was known originally as the Museu Municipal de Belles Arts, and contained mainly modern works. In 1904 it was transferred from the no longer extant Palau de Belles Arts to the former arsenal (both in the Parc de la Ciutadella, p 161), where it soon developed a speciality in medieval Catalan art. The first important medieval acquisitions—a group of Romanesque capitals and altar frontals from Tavèrnoles—were acquired between 1906 and 1908 under the directorship of the architect and historian Josep Pijoan. The nucleus of the medieval collection was however built up during the long directorship of Pijoan's successor, Joaquim Folch i Torres, assisted by Puig i Cadafalch, who was chairman of the Barcelona Museums' Board at the time.

After 1907, the Board, in combination with the Institut d'Estudis Catalans, began the work of copying, photographing and publishing the numerous Romanesque frescoes in the isolated churches of the Catalan Pyrenees. The

Catalan Romanesque had been largely ignored until around the middle of the 19C, and even then the interest had been entirely concentrated on the sculpture rather than on the painting of this period. The appreciation of Romanesque painting in Catalunya was initiated with the inauguration in 1891 of the Museu Episcopal at Vic, and became ever more widespread as a result of the publicity generated by the investigations carried out after 1907. The techniques that had recently been developed in Italy for the removal of frescoes from walls gave antique dealers the idea of buying the Romanesque frescoes from the local civic and ecclesiastical authorities and selling them abroad. Fortunately, the Board intervened at this stage. With the exception of the apse frescoes from Mur, which ended up in the Fine Arts Museum in Boston, it managed to secure for the Museu de Belles Arts all of Catalunya's important Romanesque frescoes, which were removed from their original settings between 1919 and 1923.

In 1931–34, the medieval, Renaissance and Baroque holdings of the Museu de Belles Arts were transferred to their present position in the Palau Nacional in Montjuïc, which became the Museu Nacional d'Art de Catalunya.

In 1932, the museum acquired the **collections of the industrialist Lluís Plandiura**, which comprised almost 2000 Romanesque, Gothic and modern works of art. Two years later, it received the **Francesc Fàbregas bequest** of 16C–19C paintings.

Although the museum opened in 1934, at the start of the Civil War two years later the contents were transferred to the towns of Olot and Darnius in Catalunya, and to Paris. After the war, the artworks returned to Barcelona and the collections were augmented by several important bequests, most notably that of **Francesc Cambó**.

In 1985 a complete re-organisation of the museum's collections was begun, and the architects Gae Aulenti and Enric Steegmann were entrusted with the task of remodelling the interior of the Palau Nacional. The displays are currently divided into three sections: Romanesque Art, Gothic Art and the Cambó Collection, which comprises mostly Renaissance and Baroque works. Further sections will open up as the restoration progresses. At least one temporary exhibition is also usually underway.

Romanesque Art

The reputation of the Museu Nacional d'Art de Catalunya as the finest museum of medieval art in Spain, if not in Europe, is due essentially to its unrivalled holdings of Catalan Romanesque art. The collection is remarkable above all for the frescoes, which have always been displayed in rooms emulating the shapes of the churches from which they were taken.

The displays begin with paintings from the apse of the **Sant Pere chapel in La Seu D'Urgell**. Room 3 is devoted to the Pedret Circle, with works from different churches by the Master of Pedret and his apprentices in the last decade of the 11C and the first decade of the 12C. These include a cycle from one of the side apses of the Mozarabic parish church at **Sant Quirze de Pedret**, which features the Virgin and Child in the cupola, underneath which are animated scenes representing the Wise and Foolish Virgins.

Room 5, in a downstairs space, contains one of the most outstanding exhibits: murals and liturgic furniture from the 12C Romanesque church of **Sant Climent de Taüll**. The central apse is dominated by a Christ in Majesty of mesmerising power, by the Master of Taüll. The expressiveness in the use of line, and the bold foreshortening and simplification of forms, reveal an artist of great individuality, and one who appears to have had a significant influence on the early development of both Picasso and Joan Miró.

The most extensive and among the best preserved of the frescoes are those displayed in Room 7, from the apse and wall of **Santa Maria de Taüll**, a church which was consecrated in 1123. The figure of the Virgin presides over the apse, while the side walls include scenes of the Three Kings, the Nativity and a remarkably realistic and gruesome portrayal of Hell. On the wall facing the apse are David and Goliath, the Last Judgement and two peacocks (symbolising immortality) drinking from the fountain of Paradise. Another highlight is the mid-12C **Batlló Majesty** in Room 8, a richly coloured work featuring a tunic adorned with Islamic motifs. Room 13 contains an exquisite baldachin from the 13C church at the Pyrenean village of Tavèrnoles.

Gothic Art

The museum's extensive collection of Catalan Gothic art, which dates from the 13C–15C, begins with **murals from the Aguilar palace** in the Carrer de Montcada (p 133), which depict Jaume I's conquest of Mallorca. The next two rooms show early works from monasteries in Aragon, Navarre and Castile as well as Catalunya.

Rooms 6 and 7 deal with the Italian influence in Catalunya, in particular from Florence and Siena, which reached Catalunya by way of the papal court at Avignon. This tendency was very apparent in the leading Catalan artists of the early 14C, Ferrer and Arnau Bassa. The main Italianate artists working in Catalunya in the second half of the 14C were Jaume, Joan and Pere Serra, who are represented here most notably by Pere Serra's *Virgin of Tortosa*.

Room 9 is devoted to the decorative style of c 1400 known as **Catalan International Gothic**, which mixed Italian, French and Flemish influences. One of its chief exponents was Lluís Borrassà, represented by the semicircular *Retable of Guardiola* of 1404. Other artists include Guerau Gener, Joan Mates, Joan Antigó and Bernat Despuig. Room 11 features the work of Bernat Martorell, including the *Retable of St Vincent*, who was known until recently as the Master of St George from a famous work in the Art Museum of Chicago.

Flemish influence, in painting, sculpture, music and architecture, came to predominate throughout Spain from c 1440 onwards. One of the earliest Catalan associates of the so-called Hispano-Flemish School, and the most faithful to Flemish models, was Lluís Dalmau, who is also represented in this section. He appears to have met Jan van Eyck when the latter was accompanying a diplomatic mission to Spain and Portugal in 1427–28. The direct influence of Van Eyck is at any rate apparent in Dalmau's masterpiece, the *Virgin of the Councillors*, which was painted in 1445 for the chapel of Barcelona's Town Hall, and portrays the Virgin and Child flanked by the city councillors, and Saints Eulàlia and Andrew. The figures are depicted with extreme naturalism within a minutely detailed Gothic interior. The Catalan contemporaries of Dalmau were generally more conservative artists than he was, as is exemplified in their continuing use of gold backgrounds right up to the end of the 15C.

The most prolific and important of these artists was Jaume Huguet (Room 12), whose work combines naturalistic detail, with decoratively embossed gold backgrounds, and a late medieval love of chivalry. His major work in the museum is the central panel of the **Triptych of St George and the Princess**, the wings of which are in Berlin.

The museum's culminating works of Flemish-inspired realism are by two late-15C artists who settled in Catalunya. One is the gruesome *Beheading of St Cugat* by the northern-born Anye Bru, a work of coarsely expressive brutality recalling German paintings of this period. The other is the *Descent into Limbo* by the remarkably original Cordoban-born artist Bartolomé Bermejo, whose *Pietà* in Barcelona Cathedral (p 108) has much of the pathos and grandeur characteristic of the art of Van Weyden. The *Descent into Limbo* shows the naked and realistically observed figure of Christ struggling against a chiaroscuro background of agitated bodies.

The Cambó Collection

The basement houses the bequest of the financier and politician Francesc Cambó, which comprises European artists from the 16C–19C. Spanish painters include Zurbarán, Sánchez Coello, El Greco and Goya. Italian art is represented by Tintoretto and Tiepolo, and Flemish art by Rubens, Quentyn Metsys and Lucas Cranach the Elder.

From the Palau Nacional, you can cut across to the Olympic complex or the Joan Miró museum, or return to the Plaça de Carles Buïgas to visit the Mies van de Rohe pavilion and the Poble Espanyol. To follow this walk, go back down to the Plaça de Carles Buïgas and turn along the Avinguda del Marquès de Comillas, which winds its way around the bosky slopes of Montjuïc.

At the beginning of the avenue on the left is the **Pavelló d'Alemanya**, a reconstruction in its original location of Mies van der Rohe's German Pavilion for the International Exhibition of 1929. *Open every day Apr–Oct 10.00–20.00, Nov–Mar 10.00–18.30. Fee.* The abstract simplicity of this horizontally-based marble and glass structure, its fluid use of space and lack of rigid separation between interior and exterior form a striking contrast to the pompous classicism of most of the official architecture of the Exhibition. The excellent reconstruction, carried out in 1985 by the leading Barcelona architects Cristià Cirici, Ferran Ramos and Ignasi de Solà-Morales, has had a significant impact on recent Catalan architecture and design, and has revealed to the full the richness and sensuality of a building known to the present generation only through black-and-white photographs.

The Modernista brick complex on the opposite side of the road is the **Fàbrica Casaramona**, designed in 1911 by Puig i Cadafalch. Originally a factory producing cotton thread and fabrics, the buildings were used as a police barracks until 1993. In spring 2002 the building took on a new role as **CaixaForum**, which houses the contemporary art collection of the Fundació La Caixa, as well as temporary exhibitions by major artists, architects and photographers. Mies van der Rohe's pavilion provided the inspiration for Japanese architect Arata Isozaki, who designed the Palau Sant Jordi stadium on Montjuïc, to create a spectacular entrance to the new venue, comprising two steel trees that branch out to support a glass roof over a vast courtyard. One wall of the entrance space features a mural by American artist Sol Lewitt.

Poble Espanyol

Open Mon 09.00–20.00, Tue, Wed, Thu 09.00–02.00, Fri & Sat 09.00–04.00, Sun 09.00–24.00. Fee. Bus Turístic and Barcelona Card discounts. Shops, cafés and restaurants.

You might well experience a sense of bathos as you make your way from the calming Minimalism of Mies van der Rohe to the busy kitsch of the Poble Espanyol, which lies half-way up Avinguda del Marquès de Comillas, surrounded on all sides by trees. The Poble Espanyol, which formed the part of the International Exhibition devoted to the crafts of Spain, was built in 1926–29 by the architects Francesc Folguera and Ramon Reventós, the artist Xavier Nogués and the art critic and former associate of *El Quatre Gats*, Miquel Utrillo. Though enjoying from the beginning the status of one of the city's main tourist attractions, this pseudo-Spanish walled village developed an exceedingly tacky character over the years.

A complete restoration of the complex was begun in 1987 by Sen Tato, and in the 1990s the village radically changed its image by surprisingly becoming one of the hubs of Barcelona's nightlife. A number of popular night-time bars sprung up here, including the extraordinary *Torres de Ávila*, which opened in 1990. Situated at the main entrance to the village, within the reconstruction of one of the medieval gates of the Castilian town of Ávila, the bar is another creation of the architect Alfredo Arribas and the designer Mariscal. A bar guide issued in 1991 by the design magazine *Ardi* thought that no other bar could surely equal the *Torres de Ávila* in the amount of 'design per square metre'. The interior, featuring a number of differently sized and shaped bar areas, does achieve a certain magical quality through its baffling spatial complexity and scenographic lighting. The whole place is centred around a huge egg-shaped area, but the highpoint of the bar is its roof terrace, situated among the crenellations of the towers, to one of which the designers have added a dark and luminous dome, sparkling with stars and crowned by a crescent moon. The views of Barcelona at night are magnificent, though the atmosphere of the whole bar is so dominated by the design as to be positively morgue-like. It is no longer the place to be seen, but worth a visit nonetheless. As there are several other bars and clubs nearby, this is a good area for nightlife, particularly in summer as some are outdoor.

Entering the Poble Espanyol through the **Ávila Gate**, you come immediately to the arcaded Plaça Mayor, which is made up of reproductions of buildings from all over Spain. The sloping streets to the east represent Aragon, the Basque Country and Extremadura, leading eventually to a Catalan Square. There is also a flight of steps copied from Santiago de Compostela, and a tiny but charming Barrio Andaluz inspired by the Barrios Judío and de Santa Cruz in Cordoba and Seville. With age the whole complex has acquired a remarkable authenticity in the sense that the places that it imitates, with their plethora of souvenir shops and over-restored quaintness, appear today to be no more genuine than the copies.

The **Porta del Carme**, at the top of the steps leading off the Plaza Mayor, forms the entrance to the **Fundació Fran Daurel**, a museum of contemporary art that opened at the end of 2001 and displays the collections of the Catalan industrialist of that name (*open daily 10.00–19.00. Fee*). There are paintings by leading artists including Antoni Tàpies, Miquel Barceló, Perejaume, José Maria Sicilia, Jaume Plensa, Federic Amat and Juan Uslé, as well as drawings by Dalí, ceramics by Picasso and graphic work by Miró and Chillida.

The Olympic complex

From the Poble Espanyol, the Avinguda del Marquès de Comillas winds up the hill towards the Olympic complex, known as the Anella Olímpica or Olympic Ring. After the Plaça de Sant Jordi the road becomes the Avinguda de l'Estadi.

The first building of architectural interest is the **INEFC** (National Institute of Physical Education of Catalunya). This chillingly austere example of Post-Modernism was built in 1984–90 by Ricardo Bofill and his studio. The INEFC was the first major building commissioned in Barcelona from this internationally-renowned Catalan architect, who established his reputation largely in and around Paris. It features a pedimented frontispiece set between two vast blocks inspired by classical courtyards, articulated by Doric arcading and built out of ochre-coloured pre-cast concrete, aluminium and tinted glass. Though the materials are modern, the building recalls the totalitarian architecture of Hitler, Mussolini and Franco, similarities that are reinforced by the singular officious-ness of the security guards who work here.

Just beyond it, also on the right, is the **Piscines Municipals Bernat Picornell** swimming pool complex. Originally built in 1970 for the European Swimming Championships, the indoor and outdoor pools were totally remodel-led for the Olympics by Franc Fernández and Moisés Gallego. *Open June–end Sep Mon–Sun 09.00–20.00; Oct–end May Mon–Sat 09.00–21.00, Sun & public holidays 09.00–14.30. Fee. Bus Turístic discount.*

Up ahead on the right is the **Estadi Olímpic**, a magnificent eclectic structure originally built by Pere Domènech i Roura for the sports events of the International Exhibition of 1929. It was first used in May of that year for a foot-ball match between a Catalan team and Bolton Wanderers, which the home side won by four goals to nil.

The triumphant equestrian bronze dominating the façade is the work of Pau Gargallo, and was returned here after being kept for many years in the Palau de la Virreina. The interior of the stadium was totally remodelled in 1986–90 by a team led by Vittorio Gregotti and involved lowering the foundations by eleven metres to increase the seating capacity to 60,000. Since 1997 the stadium has served as the home ground of Espanyol, one of Barcelona's two football clubs.

A curving ramp at the far side of the esplanade in front of the stadium leads down to the **Galeria Olímpica**. *Open April, May & June Tue–Sat 10.00–14.00, 16.00–19.00, Sun & public holidays 10.00–14.00; July, Aug & Sept Tue–Sat 10.00–14.00, 16.00–20.00, Sun & public holidays 10.00–14.00; Oct, Nov & Dec Tue–Fri 10.00–13.00, 16.00–18.00, Sat, Sun & public holidays 10.00–14.00 Jan, Feb & Mar Tue–Fri 10.00–13.00, 16.00–18.00, Sat, Sun & public holidays 10.00–14.00. Fee. Bus Turístic and Barcelona Card discounts.*

The space, situated underneath the stadium, contains exhibits related to the 1992 Olympic and Paralympic Games. The displays include costumes from the opening ceremony, kit and equipment used by the athletes and the arrow used to light the Olympic flame.

Adjacent is the **Palau Sant Jordi**, the most renowned of the Olympic structures. The elegant covered structure was built in 1985–90 by the Japanese architect Arata Isozaki. The main pavilion features a distinctive domed metallic mesh roof and has a capacity for 17,000 spectators. The building also contains a smaller area used for training and other activities. The sculptural installation in front of the building was created by Aiko Miyawaki, Isozaki's wife. Called '*Utsuroshi*', which means 'change', it comprises an arrangement of concrete pillars with stainless steel cords sprouting from the tops like branches of trees.

Beyond the Palau Sant Jordi at a lower level is the **Torre de Calatrava**, which looks like a sculpture but in fact has a practical use as a telecommunications aerial. The graceful steel structure, painted white, was designed by Santiago Calatrava. The curved base, decorated with broken tiles, pays homage to Gaudí, while the column leans at the same angle as the hill, making it a perfect sundial. The tower stands in a round porticoed piazza called the Plaça de Europa, where names of leading Europeans throughout history are engraved in the stone enclosing the space.

The Anella Olímpica occupies high and exposed ground commanding extensive views of a great gaunt expanse featuring a scorched semi-wasteland, distant housing developments and the city's main cemetery. Further down the hill to the south, behind the stadia, is the commemorative park known as the **Fossar de la Pedrera** (a good 30-minute walk). Designed in 1983 by Beth Galí i Camprubí, and containing a pond and monumental geometric forms, it was intended as a memorial to the executed first president of the Catalan Republic, Lluís Companys. Beyond the park is the **Montjuïc cemetery**, built in 1883, with tombstones sculpted by Eusebi Arnau, Josep Llimona and Josep Campeny.

Also south of the Olympic Stadium is the **Jardí Botànic**, or Botanical Garden. *Open July & August, Nov–Mar daily 10.00–15.00; Apr–Jun, Sept & Oct daily 10.00–17.00. Fee. Entrance on Carrer Doctor Font i Quer*. The gardens, which are still being developed, are divided into eight main sections, with plants from Australia, Chile, California and South Africa, North Africa, the Iberian Peninsula and Balearic Islands, the Eastern Mediterranean and the Canary Islands.

Fundació Joan Miró
From the Olympic complex, continue walking east along the Avinguda de l'Estadi until you reach the white and cheerful open-plan building containing the Fundació Joan Miró. *Open July–Sept Tue, Wed, Fri & Sat 10.00–20.00, Thu 10.00–21.30, Sun & public holidays 10.00–14.30; Oct–June Tue, Wed, Fri & Sat 10.00–19.00, Thu 10.00–21.30, Sun & public holidays 10.00–14.30. Fee. Included on Articket, Bus Turístic and Barcelona Card discounts. Book and gift shop. Café/restaurant.*

The Fundació Joan Miró was built in 1972–74 to house a large group of works donated by Joan Miró to his native city. In addition, the foundation was intended as a centre for the study and promotion of modern art, complete with a library, exhibition spaces, auditoria and other such facilities. Even if you do not have time to visit the museum now, it is worth having a look in the well-stocked bookshop or stopping off here for lunch or a drink in the excellent café/restaurant. The foundation also holds temporary exhibitions concentrating on particular aspects of Miró's work, as well as shows by major artists, and organises a programme of cultural events.

The building was one of only two buildings executed in Barcelona after the Civil War by the outstanding locally-born architect Josep Lluís Sert, a close friend of Miró's who had previously designed the artist's studio in Mallorca. Sert was an architect who believed passionately in the integration of a building with the landscape, and in the close collaboration between architects, sculptors and painters. These principles were the hallmark of his remarkable Maeght Foundation in St Paul-de-Vence, which provided the model for the Miró Foundation, and for which Miró had created numerous sculptures, mosaics and other works.

The foundation is beautifully set within the luxuriant shrubbery of the Montjuïc Park, and centred around a patio commanding magnificent views over Barcelona. Sculptures by Miró adorn the terraces, and the building and its grounds also incorporate works by other artists, most notably garden sculptures by Calder and Chillida. As with the Maeght Foundation, lighting for the rooms is supplied by overhead windows cut out of cylindrical forms attached to the roof. A comparable lighting system had been used by Le Corbusier, who had derived the idea from industrial architecture. The building was substantially extended in 1987–88 by Jaume Freixa, who had worked with Sert on the original scheme. Another new section was opened in 2001 to celebrate the 25th anniversary of the foundation.

The displays include paintings, sculptures, drawings, tapestries and graphic work. As well as the works donated by Miró himself, the foundation also holds the collection of his wife, Pilar Juncosa, and a range of works by leading 20C artists.

On the ground floor, one of the highlights is a large **tapestry** of 1979. The **sculpture room** contains entertaining bronze works dating from 1968–75, revealing the artist's inventiveness and sense of humour. A ramp leads to the upper level, where paintings from the late 1960s and early 1970s are displayed, including *Woman Surrounded by a Flock of Birds in the Night* (1968). The **Sala Joan Prats** contains earlier works, with paintings mainly from the 1920s and 1930s. Highlights include *Portrait of a Girl* (1919) and *The Bottle of Wine* (1924). The **Sala Pilar Juncosa** contains some powerful and disturbing Surrealist works of the 1930s and 1940s, including *The Morning Star* (1940) and *Woman Dreaming of Escape* (1945).

Miró's graphic work is the aspect of his art best represented by the foundation, with no less than 5000 drawings from his student years onwards, and a complete set of his prints (among which are a series of impressive black and white lithographs of 1939–45 commenting on the Spanish Civil War).

In the basement is the collection of works entitled **Homage to Miró**, which were donated by friends and admirers and include pieces by Léger, Motherwell, Ernst, Saura, Sam Francis, Rauschenberg, Moore, Duchamp, Millares, Penrose, Brossa and Chillida. Of particular interest is a fountain by Calder which was built by the artist for the Spanish Republican Government's Pavilion at the Paris Universal Exhibition of 1936 (the same pavilion for which Picasso had painted his *Guernica*).

The new section, called **Sala K**, opened in June 2001 and contains 23 works donated by the Japanese collector Kazumasa Katsuta, as well as a painting from Dolors Miró, the artist's daughter, and another from Juan Punyet, his grandson.

From the Fundació Joan Miró, you could walk down the hillside to visit another two museums or continue around the hill towards the castle and the cactus gardens.

For the former alternative, just head down the steps and paths leading down the hill next to the foundation, which take you through the **Parc Laribal**. This area was built by Jean Forestier and Nicolau Rubió i Tudurí in 1918–22 and is one of the more attractive stretches of the Montjuïc parkland, with shaded alleys, fountains, cascades, terraces, and an abundance of pines, cedars, eucalypti, palms, citrus trees and other luxuriant and exotic vegetation. Look out for would-be bullfighters practising in a small square right next to the Fundació Joan Miró.

Walking downhill brings you to the **Teatre Grec**, an amphitheatre built for the 1929 Exhibition by Ramon Reventós, who was inspired by that of Epidaurus. In early summer, the theatre is the main venue for the Grec Festival, which comprises a high-quality programme of concerts and theatrical performances.

Adjacent to the theatre is the **Museu Arqueològic**. *Open Tue–Sat 09.30–19.00, Sun & public holidays 10.00–14.30. Fee.* The museum occupies an arcaded pavilion built by Pelai Martínez i Paricio and Raimon Duran i Reynals in 1927–29 to house the section of the International Exhibition devoted to the Graphic Arts. As with the former Palau de l'Agricultura, on the other side of the street, the building was inspired by the architecture of the Italian Renaissance, a source of inspiration particularly appropriate to the outstanding collections of ancient art on display here. The museum, wonderfully modernised in 1985–89 by Josep Llinàs i Carmona, is centred around a white hexagonal-shaped hall, and includes an excellent group of Roman mosaics, numerous finds from the Greek settlement of Emporion (the Catalan town of Empúries), and a superb room devoted to Carthaginian finds from Ibiza, among which is the celebrated *Dama de Ibiza*, a bust richly studded with jewellery.

The former Palau de l'Agricultura, at the junction of the Passeig de Santa Madrona with the Carrer de Lleida, was built by Manuel Mayol i Ferrer in 1927–29. In 1984–85, it was converted into the theatre known as the **Mercat dels Flors**, a venue for such experimental groups as the Fura dels Baus. The inside of the dome was painted by Miquel Barceló. The building is being remodelled to become a complex with different theatre spaces and a drama school, part of a plan to turn this area into a focus for the dramatic arts known as Theatre City.

A short distance back up the hill on the Passeig de Santa Madrona is the **Museu Etnològic**. *Open Tue & Thu 10.00–19.00, Wed, Fri, Sat, Sun & public holidays 10.00–14.00. Fee.* The museum is housed in a functionalist hexagonal building of 1973, the walls of which are decorated with reliefs by Eudald Serra i Güell of anthropological scenes. The collections are displayed on two floors on a rotational basis as there are too many exhibits to show at once. Highlights include textiles, ceramics and jewellery from Morocco and carvings from Nigeria and Equatorial Guinea. The Iberian section includes sculptures by the brothers Agapit and Venanci Vallmitjana, and a collection of whistles from the Valencia region and the Balearic Islands. There are examples of specialist crafts from all over Spain, including ceramics from Almería, wrought iron from La Rioja and jewellery from Salamanca. Examples of Catalunya's rich craft tradition include candles, hats and pipes.

Back at the Fundació Joan Miró, if you continue east along the Avinguda de Miramar (the continuation of the Avinguda de l'Estadi), you come shortly to the **funicular station**, from where the funicular runs down the hill to the Avinguda del Paral·lel. You can also take a **cable car** from here up to the castle which stands at the very top of the steep hill.

The **Castell de Montjuïc** has served since 1960 as the **Museu Militar**. *Open Tue–Fri 09.30–18.30, Sat & Sun 09.30–19.30. Fee. Shop. Café.*

> The castle is situated on what was probably a Jewish burial ground, as the name Montjuïc is derived from the words '*Mont jeu*' or Jewish Mountain. Presumably there must have been some sort of watchtower here in ancient times, but the first documented fortification on the hill was built as late as 1640, at the time of the War of the Harvesters. The original structure, enlarged during the war with France, was completely rebuilt by Juan M. Cermeño between 1751 and 1759, and given its present star-shaped pentagonal plan based on French Neo-classical models. During the Civil War, the castle served as a military prison, and it was here, on October 15, 1940, that the Catalan President Lluís Companys was executed. The army abandoned the building in 1960,

The military museum contains extensive collections of weapons, helmets and uniforms, as well as paintings depicting historic military occasions. There is an equestrian statue of General Franco by Josep Viladomat and exhibits relating to the Civil War. **Room 8** contains 11,000 miniature soldiers, forming an entire Spanish division, which were displayed in the 1929 Exhibition. Archaeological exhibits found on Montjuïc are displayed on the upper floor.

From here, you can walk down to visit the cactus gardens known as the Jardins Costa i Llobera, or take the cable car to the first stop at the Mirador de l'Alcalde, then walk the rest of the way. Alternatively, from the funicular station on the Avinguda de Miramar you could hop on the Bus Turístic to Miramar, which is near the entrance to the cactus gardens.

The **Jardins Costa i Llobera** (free) are situated on the lower slope running down to the sea. One of the most important **cacti collections** in Europe, the exhibits include a large round plant with a spiky top from Mexico known as the 'mother-in-law's chair'. Near the entrance is the *Mirador café*, which has a terrace overlooking the city and the harbour and is a great spot for a drink. Adjacent is the terminus for the cable cars that will take you down to the port and Barceloneta.

9 • Pedralbes, the Palau Reial and Diagonal

▶ Start from Pedralbes Monastery. See map on p 206.

You may want to use the Bus Turístic for parts of this walk, as the route covers a large area and the bus stops at all the key points.

Of the once separate townships that make up Greater Barcelona, Pedralbes, together with the adjoining district of Sarrià, is today one of the smartest, with an abundance of wealthy villas and residential blocks set among the exotic vegetation which covers the lower slopes of the Tibidabo range.

At the top of the Avinguda de Pedralbes is a village-like square with steps leading up to the main entrance of the **Monestir de Santa Maria de Pedralbes**, the best-preserved monastic complex to survive in Barcelona and one of the finest examples of Catalan Gothic architecture. The monastery is run by the Museu d'Històra de la Ciutat and part of the building houses the **Thyssen Collection**. *The monastery and museum are both open Tue–Sun & public holidays 10.00–14.00. Fee. Bus Turístic and Barcelona Card discount and with entrance ticket from Museu d'Història de la Ciutat. Shop.*

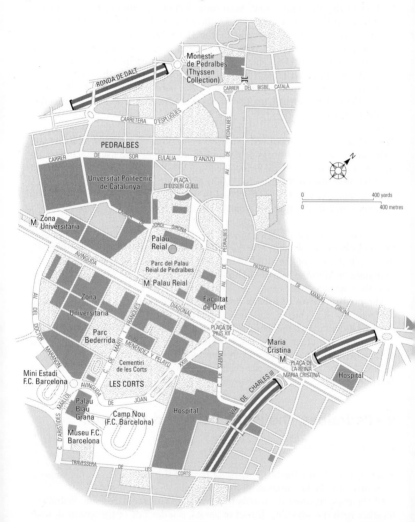

The Monestir de Santa Maria de Pedralbes was founded as a convent for Franciscan nuns of the Order of Poor Clares in 1326 by Elisenda de Montcada i de Pinós, the fourth and last wife of Jaume II the Just. The church was constructed at great speed, only one year after the convent's foundation. Following Jaume II's death in the same year, part of the convent was turned into a rather more comfortable residence, known as the Palacio de la Reina, where the Queen lived until her death.

The enormous main cloister was built as part of the original construction, though the second storey was not completed until the early 15C, when a third storey was added.

A closed order of Clarissine nuns continues to live in the convent, but they now occupy new quarters built in 1976–83 in order to facilitate access to the building for visitors.

The church is a structure of great unity and simplicity dominated on the exterior by an octagonal belltower that Le Corbusier admired for its geometrical regularity. It has a single-aisled interior and features, in a vaulted niche immediately to the right of the high altar, the fine if highly restored **tomb of Queen Elisenda**, which was completed shortly before her death in 1364, and shows the recumbent queen mourned by angels.

Entering the convent, you find yourself in the main **cloister**, which is composed of two superimposed Gothic arcades of exceptional elegance and a low upper gallery. The luxuriant cypress-shaded garden in the middle has a classical Plateresque wellhead commissioned during the rule as abbess of Teresa Enriquez (1495–1507). Walking anti-clockwise around the cloister, you come immediately to the artistic highpoint of the convent, the **Chapel of St Michael**, which is decorated with the finest surviving mural cycle from 14C Catalunya. The murals, redolent of the art of Trecento Italy, were commissioned from Ferrer Bassa in 1343 and completed in 1346, two years before the artist's death from the plague which devastated Barcelona in 1348. Featuring an upper and lower level depicting respectively the Passion of Christ and the Life of the Virgin, the murals were executed in a mixture of oil and tempera; the wall facing the chapel's entrance contains representations of saints.

Elsewhere around the cloister, there are two cells containing biblical dioramas in questionable taste, a reconstruction of the original infirmary and a refectory restored in 1894 by Joan Martorell.

In 1993 the nuns' dormitory and the great hall of the Palacio de la Reina were remodelled to house part of the impressive bequest of paintings donated to Spain by Baron Thyssen-Bornemisza (the greater part of the collection is in Madrid). The works on display here were selected specifically for their relevance to the history of the monastery and the time when it was built. The rich holdings include Fra Angelico's outstanding *Madonna of Humility*, and works by Veronese, Titian, Tintoretto, Canaletto, Guardi, Cranach, Rubens, Zurbarán and Velázquez.

On leaving the complex, before heading down Avinguda de Pedralbes you could make a short detour to the right to visit the **Nou Monestir Benedictí de la Mare de Deu de Montserrat** (Carretera d'Esplugues 101–103), which was designed by Nicolau Rubió i Tudurí in 1922, and completed in 1940 by Raimon

Duran i Reynals, following Rubió's exile after the Civil War. The structure was commissioned by Josep Nicolau d'Olzina for the monks of Montserrat, who wanted a Neo-medieval structure. The financiers, however, insisted on a monastery imbued with the Renaissance spirit of Noucentisme. The end result was a pastiche of Brunelleschi, Bramante and Michelangelo, which the monks rejected. The building was later taken over by the bishopric of Barcelona.

The Avinguda de Pedralbes leads down from the monastery to the Palau Reial complex on Diagonal, a walk of about 20 minutes, or one stop on the Bus Turístic.

Going down the Avinguda de Pedralbes, look out for the Carrer de Sor Eulàlia d'Anzizu on the right. At no. 46 is **Les Escales Park**, a luxury residential development designed in 1967–73 by Josep Lluís Sert following his return from exile in America. Despite its concessions to local building traditions such as the use of ceramics and wooden shutters, the complex remains essentially American in character, and as such did not meet with much success in Catalunya, where Sert was criticised for having lost touch with his architectural roots.

Further along this street is the **Universidad Politécnica**, built in the 1990s. The complex comprises several award-winning buildings, designed by renowned architects including Josep Benedito, Lluís Nadal and Pep Llinàs.

Returning to Avinguda de Pedralbes, on the right at **no. 15**, you reach an entrance gate, lodge and stables designed by Gaudí. These are the finest surviving elements of the Güell Estate, which is discussed below. Gaudí created these structures in 1887, at a time when he was heavily under the influence of Islamic architecture. The fantastically turretted and irregularly-shaped pavilions combine elaborate brickwork with coloured ceramics, whitewashed walls and painted decoration. The stable block (the longer of the two pavilions) is now the seat of the centre of Gaudí studies known as the Cátedra Gaudí. The main gate features some of the most extraordinary ironwork in Gaudí's whole career, the iron expressively twisted to form what is known as the *Drac de Pedralbes*, or Dragon of Pedralbes. The dragon is a reference to the myth of the Hesperides, on which the concept of the entire estate was based.

Continue to the intersection of Avinguda de Pedralbes with **Avinguda**

Drac de Pedralbes

Diagonal. The western extension of Diagonal was built in the 1920s to connect the city with the Palau Reial, and, 30 years later, came to serve the **Ciudad Universitaria** (University Campus). Turning right up Diagonal, on your right is one of the finest of the university buildings, the **Facultat de Dret** (Law Faculty) Built in 1958 by Guillermo Giráldez Dávila, Pedro López Iñigo and Xavier Subias i Fages, this light and cheerful Functionalist block is one of the finest Catalan examples of the so-called International Style. It brought a welcome breath of fresh air to Catalan architecture after the pompous heaviness and severity of so many of the buildings of the post-Civil War period.

You now come to the entrance gates of the **Palau Reial de Pedralbes**, which occupies land presented to the Spanish royal family by Gaudí's patron, Count Güell.

The former Güell residence within the estate was transformed from 1919–29 by Eusebi Bona Puig and Francesc de Paula Nebot into an imposing palace for Alfonso XIII. It is a pompous classical structure with a lavishly marbled interior and fresco decorations taken from local 18C palaces. The king slept in the palace in 1926, but the building was not finally completed until the inauguration of the International Exhibition of 1929. With the downfall of the king in 1931, the palace was handed over to the Barcelona Town Hall, which installed a museum of decorative arts here. In 1936 it was taken over by the President of the Republic and later became the Barcelona residence of General Franco. Opened again to the public in 1960, it currently houses the Museu de Ceràmica as well as the Museu d'Arts Decoratives, both of which have excellent collections that are well worth visiting.

The wonderful **gardens** were designed by the landscape architect Nicolau Rubió i Tudurí in 1925 and conceal a fountain by Gaudí, designed for the Güell estate in 1884, which was only discovered in 1983 during a clean-up operation. As you approach the palace up the central path, it is a short distance down a path to the left just before you reach the pool in front of the palace.

Museu de les Arts Decoratives and Museu de Ceràmica

Both museums are open Tue–Sat 10.00–18.00, Sun & public holidays 10.00–15.00. Fee. Bus Turístic and Barcelona Card discounts. Bookshop.

The **Museu de les Arts Decoratives** charts the development of the decorative arts from the 13C to the present day, with Romanesque, Gothic, Renaissance, Rococo, Neo-classical, Romantic, Art Nouveau, Art Déco and contemporary design sections. Exhibits include furniture, jewellery boxes, coffers and fans. Anyone interested in Barcelona's design boom of the 1980s should visit just to see the exhibits by leading designers of that decade such as Mariscal, Oscar Tusquets, Lluís Clots, Andrés Nagel and Eduardo Samsó.

The **Museu de Ceràmica**, housed in the opposite wing of the palace, contains a representative selection of Spanish ceramics from ancient times up to recent artists such as Miró and Picasso. The displays are arranged geographically, with sections devoted to the most important regions for ceramic production in Spain: Valencia, Aragón, Castile, Catalunya, Andalucía and Castellón. There are important pieces from Paterna and Manises, from the 13C–18C, including work by Mudéjar artists. The Catalan exhibits include a semicircular ceramic plaque (1710), made for a fountain on the estate of the Marqués de Castellvell in Alella, which depicts a drinking chocolate party. The Castellón section contains objects made at the Royal Factory of Ceramics and Porcelain, founded in the town of Alcora in 1727. The Modernista and contemporary displays on the second floor include pieces by Antoni Serra Fité, Venanci Vallmitjana, Josep Llorens Artigas, Antoni Cumella and Xavier Nogués, as well as jars and other works created by Joan Miró and Pablo Picasso.

Leaving the Palau Reial, you can either walk (15 minutes) or take the Bus Turístic to the stadium of the Futbol Club Barcelona. To walk there, cross to the other side of Diagonal, where there are more university faculties.

Fascist planning and architectural ideals characterise the bulk of the university complex, which was begun in 1955, but according to models formulated in the 1940s. The city's young, progressive architects were heavily critical of both the overall design of the campus and its location in an area which had not only been set apart for residential purposes but was also divided in two by the Diagonal.

The buildings on this side of Diagonal are spaciously arranged on land which was designated as one of the city's Olympic areas, on account of the important sports facilities in its lower half. The most interesting is the extension to the **Architecture School** (further north up Diagonal between Carrer Adolf Florensa and Carrer Pau Gargallo), designed by José Antonio Coderch in 1978–82, which spreads over two levels on the sloping land and features curving walls faced with vertical tiles. Opposite the Palau Reial is the Post-Modern **Biology Faculty**, designed by Joan Antoni Ballesteros, Joan Carles Cardenal and Francisco de la Guardia in 1981.

Heading south down Diagonal and turning right into the Avinguda de Joan XXIII, you pass the **Pharmacy Faculty**, at the entrance of which is a brick gate that Gaudí designed for the Güell Estate in 1887. Inside the Faculty is an interesting **pharmaceutical museum**, which is unfortunately only open by appointment (☎ 93 4024555). Exhibits include ceramic vessels from the 17C–20C, distilling apparatus and instruments. There is also a library specialising in pharmaceutical history.

The Nou Camp Stadium

Continuing down the Avinguda de Joan XXIII brings you to the Nou Camp, the home of the Futbol Club Barcelona. This vast stadium was built in 1954–57 by Lorenzo García Borbán, Francesc Mitjans Miró and Josep Soteras Mauri, and enlarged to hold 120,000 spectators for the 1982 World Cup. An adjacent building houses an enormous shop selling all manner of Barça (as the club is usually known) paraphernalia, and this is also the entrance to the **Museu del Futbol Club Barcelona**. *Open Mon–Sat 10.00–18.30, Sun & public holidays 10.00–14.00. Bus Turístic and Barcelona Card discounts.*

The museum is actually situated in the grandstand of the stadium, which you access via a covered bridge. This is a very popular attraction, and only the Picasso Museum receives more visitors. The displays chart the history of the club from its origins in 1899 up to the present day, and include trophies, photographs, programmes, posters (including one by Joan Miró), kit, a model of the stadium and an audio-visual presentation. The upper floor houses the club's art collection. Visitors can also go out into the stadium itself.

Opposite the entrance to the stadium, on the other side of the Avinguda de Joan XXIII, is the **Cementiri de les Corts**, built in 1897. The cemetery contains a Jewish burial area to the left of the main entrance.

Incongruously situated alongside the stadium as you go back up the Avinguda de Joan XXIII is one of Barcelona's surviving rural mansions known as *masías*, This one is a simple stone structure of 1702. Following restoration in 1966, it is used by the Football Club as offices and to house young players. On the lawn in front of the house is a sculpture by Josep Viladomat of a portly bearded player known as *L'Avi*, a symbolic figure who represents the team.

Further up the Avinguda de Joan XXIII on the right (on the intersecting Carrer Salvador Cardenal) there is part of another *masía* (or *mas* in Catalan). Known as the **Torre Redonda**, it dates back to 1610 and was restored in 1990. The structure now serves as an annexe to the Hotel Princesa Sofía.

Heading down Diagonal from the Princesa Sofía, at the intersection with the Gran Via de Carles III on the right, are the impressive **Torres Trade**. Built in 1966–69 by José Antonio Coderch (who designed the Architecture School mentioned above) and Manuel Valls, this complex comprises four tall towers featuring undulating curtain walls of tinted glass.

Continuing down Diagonal, you come to the vast white complex known as **L'Illa Diagonal**, the front façade of which stretches almost 300 metres down the avenue. Designed by Rafael Moneo in collaboration with Manuel Solà-Morales in 1986–93, the structure was conceived as a 'horizontal skyscraper' and features a series of staggered levels to avoid the oppressive monotony that a single block of these proportions might present. The complex, which won the coveted *FAD* (*Foment de les Arts Decoratives*) prize in 1994, contains a shopping centre, hotel, conference centre, concert hall and offices. A litle further down, at the junction with the Avinguda de Sarrià, is the **Edifici Talaia de Barcelona**, one of Barcelona's tallest skyscrapers, built in 1966–70 by Federico Correa i Ruiz, Alfonso Milà i Sagnier and José Luis Sanz Magallán. The sculpture in front of the building is by Andreu Alfaro and is called *Lines to the Wind* (1971).

The next intersection is the Plaça Francesc Macià, designed by Nicolau Rubió i Tudurí in the 1930s. The sculpture in the centre, entitled *Youth*, is by Josep Manuel Benedicto and was installed in 1953. A number of interesting modern buildings are situated on the streets north of the square. Walk up Avinguda Pau Casals and through the Turó Park to reach the Carrer de Johann Sebastian Bach, where at **no. 7** there is a shuttered residential block of 1957–61 by José Antonio Coderch and Manuel Valls, and, at **no. 28**, an influential early work by Ricardo Bofill—a block of luxury flats centred around an unusually shaped courtyard (1960–62). A year later, Bofill also designed the block at **no. 2**, on the corner of the Plaça de Sant Gregori Taumaturg.

From the block at no. 28 at the end of Carrer de Johann Sebastian Bach, you could cut along Carrer Victoria to Carrer d'Amigó, where at **no. 76** is an apartment block designed by Francesc Mitjans Miró. It may look unexceptional now, but was regarded a pioneering scheme back in 1941–43 when it was built, and was the first building in Barcelona to feature continuous balconies.

Walking two blocks east along Carrer del Rector Ubach brings you to the long Carrer de Muntaner. Turning right into the street, immediately on your left at **nos 342–348** is a block of duplex apartments dating from 1930–31. This was the first important work by Josep Lluís Sert, the most influential architect of the avant-garde group of the 1930s known as GATCPAC, which was renowned for Functionalist designs inspired by Le Corbusier. Further down the street at no. 314 is the **Clinica Barraquer**, which was built by Joaquim Lloret Homs in 1934–40. The corner structure originally comprised only the ground floor and three upper storeys, but was extended in the 1970s, which upset the elegance of the original design. The architect collaborated on the project with the ophthalmologist Joaquim Barraquer, whose ideas led to the creation of a wonderful Art Déco interior with classical decorative elements.

Continuing down the Carrer de Muntaner brings you back to Diagonal.

10 • Gràcia and Sarrià

▶ Start from Gràcia FGC station. See map on pp 214–15.

The former township of Gràcia, which extends from the top end of the Passeig de Gràcia up to the Plaça de Lesseps, was named after the 15C Monastery of Santa Maria de Jesus de Gràcia, which was destroyed in 1714 during the War of Succession. In the 19C it evolved into an industrial township with strong liberal and revolutionary traditions. By the end of that century six magazines were being published there, one devoted to feminism and another to the promotion of Esperanto. It was also a seedbed for anarchists, vegetarians, theosophists and other nonconformist groups.

In the 1960s and 70s, Gràcia became one of Barcelona's most fashionable residential districts for young middle-class intellectuals, who moved into the modest 19C apartments and houses. Lively bars, cafés, restaurants and fringe theatres soon sprang up in the network of narrow streets. Many of these places survive, joined now by new genres of social venue, which keep the streets busy with people of all ages during both day night. At the beginning of the 21C, Gràcia is one of the most coveted places to live in the city and shows no sign of losing its distinctive character. In late August it hosts a vibrant street festival with a wide range of entertainments and cultural events.

Immediately to the east of the railway station of Gràcia, on the Plaça de Llibertat, is one of the finest survivals of 19C Gràcia, the **Mercat de la Llibertat**. Although the market was originally founded in 1840, the present structure was built in 1875. The ironwork roof and frame were added in 1893 by Francesc Berenguer, who worked in close collaboration with Gaudí on a great many projects. Berenguer is one of the great unsung figures of Modernisme. Look out here for the swans decorating the roof and the Gràcia coat of arms above the two main entrances. Inside the market, there are a couple of bar stalls that serve good tapas and provide excellent vantage points for observing how the locals do their shopping.

One block downhill from the market you reach Gràcia's main east–west artery, the Travessera de Gràcia, which was originally a Roman road. Halfway along, to the south and north respectively, are the districts' two charming principal squares, the Plaça Rius i Taulet and Plaça del Sol.

To reach the **Plaça Rius i Taulet**, head one block down Carrer de Mozart. The space is popularly known as the 'Square of the Clock' (Plaça del Rellotje) from its tall, free-standing **clocktower** of 1862, which was designed by Antoni Rovira i

Trias and is decorated with terracotta reliefs representing the zodiac. A rallying-point for revolutionaries in uprisings that took place in 1870, 1873 and 1874, the tower became a famous symbol of Liberty and was reproduced on the cover of the 19C Liberal newspapers, *L'Esquella de la Torratxa* and *La Campana de Gràcia*. At the lower end is the headquarters of the Gràcia district, designed by Francesc Berenguer in 1905.

Returning to Travessera de Gràcia and walking up one block brings you to the **Plaça del Sol**, which was sensitively remodelled in 1983–86 by Jaume Bach and Gabriel Mora. This is the livelier of the two squares, particularly at night, with a plethora of bars, restaurants and pavement cafés and regular Sardana dancing. The sculpture is by Joaquim Camps and is called *Astrolabi*.

Two blocks up from the Plaça del Sol, at no. 47 Carrer de Montseny, is the **Teatre Lliure** which, since its foundation in 1976, has been one of the most important and progressive of Barcelona's small theatres. The main force behind this theatre was the director and stage-designer Fabia Puigserver (1938–91), who was responsible for the award-winning interior design of the building. In the theatre's early years, another associate of the place was the leading Spanish theatre director of today, Lluís Pasqual. At the end of 2001, the theatre transferred to the burgeoning Theatre City complex at the base of Montjuïc (p 204). These premises are however still used for certain performances.

Walk east along Carrer de Montseny and turn left into Carrer del Torrent de l'Olla, which leads after one block to the Plaça del Diamant on the right. *La Plaça del Diamant* is the title of a novel by Mercè Rodoreda (translated as *The Time of the Doves* by David Rosenthal), which is partially set in Gràcia and tells the poignant story of how the life of a girl called Colometa changes during the Civil War. The bronze sculpture in the square, called **La Colometa**, is by Xavier Medina-Campeny.

Leaving the square by heading east along either Carrer de Encarnació or Carrer d'Astúries brings you almost immediately to another square, Plaça de la Virreina. The square is named for Maria Francesca Fiveller, the young wife of the Viceroy of Peru, Manuel Amat i Junyet (p 89), who had a mansion here in the 18C. The site of the residence is now occupied by the **Església de Sant Joan**, the church that dominates the square and incorporates parts of the original structure. After being badly damaged in the uprising of 1909 known as the Setmana Tràgica (Tragic Week), the church was restored by Francesc Berenguer.

Turning right from the church along Carrer Tres Senyores, take the third left up to the Plaça Rovira i Trias, named for the renowned architect of the 19C, Antoni Rovira i Trias (1816–1889) who is commemorated here by a bronze figure, sitting on a bench. The plaque on the ground features the plan Rovira devised in the mid-19C for the development of the Eixample, a scheme which was shelved in favour of Ildefons Cerdà's grid design (p 77).

From the square, meander westwards back to Carrer Gran de Gràcia, the district's main north–south artery. You could either go along Carrer de Providència and its continuations, or walk back through the squares, perhaps stopping off at one or two of the many appealing bars in this neighbourhood. From Carrer Gran de Gràcia, turn down Carrer de les Carolines to see (from the outside only) one of Gaudí's earliest works, the **Casa Vicens**, at nos 18–24. This extraordinary house, one of the most oriental-inspired of Gaudí's structures, was built in 1883–88 for Manuel Vicens Montaner, who owned a tile factory. Gaudí

was presumably briefed to make full use of his patron's ceramic supply, and indeed the building is lavishly coated in coloured tiles. Unlike his later works, characterised by curving lines and broken tiles, here he used geometric patterns in straight lines. The fantastical ironwork on the façade includes lizards, dragons, snakes and other creatures, all with individual faces. The intricate railings, a section of which has been incorporated into the main entrance gate of the Park Güell (p 217), are now believed to be the work of Francesc Berenguer. The interior is no less ornately decorated, with a particularly opulent smoking room, but as this is a private residence it is not open to the public.

Continue to the end of Carrer Les Carolines, cross the Avinguda del Princep d'Asturies and walk down Passatge Mulet to Carrer de Saragossa. Facing you at **no. 57** is the house and studio built in 1960–63 by José Antonio Coderch and Manuel Valls for the artist **Antoni Tàpies**. From the street the house appears entirely hidden behind louvred metal shutters. The studio is on the ground floor and rises through two storeys, with the residential area above, and a library on the top floor which gives onto the interior courtyard and is hidden from the street by a curtain wall set back from the main façade.

Go back to Avinguda del Princep d'Astúries, turn right and walk down two blocks to the **Rambla del Prat** on the left. This street contains a wealth of

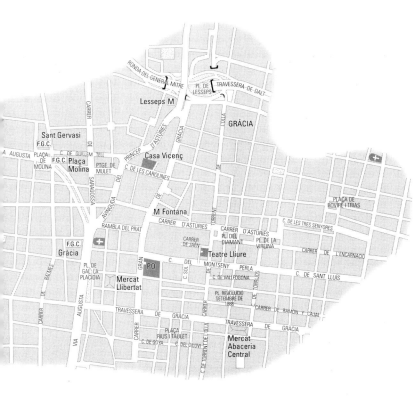

Modernista buildings, including the **Casas Cairó** from nos 4–10, which were designed by Domènec Boada in 1904 and have undulating balconies. The entrance doors, only some of which survive, feature trefoil segmental arches. Inside **no. 8**, a sculpture of St George and the Dragon adorns the marble stair-case. The **Cine Bosque** at no. 18 used to be the Teatre del Bosc, a theatre founded at the turn of the 20C and renowned for its political meetings as well as the plays and popular concerts staged there. Although the building has been substantially altered, the present façade features the original sculptural decora-tion by Pau Gargallo, which comprises four masks of Pablo Picasso, the painter Isidre Nonell, the doctor Jacint Reventós and Gargallo himself.

Sarrià

Walking one block down Avinguda del Príncep d'Astúries brings you back to Gràcia station, where you can take the train five stops up to the luxurious residential district of Sarrià. From the station, walk uphill and take the first turning on the left, Carrer Hort, which leads to Carrer Major de Sarrià, the main street of the neighbourhood. Turning right brings you to the Plaça del Consell de la Vila. The local council headquarters was was built by Francesc Mariné in 1896, when Sarrià was an independent borough. The sculpture in front of the building is by Josep Clarà, who lived in this area and whose house we will see later.

Adjacent is the Plaça de Sarrià which, although now a busy crossroads, retains some of its original character. The Neo-classical church of **Sant Vicenç** dates back to 1781, but there have been temples on this site for more than a thousand years and the structure retains architectural and decorative elements from various periods. Although the structure was partially destroyed by fire in the Civil War, inside you can still see a late-16C altarpiece by Agustí Pujol and a tabernacle by Bonet Garí surrounded by Noucentiste murals by Josep Obiols. The building with the sgraffito decoration is the **Casa Llansà**, built as the home of a noble family at the end of the 18C. The façade features a sundial and the family's coat of arms. The ground floor houses the *Foix patisserie*, which opened in 1923. Their first branch is at Carrer Major de Sarrià 57, which dates back to 1886 and is the birthplace of the poet Josep V. Foix, the son of the founder of the business.

Walk back down Carrer Major de Sarrià. Carrer de Canet, on the left, is packed with workshops where artisans make and sell their work. Continue down the hill to the Plaça Artós. Immediately beyond the square, turn right into Carrer de Santa Amèlia, which leads to some delightful **gardens**. The estate used to belong to the Folch-Girona family, who built two villas. Although blocks of flats now surround the lower part, the Villa Amèlia, the space conceals a Romantic garden with some unusual trees as well as sculptures by Jules Anthone and Ricard Sala. The upper section, the Villa Cecília, was remodelled as a public park in 1985 and features white marble paths and award-winning benches and lighting. Near the entrance is a shallow water channel, which features a sculpture by Paco López called *Drowned Ophelia*.

Returning to the Plaça Artós, walk along Carrer dels Vergós (crossing Via Augusta) and turn left up Carrer del Dr Roux. Take the second right into Carrer de Pau Alcover and turn immediately left down the unmarked path leading to the **Cementeri del Sarrià**. The cemetery dates back to 1850, when it was moved here from its previous site alongside Sant Vicenç, where the square is now. The poet Josep V. Foix and the painter Josep Obiols, whose work we saw in the church, are buried here, as well as the poet Carles Riba, whose grave features a relief by Joan Rebull.

Leaving the cemetery, turn left into Carrer de Pau Alcover and immediately right into Carrer de Calatrava. On the right at **nos 27–29** is the former home of the sculptor Josep Clarà, who specialised in classical female nudes in white marble. Born in the nearby town of Olot, he died in Sarrià in 1878, working up to the very day of his death. One of the leading sculptural associates of Noucentisme, he spent an important period in Paris at the beginning of the century, where he fell heavily under the influence first of Rodin and then of Maillol. This was his last house, which he shared with his sister Carmen. His studio was situated in the small garden. Previously a museum, the house is now used as a library, but you can go into the garden, where some of his works are installed.

You are now back at the corner of Carrer dels Vergós. Turn left, then right by the market at the end of the street, immediately left into Carrer d'Alacant, then right into Carrer de Ganduxer. You now reach the **Colegio de las Teresianas**, built by Gaudí in 1889–90. Built on a low budget in a short space of time, the structure features tall, narrow windows with louvred blinds, and characteristic pinnacles on the four corners. The rooms are flanked by corridors with parabolic arches, all set around an inner courtyard, which you may be allowed to visit (ask the nun on duty at the entrance).

From here, you could take the FGC train from Tres Torres or Bonanova stations up to Collserola (p 224) or back to the centre. If it is lunchtime, you could head for the *A Contraluz* restaurant on the nearby Carrer de Milanesat (no. 19), which serves excellent food and has a pretty garden.

11 • The Park Güell, Parc de la Creueta del Coll and Horta

▶ Start from Park Güell. To get there, take bus 24 from Passeig de Gràcia, or the metro to Lesseps, then bus 24 or 15-minute walk. Also on Bus Turístic route. See map on p 219.

Of all the many sights outside the centre of Barcelona, the most popular is perhaps the **Park Güell**. *Open daily 10.00–dusk. Free. Fee for guided tours. Bus Turístic discount. Book and giftshop. Café.*

The park, which was commissioned from Antoni Gaudí in 1900 by his great patron Eusebi Güell, was originally intended as a garden city on the lines of English models such as Bedford Park. This is why its correct name is Park Güell, using the English spelling, although the Catalan *Parc* is often now used instead. The site chosen was an estate of 16 hectares attached to the slopes of the unpromisingly named Mont Pelat or Bare Mountain. The desolate nature of the surroundings and the traditional poverty of the neighbourhood go some way towards explaining why Güell's ambitious plans for the urban renewal of the area proved ultimately to be a failure. In the end, only two of the projected 60 houses were built, and Gaudí moved into one of these himself. Gaudí completed his work here in 1914, and in 1922 the abandoned garden city was acquired by the city council for use as a municipal park. The Park Güell, despite failing its original purpose, has proved to be the most loved of all Gaudí's works, and has provided inspiration to countless visitors, including the young Salvador Dalí, who considered the place as one of the most powerful influences on his development as an artist.

If you arrive by bus, you enter the park at the side entrance. To follow the route outlined below, walk through to the main gate at the bottom of the park on the Carrer d'Olot.

The entrance is marked by two fantastically-shaped and richly-polychromed **pavilions** of gingerbread appearance. A production of *Hänsel and Gretel* was running at the Liceu theatre at the time the park was being designed, and Gaudí contributed some ideas for the sets. It is therefore likely that his sketches—for the witch's and the children's houses—were transformed into the gatehouses. The one on the right as you face the park is topped by a fly agaric mushroom, created from broken red and white tiles. Gaudí was a keen mushroom-gatherer, and there has been much specula-

Pavilion at Park Güell

tion as to why he chose this hallucinogenic variety to welcome people to the park. The left-hand gatehouse features a distinctly phallic mushroom, topped with a cross. This structure now houses a book and giftshop. The gate between the two pavilions is formed of spiky ironwork gates taken from Gaudí's Casa Vicens (p 213).

The **staircase** immediately inside the park is elaborately decorated with ceramics and fountains, dominated by a glittering multicoloured lizard. The steps lead up to the **Sala Hipóstila**, a large covered space intended to house the market serving the estate. The space, though known as the 'Hall of the 100 Columns', is in fact held up by 86 Doric columns. The ones at the front lean towards the centre, supporting an undulating entablature punctuated by dogs' heads. The intricate mosaic decoration was the work of Josep Maria Jujol, who was responsible for all the ceramic work in the park.

Above this is the famous bench-balustrade surrounding the park's central square, which is joined to the lower part of the park by flights of steps on either side of the Sala Hipóstila. The **balustrade**, which incorporates what is said to be

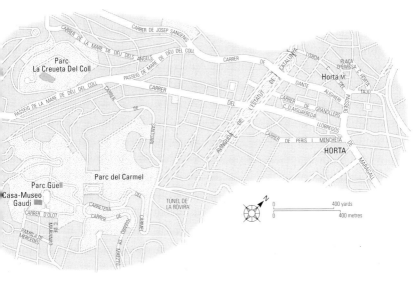

the longest bench in the world, is a typical touch of Gaudí fantasy and symbolism. Shaped like a dragon, which serves to protect the estate, it glistens with a magnificent ceramic mosaic coating executed by Gaudí in collaboration with Jujol. There is a panoramic view of Barcelona from the square, and there are few better places from which to admire the city than the sinuous bench. On either side of the square are viaducts with leaning columns and an overall rustic appearance.

The path to the east of the square takes you to the **Casa-Museu Gaudí**. *Open daily May–Sept 10.00–20.00, Oct, March & Apr 10.00–19.00, Nov–Feb 10.00–18.00. Fee. Free with Ruta del Modernisme voucher.* The museum is housed in a building designed by Francesc Berenguer in 1904, which Gaudí acquired as a family home in 1906. The displays include furniture designed by Gaudí for other buildings, as well as his own wardrobe, iron bed and personal belongings.

The summit of the park was originally to have been crowned by a chapel, but in its stead there is now a large cross, from where a further extensive panorama can be enjoyed.

Depending on how much time you have, on leaving the Park Güell you could either walk downhill to explore the Gràcia district (p 212) or continue uphill to visit two lesser known parks and the Horta neighbourhood.

On the slopes of the hill immediately to the north west of the Park Güell is one of Barcelona's more recent attractions, the **Parc de la Creueta del Coll** (reached by bus 28 from the stop at the side entrance of the Park Güell). Of all Barcelona's many recent squares and parks, this is in many ways the most attractive, not least because its major element is a large palm-lined and irregularly-shaped swimming pool, one of Barcelona's most seductive open-air pools. The park, which occupies the crater of an abandoned quarry, was built in 1981–87 by Josep Martorell, Oriol Bohigas and David Mackay. The place is greatly enhanced by two monumental sculptures, one a vertical piece by

Ellsworth Kelly, the other a huge concrete claw by Eduardo Chillida. This latter work is suspended from the cliff-slope by four cables. On the summit of the hill there is an immense female face by Roy Lichtenstein.

Horta

Two kilometres east of the Coll de la Creueta begins the lively district of Horta. On leaving the park, turn left along the Carrer de la Mare de Dèu del Coll. After a couple of minutes you come to a crossroads, where you can get bus 87 to the centre of Horta, the Plaça de Eivissa.

Horta became part of Barcelona in 1904, but had existed as a village for at least a thousand years by then. Meandering through the streets around the metro station, you will come across many buildings that date back hundreds of years. One of the oldest houses in the area is the **Can Mariner** on the Carrer de Horta, which was originally built in 1050. One of the most interesting streets is the pretty Carrer de Aiguafreda (the continuation of Carrer de Granollers off the Passeig de Maragall), one side of which is lined with wash-houses. Before the days of washing machines in every home, the woman of Horta used to do the laundry for families living in the more well-to-do areas of Barcelona. Returning to the Passeig de Maragall and turning right brings you shortly to the corner of Carrer Peris Mencheta, where there is one of the best-preserved houses in the district, which was once a farmhouse at the centre of a vineyard.

From the Plaça de Eivissa, take bus 85 up to the **Velòdrom d'Horta** on the Passeig de Vall d'Hebró, which forms part of the network of dual carriageways surrounding Barcelona. The Velòdrom, a light and elegant stadium designed in 1983 by Esteve Bonell i Costa and Francesc Rius i Camps, is the centrepiece of another of Barcelona's Olympic areas. This one features not only sports facilities but also a large residential block, constructed with the initial intention of housing journalists during the Games.

On the slopes of the hill above the stadium hover two large round **gasometers** colloquially known as the *Huevos de Porcioles*, a reference to the testicles of the notorious Fascist Mayor of Barcelona, Porcioles, who was responsible for some of the more brazen building developments of the post Civil-War period. Scattered on the lawn on the western side of the stadium is a visual poem by Joan Brossa, comprising a group of blocks representing letters and question marks.

Immediately above the stadium, hidden among trees, is the **Parc del Laberint d'Horta**, a bosky late-18C park which in its own way is no less magical a place than the Park Güell, and a considerably less visited one. The Laberint d'Horta was the creation of the learned and enlightened Joan Antoni Desvalls, marquis of Alfarràs i Llupià (1740–1820). The marquis himself was responsible for designing and supervising the laying out of the park, though the complex nature of the steeply sloping site, and the need for elaborate water systems, forced him to enlist the help of the Italian engineer Domenico Bagutti. Work on the park was begun in 1793 and completed in 1804. Large plaques inside the park commemorate festivities organised here in honour of both Charles IV in 1802 and Alfonso XIII in 1929. At the entrance to the park stands the **former country mansion** of the Marquises of Llupià, which dates back to a castle built in the 14C for the Vallseca family, but owes its present appearance largely to Neo-Moorish remodelling carried out in the mid-19C. The building, like the park itself, now belongs to the Barcelona city council. Both were restored in 1993.

On the steep wooded slopes behind the house extends a complex of cypress avenues, ponds, fountains, classical pavilions, statuary and enigmatic inscriptions. The park's creator, a true man of the Enlightenment, was greatly interested in philosophy, and the whole layout of the park can be interpreted as an initiation into the different forms of love. At the very centre of the park, preceded by a grotto containing statues of Echo and Narcissus, is the park's famous *laberint* or **maze**, in the middle of which is a representation of Eros. 'The Labyrinth is simple', an inscription outside assures you, 'you will have no need of the ball of thread which Ariadne gave to Theseus'. Tourists in a hurry, however, might well have to resort to taking short-cuts through gaps in the tightly clipped cypress hedges. The progress of visitors stumbling through the maze is observed by Venus, whose statue stands on a raised terrace, enclosed within a *tempietto*. Further up is a classical pavilion, beyond which is a shaded rectangular pool, featuring at its furthest end a statue of a nymph, whose stance of quiet repose signifies the peace at the end of Love's journey.

From here, you could continue to Tibidabo and Collserola to follow the next walk. Take bus 17, 73 or 85 west along the Passeig de Vall d'Hebron to the Plaça John F. Kennedy.

12 • Tibidabo and Collserola

▶ Start from Avinguda del Tibidabo FGC station on Plaça de John F. Kennedy. See map on p 222.

When you emerge from the station on the Avinguda del Tibidabo, you can either go straight up the hill on the tram, or first explore the route outlined below, which takes in one of Gaudí's best buildings.

The avenue is a long, steep hill lined with imposing early 20C villas and gardens. On the right of the avenue at no. 28 is the **Casa Coll**, designed by Enric Sagnier i Villavecchia in 1918 and now a school. Halfway up on the left, at **no. 31**, is an outstanding Modernista house built in 1903–13 by Joan Rubió for the Roviralta family. It is popularly known as '*El Frare Blanc*' or 'White Friar', not because of its white coat of plaster but because a Dominican convent previously stood on the site. The exterior comprises a fantastical interpretation of the Catalan Gothic style, with widely projecting eaves. The whitewashed, revamped interior now houses a renowned restaurant, *El Asador de Aranda*.

The quiet residential street by the side of the building, the Carrer Teodor Roviralta, will take you to the excellent **Museu de la Ciència de la Fundació La Caixa**. *Open Tue–Sun 10.00–20.00. Fee. Barcelona Card discount. Shop. Café.* The museum occupies an early 20C building by Domènech i Estapà which was beautifully remodelled and enlarged in 1980. It presents science in a genuinely imaginative and accessible way through the use of hundreds of interactive exhibits. There is also a planetarium and a special section for children. There are plans to close the museum from September 2002 to October 2003, when the displays will be transferred to the Fundació La Caixa's premises at Passeig de Sant Joan 108 (p 185).

From the museum, turn right into Carrer dels Quatre Camins. You shortly reach the Plaça Calvo, off which is the Carrer de la Infanta Isabel. At no. 4 is the

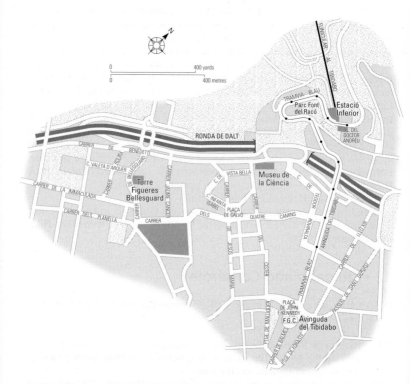

fashionable restaurant *La Balsa*, an almost Japanese-like glass, wood and brick structure, beautifully set amidst dense and luscious vegetation. This award-winning building was designed in 1978 by Lluís Clotet and Oscar Tusquets.

Continue along Carrer dels Quatre Camins and turn right into Carrer de Bellesguard, where at nos 16–20, is the **Casa Bellesguard**, built by Gaudí in 1900–02. The structure was built as a private house over the scant remains of a summer residence commissioned in 1409 by Martí I, the last of the Catalan kings. The palace was known as Bellesguard after the Catalan for 'beautiful view'. The medieval site inspired Gaudí to create a Neo-Gothic castle-like structure, the whole surmounted by a tall spire supporting a cross. The building, regarded by some as Gaudí's secular masterpiece, is also one of this architect's least known works. The structure has always been in private ownership, and until recently was hidden behind a large walled enclosure. The well-preserved interior, which is now divided into apartments, is still inaccessible to the public, but the present owners do at least allow visitors to walk around the large garden, thus allowing you an excellent view of the building's exterior. It is also worth walking around the corner into Carrer Valeta d'Arquer to get another perspective.

Adjacent is the **Convento del Redemptor**, a curious Modernista complex built by Bernardí Martorell Puig in 1926. Return to the Avinguda del Tibidado.

The picturesque **Tramvia Blau** (Blue Tram) runs the length of the avenue. Dating back to the beginning of the 20C, this is Barcelona's last surviving tram, as the others ceased functioning in the 1960s. It terminates at the top of the Avinguda del Tibidabo in a charming small square, the Plaça del Doctor Andreu. An old funicular station stands alongside a palm-lined terrace containing the pretty restaurant *La Venta*, where some of the tables are on a covered terrace, with partitions covered in flowers and fragments of glazed tiles. The restaurant's owner, Paco d'Ors, also runs the intimate adjoining bar, *Merbeyé*, which was opened in 1978 and features one of the first interiors to be associated with the designer Mariscal. It contains not only graphic designs by him, but also such whimsical features as two large fans, one of which appears to have carved a dent through one of the bar's columns, while the other seems to have cut through a column completely.

On the other side of the square, overhanging the steep slopes of the hill, is *Mirablau*, an elegant bar with floor-to-ceiling windows, providing a panoramic view of Barcelona. Sitting on a stool by the window at night, the view is particularly magical.

The last stage of the ascent up to the summit of **Tibidabo** (542m) is usually done by funicular, which climbs through a dense forest of pines and passes near the **Fabra Observatory**, an early 20C structure by Domènech i Estapà. The mountain of Tibidabo derives its name from the Latin words, '*Haec omnia tibi dabo si cades adoraberis me*' ('All this shall I give you if you but adore me'), the words of the devil as quoted in St Matthew's Gospel. A road to its summit was created in 1868, and among those who subsequently made the ascent was Saint John Bosco, the founder of the Salesian Order, who came here in 1886 and dedicated the mountain to the Sacred Heart. The Queen of Spain visited the mountain in 1888, on the occasion of the World Exhibition.

The development of Tibidabo as a popular place of recreation for the people of Barcelona was due to the celebrated pill manufacturer Dr Andreu. In 1900, he created the *Sociedad Anónima del Tibidabo*, which not only promoted the garden suburb on the slopes of the mountain, but was also responsible both for the Blue Tram and the funicular. A public park was laid out in 1908 on the upper reaches of Tibidabo, and near the top an **amusement park** was built, which was thoroughly overhauled in 1989. *Open summer daily 12.00–dusk, weekends only in winter. Fee. Barcelona Card discount.* The traditional rides are great fun and much more hair-raising than usual owing to the great height. The park also contains the **Museu dels Autòmates**. This entertaining museum contains automatons dating back to the beginning of the 20C. Exhibits include coin-operated mechanised dolls from funfairs, theatrical scenes and musicians. *Open daily 12.00–20.00. Fee. Admission included with funfair ticket*.

The summit of the mountain is marked by the **Temple del Sagrat Cor**, which was founded in 1902. This building of singular hideousness was designed by Enric Sagnier i Villavecchia and intended as Barcelona's answer to the Sacré Coeur in Montmartre. Its sole attraction is that you are able to climb almost to the top of its main spire, from where you can admire potentially extensive views that are unfortunately sometimes marred by pollution.

From the Plaça del Tibidabo, take bus 211 across to the **Torre de Collserola**, which crowns the summit of the neighbouring mountain. This significant addition to Barcelona's skyline is the city's telecommunications' tower. *Open Wed–Sun 11.00–14.30, 15.30–20.00. Fee. Café*.

The tower, used to broadcast radio and television programmes across Catalunya, was designed by Norman Foster and built in 1989–92. The structure is faithful to Foster's belief in achieving the maximum of effect through the minimal of structural means and comprises a mast-like central shaft of pre-cast concrete supporting a skeletal framework of exceptional elegance. It is 288m high, and stands on a hill that is 445m above sea level. The observation deck is on the 10th floor (reached in two minutes by lift), and affords views across more than 70km of the city, sea and countryside.

Collserola hill is actually a municipal park, with a wealth of flora and fauna, as well as archaeological remains, old farmhouses and more than 200 natural springs. Take the 211 bus on to the **Vallvidrera funicular station**, a Modernista gem designed by Arnau Calvet and Bonaventura Conill in 1905, with distinctive curved windows framed in brick. From here you can walk (or get a taxi) up to the information centre, where you can pick up maps and information on walking routes.

Nearby is the **Museu Verdaguer**. *Open Jun–Sep Sat 11.00–14.00, 15.00–18.00, Sun 11.00–15.00; Oct–May Sat & Sun 11.00–15.00. Free.* This was the final home of another great Catalan poet, Jacint Verdaguer. The large Renaissance-style house of 18C origin where the poet died on 10 June, 1902, is known as the Vil-la Joana. As well as numerous mementoes relating to the poet, it features an outdoor gallery with wonderful views towards Montserrat, a place which inspired a number of his works.

From Collserola you can return to the city centre by FGC train from Baixador de Vallvidrera station, about ten minutes walk downhill from the information centre.

Days out

Catalunya's combination of coastal and spectacular mountain scenery, and its wealth of monuments—particularly from the Romanesque, Gothic and Modernista periods—allow for an exceptional range of excursions from Barcelona. The places included here can all be visited in a day, and all can be reached by public transport. A detailed description of Catalunya's many riches is beyond the scope of this guide, as you could easily spend a couple of weeks exploring the region. The Catalunya Tourist Office in Barcelona (see p 13) provides further practical and general information on all the places listed below.

Colònia Güell

23km south-west of Barcelona.

Getting there
By train

FGC line S33 (pink), S4 (mustard) or S8 (light blue) from Plaça d'Espanya to Colònia Güell. Journey time approximately 20 minutes.

Information
☎ 93 6852400 or 93 6402936.
Visitors are free to wander around the complex at any time. There are plans to open the crypt on a daily basis (hitherto open on Sunday mornings only). Check with the Barcelona tourist office for details.

Anyone interested in Antoni Gaudí should visit the Colònia Güell, just outside Barcelona. The colony was built in the 1890s for the workers at Eusebi Güell's textile factory, which was transferrred here from Barcelona in 1891. The residential area of the colony, with its curious brick buildings, central monument commemorating Güell himself, and its general character of decay, has a quiet haunting charm, but the main object of a visit here is to see Gaudí's unfinished church, which stands on a pine-shaded mound outside. The only part of the ambitious building to be completed was the crypt, an expressively shaped brick structure that rises above the ground like a monstrous crab. It was restored in 2001 in preparation for the Gaudí Year in 2002. The sombre, grotto-like interior features stained-glass windows that open up like butterfly wings, stalls shaped like butterflies, and a museum documenting Güell, Gaudí and the colony. Other buildings in the colony were designed by Francesc Berenguer and Joan Rubió Bellver, and are also worth seeing.

Montserrat

60km west of Barcelona.

Getting there
By train

FGC line R5 (turquoise) from Plaça d'Espanya to Aeri de Montserrat, then cable car. Journey time approximately one hour. Trains leave at 36 minutes past every hour.

The *Tot Montserrat* ticket includes metro ride to and from station, train, cable car, funicular rides, museum entrance and self-service lunch. Approximately €35. Also available is the

Trans Montserrat ticket, which does not include the museum or lunch. Approximately €21. Available from Plaça d'Espanya and Plaça de Catalunya stations, or from FGC shop in the Triangle shopping centre (corner of C/Pelai and Plaça de Catalunya).

By bus

Julià company from Sants bus station (☎ 93 4904000). Bus leaves at 09.00 and returns at 17.00 (18.00 in July & August). Journey time approximately 90 mins.

Information

Pl. de la Creu. ☎ 93 8777777 or 8777701, www.abadiamontserrat.net.

One of the most popular excursions from Barcelona, the Monastery of Montserrat is set against an extraordinary background of eroded sandstone pinnacles that inspired Gaudí's plans for both the Sagrada Família and the Colònia Güell. The Benedictine monastery is more interesting for its magnificent views and historical and symbolical associations than for its architecture, as most of the complex was pompously transformed in the late 19C.

Owing to the altitude, it is colder here than in Barcelona, so bring an extra layer of clothing. There are several walking routes along tracks in the surrounding countryside, so wear suitable shoes if you want to explore. The local tourist office provides a leaflet detailing the walks, as well as general information including a map marking the monuments. If visiting in warm weather, a picnic lunch is probably a better idea than the touristy options available.

The monastery was founded in the 1025 following the apparition of the Virgin Mary here. Around 80 monks live there now. The **Basilica** contains a 12C Romanesque figure of the Virgin Mary, patron saint of Catalunya, also known as the Black Virgin (*La Moreneta*). The **Escolans** is a choir of boys from the monastery's school and claims to be the oldest boys' choir in Europe. Mass takes place every day at 11.00, and the choir sings Mon–Sat 13.00, Sun & public holidays 12.00.

The **Museum** contains archaeological finds from Mesopotamia, Egypt, Cyprus and the Holy Land and liturgical items dating from the 15C–20C. The 13C–18C painting collection includes works by El Greco, Caravaggio, Tiepolo and Berruguete. The section devoted to modern painting and sculpture includes work by Picasso, Dalí, Rusinyol, Casas, Nonell and Mir. There is also a display of Impressionists, with paintings by Monet, Degas, Pissarro and Sisley. *Open Mon–Fri 10.00–18.00, Sat, Sun & public holidays 09.30–18.30. Fee.*

Terrassa

33km west of Barcelona.

Getting there
By train

Rodalies/Cercanías line C-4 (gold), or *FGC* line S1 (red) from Plaça de Catalunya. Journey time approximately 40 minutes.

Information

Ajuntament de Terrassa, Raval de Montserrat 14. ☎ 93 7397019, www.terrassa.org.

This industrial town is not on the mainstream tourist beat, but is well worth visiting for the Visigothic and Romanesque churches and the outstanding Modernista industrial architecture. All points of interest are marked on a map provided by the tourist office.

In the centre of town there is a small park, the Parc de Sant Jordi, which contains Terrassa's most well-known building, the **Masia Freixa**, which is now the Municipal Conservatory of Music. This fantastical white structure of parabolic arches was built as a textile mill, but was converted in 1907–10 into a family residence for the mill's owner, Josep Freixa Argemí. The architect who undertook the conversion, Lluís Muncunill, was also responsible for the **Vapor Aymerich, Amat i Jover** factory of 1907–08, situated at no. 270 of the **Rambla d'Egara**, the town's main street. This large and curious Modernista structure, one of the most important industrial buildings in Catalunya, houses the fascinating and evocative **Museu Nacional de la Ciència i de la Tècnica de Catalunya**. *Open July & Aug Tue–Sun 10.00–14.30; Sept–June Tue–Fri 10.00–19.00, Sat, Sun & public holidays 10.00–14.30. Fee.* The displays at this industrial museum include sections dealing with power generation, the textile production process and transport.

Anyone interested in textiles could also visit the **Centre de Documentació i Museu Tèxtil** at Carrer de Salmerón 25, which charts the development of weaving and clothing from the 3C to the present day. *Open Tue, Wed & Fri 09.00–18.00, Thu 09.00–21.00, Sat & Sun 10.00–14.00. Fee.*

Near this museum is a remarkable group of buildings, known collectively as the **Esglésies de Sant Pere**, situated in the Plaça del Rector Homs. *Open Tue–Sat 10.00–13.30, 16.00–19.00, Sun 11.00–14.00.* This site was an Iberian settlement and the hub of the Roman town of Egara. Dating back to the foundation of the town's bishopric in the 6C, the Romanesque and pre-Romanesque buildings are set within a quiet, verdant area, reached by crossing the 17C **Pont de Sant Pere**, a tall bridge spanning a lush, fertile enclave. The parish church of **Sant Pere** is a Romanesque remodelling of a 6C structure, of which the triple apse remains. Next to this is **Sant Miquel**, a 6C baptistery, the interior of which features marble arcading and murals of Byzantine inspiration. A Romanesque sarcophagus serves as a font. The third church is **Santa Maria**, which was consecrated in 1122. Fragments of Romanesque frescoes can be seen in its apse, but the building is remarkable above all for its altarpiece of Sts Abdón and Sené, which was painted by Jaume Huguet in 1460.

If you return to Barcelona on the *FGC* train, you could stop off at Sant Cugat to see the **Monastery of Sant Cugat del Vallès**, which has a celebrated Romanesque cloister containing 145 carved capitals.

Sant Sadurní d'Anoia and Vilafranca del Penedès

40km south-west of Barcelona.

Getting there
By train

Rodalies/Cercanías line C-4 (gold) from Plaça de Catalunya or Sants. Journey time approximately 40 minutes to Sant Sadurní, 1 hour to Vilafranca.

Information
Sant Sadurní: Ajuntament de Sant Sadurní d'Anoia, Plaça Ajuntament. ☎ 93 8910325; Vilafranca: Plaça de la Vila, ☎ 93 8920358.

Sant Sadurni d'Anoia

The small town of Sant Sadurni d'Anoia, in the heart of the Penedès region, is the centre of production for **cava**, the Catalan version of champagne. More than a hundred wineries are based there, dominated by the two major producers, *Codorníu* and *Freixenet*.

Cava is made by the *méthode champenoise*, whereby yeast and a small amount of sugar are added to the base wine in the bottle, which then undergoes a second fermentation. After an ageing period of between nine months and five years in underground cellars, the bottles are gradually turned and upended to allow the yeast to accumulate in the neck for removal at the end of the process. This is done by hand in smaller wineries, while the large companies use computerised gyrating palettes.

The similarity with champagne ends there, however. The soil and climate are obviously different, but the most important factor is the use of local grape varieties. Unlike sparkling wines from California, Australia, New Zealand and South Africa, which are made from the same grapes as champagne—Chardonnay, Pinot Noir and Meunier—cava is traditionally made from varying combinations of Macabeo, Xarelló and Parellada grapes, all native to the Penedès region.

Although a few sparkling wines appeared in Spain in the 1860s, it was Josep Raventós of *Codorníu* who really got the ball rolling after a visit to France in 1872 to check out what sort of wines were doing well there. His family had been producing wine since the 16C, but their vineyards had had to be replanted following the devastating phylloxera epidemic, and new ideas were needed. Impressed by the popularity of champagne, he decided to follow the same process with his own grape varieties. After a decade or so of experiments, *Codorníu* launched its first cava commercially in 1885.

More than a century later, it has the largest underground cellars in the world at its plant in Sant Sadurní, covering an area of 28km. The winery is still experimenting, a policy that has led to bitter wrangles with its chief rival, *Freixenet*. *Codorníu* has always supported Catalan culture, using the work of local artists for its advertising campaigns and commissioning Josep Puig i Cadafalch, one of the leading exponents of Modernisme, to design its head-quarters at the beginning of the 20C. This enthusiasm for all things Catalan has not, however, stopped the winery from using Chardonnay in some of its cavas, a practice that is becoming increasingly widespread throughout the industry.

Visiting bodegas

The tourist office provides a map and list of wineries. *Freixenet* and *Codorníu* have guided tours, but you should make appointments anywhere else. *Freixenet* is near the train station, but you need to take a taxi to *Codorníu*, which is just outside the town. If you plan to visit several places, it would be advisable to hire a car.

Codorníu (Avda. Jaume Codorníu, ☎ 93 8183232). Tours Mon–Thur 08.00–12.00, 13.00–16.30; Sat and Sun 10–13.30.

Freixenet (C/Joan Sala 2, ☎ 93 8183200). Tours Mon–Thur at 09.00, 10.00, 11.30, 15.30 and 17.30; Fri at 09.00, 10.00 and 11.30.

Raventós i Blanc (Plaça del Roure, ☎ 93 8183262). This house has only been going for 20 years, since the founder broke away from the *Codorníu* dynasty, but already has quite a reputation.

Agustí Torelló (La Serra, ☎ 93 8911173). Agustí Torelló has been in the cava business since he was a teenager and now heads the family firm, founded in 1955, which has gained a reputation as one of the most innovative cava wineries.

Juvé y Camps (C/Sant Venat 1, ☎ 93 8911000). Family-run house renowned for complex, aged cavas.

Gramona (C/Industria 38, ☎ 93 8910113). Another family business, with the emphasis on high standards and maintaining traditions.

Joan Raventós Rosell (Carretera Sant Sadurní-Masquefa, km 6.5, ☎ 93 772 5251). Although only founded in 1987, this is one of the most exciting wineries in the Penedès region, producing both still and sparkling wines.

Vilafranca del Penedès

From Sant Sadurní, you could take the train down to the larger and livelier town of Vilafranca del Penedès (20 minutes), which is the centre of the Penedès wine region. Head for the Plaça Jaume I in the charming old town, where you will find the **Museu del Vi**. *Open Tue–Sat 10.00–14.00, 16.00–19.00, Sun 10.00–14.00. Fee.* Housed in the Palau dels Comtes-Reis (12C–13C), the museum charts the history of wine-making in the region, with the emphasis on sociological development. The displays are complemented by collections of paintings, sculpture, ceramics and archaeological finds. You could also visit the *Miguel Torres* winery (C/Comercio 22, ☎ 93 8177487 or 93 8177400), which runs several guided tours daily. Call to book or check with tourist office. *Torres* is the major wine-producer in the region, founded in 1870, and is renowned worldwide for its red and white wines.

Sitges

37km south of Barcelona

approximately 35 minutes.

Getting there
By train

Rodalies/Cercanías line C-2 (green) from Passeig de Gràcia or Sants. Journey time

Information

C/Sínia Morera 1, ☎ 93 8945004 or 93 8944251, www.sitges.org.

Despite being a very popular tourist centre, Sitges is home to many artists and has retained an elegant early 20C character. In summer, it is one of Europe's foremost gay resorts and in October hosts a prestigious film festival. The seafront is flanked by a palm-lined promenade which is bordered to the north by a rocky promontory on which stand both its cheerful Baroque church and the warren of tiny streets and alleys comprising the old town.

A visit to Sitges is compulsory for anyone seriously interested in Modernisme, as the artist Santiago Rusinyol lived and worked there in a grand house of medieval origin. Spectacularly situated overlooking the sea, the house has been perfectly conserved as the **Museu Cau Ferrat**. *Open mid-June–mid-Oct Tue–Sun 10.00–14.00, 17.00–21.00; mid-Oct–mid-June Tue–Fri 10.00–13.30, 15.00–18.30, Sat 10.00–19.00, Sun 10.00–15.00. Fee. Ticket covering admission to the two adjacent museums also available.*

The museum is an atmospheric treasure trove with dark-blue walls, beamed ceilings and an abundance of ceramic decorations, early 20C mementoes and old master paintings. These include two works by El Greco, *The Tears of Saint Peter* and *Mary Magdalene, Repentant*, the latter of which was paraded through the streets of Sitges during the first of the *Festes Modernistes*, artistic gatherings organised by Rusinyol. In addition to his own drawings and paintings, the displays also include Rusinyol's substantial collection of wrought-iron objects, as well as paintings and sculptures by Picasso, Ramon Casas, Miquel Utrillo, Joan Llimona, Isidre Nonell, Ignacio Zuloaga and others.

The house was a meeting place for poets, writers, artists and musicians. On display is a piano on which Manuel de Falla composed part of *Love, the Magician* and *Nights in the Gardens of Spain*.

No less interesting is the adjoining **Museu Maricel** (same hours as above), a former private residence which was remodelled by Rusinyol's friend and colleague Miquel Utrillo to house a most varied collection ranging from 14C Catalan altarpieces to murals by Josep Maria Sert. The museum also contains the municipal collections, including works by artists with links to Sitges from the 19C to the present day.

Nearby in the lower town, at C/de Sant Gaudenci 1, is the charming late-18C residence known as Can Llopis, which now houses the **Museu Romàntic** (same hours as above). The interior has been little altered since the beginning of the 19C and contains furniture, musical instruments, paintings and sculpture dating mainly from that century. There is also a collection of dolls, mainly from the 17C–19C, made in Catalunya, Germany and France.

Although you may now be tempted by the beach or the abundant cafés, restaurants and shops, you could also have a look at some of the many Modernista buildings in Sitges. These include the **Casa Pere Carreras i Robert**

(C/Francesc Gumà 23), the **Casa Manuel Planas i Carbonell** (C/Illa de Cuba 21) and the **Casa Bartomeu Carbonell i Mussons** (Plaça del Cap de la Vila 7-8). The tourist office provides a useful booklet and map on Modernista architecture in the town.

Tarragona

98km south of Barcelona.

Getting there
By train
Regional and some *Largo Recorrido* trains from Passeig de Gràcia or Sants. Journey time approximately 1 hour 15 mins.

Information
Municipal tourist office at C/Major 39,

☎ 977 241953, Provincial tourist office at C/Fortuny 4, ☎ 977 233415, www.tarragona.net. At the tourist offices you can buy a ticket covering six major sights, which can be used on different days. Monuments open all day 09.00–20.00, Sun 0.9.00–15.00. All monuments except the Cathedral are closed on Mondays.

A far more important city than Barcelona in Roman times, Tarragona was made capital of *Hispania Citerior* by the Emperor Augustus. Its wines were praised by Pliny, and Martial referred to its sunbaked shores and the fertility of its surroundings. Today a provincial capital and a popular resort, Tarragona has undergone extensive development but still boasts remarkably extensive Roman remains.

From the train station, turn right and walk up the hill to the Rambla Nova promenade. Continuing north up the C/Sant Agustí brings you to the Plaça de la Font, north of which is the C/Major (where the tourist office is situated). This pedetrianised shopping street leads up to the Cathedral, in the heart of the evocative medieval quarter.

The **Cathedral** was founded in 1171 and largely completed by the late 14C. *Open mid-Mar–end June Mon–Sat 10.00–13.00, 16.00–19.00; July–mid-Oct 10.00–19.00; mid-Oct–mid-Nov 10.00–12.30, 15.00–18.00; mid-Nov–mid Mar 10.00–14.00. Fee.* The west façade is enlivened by a magnificent Gothic portal of 1289, covered with representations of prophets and apostles by Barthélemy 'le Nourmand'. The rest of the building, blending Gothic and Romanesque elements, features an especially gloomy interior centred on a fine Romanesque apse, and a splendid 13C–14C cloister with capitals adorned with a myriad of curious carvings, including one of a cat's funeral conducted by rats. The sacristy and chapterhouse contain the **Museu Diocesà** (hours same as above). Displays include tapestries, liturgical objects from churches all over the bishopric of Tarragona, and Roman, Visigothic and Islamic exhibits, including a 10C sculpted alabaster arch.

The stretch of the town's ramparts beyond the cathedral has been laid out with gardens and archaeological finds to form the **Passeig Arqueològic**, which offers excellent views of the hinterland and the sea. The promenade is flanked by the 3C BC walls and the fortifications erected by British engineers during the War of the Succession in the early 18C. The walls also incorporate Megalithic vestiges.

Re-entering the town through the Portal del Roser, nearby at C/Cavallers 14 is the **Museu Casa Castellarnau**. *Open June–Sept Tue–Sat 09.00–20.00, Sun 09.00–15.00; Oct–May Tue–Sat 10.00–13.00, 16.00–19.00, Sun 10.00–14.00. Fee*. Built in the 17C and restored in the 18C and 19C, this former family mansion contains permanent exhibitions on Roman, Visigothic and medieval Tarragona, as well as temporary displays.

Continuing east along this street and its continuation, C/Nau, brings you to the Plaça del Rei, and the **Museu Nacional Arqueològic de Tarragona**. *Open June–Sept Tue–Sat 10.00–20.00, Sun & public holidays 10.00–14.00; Oct–May Tue–Sat 10.00–13.30, 16.00–19.00, Sun & public holidays 10.00–14.00. Fee*. The museum, which is attached to the defensive walls, contains an impressive collection of mosaics, sarcophagi, statuary and other Iberian, Greek and Roman finds.

Just off the square, on C/Santa Anna, is the **Museu d'Art Modern**, which concentrates on Catalan artists. *Open Tue–Fri 10.00–20.00, Sat 10.00–15.00 & 17.00–20.00, Sun 11.00–14.00. Free*. A passage opposite the museum entrance leads to the atmospheric **Barri Jueu**, the former Jewish quarter, which retains several Gothic arches.

South of the Plaça del Rei, on the corner with Rambla Vella are the restored remains of a 1C Roman Circus. Nearby is the vast **Amphitheatre**. Beautifully situated in lush parkland rolling directly down to the sea, the amphitheatre dates back to 2C and was mainly used for gladiatorial fights. It was substantially restored in 1970. *Open June–Sept Tue–Sat 09.00–20.00, Sun 09.00–15.00; Oct–Mar Tue–Sat 10.00–13.00, 15.00–17.00, Sun 10.00–14.00; Apr & May Tue–Sat 10.00–13.00, 15.00–19.00, Sun 10.00–14.00. Fee*.

South of the Rambla Nova, there are remains of the **Roman Forum** on C/Soler. Beyond this, at Avinguda de Ramón y Cajal 80, is the **Museu i Necròpolis Paleocristians**. The Romano-Christian necropolis of the 3C–6C is considered to be the most important in the western half of the Roman Empire. *Open June–Sept Tue–Sat 10.00–20.00, Sun & public holidays 10.00–14.00; Oct–May Tue–Sat 10.00–13.30, 16.00–19.00, Sun & public holidays 10.00–14.00. Fee*.

The Roman remains around Tarragona include a magnificent **Triumphal Arch** of the 2C AD, situated 4km outside the city on the old Barcelona road (the Via Augusta). 6km beyond the arch is the **Tower of the Scipios**, an imposing funerary monument of the same period. 4km from the city on the Lleída road is a two-storeyed **Aqueduct** which is 217 metres long and possibly dates back to Trajan's reign.

If you are in the mood for a slap-up lunch, take a taxi to the waterfront at Serralló, just beyond the port, where there is a strip of upmarket restaurants serving first-rate fresh fish.

Girona

100km north of Barcelona.

Getting there
By train
Regional from Passeig de Gràcia or Sants. Fastest journey time 1 hour 10 mins.

By bus
Barcelona Bus (☎ 93 2320459) from Estació del Nord (C/Alí Bei 80). Journey time 1 hour 15 mins.

Information
Rambla de la Llibertat 1, ☎ 972 226575. A ticket is available covering access to six museums.

The lively city of Girona is a large provincial capital with one of Catalunya's finest medieval districts, containing a well-preserved Jewish quarter. The old town is on the east side of the River Onyar, and is joined to the Neo-classical Plaça de Independencia in the new town by the Pont de Sant Agustí. The bridge affords an excellent view of the tall and brightly-coloured late medieval houses that line the river's east bank.

On turning right at the end of the bridge you come almost immediately to a shaded riverside promenade, the Rambla de la Llibertat, where the tourist office is situated. Behind this stretches the part of the old town known as the Ciutat Gremial after the medieval guilds that were once situated here. As with the Barcelona district of Sant Pere, this is an area combining commercial vitality with corners of considerable medieval charm—such as the flight of steps leading up from the quaintly irregular Plaça de l'Oli towards the early Gothic convent of Sant Domènec.

In contrast, the medieval area to the left of the Pont de Sant Agustí has the museum-like character of Barcelona's Barri Gòtic, with a stunning wealth of lovingly restored monuments, and a series of narrow pedestrian streets and alleys that seem almost too pretty and well-maintained to be those of a real town.

The second street to your left after crossing the bridge is the long and narrow Carrer de la Força, which was once the main street of one of Spain's most important Jewish centres, **El Call**. Much of the claustrophobic character of the quarter has survived, in particular in the dark and ivy-covered ascending alleys leading off the Carrer de la Força. On the first of these, the Carrer de Sant Llorenç, is the **Centre Bonastruc ça Porta**. *Open May–Oct Mon–Sat 10.00–20.00, Sun & public holidays 10.00–15.00; Nov–Apr Mon–Sat 10.00–18.00, Sun & holidays 10.00–14.00. Fee.* Named after a 13C Cabbalist, philosopher and mystic, and believed to be the site of the last synagogue, the centre houses both the **Museum of Jewish History** and the **Institute of Sephardic Studies**. The displays at this dynamic and expanding institution document the six centuries of the Jewish presence in Girona.

At no. 27 of Carrer de la Força is the **Museu d'Historia de la Ciutat**. *Open Tue–Sun 10.00–14.00, 17.00–19.00, Sun & public holidays 10.00–14.00. Fee.* Housed in an 18C Capuchin monastery, the displays at this fascinating museum include sections on the city's Roman, Christian and Visigothic past, as well as its more recent industrial heritage.

Just beyond the museum is the **Catedral de Santa Maria** (*open July–Sept Tue–Sat 10.00–20.00, Sun & public holidays 10.00–14.00; Oct–Feb Tue–Sat 10.00–*

14.00, 16.00–18.00, Sun 10.00–14.00; Mar–Jun Tue–Sat 10.00–14.00, 16.00–19.00, Sun & public holidays 10.00–14.00. The Cathedral is one of the great architectural jewels of Catalunya. Its Baroque west façade, an unusually dramatic work for this region, features an elaborate frontispiece crowning a steep and monumentally tall flight of steps of 1607–90. The highly theatrical façade shields a single-aisled Gothic interior of unusual harmony and echoing proportions. This atmospherically lit and elegantly austere interior was begun in the early 14C and brought to completion 100 years later by Antoni Canet and Guillem Bofill. The cloister is adorned with one of the most important series of Romanesque carvings in Catalunya. The museum (same hours as above. Fee) contains a rich collection of liturgical exhibits from the 9C–19C. Highlights include a 10C Arab coffer and the 12C Romanesque Tapestry of the Creation.

Next door to the Cathedral is the former Bishop's Palace, which houses the **Museu d'Art de Girona**. *Open July–Sept Tue, Thur, Fri & Sat 10.00–19.00, Wed 10.00–24.00, Sun & public holidays 10.00–14.00; Oct–Feb Tue–Sat 10.00–18.00, Sun & public holidays 10.00–14.00; Mar–June Tue–Sat 10.00–19.00, Sun & public holidays 10.00–14.00. Wheelchair access. Information in braille. Activity packs for children. Fee.* The collections are beautifully and spaciously arranged in well-restored rooms. The high-quality displays range from Gothic altarpieces by the likes of Bernat Martorell and Lluís Borrassà to 19C Catalan masters such as Fortuny and Rusinyol. Several temporary exhibitions are running at any given time.

Going back down the Cathedral steps, in front of you is the enormous **Església de Sant Feliu**, parts of which date from the 13C. The Baroque west façade features only one tower, as the second was never built.

Follow signs to the adjacent **Banys Arabs** on C/Ferran el Català. *Open Apr–Sept Mon–Sat 10.00–19.00, Sun & public holidays 10.00–14.00; Oct–Mar Tue–Sun 10.00–14.00. Fee.* The name is misleading, as the baths were built by Christians in the 12C and 13C, inspired by Roman and Moorish designs. The restored complex features an *apodyterium*, or changing room, with an octagonal pool surrounded by eight slender columns.

A bridge just beyond the baths leads to the Romanesque **Monestir de Sant Pere de Galligants** (11C–12C) in the Plaça Santa Llúcia. The Benedictine monastery houses the **Museu de Arqueologia de Catalunya-Girona**. *Open June–Sept Tue–Sat 10.30–13.30, 16.00–19.00, Sun & public holidays 10.00–14.00; Oct–May Tue–Sat 10.00–14.00, 16.00–18.00, Sun & public holidays 10.00–14.00. Fee.* The museum is situated in the church and contains exhibits from prehistoric to medieval times, including Palaeolithic finds and Roman mosaics. The cloister features Hebrew inscriptions from tombstones in the Jewish cemetery. Adjacent is the 12C Romanesque **Església de Sant Nicolau**, which has an octagonal dome and a trefoil apse.

Crossing back over the bridge you could climb the steps to the **Passeig Arqueològic**, a path following the medieval ramparts, which eventually leads around to the Gothic **Convent de Sant Domènec** (13C–17C), which is now part of the university. From here steps lead back down to the Carrer de la Força and the Rambla de la Llibertat.

Figueres and Cadaqués

Figueres 138km, Cadaqués 174km
north of Barcelona.

Getting there
By train
Regional from Passeig de Gràcia or
Sants to Figueres. Fastest journey time
1 hour 40 mins.
By bus
Barcelona Bus ☎ 93 2320459) from
Estació del Nord (C/Alí Bei 80) to
Figueres. Journey time 2 hours 20 mins.
Sarfa ☎ 902 302025) runs an
infrequent service to Cadaqués from

Barcelona Estació del Nord (departures
at 11.15 and 20.25 only. Return at
07.15 & 16.15). Journey time 2 hours
15 mins. Sarfa also runs buses from
Figueres to Cadaqués (departures at
11.00, 13.00 & 19.15 only. Return at
07.15, 14.25 & 17.00). Journey time
1 hour 5 mins.

Information
Figueres: Plaça del Sol, ☎ 972 503155.
Cadaqués: C/Cotxe 2-A, just off Plaça
Frederic Rahola, ☎ 972 258315.

Visiting both places in one day using public transport is a bit of a rush, but is just
about possible if that is all the time you have. The best option is to get an early
train to Figueres and spend the morning there, then get the 13.00 bus to
Cadaqués. If you reserve your visit to Dalí's house for 15.00 or 15.30 (see below),
you will be able to catch the 17.00 bus back to Figueres.

Figueres
Figueres is best known as the birthplace of Salvador Dalí (1904–89), who turned
the town's old municipal theatre in the Plaça Gala-Salvador Dalí into the
eccentric and extremely popular **Teatre-Museu Dalí**, ☎ 972 677500,
www.salvador-dalí.org. *Open July–Sept Mon–Sun 09.00–19.45; Oct–Jun Tue–Sun
10.30–17.45. Fee. Book and gift shop.*

Dalí wanted the work to speak for itself, so only a minimum of written
information is provided. He thought that visiting his museum should be a
stimulating rather than an educational experience. The exhibits are displayed in
a series of indoor and outdoor spaces. There are several key works in the Sala del
Tresor, including *The Spectre of Sex Appeal*, *The Bread Basket* and *Galarina*.
The Sala de les Peixateries contains the *Portrait of Picasso* and *Soft Self-Portrait
with Fried Bacon Rasher*. Dalí's tomb is in the crypt. The Sala de Mae West
contains the famous representation of the actress, including the *Sofa-Saliva-
Lips*.

Figueres is a pleasant town to stroll around, and there are another two
museums worth visiting. The **Museu de l'Empordà** is at La Rambla 2. *Open
July–Sept Tue–Fri 11.00–13.00, 16.00–21.00, Sat, Sun & public holidays 17.00–
21.00; Oct–June Tue–Fri 11.00–13.00, 15.30–19.00, Sat, Sun & public holidays
11.00–14.00. Fee.* The archaeological displays chart the development of the
Empordà region from Neolithic to Roman times, including ceramics and
fragments of murals from the Greek and Roman town of Empúries. The art
collections include paintings by Anton Raphael Mengs, Antoni Tàpies and Joan
Miró.

Adjacent is the **Museu dels Joguets** at Rambla 10. *Open July–Sept Mon–Sat
10.00–13.00, 16.00–19.00, Sun & public holidays 11.00–13.30, 17.00–19.30;*

Oct–June Mon, Wed–Sat 10.00–13.00, 16.00–19.00, Sun & public holidays 11.00–13.30. Fee. The museum displays the extensive collection of toys and games donated by Josep Maria Joan Rosa. Exhibits include toys found at archaeological sites and a teddy bear that belonged to Salvador Dalí.

The **Hotel Durán**, at C/Lasauca 5 off the Rambla, was a favourite haunt of Dalí's, with a room full of memorabilia and photographs. This is also a good place for lunch.

Cadaqués

Cadaqués is situated on a craggy peninsula on the wildest part of the Costa Brava. Although still a fishing village, it has been a magnet for artists, writers and bohemian types for nearly a century, attracted by the unique quality of the light. It is now a rather chic resort, but charming nevertheless, and the light is of course as magical as ever.

The **Casa-Museu Salvador Dalí**, where Dalí lived intermittently from 1930 until his death, is situated 2km away in Port Lligat. Visitor numbers are strictly limited, so telephone in advance to reserve a place, ☎ 972 677500, www. salvador-dalí.org. *Open mid-Mar–mid-June Tue–Sun 10.30–18.00; mid-June– mid-Sept daily 10.30–21.00; mid-Sept–6 Jan Tue–Sun 10.30–18.00. Closed 7 Jan– mid-Mar. Fee. Book and gift shop.* You must collect your tickets half an hour before the allotted time.

The light, airy house is right on the waterfront, at the easternmost point in Spain. As you enter, you are greeted by a stuffed bear, adorned with necklaces, which rather sets the tone for the whole visit. The studio has a big window overlooking the bay and a frame showing a work supposedly in progress. Other boldly-decorated rooms contain cages, more stuffed animals and photographs of Dalí and Gala with their famous friends, including Gregory Peck, Ingrid Bergman, Picasso and Franco.

Vic, Ripolles and Rupit

Vic 70km, Ripoll 95km and Rupit 98km north-west of Barcelona

Getting there
By train

Regional from Plaça de Catalunya or Sants to Vic and Ripoll. Fastest journey time 1 hour 20 mins to Vic, 2 hours to Ripoll. Vic to Ripoll approximately 40 mins.

By bus

Sagalès (☎ 93 8892577) from Plaça de Urquinaona in Barcelona to Vic. Journey time 1 hour 45 mins. Pous (☎ 93 8506063) runs a very limited service from Vic to Rupit (departures Mon–Fri 19.00, Sat 12.30, Sun 09.00 & 19.00. Return Sat & Sun 17.00 , every day 08.00). Journey time approximately 1 hour 10 mins.

Information

Vic: C/Ciutat 4 (just off Plaça Major), ☎ 93 8862091.
Ripoll: Plaça Abat Oliba, ☎ 972 702351.
Rupit: Plaça Era Nova, ☎ 938 522083.

Vic

Vic is an easy day trip with frequent trains, but if you want to go on to Rupit, Saturday is the only feasible day given the bus times.

Now a busy commercial and industrial hub, Vic is an ancient town with a well-preserved old quarter. The **Plaça Major**—also known as El Mercadal—is framed by Gothic, Baroque and Modernista buildings. A lively market has been held there on Tuesdays and Saturdays for more than a thousand years.

The **Cathedral**, which was largely rebuilt in the Neo-classical period, has a Romanesque crypt and cloister, and a nave decorated with powerful murals by Josep Maria Sert (1876–1945), who was born here. *Open daily 10.00–13.00, 16.00–19.00.*

Adjacent in the Plaça Bisbe Oliba is the **Museu Episcopal**. *Open mid-May–mid-Oct Mon–Sat 10.00–13.00, 16.00–18.00, Sun & public holidays 10.00–13.00; mid-Oct–mid-May daily 10.00–13.00. Fee.* The museum contains an important collection of Catalan 12C–15C paintings, including works by Arnau Bassa, Lluís Borrassà, Bernat Martorell and Jaume Huguet. Also of interest is the **Museu de l'Art de la Pell**, just north of Plaça Major at C/Arquebisbe Alemany 5. *Open Tue–Sat 11.00–14.00, 17.00–20.00, Sun & public holidays 11.00–14.00. Free.* The permanent displays at this unusual new museum in a former convent comprise the collections of leather artworks and objects donated by Andreu Colomer Munmany. Temporary photography, architecture and art exhibitions are also held. The **Sala Sert** at C/Ramon d'Abadal i de Vinyals 5. has changing displays of Sert's work. *Open Mon–Sat 09.00–13.00, 16.00–18.00. Free.*

Ripoll

Ripoll, situated at the confluence of the Freses and Ter rivers, was called the Cradle of Catalunya by the poet Jacint Verdaguer (1845–1902), owing to the important cultural and economic role played by its monastery in medieval times. The Benedictine **Monestir de Santa Maria de Ripoll** was founded in 879 by Wilfred the Hairy, whose bones are in a sarcophagus on the wall of the left transept. *Open daily 08.00–13.00, 15.00–20.00.* The church was partially destroyed by an earthquake in 1428, and was rebuilt and badly restored in the 1820s, before falling into disrepair following the disentailment of the monasteries in 1835. In the 1880s, riding the new wave of Catalan nationalism, it was restored by Elias Rogent i Amat. The Romanesque structure has extensive carvings in its cloister and an outstanding west portal richly carved with grotesques and bands of sculpture illustrating the scriptures. *Open daily 10.00–13.00, 15.00–19.00. Fee.*

The adjacent **Museu de les Pireneus** charts Ripoll's importance in the production of weapons and ironmongery in the 16C–18C, as well as the history of the region. *Open July–Sept Tue–Sun 09.30–19.00; Oct–June Tue–Sun 09.30–13.30, 15.30–18.00. Fee.*

Rupit

Rupit is a picturesque village with cobbled streets and distinctive stone architecture, set in a spectacular landscape with extensive views of distant snow-capped peaks. These fortunate circumstances have made it very popular with artists and tourists alike. After a morning in Vic, it is very pleasant to come here for lunch and a stroll around the village and surrounding countryside. The perfectly-preserved balconied houses, dating from the 16C and 17C, perch above a rushing stream, crossed by means of a perilous-looking swinging footbridge with wooden slats.

Glossary of art and architectural terms

ajuntament city hall
apse semicircular or polygonal rear wall of chancel or chapel
artesonado coffered wooden ceiling
azulejo glazed tile
baldachin canopy over altar or tomb
bargueño elaborate chest with lots of small drawers
barri neighbourhood
Call Jewish quarter
capella chapel
capital element crowning a column
caryatid sculpture of female figure used as support element
console ornamental bracket
Corinthian column with fluted shaft and elaborately sculpted capital
Doric column with fluted shaft and unadorned capital
entablature band at top of columns, comprising architrave, frieze and cornice
església church
Gothic medieval architectural style, characterised by pointed arches, rib vaults and flying buttresses
Ionic column with fluted shaft and capital adorned with volutes
mirador glassed-in balcony
Modernisme the Catalan form of Art Nouveau, also described as Jugendstil, Sezessionstil and Stile Liberty
monstrance receptacle for consecrated host
Mudéjar style of architecture and craft of Muslims who remained in Spain under Christian rule
Neo-classical late 18C architectural style that revived classical forms
Neo-Mudéjar late-19C architecture using Mudéjar elements such as red brick, horseshoe arches and tiling
Noucentisme a term coined by Eugeni d'Ors (1882–1954) to describe the work of Catalan artists, architects and writers associated with the revival of classical forms and themes in the first quarter of this century
order type of column (shaft, capital, entablature and sometimes base)
polychrome multicoloured, used to describe painted religious figures
portico roofed entrance, often with columns
predella compartmented band at base of altarpiece
retable altarpiece, usually lavishly carved and embellished
Renaissance revival of ancient Roman motifs in 15C Italy, which spread to Spain in the early 16C
Romanesque architectural style drawing on Roman characteristics, used in Spain from the early 11C to the late 13C
Sardana Catalan dance
Trencadis broken-tile mosaic technique pioneered by Gaudí
Visigothic art and architecture of the Western Goths who settled in Spain in the 5C, remaining until the 8C.

Index

This detailed index of buildings, monuments, people from history, artists and architects includes sub-indexes for cafés, churches and chapels, markets, museums, palaces (Palau), restaurants, squares (Plaça), and streets (Avinguda, Bajada, Carrer, Passatge, Passeig and Rambla).

A

B

City Guide
Madrid

- let Blue Guide author Annie Bennett also guide you around Madrid. Packed with information about the city's history, art and architecture. 10 detailed walks ensure you don't miss a thing. Fascinating detail about Madrid's writers and rulers, artists and architects. Take day trips to Toledo, Segovia or Ávila.

- Annie Bennett
  2nd edition, 2000
  288pp
  ISBN 0–7136–5212–8
  £11.99

City Guide
Venice

- detailed walks, providing a fascinating tour of this stunningly beautiful city, are accompanied by a comprehensive street map and plans of museums and monuments. Includes day trips to the lagoon, and full practical advice to make the most of your visit.

- Alta Macadam
  7th edition, 2001
  304pp
  ISBN 0–7136–5445–4
  £12.99

City Guide
Vienna

- detailed walks offer a leisurely tour around Vienna's glorious sights, with information about the artists, writers, composers and historical figures who have played a significant roles in the development of the city. Visit the world famous museums and the exciting new MuseumsQuartier

- Nicholas T. Parsons
  2nd edition, 2002
  224pp
  ISBN 0–7136–6128–3
  £11.99